BUSINESS MATHEMATICS

BUSINESS MATHEMATICS

Flora M. Locke

*Merritt College
Oakland, California*

John Wiley & Sons, Inc.
New York • London • Sydney • Toronto

Copyright © 1972, by John Wiley & Sons, Inc.

All rights reserved. Published simultaneously in Canada.

Reproduction or translation of any part of this work beyond that permitted by Sections 107 or 108 of the 1976 United States Copyright Act without the permission of the copyright owner is unlawful. Requests for permission or further information should be addressed to the Permissions Department, John Wiley & Sons, Inc.

Library of Congress Catalog Card Number: 72-180272

ISBN 0-471-54301-2

Printed in the United States of America.

10 9 8 7 6

Preface

This book provides self-directed instruction in the use of mathematics for solving personal and professional business problems. After completing this program you will be able to solve problems dealing with income, property, and sales taxes; to understand various kinds of problems dealing with fire, automobile, and life insurance; to use credit more wisely; to understand the principles involved in the lending or borrowing of money; and to solve problems dealing with payroll, depreciation, and merchandising.

In the course of your work you will improve your ability to perform the fundamental operations of arithmetic and to evaluate and prove answers. You will develop a greater appreciation of number relationships. In addition, your background of business terminology will be increased by exposure to a variety of business problems in which mathematics is applied.

It is assumed that you have completed courses in arithmetic and basic mathematics before starting this program. The first chapter is a review of basic processes, with emphasis on methods of improving speed and accuracy in all computational work. A great deal of pencil and paper work is required today, even though you may have the use of a calculator or adding machine. Furthermore, to solve a problem it is essential first to understand what is wanted and the process or method by which a solution can be obtained.

You can tailor this book to your particular needs because the order of the chapters is flexible. (Chapters 3 through 8 are independent of one another; Chapters 10 and 11 must follow Chapter 9.) If you work in accounting or bookkeeping, for example, you may concentrate on chapters covering depreciation, payroll, taxes, and notes and drafts. Chapters on merchandising and discounts may be particularly interesting to those in retail and wholesale businesses, and so on. If you want further references in business mathematics, or if you are using this program with a course textbook, a reference chart provides a chapter-by-chapter correlation with some popular textbooks. So your pace through *Business Mathematics* depends on your interests and experience.

FLORA M. LOCKE

Sebastopol, California
December 1971

How to Use This Book

Your progress through *Business Mathematics* will depend on your background: how well you remember basic mathematics, how recently you have studied or used it, and your interests and experience. At the beginning of each chapter are objectives that describe what you will be learning. Certain units offer pretests. If you do well on a pretest, you may "bypass" portions of the material; the results of the pretest will show what sections you need to study.

The chapters are arranged in units that are broken down into short steps, called frames, which call for your active participation in learning the material. Following explanations and examples, you will be given a question or problem. After you have written your answer in the space provided, compare it with the one given below the dotted line. If the answers do not agree, check your arithmetic. If they still do not agree, review the preceding frames. Be sure you understand the solution before you go on. (Your learning will be most effective if you actually write out your answer before looking at the answer given; you may wish to use an index card or a folded piece of paper to cover the area below the dotted line until you have answered.)

At the end of each unit or chapter is a test for self-evaluation. When appropriate, both answers *and* solution are provided. As before, if your answer does not agree with the one given, check your arithmetic. If your answer still does not agree, try to find the correct method of solution on your own before checking the solution in the book. A final test is offered at the end of the book.

REFERENCE CHART FOR SELECTED TEXTBOOKS IN BUSINESS MATHEMATICS

The following table identifies the chapters in this book with corresponding material in some widely used texts. You may find it useful in looking for different treatments or additional coverage of specific topics or in relating work in this book to a course that uses one of the texts listed below.

Chapter in Locke	Beighey and Borchardt	Diamond and Pintel	McCready	Rice, Boyd, and Mayne	Rosenberg
1 A Review of Fundamentals	1,2	1,2	1,3	I,II	1,2
2 Percentage	2,3	2,3	4	III	3
3 Trade and Cash Discounts	4	10	6	III	4
4 Merchandising	5	7,8	7	III	5
5 Depreciation	7	11	5	III	13
6 Payroll	4,7	9,10	2	VI	6
7 Property and Sales Taxes	8	6	...	VI	21
8 Insurance	8	6,12	13	V	12,22
9 Interest	6	4	8,9	IV,V	7,18
10 Notes and Drafts	6	12	8	IV	8,10
11 Installment Purchases and Periodic Loan Payment Plans	...	5	11,12	IV	19,23

REFERENCES

Beighey, Clyde, and G. C. Borchart, *Mathematics for Business: College Course*, 4th ed. (New York: Gregg Division, McGraw-Hill, 1965).

Diamond, Jay, and Gerald Pintel, *Mathematics of Business* (Englewood Cliffs: Prentice-Hall, 1970).

McCready, Richard R., *Business Mathematics* (Belmont, Calif.: Wadsworth Publishing Company, 1968).

Rice, Louis A., A. C. Boyd, and F. Blair Mayne. *Business Mathematics for Colleges*, 5th ed. (Cincinnati: South-Western Publishing Company, 1966).

Rosenberg, R. Robert, *College Mathematics*, 4th ed. (New York: Gregg Division, McGraw-Hill, 1967).

Contents

Chapter 1 Review of Fundamentals   1

    Unit 1. Whole Numbers and Decimals, 7
    Unit 2. Rounding Numbers, Estimating Answers, 40
    Unit 3. Fractions, 51
    Unit 4. Decimals or Decimal Fractions, 73

Chapter 2 Percentage   87

    Unit 1. Changing Percents to Decimals or Fractions and Conversely, 89
    Unit 2. Basic Elements of Percent Problems, 96

Chapter 3 Trade and Cash Discounts   119

    Unit 1. Meaning of Terms, 119
    Unit 2. Single Trade Discount, 121
    Unit 3. Trade Discounts Series (Chain Discounts), 129
    Unit 4. Cash Discounts, 145

Chapter 4 Merchandising   167

    Unit 1. Markup, 167
    Unit 2. Markdown, 185
    Unit 3. Profit and Loss, 191

Chapter 5 Depreciation   202

    Unit 1. Introduction to Depreciation: the Straight-Line Method, 202
    Unit 2. Accelerated Methods of Depreciation:
             The Sum-of-the-year's-digits Method, 210
             The Declining-Balance Method, 221
    Unit 3. Additional First-year Depreciation, 229

Chapter 6   Payroll   236

    Unit 1. Time Payment Payroll System, 236
    Unit 2. Payroll Deductions, 248
    Unit 3. Piece-rate Payroll System, Commissions, 259
    Unit 4. Cash Payrolls, 265

Chapter 7   Property and Sales Taxes   280

    Unit 1. Property Taxes, 280
    Unit 2. Sales Taxes, 292

Chapter 8   Insurance   302

    Unit 1. Fire Insurance, 302
    Unit 2. Automobile Insurance, 326
    Unit 3. Life Insurance, 330

Chapter 9   Interest   344

    Unit 1. Simple Interest, 345
    Unit 2. Compound Interest, 376

Chapter 10   Notes and Drafts   398

    Unit 1. Promissory Notes, 398
    Unit 2. Drafts, 412

Chapter 11   Installment Purchases and Periodic Loan Payment Plans   425

    Unit 1. Installment Purchases, 426
    Unit 2. Periodic Loan Payment Plans, 441

Final Examination   455

Index   461

BUSINESS MATHEMATICS

CHAPTER ONE
A Review of Fundamentals

OBJECTIVES

The ability to perform the fundamental operations of arithmetic with reasonable skill is essential to success in the study of business mathematics. It requires knowledge of the methods for each situation and practice in using them.

When you have completed this chapter, you will be able to

(1) perform fundamental operations of arithmetic for all computations involving whole numbers, decimals, and fractions,
(2) improve speed and accuracy in computations by the use of short cuts,
(3) estimate answers to problems involving the four fundamental processes.

The first unit deals with whole numbers and decimals, reading and writing, addition, subtraction, multiplication, and division. A test on this material is offered in the following pages if you wish to take it. It will be a source of satisfaction to you if your score is acceptable, for you will be able to skip some of this unit. If not, those areas in which more practice is needed to complete this course of study successfully will be indicated. Your progress will depend on how well you remember fundamentals.

If you *do not* take the test, go to frame 1, page 7.

PRETEST

Whole Numbers and Decimals

Instructions: Record answers in the spaces provided. When you have completed the test, check your answers with those shown in the following pages:

I. 3.06 is read "three and six hundredths."
3108 is read "three thousand, one hundred eight."

The following numbers are read as

    15   _____

    22.5   _____

    306.03   _____

    2540.096   _____

    .10035   _____

II. Arrange the following numbers in a column and add:

    1. 13.75, 8.9, .006, 52.009, 21, 5.6098
    2. Two and nine tenths, three thousand fifty six, eighty-two ten-thousandths, nine thousand, four hundred ten, and one hundred twenty-one thousandths.

                                                             Totals

III. Add (use combinations of 10 when possible). Check answers by reverse addition.

    1. 524   2. 872.15
        619   250.08
        790   852.22
        297   96.55
        713   180.09
        624   21.01

IV. Record the subtotal where indicated and total. Check your answers by adding the column without the use of subtotals.

```
        211
         89
        664  _____ subtotal
       8117
        988
       1052  _____ subtotal
        782
       3198  _____ subtotal
Total              total
```

V. Complete the following report and check by adding each column down and each line across. Check the grand total by adding the total column and total line. The sum should be the same.

	A	B	C	D	Total
Line A	323	566	821	900	_____
B	56	821	919	1066	_____
C	567	789	507	899	_____
Total	___	___	___	___	_____ Grand total

VI. Subtract. Check answers mentally by addition, i.e., $26 - 12 = 14$; check: $14 + 12 = 26$.

1. $92 - 16 =$ _____ .
2. $180 - 99 =$ _____ .
3. $\quad$ 816.21
   $\underline{-\ 36.09}$
4. $\quad$ 186.21
   $\underline{-\ 99.99}$

4 PRETEST

VII. Multiplication (use short cuts when possible):

1. 21.6 × 10 = _____. 2. 15 × 20 = _____.
3. 125 × 100 = _____. 4. 8.4 × 125 = _____.
5. .96 × 50 = _____. 6. 89.65 × .50 = _____.
7.   196
  × 28

8.   8.96
  × .072

VIII. Division (show remainder, if any, i.e., $26 \div 5 = 5\frac{1}{5}$). Verify answers for 5 and 6 by multiplication. Use short cuts when possible.

1. 840 ÷ 50 = _____. 2. 9.06 ÷ 10 = _____.
3. 1000 ÷ 125 = _____. 4. 2.27 ÷ 100 = _____.
5. 218)620   Check: 218 × _____ = 620.

6. .21)32.78   Check: .21 × _____ = 32.78.

Answers

After you check your answers, follow the instructions below and review the frames covering the appropriate sections.

I. Frames 5 to 8, pages 9 to 10.

15 is read as "fifteen."
22.5 is read as "twenty-two and five tenths."
306.03 is read as "three hundred six and three hundredths."
2540.096 is read as "two thousand five hundred forty and ninety-six thousandths."
.10035 is read "ten thousand thirty-five hundred thousandths."

II. Frame 9, page 11.

1.   13.75
      8.9
       .006
     52.009
     21.
      5.6098
    ─────────
    101.2748

2.   2.9
      3,056.
          .0082
      9,000.
        410.121
    ─────────
    12,469.0292

III. Frame 10, page 12.

1.
```
  5  2  4
  6  1ᵣ 9
  7  9ᴸ 0
 2ᵣ 9ᵣ 7ᵣ
  7  1ᴸ 3ᴸ
 6ᴸ 2  4
 2ᴸ 2
─────────
 35  6  7
```

2.
```
 8ᵣ 7  2ᵣ 1  5
 2ᴸ 5ᵣ 0. 0  8ᵣ
  8  5ᴸ 2.ᵣ 2ᵣ 2ᴸ
        9ᵣ 6.ᴸ 5ᵣ 5
  1  8ᵣ 0. 0  9ᵣ
        2ᴸ 1. 0  1ᴸ
  3ᴸ 1  1  3ᴸ
─────────────
 22  7  2. 1  0
```

IV. Frames 11 and 12, page 13.

```
  211
   89
  664     964    subtotal
 8117
  988
 1052   10157    subtotal
  782
 3198    3980    subtotal
─────   ─────
15101   15101    total
```

V. Frames 14 to 19, pages 17 to 20.

Line totals
$$A = 2610$$
$$B = 2862$$
$$C = 2762$$
Grand total   8234

Column totals
$$A = 946$$
$$B = 2176$$
$$C = 2247$$
$$D = 2865$$
Grand total   8234

VI. Frames 20 to 23, pages 21 to 22.

1. 76
2. 81
3. 780.12
4. 86.22

VII. Frames 24 to 35, pages 23 to 29.

1. 216
2. 300
3. 12,500
4. 1050
5. 48
6. 44.825
7. 5488
8. .64512

VIII. Frames 36 to 48, pages 30 to 37.

1. 16.8
2. .906
3. 8
4. .0227
5. $2\frac{184}{218}$ check: $(218 \times 2) + 184 = 620$
6. $156\frac{2}{21}$ check: $(.21 \times 156) + .02 = 32.78$

Instructions: If you made a perfect score or no more than two errors, skip to Unit 2, frame 1, page 40.

If you made one error or more in any section of problems, study all the frames for that section.

Examples: If you missed one or more problems in Section I, complete the first 10 frames, beginning with frame 1, page 7.
If you missed *none* in Section I but did miss one or more in Section II, skip to frame 9, page 10.

Proceed in this manner for all sections.

Section III: Did you use combinations of 10? If not, even though your answers were correct, you should review frame 10, page 16.

Section VII: If you did not use shortcuts for problems 1 to 6, study frames 29 to 34, pages 25 to 28, even though your answers were correct.

Section VIII: If you did not use shortcuts for problems 1 to 4, study frames 42 to 48, pages 35 to 37, even though your answers were correct.

After you have reviewed all sections in which errors occurred go to Unit 2, frame 1, page 40.

UNIT 1. WHOLE NUMBERS AND DECIMALS

1. Underscore the correct answer for each of the following statements:

   25 is a (whole/decimal/mixed) number.
   31.6 is a (whole/decimal/mixed) number.
   .27 is a (whole/decimal/mixed) number.

   If your answers are correct, skip to frame 5. Otherwise, continue on here.

   _____

   whole, mixed, decimal

Reading Numbers

Our number system is called the decimal system (from the Latin *decem* which means ten), since it is based on 10 symbols or digits—0, 1, 2, 3, 4, 5, 6, 7, 8, 9. The base is 10 because it takes 10 in any one place to equal 1 in the next higher place; for example, it takes 10 ones to equal 10, 10 tens to equal 100, 10 hundreds to equal 1000.

2. A number consists of one or more digits. A whole number is a digit from 0 to 9 or a combination of two or more digits such as 25 or 1037.

231 is a _____ number.

----

whole

3. A decimal, which is less than a whole number, is indicated by the decimal point and may consist of one or more digits. Examples are .5, .52, .678, .008.

.059 is a _____ number.

----

decimal

4. The decimal point separates whole numbers from decimal numbers. A number such as 23.056 is called a mixed number, since it consists of a whole number part (23) and a decimal part (.056).

52 is a _____ number.
2.067 is a _____ number.
.825 is a _____ number.

----

whole, mixed, decimal

Digit positions to billions (whole numbers) and to billionths (decimal numbers) are illustrated in the chart.

Billions	Hundred millions	Ten millions	Millions	Hundred thousands	Ten thousands	Thousands	Hundreds	Tens	Units	DECIMAL POINT	Tenths	Hundredths	Thousandths	Ten-thousandths	Hundred-thousandths	Millionths	Ten-millionths	Hundred-millionths	Billionths
←				Whole numbers					→	·	←				Decimal numbers				→

WHOLE NUMBERS AND DECIMALS 9

Examples in reading: 8 is read "eight."
  23 is read "twenty-three."
  458 is read "four hundred fifty-eight."
  6108 is read "six thousand, one hundred eight."

The word "and" is used to indicate the decimal point for numbers that include digits to the *right* of the decimal; for example,

  2.5 is read "two and five tenths."
  167.09 is read "one hundred sixty-seven and nine hundredths."
  6030.4 is read "six thousand thirty and four tenths."
  .305 is read "three hundred five thousandths."

5. The following numbers are read as

  2.6 _____
  30.07 _____
  .08 _____
  400.56 _____
  10,906.7 _____

- -

"two and six tenths," "thirty and seven hundredths," "eight hundredths," "four hundred and fifty six hundredths," "ten thousand, nine hundred six and seven tenths."

6. Zeros may be added after the decimal point without changing its value. Thus 2.5 = 2.50 = 2.5000, etc., 56 = 56.0 = 56.00, etc., .5 = <u>50</u> hundredths.

  .03 = _____ thousandths.

  12.5 = twelve and _____ hundredths.

  .5500 = five thousand, five hundred ten-thousandths or _____ hundredths.

- -

thirty, fifty, fifty-five

7. Large numbers are generally easier to read when the comma is used to group hundreds, thousands, millions, and so on; for example, the number 3678458 is easily and quickly read when written as 3,678,458, i.e., "three million, six hundred seventy-eight thousand, four hundred fifty-eight."

   4589065 written as 4,589,065 is read _____

   _____

   -

   four million, five hundred eighty-nine thousand, sixty-five

8. Eight hundred twenty-five and sixteen thousandths is written as _____.

   Nine thousand fifty-six and eight ten-thousandths is written as _____.
   Ten thousand, one hundred six and two hundred fifty thousandths is written as

   _____.

   -

   825.016, 9,056.0008, 10,106.250

Adding Numbers

Addition is the means by which two or more numbers are combined and expressed as a single quantity called a *sum* or *total*. The *plus* (+) sign is used to denote addition.

When a group of numbers is to be added, units are added to units, tens are added to tens, hundreds are added to hundreds, and so on. Therefore they should be aligned so that whole numbers and decimals are properly placed in relation to one another.

Examples: 3 + 45 = 48   or $\begin{array}{r} 3 \\ +45 \\ \hline 48 \end{array}$ $\begin{array}{r} 5.9 \\ + .013 \\ \hline 5.913 \end{array}$ sum or total

   To add 3.5, .006, 1265, 9.0965 line up the columns *exactly* as they are shown here.

$$\begin{array}{r} 3.5 \\ .006 \\ 1265. \\ 9.0965 \\ \hline 1277.6025 \end{array}$$ sum or total

9. (a) Copy the following numbers in a column and add: 375, 80, .05, 2.65, 82.009

(b) Write in a column and add the following: seven tenths, nine hundred sixty, five thousandths, and three and five tenths.

- -

(a) 375
      80
        .05
       2.65
     82.009
     ──────
     539.709

(b)   .7
     960.
        .005
       3.5
     ──────
     964.205

Developing Speed and Accuracy in Addition, Grouping by Tens

Look for and combine two or more numbers that add to 10 in the same column. In the example shown at the right note that 7 and 3 add to 10 and that 6 plus 4 equals 10 in the units column. Add the remaining numbers in that column. The result is 24. The digit 2, which is carried to the 10's position, combines with 8 to equal 10, to which other digits in that column are added.

```
 37⎤
 53⎦
 46⎤
 91⎦
⎡84⎦
⎢93
⎣ 2
———
404
```

It is a good idea to record the number to be carried to the next column [(2 in this problem) to the 10's position] as a check when re-adding or interrupted.

Other number combinations that tend to repeat themselves may be used in the same manner.

10. Find the sum of each of the following, using combinations of 10 whenever possible. Show combinations of 10s as illustrated above.

(a)	8.36	(b)	19	(c)	16	(d)	1.02
	1.03		6		8		3.25
	9.21		25		20		4.53
	16.14		71		72		.18
					9		5.22
					22		

- -

(a) 8.36⎤
    ⎡1.03⎦
    ⎣9.21⎦ or
     16.14
     2 1
     ————
     34.74

(b) ⎡19⎤
    ⎢ 6
    ⎢25
    ⎣71⎦
      2
     ———
     121

(c) ⎡16⎤
    ⎢ 8⎦
    ⎢20
    ⎣72⎦
      9 or
     22
      2
     ———
     147

(d) 1.02⎤
     3.25⎦
    ⎡4.53⎦
    ⎢ .18⎤
    ⎣5.22⎦
     1 2
     ————
     14.20

Developing Speed and Accuracy in Addition, Using Subtotals

When a long column of numbers is to be added (a) add part of the column and record to the side and (b) add these partial totals (subtotals) to get a final total. This method is helpful, since you may be interrupted, in which case the whole column need not be re-added.

Example: 328
422
<u>511</u> 1261 subtotal
741
108
62
<u>1550</u> 2461 subtotal
145
22
2100
914
<u>62</u> <u>3243</u> subtotal
6965 6965 total

11. In the example shown above the subtotal 1261 is the total of the first three numbers, 2461 is the total of the next four numbers, and 3243 is the total of the last _____ numbers.

― ―

5

12. In the following problems record the subtotals and total as indicated.
 (a) 36   (b) 3.17
      127   22.09
      890   55.43 _____
      3110 _____   9.44
      346   8.69
      578   83.75 _____
      289 _____   2.09
      64   18.26 _____
      <u>22</u> _____   total
              total

― ―

 (a) 4163   (b) 80.69
      1213   101.88
      <u>86</u>   <u>20.35</u>
      5462   202.92

Checking Answers

Checking answers in addition by the reverse-order method is the most common. This means that if you have added a column of numbers from the top down, you must re-add by starting from the bottom and adding up.

13. Add this column and check by the reverse-order method.

```
   _____      (b)  Add from the bottom to the top and record total here.
   2365
    821       Obviously, if your two totals are not the same, you have made an
   9067       error.
    544
   8178
    975
   1819
   _____      (a)  Add from the top down and record total here.
```

23,769

EXERCISE 1

See how many minutes it takes you to complete this exercise.

1.	823 569 5460 5421	2.	4528 980 5990 659	3.	1074 4208 878 582	4.	.0078 .6954 .0708 .1538
5.	87.87 9.19 41.19 .89	6.	18.67 102.21 55.55 3.78	7.	42.68 5.33 2.47 77.12	8.	27,889 1,342 31,178 8,556 36,230
		9.	31.27 8.99 45.44 82.14 9.56 118.06 67.55 63.16	10.	879.25 23.30 638.17 61.53 452.00 78.56		

16 UNIT 1

1.
```
          8  2⌐ 3
          5⌐ 6⌐ 9⌐
    5⌐  4  6  0
    5⌡ 4⌡ 2⌡ 1⌡
    ₂   ₁  ₁
   12,  2  7  3
```

2.
```
       4  5  2⌐ 8
             9  8⌡ 0
       5  9  9⌐ 0
             6  5⌡ 9
       ₃    ₂   ₁
      12,  1  5  7
```

3.
```
    1  0  7  4
    4  2⌐ 0  8
       8⌡ 7  8⌐
       5  8⌐ 2⌡
    ₁  ₂  ₂
    6, 7  4  2
```

4.
```
    .0  0  7⌐ 8
    .6  9⌐ 5  4⌐
    .0  7  0  8⌡
    .1  5⌡ 3⌡ 8⌡
    ₂   ₁  ₂
    .9  2  7  8
```

5.
```
       8  7. 8  7
          9.⌐ 1⌐ 9
       4  1.⌡ 1⌡ 9
          .   8⌡ 9
          ₁  ₂  ₃
      13  9. 1  4
```

6.
```
       1  8.⌐ 6⌐ 7
    1  0  2.⌡ 2⌡ 1
       5  5.⌐ 5  5
             3.⌡ 7  8
       ₂    ₂  ₂
    1  8  0. 2  1
```

7.
```
    4  2.  6  8⌐
       5.  3⌐ 3⌡
       2.⌐ 4⌐ 7⌡
    7  7.⌡ 1⌡ 2⌡
       ₁   ₁  ₂
   12  7.  6  0
```

8.
```
    2⌐ 7  8  8  9
       1  3  4  2⌐
    3⌐ 1  1⌐ 7  8⌡
       8  5⌡ 5⌐ 6
    3⌐ 6  2⌡ 3⌡ 0
    ₂   ₂  ₂  ₂
    10 5, 1  9  5
```

9.
```
       3  1. 2  7
          8. 9⌐ 9
       4⌐ 5. 4  4⌐
       8  2.⌐ 1⌡ 4⌐
          9.  5  6⌡
    1  1  8.⌡ 0  6⌡
       6⌐ 7.⌐ 5⌐ 5
       6  3.⌡ 1⌡ 6
    ₃  ₄  ₃   ₄
    4  2  6.  1  7
```

10.
```
          8  7⌐ 9. 2⌐ 5
          2  3. 3⌡ 0
       6⌐ 3⌡ 8.⌐ 1  7⌐
          6   1.⌡ 5⌡ 3⌡
       4⌡ 5   2.⌐ 0  0
          7⌐ 8.⌐ 5  6
       ₃  ₃   ₁  ₂
      21  3   2.  8  1
```

If you completed this exercise in 3 or 4 minutes, you are doing fine and, if all of your answers are correct, good for you. If you missed only one, that is good, too. The number of problems completed correctly per minute is the important measure. If you completed fewer than 7 correctly in 3 minutes, you need to practice.

Go to page 17.

Crossfooting: Vertical and Horizontal Addition

One definition of the word "foot" is to add (a column of figures) and set down a total. To crossfoot means to add horizontally and set down a total.

Many business reports require both vertical and horizontal addition. Data are arranged to provide more than one kind of information, besides including a check against totals.

The following report provides (a) the total sales for each district for the week and (b) the total sales for each day of the week. It is also a convenient means of making comparisons between districts or days and other weekly periods during the year.

The total of the line or district totals ($1327.02) is also the total of the column or daily totals and is referred to as the *grand total*.

MANLY CATERING SERVICE

Sales   Week Ending June ____, 19 ____

District	Monday	Tuesday	Wednesday	Thursday	Friday	Saturday	Total
A	$ 43.20	$ 92.52	$ 78.69	$ 86.98	$ 99.35	$120.50	$ 521.24
B	71.15	76.56	68.25	$ 91.00	82.52	99.20	488.68
C	55.17	66.42	45.98	54.13	45.00	50.40	317.10
Total	$169.52	$235.50	$192.92	$232.11	$226.87	$270.10	$1327.02

14. In the example above, $169.52 is a (district/daily) total   _____

$317.10 is a (district/daily) total   _____

The grand total is $ _____

The sum of the district totals is $ _____

The sum of the daily totals is $ _____

---

daily
district
$1327.02
$1327.02
$1327.02

Since the sum of the district totals equals the sum of the daily totals, the report is assumed to be correct. (It is possible but rare to have a compensating error.)

Identifying and Correcting Errors in Crossfooting

A great deal of time can be saved if you know how to locate an error. The possibilities depend on the type of problem. In the problem illustrated proceed as follows:

1. Find the difference between the sum of the line totals and the sum of the column totals.

   (a) If the difference appears in the units column, re-add that column only; if it appears in the tens column, re-add the first two columns, and so on.
   (b) If the difference equals any one number in the report, it is likely that it was omitted in adding.
   (c) An error of 1, 10, or any power of 10 is almost always an error in addition rather than in copying or omitting a number.

2. If the error cannot be localized, re-add the total column and verify the line totals.

3. As a last resort check each column total and then check each line total.

15. Find the error in the following report. Draw a line through the incorrect total and record the correct amount directly above it. Record the correct grand total.

A & C BUILDERS

Contracts for July

Type of Contract	District			Total
	A	B	C	
1-A	36	77	49	162
3-Z	109	82	76	267
2-C	25	56	40	121
Total	170	205	165	——

(a) The sum of the total line as shown is _____.

(b) The sum of the total column as shown is _____.

(c) The correct grand total is _____.

(a) 540, (b) 550, (c) 550
Total of column B should be 215.

16. One common fault in copying numbers is transposing digits—reversing their order. When this occurs, the difference from the control figures will be a multiple of 9 (e.g., 9, 18, 27).

If 36 is copied as 63, the difference will be ____. Is this a multiple of 9? ____. If the digits in the number 91 are transposed when copied, the number will be ____. The difference will be ____ which is a multiple of ____.

27, yes, 19, 72, 9

17. These figures were copied from other records. One number has been transposed. Add each column and line. Then compare your totals with the correct totals shown at the right. Locate the error, draw a line through it, and record the correct number directly above it. Correct the totals affected by this error in the same manner.

A	B	C	Total		A	B	C	Total
36	98	32	___					157
57	27	49	___					133
19	38	51	___		___	___	___	108
					112	154	132	398

A	B	C	Total
	89		157
36	~~98~~	32	~~166~~
57	27	49	133
19	38	51	108
	154		398
112	~~163~~	132	~~407~~

18. A & B MERCHANTS

Sales Report				Week Ending January ____, 19____
District	Department			Total
	A	B	C	
Anza	$ 2,316.94	$ 7,546.18	$ 5,627.93	$15,491.05
Ballard	8,140.06	10,092.22	7,901.01	26,133.29
Manor	9,200.10	8,654.55	7,598.66	25,453.31
Hayes	5,476.18	7,078.00	3,950.75	16,504.93
Total	$25,133.28	$33,370.85	$25,078.35	$83,582.58

The total of the column totals equals $83,582.48, a difference of 10¢ from the total shown in the total column. This suggests an error in addition. Since it is easier to add vertically than horizontally, begin by checking the department totals, adding just the first two columns of digits (cents columns). Find it? Good for you. The error was in Department ___. The total should read $_____.

Department B; the total should be $33,370.95

19. When errors are a multiple of 10, it suggests an error in _____ rather than an omission or a number copied incorrectly.
When the error cannot be identified check the (horizontal/vertical) addition first.

----

addition, vertical

Subtracting Numbers

Subtraction is the process of finding the difference between numbers. Unless otherwise stated, the minus (−) sign is used to indicate subtraction. To check answers add mentally the difference (answer) to the subtrahend, which should, of course, equal the minuend.

$$\begin{array}{rl} 36.16 & \text{minuend} \\ -20.75 & \text{subtrahend} \\ \hline 15.41 & \text{difference or remainder} \end{array}$$

OR   36.16 − 20.75 = 15.41.

Check   15.41 + 20.75 = 36.16.

WHOLE NUMBERS AND DECIMALS 21

20. Circle answers that are incorrect in the following examples:

(a) 489
    −237
    ———
    252

(b) 101.56
    − 39.59
    ———
    61.87

(c) 31,377
    −18,788
    ———
    12,689

(d) 631.45
    −238.83
    ———
    392.62

(e) 4007
    −3110
    ———
    997

(f) 504.18
    −231.07
    ———
    263.11

(b), (c), (e), (f)

21. Subtract. Check results mentally.

(a) 61.53
    49.02

(b) 50,677
    33,786

(c) .00583
    .00505

(d) 10,017
    9,009

(e) 21,054
    11,009

(f) 234.56
    88.05

(a) 12.51   (b) 16,891   (c) .00078
(d) 1008   (e) 10,045   (f) 146.51

22. Complete the following report. It represents dollar sales for the Havens-court Services for the current year, compared with the same period for the preceding year.

HAVENSCOURT SERVICES

Comparative Sales Report

	This Year	Last Year	Difference
First 6 months	$2,316,820.08	$3,516,008.20	$_____ decrease
Last 6 months	$4,008,920.00	$3,927,111.19	$_____ increase
Total	$_____	$_____	$_____

- -

This Year $6,325,740.08, Last Year, $7,443,119.39, Difference, $1,117,379.31

23. Find the net weight of the following carriers. (Gross weight equals the weight of the carrier plus the contents; tare weight equals the weight of the carrier; net weight equals the weight of the contents—grows weight less tare weight.) Verify the total net weight for the five carriers listed by the principle of crossfooting.

Gross	*Tare*	*Net*
13,620	462	_____
27,317	462	_____
18,504	462	_____
35,614	462	_____
34,250	462	_____

Total

- -

Gross total, 129,305, Tare total 2310, Net total, 126,995

Multiplying Numbers

Multiplication is a short method of repeat addition; for example, 3 multiplied by 4 equals 12, which is the same as 3 added 4 times (3 + 3 + 3 + 3) or 4 added 3 times (4 + 4 + 4).

The result of multiplying two numbers (called *factors*) by one another is called the *product*. Since the result is the same, regardless of the factor used as the multiplier, it is easier to use the smaller number.

24. In the problem 3 × 6 = 18, 3 and 6 are called _____. The result, 18, is called the _____.

----

factors, product

25. *Multiplication of whole numbers with two or more digits*

 Example: Multiply 365 by 54 **Problem:** Complete the following multiplication.

```
        365   multiplicand                  296
         54   multiplier                     32
       ————                                 ———
       1460
       1825
       ————
      19710   answer (product)
```

```
    296
     32
    ———
    592
    888
    ————
   9472
```

26. *Multiplication of decimal numbers with two or more digits*

When decimal numbers are multiplied, the product must have as many decimals as there are in both factors.

24 UNIT 1

Example: Multiply 3.605 by 1.27

```
    3.605   multiplicand (3 decimals)
    1.27    multiplier (2 decimals)
   -----
   25235
    7210
    3605
   ------
   457835
   4.57835  answer or product
            (5 decimals)
```

Problem: Complete the following multiplication.

```
   2.064
   13.2
   ----
```

_____

```
   2.064
   13.2
   -----
   4128
   6192
   2064
   ------
   272448
   27.2448   answer or product
```

27. Indicate the position of the decimal point in the answers for the following problems:

3.16 ×	20	6320
52 ×	.0078	4056
21.96 ×	5.34	1172664
1.85 ×	6.257	1157545
.18 ×	.07	126

_____

```
    63.20
     .4056
  117.2664
   11.57545
     .0126
```

28. Answers may be checked in multiplication work by (a) reversing the factors or (b) dividing the product by either factor to obtain the other. Because multiplication is an easier process than division, the first method is usually preferred.

Example: If 3 × 40 = 120, then 40 × 3 = 120 or 120 ÷ 3 = 40.

Verify the answers to the following problems by reversing the factors.

(a) 3.25   Check: 5.6   (b) 13.75   Check: 23.9
     5.6   3.25   23.9   13.75
     ────   ────   ─────   ─────
     1950   12375
     1625   4125
     ────   2750
     18.200   ───────
                                  328.625

- -

(a)   5.6   (b)   23.9
      3.25   13.75
      ────   ─────
      280   1195
      112   1673
      168   717
      ────   239
      18.200   ───────
                     328.625

Multiplying by Any Power of 10 (10, 100, 1000, etc.)

Whole numbers: If a number is to be multiplied by 10, 100, 1000, etc., simply add to the multiplicand the number of zeros in the multiplier.

Examples: 96 ×   10 =   960
               96 ×   100 =   9600
               96 × 1000 = **96000**

Decimal numbers: If the multiplicand is a decimal, move the decimal point to the right one place for each zero in the multiplier.

Examples: 3.167 ×   10 =   31.67
               3.167 ×   100 =   316.7
               3.167 × 1000 = 3167

29. When a number is multiplied by 100, add _____ zeros to the multiplicand.
4608 × 100 = _____, 960 × 100 = _____.

2,   460,800,   96,000

30. 162 × 10 = _____, 36 × 1000 = _____, 126 × 100 = _____.

1620,   36000,   12600

31. If 16.5 is multiplied by 10, move the decimal point _____ places to the right to obtain the product.
2.64 × 10 = 26.4,   8.25 × 10 = _____,   .19 × 10 = _____.

1
82.5,   1.9

32. 80.5 × 10000 = _____, 10.645 × 100 = _____, .0368 × 1000 = _____.

805,000,   1064.5,   36.8

Multiplying by Any Factor of 10, 100, 1000, etc., such as 5, 25, 50, $16\frac{2}{3}$, and 125

1. 629 × 5
   629 × 10 = 6290
   6290 ÷ 2 = 3145 (answer)

   Multiply by 10 and then divide the result by 2, since 10 is 2 times as great as 5.

2. 45 × 25
   45 × 100 = 4500
   4500 ÷ 4 = 1125 (answer)

   Multiply by 100 and then divide the result by 4, since 100 is 4 times as great as 25.

3. 562 × 50
   562 × 100 = 56,200
   56,200 ÷ 2 = 28,100 (answer)

   Multiply by 100 and then divide the result by 2, since 100 is 2 times as great as 50.

4. 36 × $16\frac{2}{3}$
   36 × 100 = 3600
   3600 ÷ 6 = 600 (answer)

   Multiply by 100 and then divide the result by 6, since 100 is 6 times as great as $16\frac{2}{3}$.

5. 912 × 125
   912 × 1000 = 912,000
   912,000 ÷ 8 = 114,000 (answer)

   Multiply by 1000 and then divide the result by 8, since 1000 is 8 times as great as 125.

33. Study the above examples and then test yourself with the following statements.

  (a) An easy way to multiply by 25 is to multiply by _____ and then divide by _____.

  (b) To multiply 725 by 20 add _____ zeros and then divide by _____.

  (c) An easy way to multiply a number by 50 is to multiply by _____ and then divide by _____.

(a) 100, 4, (b) 2, 5, (c) 100, 2

28 UNIT 1

34. Perform the following calculations, using shortcut methods.

(a) 16 × 5 =   160 ÷ 2 = _____.
     27 × 50 =   2700 ÷ 2 = _____.
     16 × 25 =   1600 ÷ 4 = _____.
     48 × 125 =   48,000 ÷ 8 = _____.

(b) 316 × 50 = _____ ÷ __ = _____.
     82 × 125 = _____ ÷ __ = _____.
     126 × 5 = _____ ÷ __ = _____.
     3.28 × 25 = _____ ÷ __ = _____.

(c) 96.4 × 125 = _____ ÷ __ = _____.
     8.55 × 5 = _____ ÷ __ = _____.
     15.24 × 50 = _____ ÷ __ = _____.
     218 × 25 = _____ ÷ __ = _____.

- -

(a) 16 × 5 =   160 ÷ 2 =   80.
     27 × 50 =   2700 ÷ 2 =   1350.
     16 × 25 =   1600 ÷ 4 =   400.
     48 × 125 =   48,000 ÷ 8 = 6,000.

(b) 316 × 50 = 31,600   ÷ 2 = 15,800.
     82 × 125 = 82,000   ÷ 8 = 10,250.
     126 × 5 = 1260   ÷ 2 = 630.
     3.28 × 25 = 328   ÷ 4 = 82.

(c) 96.4 × 125 = 96,400 ÷ 8 = 12,050.
     8.55 × 5 =   85.5   ÷ 2 = 42.75.
     15.24 × 50 = 1524   ÷ 2 = 762.
     218 × 25 = 21,800   ÷ 4 = 5450.

Multiplying by 9, 99, 101, 90, 110

Such numbers as these (there are many others) can be multiplied quickly by some other number. Any number may be expressed as the sum or difference of two numbers; for example,

$$9 \text{ has the same value as } 10 - 1$$
$$99 \text{ has the same value as } 100 - 1$$
$$101 \text{ has the same value as } 100 + 1$$
$$90 \text{ has the same value as } 100 - 10$$
$$110 \text{ has the same value as } 100 + 10$$

Therefore the following examples may be solved as illustrated.

1. $26 \times 9 = 26 \times (10 - 1)$ OR $26(10 - 1) = 260 - 26 = 234$.
2. $546 \times 99 = 546(100 - 1) = 54{,}600 - 546 = 54{,}054$.
3. $214 \times 101 = 214(100 + 1) = 21{,}400 + 214 = 21{,}614$.
4. $763 \times 90 = 763(100 - 10) = 76{,}300 - 7630 = 68{,}670$.
5. $3.54 \times 110 = 3.54(100 + 10) = 354 + 35.4 = 389.4$.

35. Perform the following calculations, using shortcut methods.

(a)
$36 \times 9 = 360 - 36 = \underline{}$.
$29 \times 99 = 2900 - 29 = \underline{}$.
$75 \times 90 = 7500 - 750 = \underline{}$.
$8.7 \times 101 = 870 + 8.7 = \underline{}$.
$123 \times 110 = 12{,}300 + 1230 = \underline{}$.

(b)
$3.42 \times 90 = \underline{} - \underline{} = \underline{}$.
$132 \times 99 = \underline{} - \underline{} = \underline{}$.
$96.2 \times 101 = \underline{} + \underline{} = \underline{}$.
$42.5 \times 110 = \underline{} + \underline{} = \underline{}$.
$387 \times 9 = \underline{} - \underline{} = \underline{}$.

(a)   36 × 9   =   360 −   36   =   324.
      29 × 99 =   2900 −   29   = 2871.
      75 × 90 =   7500 −   750   = 6750.
     8.7 × 101 =   870 +   8.7   = 878.7.
     123 × 110 = 12,300 + 1230   = 13,530.

(b) 3.42 × 90 =   342 − 34.2   = 307.8.
      132 × 99 = 13,200 −   132   = 13,068.
     96.2 × 101 =   9620 + 96.2   = 9716.2.
     42.5 × 110 =   4250 +   425   = 4675.
      387 × 9   =   3870 −   387   = 3483.

Dividing Whole Numbers

Division is a short method of repeat subtraction. It is the inverse operation of multiplication; for example, 20 divided by 5 is the same as saying: "How many times can the number 5 be subtracted from 20?" In this case the number is 4.

Any division problem may be expressed as follows:

$$362 \div 15, \quad \frac{362}{15}, \quad \text{or} \quad 15\overline{)362}$$

Ability to divide quickly and accurately is dependent on a thorough knowledge of the multiplication tables.

36. (a) The number 14 can be subtracted from 70 *five* times. Then 70 divided by 5 = _____ and 70 divided by 14 = _____.

  (b) 24 ÷ 6 is the same as asking how many times 6 can be _____ from 24. The answer is _____.

- -

(a) 14, 5
(b) subtracted, 4

37. Perform the following computations, giving the remainder, if any, as shown in the example. Show your work in the space provided.

Example:

$$\begin{array}{r}24\text{ quotient}\\15\overline{)362}\text{ dividend}\\30\\\hline 62\\60\\\hline 2\text{ remainder}\end{array}$$

(a) $57\overline{)9090}$ (b) $26\overline{)735}$

(a) $\begin{array}{r}159\\57\overline{)9090}\\57\\\hline 339\\285\\\hline 540\\513\\\hline 27\end{array}$

(b) $\begin{array}{r}28\\26\overline{)735}\\52\\\hline 215\\208\\\hline 7\end{array}$

Dividing Decimal Numbers

After the decimal point has been determined proceed as with whole numbers.

When the number of decimals in the divisor is equal to or less than those in the dividend, mentally move the decimal point in the dividend as many places as there are decimal places in the divisor to locate the decimal point in the quotient.*

---

*The dividend and divisor or, in fraction form, the numerator and denominator may be multiplied by any number without changing its value; that is,

$$\frac{.2815 \times 100}{.05 \times 100} = \frac{28.15}{5} = 5.63.$$

Examples: $4.00\overset{3.}{\overline{1)12.003}}$ $136\overline{)2805.1}^{20.6+}$ $.0\overset{5.63}{\overline{5).2815}}$

$.00\overset{.09}{\overline{9).00081}}$ $.01\overset{.05}{\overline{8).00090}}$ $4.00\overset{3.}{\overline{1)12.003}}$

When the number of decimals in the divisor is greater than in the dividend, add decimal places in the dividend to equal those in the divisor. Zeros added to any number after the decimal point do not change its value.

Examples: (a) Divide 1026 by .15   (b) Divide 80.26 by 2.016

$.15\overline{)1026.00}^{6840.}$ $2.016\overline{)80.260}^{39.+}$

38. Indicate the position of the decimal point in the quotient for the following, as illustrated in the example. Add zeros to the dividend when necessary.

Example: $.26\overline{)36.056}$

(a) $36.5\overline{)29.0078}$ (b) $.15\overline{)7563}$ (c) $23\overline{)7.896}$

(d) $.52\overline{)9580.46}$ (e) $.036\overline{)21.6}$ (f) $4.27\overline{)369}$

(g) $2.017\overline{)8.25}$ (h) $46\overline{).00789}$ (i) $.0036\overline{)78.01}$

(a) $36.5\overline{)29.0078}$ (b) $.15\overline{)7563.00}$ (c) $23\overline{)7.896}$

(d) $.52\overline{)9580.46}$ (e) $.036\overline{)21.600}$ (f) $4.27\overline{)369.00}$

(g) $2.017\overline{)8.250}$ (h) $46\overline{).00789}$ (i) $.0036\overline{)78.0100}$

39. Divide as indicated. Show remainder.

(a) $19\overline{)4.205}$ (b) $3.55\overline{)21.65}$ (c) $.42\overline{).0076}$

(d) $.026\overline{)28.4}$ (e) $2.014\overline{)82.6}$

(a)
```
        .221
    19)4.205
       3 8
       ---
         40
         38
         --
         25
         19
         --
          6
```

(b)
```
          6.
     3.55)21.65
          21 30
          -----
             35
```

(c)
```
          .01
     .42).0076
          42
          --
          34
```

(d)
```
         1092.
    .026)28.400
         26
         --
          2 40
          2 34
          ----
             60
             52
             --
              8
```

(e)
```
         41.
    2.014)82.600
          80 56
          -----
           2 040
           2 014
           -----
              26
```

Checking Answers in Division

Multiply the quotient by the divisor and add the remainder (if any). The result should equal the dividend.

Example: $953 \div 22 = $ 43 with a remainder of 7.
  Check: $43 \times 22 = 946$; $946 + 7 = 953$.

40. If $615 \div 36 = 17$ with a remainder of 3, then $17 \times$ ____ = ____ and ____ + 3 = 615.

_ _

  $17 \times 36 = 612$ and $612 + 3 = 615$

41. Divide 3828 by 255 and verify. Show work in space provided.

$$255\overline{)3828} \underset{}{\overset{15}{}} \text{ with a remainder of 3}$$

Check: (255 × 15) + 3 = 3828.

Dividing by Any Power of 10 (10, 100, 1000, etc.)

Whole numbers: Mark off as many decimal places as there are zeros in the divisor.

Examples: 54 ÷   10 = 5.4.
216 ÷ 100 = 2.16.
 29 ÷ 1000 = .029.

Decimal numbers: Move the decimal point to the left as many places as there are zeros in the divisor.

Examples: 2.19 ÷   10 = .219.
436.54 ÷ 100 = 4.3654.
 92.7 ÷ 1000 = .0927.

42. Divide 3168 by   10 = _____ ,

3168 by 100 = _____ ,

3168 by 1000 = _____ .

316.8, 31.68, 3.168

43. Divide 417.55 by 10 = _____,

    46.789 by 100 = _____,

    358.090 by 1000 = _____.

41.755, .46789, .358090

Dividing by Any Factor of 10, 100, 1000, etc.

1. 962   ÷ 5   Divide by 10 and then multiply the
    962   ÷ 10 = 96.2   result by 2, since 10 is 2 times as
    96.2   × 2 = 192.4   great as 5.

2. 3620   ÷ 25   Divide by 100 and then multiply by 4,
    3620   × 100 = 36.20 since 100 is 4 times as great as 25.
    36.20   × 4   = 144.80

3. 854   ÷ 125   Divide by 1000 and then multiply by 8,
    854   ÷ 1000 = .854 since 1000 is 8 times as great as 125.
    .854   × 8   = 6.832

44. To divide any number by 5 first divide by ____ and then multiply by ____.

10, 2

45. When a number is divided by 25, the result equals four times the amount when divided by _____.

100

46. A quick method of dividing by 250 is first to divide by 1000 and then multiply by ____.

4

47. Using the method illustrated above, divide 3680 by 12.5.

3680 ÷ _____ = 36.80, _____ × 8 = _____.

- -

3680 ÷ 100 = 36.80, 36.80 × 8 = 294.40

48. Work the following problems, using shortcut methods. Show remainder for those problems with uneven answers.

(a) 735 ÷ 25 = (735 ÷ _____) × __ = _____.
(b) 5106 ÷ 100 = _____.
(c) 375 ÷ 1000 = _____.
(d) 2125 ÷ 125 = _____.
(e) 3278 ÷ 5 = _____.

- -

(a) 735 ÷ 25 = (735 ÷ 100) × 4 = 7.35 × 4 = 29.40.
(b) 5106 ÷ 100 = 51.06.
(c) 375 ÷ 1000 = .375.
(d) 2125 ÷ 125 = (2125 ÷ 1000) × 8 = 2.125 × 8 = 17.000.
(e) 3278 ÷ 5 = (3278 ÷ 10) × 2 = 327.8 × 2 = 655.6.

EXERCISE 2

General Instructions: Work the following problems as quickly as you can. Use shortcuts when appropriate. Record answers in the spaces provided. *Time yourself.* Check your answers with those shown at the end of this exercise.

I. Multiplication

1. 23 × 25 = _____.
2. 319 × 5 = _____.
3. 27.5 × 101 = _____.
4. .0675 × 10 = _____.
5. 976 × 50 = _____.
6. 51.32 × 1000 = _____.
7. 700 × 125 = _____.
8. 3.167 × 100 = _____.
9. 74 × 110 = _____.
10. 90 × 96 = _____.
11. 46 × 35 = _____.
12. 38 × 62 = _____.
13. 47.36 × 80.2 = _____.
14. .189 × 14.6 = _____.
15. 37.5 × 4.06 = _____.

II. Division

1. Find the quotients for the following correct to 2 decimals. Division must be carried to 1 more decimal than is required in the answer. If the third decimal is less than 5, drop it; if it is more than 5, increase the second decimal by 1: for example, (1) 17.428 ÷ .24 = 72.616 (to 3 decimals) or 72.62 corrected to 2 decimals; (2) 5.6 ÷ 92 = .060. Record as .06.

   (a) .24 ÷ 2.7 = _____.
   (b) 72 ÷ 26.4 = _____.
   (c) 8.7 ÷ 15.7 = _____.
   (d) 6.6 ÷ .75 = _____.
   (e) 23.86 ÷ 375 = _____.
   (f) 148 ÷ .026 = _____.

2. Record all answers correct to the nearest thousandth. Carry quotient to 4 decimals and increase or drop the third decimal as illustrated. (1) 48 ÷ 58 = .8275. Record as .828. (2) 6.795 ÷ 12 = .5662. Record as .566.

   (a) .90 ÷ 3.2 = _____.
   (b) 100 ÷ 3.85 = _____.
   (c) 48 ÷ .16 = _____.
   (d) 62 ÷ 1.50 = _____.
   (e) .648 ÷ 4.86 = _____.
   (f) 49 ÷ .54 = _____.

Answers

I. Multiplication

1. 575	2. 1595	3. 2777.5
4. .675	5. 48,800	6. 51,320
7. 87,500	8. 316.7	9. 8140
10. 8640	11. 1610	12. 2356
13. 3798.272	14. 2.7594	15. 152.250

II. Division

1. (a) .09
   (b) 2.73
   (c) .55
   (d) 8.80
   (e) .06
   (f) 5692.31

2. (a) .281
   (b) 25.974
   (c) 300.000
   (d) 41.333
   (e) .133
   (f) 90.741

Solutions to Section I

1. $23 \times 25 = (23 \times 100) \div 4 = 2300 \div 4 = 575.$
2. $319 \times 5 = (319 \times 10) \div 2 = 3190 \div 2 = 1595.$
3. $27.5 \times 101 = (27.5 \times 100) + (27.5) = 2750 + 27.5 = 2777.5.$
4. $.0675 \times 10 = .675.$
5. $976 \times 50 = (976 \times 100) \div 2 = 97,600 \div 2 = 48,800.$
6. $51.32 \times 1000 = 51,320.$
7. $700 \times 125 = (700 \times 1000) \div 8 = 700,000 \div 8 = 87,500.$
8. $3.167 \times 100 = 316.7.$
9. $74 \times 110 = (74 \times 100) + (74 \times 10) = 7400 + 740 = 8140.$
10. $90 \times 96 = (96 \times 100) - (96 \times 10) = 9600 - 960 = 8640.$
11. $46 \times 35 = 1610.$
12. $38 \times 62 = 2356.$
13. $47.36 \times 80.2 = 3798.272.$
14. $.189 \times 14.6 = 2.7594.$
15. $37.5 \times 4.06 = 152.250$ OR $\frac{3}{8} \times (4.06 \times 100) = \frac{3}{8} \times 406 = 152.25.$

UNIT 2. ROUNDING NUMBERS, ESTIMATING ANSWERS

Rounding Numbers

The number of significant figures desired depends on their use. If the part of the number that is to be dropped begins with 5 or more, add 1 to the preceding digit; if the number to be dropped begins with some digit less than 5, drop it and record the preceding digits unchanged.

The following numbers illustrate this principle:

Rounded to Hundreds	*Rounded to Thousands*
863 to 900	821,862 to 822,000
450 to 500	37,500 to 38,000
319 to 300	9,499 to 9,000

Rounded to Units	*Rounded to Hundredths*
32.50 to 33	0.7349 to 0.73
41.25 to 41	0.10409 to 0.10
70.92 to 71	3.5 to 3.50
6.499 to 6	44.0653 to 44.07

1. 925 rounded to the nearest hundreds is 900 because the next digit 2 is *less than* 5. In this case the digits 2 and 5 are dropped. Then, according to this rule, 916 rounded to the nearest hundreds equals _____ because the next digit 1 is equal to/less than/more than) 5.

   _____

   900, less than

2. 856 equals 900 rounded to the nearest hundreds because the second digit is 5. Therefore raise the digit 8 to 9. According to this rule, 857 rounded to hundreds equals _____ because the second digit is (equal to/less than/more than)5.

   _____

   900, equal to

3. 6.899 rounded to the nearest whole number equals 7 because the digit 8 is *more than* 5. Then 17.699 rounded to the nearest whole number is _____.
   Round 8.52 to the nearest whole number   _____,
       1678 to the nearest hundreds   _____,
       2189 to the nearest thousands   _____.

   _____

   18, 9, 1700, 2000

4. Round the following numbers to the nearest hundreds: 217, 865, 1009.

   _____

   200, 900, 1000

5. Round the following numbers to the nearest thousandths: .0076, 31.1541, 16.05449.

   _____

   .008, 31.154, 16.054

6. Round the following numbers to the nearest units or whole numbers: 56.5, 102.4, 7.499.

   _____

   57, 102, 7

7. The number 1277.65 rounded to the nearest whole number is (1277/1278?).

   _____

   1278

8. 8249 rounded to the nearest hundreds is (8200/8300).

    _____

    8200

9. The number 62.499 corrected or rounded to the nearest tenth is (62.5/62.4).

    _____

    62.5

Estimating Answers

An approximation is a value that is nearly but not exactly correct. There are many occasions, such as in comparative studies, decision making, and checking against gross errors in computational work, when exact figures are neither desirable nor necessary.

The report of stock market sales for any day may be 12 million shares when actually 12,426,429 shares may have been sold. The population of a certain city is reported to be 350,000, whereas 345,263 may be the exact number. In both cases the approximate figures are more meaningful to the general public. They also mean more when comparisons are made.

Although the exact answer is required in a business transaction when a settlement is made, rough estimates are used by many people in the trades, such as carpenters, repair men, plumbers. This is regular practice when bidding on a job.

The ability to estimate the answer to a problem involving computations can prevent a serious error, since it serves as a guide to the correct solution. With a little practice you can develop skill in detecting errors that might be missed otherwise.

Estimating Answers in Addition

Suppose we wanted to know the approximate total of the following list of numbers.

$$367, 125, 820, \text{ and } 578$$

Consider the first digit only. Since these numbers are all 3-digit numbers, we round them to the nearest 100, i.e., 400, 100, 800, and 600, respectively. Then

$$400 + 100 + 800 + 600 = 1900 \text{ } estimated \text{ total}$$

and

$$367 + 125 + 820 + 578 = 1890 \text{ } exact \text{ total}$$

10. What is your estimate of the following list? What is the actual total?

420, 106, 834, and 576

Estimated total = ___ + ___ + ___ + ___ = ___ .

Exact total = 420 + 106 + 834 + 576 = ___ .

Estimated total = 400 + 100 + 800 + 600 + = 1900.
Exact total = 1936.

11. If we wished to estimate the total of the following column of numbers, we would find that the values differ considerably. A good general rule is to group them and round to the most common multiple of 10, i.e., 100, 1000.

Example:	*Exact*	*Estimate*	**Problem:**	What is your estimate of the following?
	26 ⎫			22
	840 ⎭	900		368
	35 ⎫			109
	156 ⎭	200		8
	96 ⎫			19
	805 ⎭	900		625
	212 ⎫			35
	56 ⎬			82
	8 ⎭	300		192
	2234	2300		___ exact ___ estimate

Exact	Estimate		Exact	Estimate
22 ⎫			22 ⎫	
368 ⎭	400		368 ⎭	400
109	100		109 ⎫	
8 ⎫			8 ⎬	
19 ⎬		OR	19 ⎭	100
625 ⎭	600		625 ⎫	
35 ⎫			35 ⎭	700
82 ⎬			82 ⎫	
192 ⎭	300		192 ⎭	300
1460	1400		1460	1500

12. The total operating costs of a certain business for the week were $360.25, $1068.25, $8260.50, and $82.60. What is your estimate of the total? Ignore cents column; treat as $360, $1068, and so on.

```
    Exact           Estimate
  $ 360.25
    1068.25
    8260.50
      82.60
  ─────────       ─────────
  $               $
```

```
    Exact          Estimate
  $ 360.25         $ 400
    1068.25          1100
    8260.50          8300
      82.60           100
  ─────────       ─────────
  $9771.60         $9900
```

Estimating Answers in Subtraction

Mr. Jones wanted to remodel his kitchen. One company offered to do the job for $876, and another company wanted $1052, or a difference of approximately $200 ($1100–$900). The actual difference was $176.

```
      Exact                        Estimate
    $1052   minuend               $1100
  −  876    subtrahend           −  900
  ───────                        ───────
  $ 176     difference            $ 200
```

In estimating differences, always consider the smaller number (subtrahend) and round it to the nearest multiple of 10. Then round the larger number (minuend) to the same degree.

Examples:

```
    Exact      Estimate      Exact       Estimate
    9836        9800         436.50        440
  −  146      −  100        −  25.00     −  30
  ──────      ──────        ───────     ───────
    9690        9700         411.50        410
```

13. Estimate the differences for the following problems. Show your work as illustrated above.

(a) Exact   Estimate   (b) Exact   Estimate
     658   _____   768.50   _____
   − 43   _____   − 29.42   _____
                       difference

- -

(a) 615, 660 − 40 = 620, (b) 739.08, 770 − 30 = 740

14. To arrive at a closer estimate when both numbers are of the same magnitude you may want to round to the second digit from the left rather than the first; for example, in the problem below you would round to the nearest 100 rather than 1000.

Example: Exact   Estimate
               2683   2700   Since both numbers are 4-
             − 1421   − 1400   digit numbers, they are
               ────   ────   not rounded to thousands
               1262   1300   but instead, to hundreds.

Estimate the difference for the following problems.

(a) Exact   Estimate   (b) Exact   Estimate   (c) Exact   Estimate
     7342   22106   8206
   − 6250   − 19842   − 4310
     ────   ─────   ────
     1092   2264   3896

- -

(a) 7300 − 6300 = 1000, (b) 22,000 − 20,000 = 2000, (c) 8200 − 4300 = 3900

15. What is your estimate for the following?

	(a)	Exact	Estimate	(b)	Exact	Estimate	(c)	Exact	Estimate
		3168			896.50			2963	
		− 236	_____		− 76.20	_____		− 1983	_____
		2932			820.30			980	

(a) 3200 − 200 = 3000, (b) 900 − 80 = 820, (c) 3000 − 2000 = 1000

Estimating Answers in Multiplication

As in addition and subtraction, it is easy, with a little practice, to estimate answers in multiplication. An estimate tells us if our answer is approximately correct or in some cases that it is incorrect. The closer your estimate to the true answer, the better, in checking errors.

Example: 562 × 43 = 24,166.

Round each factor to the *same number* of digits. In this example round the number 43 first (since it has only two digits) to the nearest 10s and then round the larger factor to the same place.

Then 560 × 40 = 22,400 *estimate*.

16. What is your estimate and actual answer for the following?

   (a) 413 × 26 = _____.   Estimate _____ × _____ = _____.
   (b) 857 × 75 = _____.   Estimate _____ × _____ = _____.
   (c) 853 × 47 = _____.   Estimate _____ × _____ = _____.

   (a) 413 × 26 = 10,738.   Estimate 410 × 30 = 12,300.
   (b) 857 × 75 = 64,275.   Estimate 860 × 80 = 68,800.
   (c) 853 × 47 = 40,091.   Estimate 850 × 50 = 42,500.

17. Sometimes an allowance or adjustment has to be made in rounding one factor or the other to obtain a good approximate.

Example: 836 × 403 = 336,908

If both are rounded to hundreds, then 800 × 400 = 320,000. A closer estimate can be made mentally however, by rounding 836 to 840 and 403 to 400; then 840 × 400 = 336,000.

What is your estimate of (a) 875 × 403 = 352,625?

___ × ___ = _____ estimate.

(b) 907 × 585 = 530,595?

OR ___ × ___ = _____ estimate.

_ _

(a) 880 × 400 = 352,000, (b) 900 × 600 = 540,000 or 900 × 590 = 531,000

18. When multiplying decimals such as 32.56 × 5.80, drop the decimal and treat as whole numbers.

    Example: 32.56 × 5.80 = 188.848; treat as 33 × 6, then 30 × 6 = 180 (estimate)

    What is your estimate of 93.06 × 25.86 = 2406.5316?

    Estimate: ___ × ___ = _____.

    What other shortcut method might you use to make this estimate? _____.

_ _

90 × 30 = 2700, ¼ of 9300 = 2325.

Estimating Answers in Division

The procedure in estimating answers in division is simple but, except under certain conditions, it is more difficult to get a good approximation to the exact answer than in multiplication.

Estimates are generally more accurate if both the dividend and divisor are rounded up (example a) or both are rounded down (example b).

Round the dividend to *one more digit* than the divisor.

Example a: 38)4978 = 131   **Example b :** 230)3220 = 14

Estimate: 40)5000 = 125   **Estimate:** 200)3000 = 15

19. When estimating an answer in division, if the divisor is rounded to 10s the dividend is rounded to 100s; if the divisor is rounded to 100s, the dividend is rounded to _____.

1000s

20. Estimate the answer to the following:

              53
Example: 86)4558   **Problem:** (a) 226)5198   (b) 319)49,764

              51
Estimate: 90)4600   **Estimate:** (a)   (b)

(a) $5000 \div 200 = 25$,   (b) $50{,}000 \div 300 = 167$ or $49700 \div 320 = 155$

21. When estimating an answer in decimals for a problem such as $77.4656 \div 3.56 = 21.76$, either round to the nearest whole number, $77 \div 4 = 19\frac{1}{4}$, or estimate, $80 \div 4 = 20$. Then to estimate the answer for $1389.0 \div 92.6$.

   round to whole numbers   _____ ÷ _____ = _____.

   or estimate   _____ ÷ _____ = _____.

   The exact answer is   = _____.

----

rounded, $1389 \div 93 = 14\frac{87}{93}$, estimate, $1400 \div 90 = 15\frac{5}{9}$, exact answer = 15.

EXERCISE 3

1. Find the exact and estimated total to the nearest $100 for the following:

   Exact: $326 + $115 + $25 + $720 + $196 = _____.

   Estimate: ____ + ____ + ____ + ____ + ____ = _____.

2. What is the estimate to the nearest $100 of the following list by grouping two or more numbers?

   Problem: 3168   Show work here
                  420   Estimate
               9006
                   35
                 826
               1207
                   99
              14761

3. The approximate difference between $2662.43 and $834.42 is $_____.

4. If Mr. James deposited $3146.75 in his checking account this month and spent $2036.50 during the same period, how much was his balance approximately?

   _____

5. When estimating the answer to 356 × 8135, if 356 is rounded to 400, then 8135 is rounded to _____. The estimate is _____ ; the exact answer is _____ .

6. Mrs. Haynes ordered carpet for her living room. If it cost $6.78 a sq yd and her living room contained 125 sq yd, what was the approximate cost?

7. The students at Lane High School collected $6102 to send the school band on a trip. If there were 678 students enrolled, what was the approximate amount collected from each student?

Answers

1. Exact, $1382; estimate, $300 + $100 + $700 + $200 = $1300.

2. 3200
    400
    9000
    900
    1300
    ——
    14800

3. $2662.43 − $834.42 = $1828.01; estimate is $2700 − $800 = $1900.

4. $3000 − $2000 = $1000.

5. 8100; estimate is 3,240,000; exact answer is 2,896,060.

6. 120 × 7 = $840.

7. 6000 ÷ 700 = 8+ dollars.

UNIT 3. FRACTIONS

It may be that you do not need to go over this unit on fractions. The following test will help you to determine this fact.

If you *do not* take the test, go to frame 1, page 54.

If you take the test, (1) record answers in spaces provided. (a) Check your answers with those shown on pages that follow.

PRETEST

Fractions

1. Which of the following are (a) proper fractions, (b) improper fractions, (c) mixed numbers, (d) complex fractions?

    $\dfrac{3}{5}$ $\dfrac{21}{8}$ $\dfrac{3\frac{1}{2}}{2}$ $\dfrac{11}{12}$ $\dfrac{12}{11}$ $\dfrac{3}{9}$ $\dfrac{2\frac{1}{2}}{4}$ $\dfrac{6}{42\frac{1}{2}}$ $3\frac{1}{8}$ $\dfrac{21}{7}$ $5\frac{3}{7}$ $\dfrac{4\frac{1}{4}}{3\frac{1}{2}}$ $\dfrac{9}{4}$

    (a) _____   (b) _____

    (c) _____   (d) _____

2. Reduce the following fractions to the lowest terms:

    (a) $\dfrac{12}{22} =$ (b) $\dfrac{33}{177} =$

    (c) $\dfrac{20}{45} =$ (d) $\dfrac{27}{108} =$

3. Change each of the following improper fractions to a whole or mixed number:

    (a) $\dfrac{22}{4} =$ (b) $\dfrac{327}{3} =$

    (c) $\dfrac{17}{5} =$ (d) $\dfrac{110}{8} =$

4. Change each of the following mixed numbers to an improper fraction:

    (a) $5\frac{2}{5} =$ (b) $3\frac{4}{5} =$

    (c) $6\frac{1}{3} =$ (d) $14\frac{3}{4} =$

5. Change each of the following fractions to higher terms as indicated:

   (a) $\dfrac{2}{5} = \dfrac{}{20}$.

   (b) $\dfrac{3}{8} = \dfrac{}{40}$.

   (c) $\dfrac{4}{6} = \dfrac{}{12}$.

   (d) $\dfrac{2}{9} = \dfrac{}{27}$.

6. Add the following:

   (a) $2\tfrac{1}{3}$
   $3\tfrac{2}{3}$
   $12\tfrac{1}{3}$
   6

   (b) $12\tfrac{1}{6}$
   $8\tfrac{3}{20}$
   $4\tfrac{1}{5}$

   (c) $10\tfrac{2}{3}$
   $42\tfrac{1}{8}$
   $3\tfrac{5}{6}$
   $28\tfrac{1}{12}$
   $4\tfrac{1}{9}$

7. Subtract the following:

   (a) $26\tfrac{6}{8}$
   $- 5\tfrac{3}{8}$

   (b) $520\tfrac{5}{9}$
   $- 19\tfrac{7}{9}$

   (c) 616
   $- 20\tfrac{3}{5}$

8. Multiply the following fractions:

   (a) $\dfrac{9}{10} \times \dfrac{7}{3} =$

   (b) $\dfrac{22}{8} \times \dfrac{2}{11} =$

   (c) $16 \times \dfrac{5}{9} =$

   (d) $\dfrac{2}{3} \times 12\tfrac{1}{2} =$

   (e) $3\tfrac{1}{3} \times 9\tfrac{3}{11} =$

9. Divide the following fractions and reduce to lowest terms:

   (a) $\dfrac{2}{5} \div \dfrac{1}{3} =$

   (b) $\dfrac{8}{9} \div \dfrac{4}{12} =$

   (c) $25 \div 3\tfrac{1}{3} =$

   (d) $15\tfrac{1}{2} \div 6\tfrac{1}{8} =$

   (e) $8\tfrac{1}{6} \div 5\tfrac{1}{2} =$

10. Simplify (division):

(a) $\dfrac{4\tfrac{1}{3}}{22} =$

(b) $\dfrac{10}{3\tfrac{1}{2}} =$

(c) $\dfrac{5\tfrac{1}{6}}{8\tfrac{2}{7}} =$

(d) $\dfrac{\tfrac{2}{9}}{\tfrac{7}{6}} =$

Answers

After you check your answers, follow the instructions below and review the frames covering the appropriate section.

1. Frames 1 to 9, pages 54 to 57.

    (a) $\dfrac{3}{5}, \dfrac{11}{12}, \dfrac{3}{9}$ (b) $\dfrac{21}{8}, \dfrac{12}{11}, \dfrac{21}{7}, \dfrac{9}{4}$

    (c) $3\tfrac{1}{8}, 5\tfrac{3}{7}$ (d) $\dfrac{3\tfrac{1}{2}}{2}, \dfrac{2\tfrac{1}{2}}{4}, \dfrac{6}{42\tfrac{1}{2}}, \dfrac{4\tfrac{1}{4}}{3\tfrac{1}{2}}$

2. Frames 10 and 11, page 57.

    (a) $\dfrac{6}{11}$ (b) $\dfrac{11}{59}$

    (c) $\dfrac{4}{9}$ (d) $\dfrac{1}{4}$

3. Frame 12, page 59.

    (a) $5\tfrac{1}{2}$ (b) 109

    (c) $3\tfrac{2}{5}$ (d) $13\tfrac{3}{4}$

4. Frame 13, page 59.

    (a) $\dfrac{27}{5}$ (b) $\dfrac{19}{5}$

    (c) $\dfrac{19}{3}$ (d) $\dfrac{59}{4}$

5. Frames 14 and 15, page 60.

(a) $\frac{8}{20}$ (b) $\frac{15}{40}$

(c) $\frac{8}{12}$ (d) $\frac{6}{27}$

6. Frames 16 to 24, pages 61 to 65.

(a) $24\frac{1}{3}$ (b) $24\frac{31}{60}$

(c) $88\frac{59}{72}$

7. Frames 25 to 27, page 66.

(a) $21\frac{3}{8}$ (b) $500\frac{7}{9}$

(c) $595\frac{2}{5}$

8. Frames 28 to 31, pages 67 to 69.

(a) $2\frac{1}{10}$ (b) $\frac{1}{2}$

(c) $8\frac{8}{9}$ (d) $8\frac{1}{3}$

(e) $30\frac{10}{11}$

9. Frame 32, page 70.

(a) $1\frac{1}{5}$ (b) $2\frac{2}{3}$

(c) $7\frac{1}{2}$ (d) $2\frac{26}{49}$

(e) $1\frac{16}{33}$

10. Frame 33, page 71.

(a) $\frac{13}{66}$ (b) $2\frac{6}{7}$

(c) $\frac{217}{348}$ (d) $\frac{4}{21}$

Instructions

1. If you made no more than one error in any group of problems and not more than 5 errors for the entire test, skip to Unit 4, frame 1, page 73.
2. If you did not meet this requirement, you will have an opportunity to test yourself again after you have completed this unit. Go to Unit 3, frame 1, page 54.

Fractions

A fraction is another way of writing division; for example, $\frac{9}{11}$ is called a fraction but it is also another way of saying that 9 is to be divided by 11.

It may be expressed as a number (called the numerator) written above another number (called the denominator), such as $\frac{1}{2}$ and $\frac{3}{4}$ or in decimal form as .50 and .75, respectively.

1. In the fraction $\frac{7}{8}$, 7 is called the——————and 8 is called the——————.
   _

   numerator, denominator

FRACTIONS 55

2. .875 is the _____ form of $\frac{7}{8}$.

- -

decimal

Proper and Improper Fractions

A *proper fraction* has a value less than 1 because, by definition, it has a numerator that is less than the denominator (also called the divisor). Some examples are $\frac{3}{8}$, $\frac{5}{6}$, and $\frac{11}{12}$.

An *improper fraction* has a value equal to or greater than 1 because, by definition, it has a numerator that is equal to or greater than the denominator. Some examples are $\frac{5}{4}$, $\frac{7}{6}$, $\frac{4}{3}$, and $\frac{8}{8}$.

3. (a) A proper fraction is one in which the numerator is (less than/greater than) the denominator.
(b) An improper fraction is one in which the numerator is (greater than, less than, or equal to) the denominator.

- -

(a) less than, (b) greater than or equal to

4. Group the following fractions as proper and improper fractions: $\frac{2}{3}, \frac{9}{5}, \frac{11}{6}, \frac{4}{6}, \frac{12}{12}, \frac{3}{9}, \frac{7}{5}, \frac{5}{3}, \frac{1}{8}$.

Proper fractions _____.

Improper fractions _____.

- -

Proper fractions $\frac{2}{3} \ \frac{4}{6} \ \frac{3}{9} \ \frac{1}{8}$
Improper fractions $\frac{9}{5} \ \frac{11}{6} \ \frac{12}{12} \ \frac{7}{5} \ \frac{5}{3}$

Mixed Numbers

A *mixed number* is a number containing a whole number and a fraction. Some examples are $3\frac{1}{2}$, $4\frac{1}{4}$, $8\frac{1}{5}$.

5. If a mixed number contains a whole number and a fraction, then $2\frac{5}{6}$ is a _____ number.

----

mixed

6. In a mixed number $2\frac{5}{6}$, $\frac{5}{6}$ is a _____ fraction.

----

proper

7. Five and one fourth written as a mixed number is _____.

$5\frac{1}{4}$

Simple and Complex Fractions

A simple fraction is one in which both the numerator and denominator are whole numbers such as $\frac{9}{13}, \frac{5}{8}, \frac{6}{9}, \frac{8}{3}, \frac{5}{4}$.

A *complex fraction* is one in which the numerator or denominator, or both, is a mixed number.

$$\frac{5\frac{1}{4}}{6\frac{1}{2}} \qquad \frac{4}{2\frac{1}{3}} \qquad \frac{10\frac{1}{2}}{5} \qquad \frac{27\frac{2}{3}}{\frac{8}{9}}$$

8. In the fraction $\frac{2}{9}$ the numerator and denominator are both whole numbers. Then $\frac{2}{9}$ is a _____ fraction. It is also a _____ fraction.

Is $\frac{7}{4}$ a simple or a complex fraction? _____

$\frac{7}{4}$ is also called an _____ fraction.

----

simple, proper, simple, improper

FRACTIONS 57

9. (a) Which of the following fractions are simple, complex?

$$\frac{12\frac{1}{2}}{4\frac{1}{4}} \quad \frac{2}{3} \quad \frac{5\frac{1}{2}}{3} \quad \frac{42}{42\frac{1}{4}} \quad \frac{14}{8} \quad \frac{5}{9} \quad \frac{3\frac{1}{3}}{10\frac{1}{2}} \quad \frac{4}{13}$$

Simple: _____

Complex: _____

(b) Which of the simple fractions listed under (a) are proper, improper?

Proper: _____ Improper: _____

(a) Simple: $\frac{2}{3} \quad \frac{14}{8} \quad \frac{5}{9} \quad \frac{4}{13}$ Complex: $\frac{12\frac{1}{2}}{4\frac{1}{4}} \quad \frac{5\frac{1}{2}}{3} \quad \frac{42}{42\frac{1}{4}} \quad \frac{3\frac{1}{3}}{10\frac{1}{2}}$

(b) Proper: $\frac{2}{3} \quad \frac{5}{9} \quad \frac{4}{13}$ Improper: $\frac{14}{8}$

Reducing Fractions

To reduce a fraction to its lowest terms divide the numerator and denominator by the largest whole number common to both.

Example: Reduce $\frac{12}{18}$ to its lowest terms. Since 6 is the largest divisor of 12 and 18, divide each by 6, i.e.,

$$\frac{12 \div 6}{18 \div 6} = \frac{2}{3}.$$

If the largest common divisor or factor is not recognized, the same result will be obtained by dividing both the numerator and denominator of the fraction by any common divisor and repeating the process until the fraction is reduced to its lowest terms. In the example given above 3 is a common divisor of both 12 and 18, in which case $12 \div 18 = 4 \div 6$. Since both 4 and 6 may be divided by 2, then $4 \div 6 = 2 \div 3$. In this case an additional step in the process is required, but the final result is, of course, always the same.

10. In the fraction $\frac{21}{28}$ the largest factor that both the numerator and denominator may be divided by is ____. Then $\frac{21 \div}{28 \div} = \frac{}{}$.

7, $\frac{21 \div 7}{28 \div 7} = \frac{3}{4}$.

58 UNIT 3

When reducing or changing fractions to lower terms, the following suggestions may be helpful if you do not recognize common divisors of the numerator and denominator.

When both the numerator and denominator are *even*, they can *always* be divided by 2 and sometimes by a multiple of 2.

Examples: $\dfrac{10}{12} = \dfrac{10 \div 2}{12 \div 2} = \dfrac{5}{6}$, $\dfrac{20}{24} = \dfrac{20 \div 4}{24 \div 4} = \dfrac{5}{6}$.

When either the numerator or denominator is even and the other is odd or both are odd numbers, they cannot be divided by an even number. If there is a common divisor, it must be an odd number such as 3, 5, or 7.

Examples: $\dfrac{21}{49} = \dfrac{21 \div 7}{49 \div 7} = \dfrac{3}{7}$, $\dfrac{18}{63} = \dfrac{18 \div 9}{63 \div 9} = \dfrac{2}{7}$.

When the numerator and denominator both end in 0 and/or 5, a common factor or divisor is 5 or a multiple of 5.

Examples: $\dfrac{20}{45} = \dfrac{20 \div 5}{45 \div 5} = \dfrac{4}{9}$, $\dfrac{85}{135} = \dfrac{85 \div 5}{135 \div 5} = \dfrac{17}{27}$.

Changing an Improper Fraction to a Whole or Mixed Number

Divide the numerator by the denominator and write the remainder, if any, as a fraction.

Examples: $\dfrac{12}{7} = 1\tfrac{5}{7}$ (mixed number).

$\dfrac{15}{5} = 3$ (whole number).

11. Change the following improper fractions to a whole or mixed number:

 (a) $\dfrac{22}{5} =$ (b) $\dfrac{14}{3} =$

 (c) $\dfrac{21}{7} =$ (d) $\dfrac{124}{3} =$

(a) $4\tfrac{2}{5}$, (b) $4\tfrac{2}{3}$, (c) 3, (d) $41\tfrac{1}{3}$

Changing a Mixed Number to an Improper Fraction

Multiply the whole number by the denominator of the fraction; add the numerator of the fraction and place over the denominator.

Examples: $\quad 4\frac{3}{4} = \frac{19}{4}. \qquad 5\frac{1}{6} = \frac{31}{6}.$

Solution: $\quad 4 \times 4 = 16. \qquad 5 \times 6 = 30.$
$\qquad\qquad\quad 16 + 3 = 19. \qquad 30 + 1 = 31.$

12. Complete the following:

(a) $5\frac{2}{3} = \frac{?}{3}.$ (b) $12\frac{1}{2} = \frac{?}{2}.$ (c) $3\frac{2}{7} = \frac{?}{7}.$

(d) $8\frac{3}{4} = \frac{?}{4}.$ (e) $5\frac{2}{7} = \frac{?}{7}.$ (f) $6\frac{3}{8} = \frac{?}{8}.$

(a) 17, (b) 25, (c) 23, (d) 35, (e) 37, (f) 51

13. Reduce each of the following fractions to its lowest terms.

(a) $\frac{12}{20} =$ (b) $\frac{25}{45} =$

(c) $\frac{18}{36} =$ (d) $\frac{27}{81} =$

(e) $\frac{120}{225} =$ (f) $\frac{432}{1608} =$

(g) $\frac{258}{654} =$

(a) $\dfrac{12}{20} = \dfrac{12 \div 4}{20 \div 4} = \dfrac{3}{5}.$ (b) $\dfrac{25}{45} = \dfrac{25 \div 5}{45 \div 5} = \dfrac{5}{9}.$

(c) $\dfrac{18}{36} = \dfrac{18 \div 18}{36 \div 18} = \dfrac{1}{2}.$ (d) $\dfrac{27}{81} = \dfrac{27 \div 27}{81 \div 27} = \dfrac{1}{3}.$

(e) $\dfrac{120}{225} = \dfrac{120 \div 5}{225 \div 5} = \dfrac{24}{45}.$ (f) $\dfrac{432}{1608} = \dfrac{432 \div 8}{1608 \div 8} = \dfrac{54}{201}.$

$\dfrac{24}{45} = \dfrac{24 \div 3}{45 \div 3} = \dfrac{8}{15}.$ $\dfrac{54}{201} = \dfrac{54 \div 3}{201 \div 3} = \dfrac{18}{67}.$

OR OR

$\dfrac{120}{225} = \dfrac{120 \div 15}{225 \div 15} = \dfrac{8}{15}.$ $\dfrac{432}{1608} = \dfrac{432 \div 24}{1608 \div 24} = \dfrac{18}{67}.$

(g) $\dfrac{258}{654} = \dfrac{258 \div 2}{654 \div 2} = \dfrac{129}{327}, \dfrac{129 \div 3}{327 \div 3} = \dfrac{43}{109}.$

OR

$\dfrac{258}{654} = \dfrac{258 \div 6}{654 \div 6} = \dfrac{43}{109}$

For problems (e) and (f) it is not practical to look for factors as large as 15 and 24.

Changing a Fraction to Higher Terms

Follow the procedure as illustrated.

Examples: $\dfrac{1}{4} = \dfrac{?}{20}.$ $\dfrac{3}{8} = \dfrac{?}{24}.$

Procedure: $20 \div 4 = 5.$ $24 \div 8 = 3.$

Answers: $\dfrac{1 \times 5}{4 \times 5} = \dfrac{5}{20}.$ $\dfrac{3 \times 3}{8 \times 3} = \dfrac{9}{24}.$

14. $\dfrac{15}{17} = \dfrac{}{34}.$ (a) 34 divided by 17 = ___.

(b) then $\dfrac{15 \times }{17 \times } = \dfrac{}{34}.$

(a) 2, (b) $\dfrac{15 \times 2}{17 \times 2} = \dfrac{30}{34}$

FRACTIONS 61

15. Change each of the following fractions to the higher terms shown:

(a) $\dfrac{1}{5} = \dfrac{}{20}.$ (b) $\dfrac{5}{9} = \dfrac{}{27}.$

(c) $\dfrac{2}{3} = \dfrac{}{12}.$ (d) $\dfrac{3}{4} = \dfrac{}{24}.$

- -

(a) $\dfrac{4}{20}$, (b) $\dfrac{15}{27}$, (c) $\dfrac{8}{12}$, (d) $\dfrac{18}{24}$

Adding Fractions when the Denominators Are the Same

Example: $4\tfrac{1}{4}$
$5\tfrac{2}{4}$
$12\tfrac{3}{4}$
———
$22\tfrac{6}{4}$ or $22\tfrac{1}{2}$ (answer)

Procedure: Add the numerators of the fractions. Result is $\tfrac{6}{4}$ or $1\tfrac{2}{4}$. Carry the 1 to the units column and add. Reduce the fraction to its lowest terms.

16. *One* fourth plus *two* fourths plus *three* fourths = *six* fourths, or $\tfrac{1}{4} + \tfrac{2}{4} + \tfrac{3}{4} = \tfrac{6}{4}$.
Then *one* sixth plus *three* sixths plus *five* sixths is the same as $\tfrac{1}{6} + \tfrac{3}{6} + \tfrac{5}{6} = $ _____
or _____ reduced to lowest terms.

$\tfrac{5}{8} + \tfrac{3}{8} = $ _____ expressed as a whole number.

$\tfrac{3}{12} + \tfrac{1}{12} + \tfrac{5}{12} = \dfrac{}{12}$ or $\dfrac{}{4}$ when reduced to lowest terms.

- -

$\tfrac{9}{6}$ or $\tfrac{3}{2} = 1\tfrac{1}{2},\ 1,\ \tfrac{9}{12}$ or $\tfrac{3}{4}$

17. Add the following:

    (a) $4\frac{2}{5}$ (b) $5\frac{1}{9}$ (c) $2\frac{1}{4}$
           $18\frac{3}{5}$ $14\frac{2}{9}$ $5\frac{3}{4}$
           $\underline{9\frac{1}{5}}$ $\underline{6}$ $\underline{10\frac{2}{4}}$

- -

(a) $32\frac{1}{5}$, (b) $25\frac{1}{3}$, (c) $18\frac{1}{2}$

Adding Fractions when the Denominators Are Not the Same

Fractions with unlike denominators cannot be added until the denominators are changed to the same value.

Example: $5\frac{1}{6}$ $\frac{4}{24}$

              $20\frac{3}{8}$ $\frac{9}{24}$

              $\underline{15\frac{3}{4}}$ $\underline{\frac{18}{24}}$

              $41\frac{7}{24}$ $\frac{31}{24}$ $1\frac{7}{24}$

Procedure: First find the smallest number that can be divided by 6, 8, and 4. This is called the least common denominator (LCD). In this case it is 24. Then change each fraction to 24ths and add as illustrated.

18. The smallest number that can be divided by 3, 4, and 2 is 12; 12 is called the

    _____ _____ _____ .

    The LCD of 2, 6, and 3 is ___.
    In the series 4, 6, 12, and 8 is the LCD 24 or 36?

- -

least common denominator, 6, 24

19. Add (a) $4\frac{2}{3}$ $\frac{}{6}$ (b) $5\frac{1}{8}$ (c) $22\frac{1}{5}$
$16\frac{1}{6}$ $\frac{}{6}$ $16\frac{3}{4}$ $10\frac{2}{5}$
$5\frac{2}{6}$ $\frac{}{6}$ $22\frac{1}{12}$ $5\frac{3}{10}$
     $56\frac{3}{8}$ $4\frac{1}{4}$
     $\frac{5}{12}$ $\frac{6}{10}$
                            $16\frac{2}{4}$
                            9

- -

(a) $26\frac{1}{6}$, (b) $100\frac{3}{4}$, (c) $68\frac{1}{4}$

Finding the Least Common Denominator for a Series of Numbers

When the denominators are *prime* to one another, the least common denominator is their product. (Numbers are said to be prime to one another if they have no common denominator except 1.) The numbers 7, 9, and 13 are prime to one another, since they have no common denominator except 1. The series 4, 5, and 9 is prime for the same reason.

Example: Find the LCD (least common denominator) for the following fractions: $\frac{5}{6}, \frac{1}{7},$ and $\frac{4}{5}$

Solution: Since 6, 7, and 5 are prime to one another, the LCD = 6 × 7 × 5 = 210.

20. What is the LCD for $\frac{2}{3}, \frac{7}{11},$ and $\frac{1}{5}$? _____

- -

LCD for $\frac{2}{3}, \frac{7}{11},$ and $\frac{1}{5}$ is 3 × 11 × 5 = 165

21. When one denominator can be divided exactly by the others, the LCD can be found by inspection.

Example: $\frac{2}{3}$ and $\frac{5}{6}$. The LCD = 6, since it can be divided exactly by 3 and 6. $\frac{1}{3}, \frac{2}{9},$ and $\frac{1}{18}$. The LCD = 18 since it can be divided exactly by 3, 9, and 18.

What is the LCD for $\frac{2}{5}, \frac{1}{15}, \frac{2}{30}$? _____

- -

The LCD for $\frac{2}{5}, \frac{1}{15},$ and $\frac{2}{30}$ is 30, since it is divisible by 5, 15, and 30.

When the denominators are neither prime to one another nor factors of one another, follow the procedure outlined below.

Example: $\frac{4}{5}, \frac{7}{12}, \frac{2}{9}, \frac{5}{8}.$

Procedure:
1. Arrange the denominators in a row.
2. Divide by the smallest number that can be divided into two or more denominators and bring down to the next row with any denominators that were not divided.
3. Continue this process until there are no divisors.
4. Multiply all divisors and the numbers in the last row.

$2 \times 2 \times 3 \times 5 \times 1 \times 3 \times 2 = 360$ LCD

```
           5    12   9   8
        2)5    12   9   8
           5     6   9   4
        2)5    12   9   8
        2)5     6   9   4
        3)5     3   9   2
           5     1   3   2
```

22. (a) The LCD for $\frac{2}{3}, \frac{5}{7},$ and $\frac{2}{4}$ is $3 \times 7 \times 4 = $ _____ because 3, 7 and 4 are _____ to one another.

    The LCD for $\frac{1}{8}, \frac{5}{9},$ and $\frac{4}{5}$ is _____.

    (b) The LCD for $\frac{3}{16}$ and $\frac{5}{8}$ is 16 because 16 is divisible by 8 and 16 exactly. Then the LCD for $\frac{3}{5}$ and $\frac{1}{10}$ is _____ and the LCD for $\frac{8}{11}$ and $\frac{2}{33}$ is _____ .

_ _

(a) $3 \times 7 \times 4 = 84$ because 3, 7, and 4 are prime to one another. LCD for $\frac{1}{8}, \frac{5}{9},$ and $\frac{4}{5}$ is $8 \times 9 \times 5 = 360$.

(b) LCD for $\frac{3}{5}$ and $\frac{1}{10}$ is 10 and for $\frac{8}{11}$ and $\frac{2}{33}$, 33.

In the series $\frac{3}{4}, \frac{5}{7}, \frac{2}{9},$ and $\frac{1}{6}$, the LCD is found as follows:

1. Arrange in this order _____ →

```
        2)4   7   9   6
        3)2   7   9   3
           2   7   3   1
```

2. What is the smallest number that can be divided into two or more of these numbers? The answer is 2. Divide 4 and 6 by 2. Bring down the other numbers.
3. 9 and 3 are divisible by 3.
4. Since there are no more divisors, multiply $2 \times 3 \times 2 \times 7 \times 3 \times 1 = 252$ LCD.

23. Find the LCD for the following series:

(a) $\frac{2}{7}, \frac{5}{6}, \frac{4}{8}, \frac{3}{9}, \frac{2}{3}$

(b) $\frac{1}{15}, \frac{2}{3}, \frac{1}{5}, \frac{2}{6}$

- -

(a) 2)7 6 8 9 3
    3)7 3 4 9 3
       7 1 4 3 1
    LCD = 2 × 3 × 7 × 4 × 3 = 504

(b) 3)15 3 5 6
    5) 5 1 5 2
       1 1 1 2
    LCD = 3 × 5 × 2 = 30

24. Add the following numbers:

$3\frac{1}{3}$
$15\frac{1}{5}$
$27\frac{1}{2}$
$402\frac{3}{4}$
$98\frac{1}{10}$

Show work here:

) 3 5 2 4 10

LCD =

- -

Total = $546\frac{53}{60}$

2)3   5   2   4   10
5)3   5   1   2   5
   3   1   1   2   1
LCD = 2 × 5 × 3 × 2 = 60

Subtracting Fractions when the Denominators Are the Same

Example 1: $12\frac{4}{9}$
$\underline{5\frac{1}{9}}$
$7\frac{3}{9}$ or $7\frac{1}{3}$ answer

Procedure: Subtract $\frac{1}{9}$ from $\frac{4}{9}$ and reduce.
Subtract 5 from 12.

Example 2: $10\frac{17}{12}$
$11\frac{5}{12}$
$\underline{3\frac{7}{12}}$
$7\frac{10}{12}$ or $7\frac{5}{6}$ answer

Procedure: Since 7 is greater than 5, borrow 1 whole number from the minuend, change to 12ths, and add to $\frac{5}{12}$ths. Proceed as illustrated.

---

25. *Nine* fifteenths less *six* fifteenths equals *three* fifteenths
OR $\frac{9}{15} - \frac{6}{15} = \frac{3}{15}$. Try these; be sure to reduce fractions if possible:

(a) $\frac{7}{8} - \frac{2}{8} =$ _____   (b) $\frac{5}{9} - \frac{3}{9} =$ _____

(c) $\frac{8}{12} - \frac{5}{12} =$ _____   (d) $1\frac{4}{5} - \frac{2}{5} =$ _____

(e) $19\frac{7}{8}$ (f) $26\frac{4}{8}$
$\underline{-11\frac{2}{8}}$ $\underline{-10\frac{2}{8}}$

(a) $\frac{5}{8}$,   (b) $\frac{2}{9}$,   (c) $\frac{3}{12}$ or $\frac{1}{4}$,   (d) $1\frac{2}{5}$,   (e) $8\frac{5}{8}$,   (f) $16\frac{1}{4}$

26. These problems are similar to the one in Example 2 above.

(a) $23\frac{5}{12}$ (b) $56\frac{1}{9}$
$\underline{-18\frac{9}{12}}$ $\underline{-40\frac{4}{9}}$

(a) $4\frac{2}{3}$,   (b) $15\frac{2}{3}$

Subtracting Fractions when the Denominators are not the Same

Example: $90\frac{5}{6}$ | $\frac{15}{18}$
$-27\frac{1}{9}$ | $\frac{2}{18}$
$63\frac{13}{18}$ | $\frac{13}{18}$

Procedure: The LCD of 6 and 9 is 18. Therefore change $\frac{5}{6}$ and $\frac{1}{9}$ to 18ths and proceed as illustrated.

27. Subtract   (a) $32\frac{7}{9}$ (b) $27\frac{5}{8}$
     $5\frac{2}{3}$ $6\frac{3}{5}$

_ _

(a) $27\frac{1}{9}$ (b) $21\frac{1}{40}$

Multiplying Fractions

$\frac{3}{8} \times \frac{5}{7} = ?$

1. Multiply the numerators (3 and 5) by each other; i.e., $3 \times 5 = 15$.
2. Multiply the denominators (8 and 7) by each other; i.e., $8 \times 7 = 56$.

   We now have $\frac{3 \times 5}{8 \times 7} = \frac{15}{56}$

3. Reduce $\frac{15}{56}$, if possible, to its lowest terms. In this case 15 and 56 have no common factor or divisor.

28. What is $\frac{4}{9} \times \frac{5}{11} =$

_ _

$\frac{4}{9} \times \frac{5}{11} = \frac{4 \times 5}{9 \times 11} = \frac{20}{99}$

When a whole number is multiplied by a fraction or mixed number, proceed as follows:

Example: $7 \times 3\frac{1}{8}$

Solution: Think of 7 as $\frac{7}{1}$.

Change $3\frac{1}{8}$ to an improper fraction, i.e., $\frac{25}{8}$. Then

$$7 \times 3\frac{1}{8} = \frac{7}{1} \times \frac{25}{8} = \frac{175}{8} = 21\frac{7}{8}$$

When the result is an improper fraction, always change it to a mixed number.

29. Try these problems: (a) $12 \times \frac{5}{11}$, (b) $8 \times \frac{5}{6}$

(a) $12 \times \dfrac{5}{11} = \dfrac{60}{11} = 5\frac{5}{11}$,   (b) $\overset{4}{\cancel{8}} \times \dfrac{5}{\underset{3}{\cancel{6}}} = \dfrac{20}{3} = 6\frac{2}{3}$

Sometimes a fraction can be reduced before it is multiplied by another.

Example 1: $\dfrac{4}{10} \times \dfrac{5}{6} =$

In this case $\frac{4}{10}$ can be reduced to $\frac{2}{5}$, since 4 and 10 have a common divisor 2. Our problem now becomes

$$\frac{2}{5} \times \frac{5}{6} = \frac{2 \times 5}{5 \times 6} = \frac{10}{30} = \frac{1}{3}.$$

The solution can be simplified, however by "canceling" the factors 5 and 2 which are common to both fractions.

Then $\dfrac{\overset{1}{\cancel{2}}}{\underset{1}{\cancel{5}}} \times \dfrac{\overset{1}{\cancel{5}}}{\underset{3}{\cancel{6}}} = \dfrac{1 \times 1}{1 \times 3} = \dfrac{1}{3}$

OR going back to

$$\frac{4}{10} \times \frac{5}{6} = \frac{\overset{2}{\cancel{4}}}{\underset{2}{\cancel{10}}} \times \frac{\overset{}{\cancel{5}}}{\underset{3}{\cancel{6}}} = \frac{1}{3}.$$

Usually the 1 shown here is understood and is therefore not recorded. This process is called "canceling out" common factors.

Example 2. $\dfrac{\cancel{10}^{\,5}}{\cancel{12}_{\,2}} \times \dfrac{\cancel{6}}{\cancel{2}} = \dfrac{5}{2} = 2\tfrac{1}{2}$ $\begin{cases} \text{12 and 6 are divided by the common factor 6,} \\ \text{10 and 2 are divided by the common factor 2.} \end{cases}$

30. Try these: $\dfrac{10}{15} \times \dfrac{3}{7} =$ $\dfrac{7}{8} \times \dfrac{4}{11} =$

- -

$\dfrac{\cancel{10}^{\,2}}{\cancel{15}_{\,3}} \times \dfrac{3}{7} = \dfrac{2}{7}$, $\dfrac{7}{\cancel{8}_{\,2}} \times \dfrac{\cancel{4}}{11} = \dfrac{7}{22}.$

31. Solve the following:

   (a) $\dfrac{10}{15} \times \dfrac{3}{11} =$

   (b) $\dfrac{2}{16} \times \dfrac{3}{4} =$

   (c) $\dfrac{11}{12} \times \dfrac{3}{5} \times \dfrac{6}{22} =$

   (d) $6 \times \dfrac{8}{9} =$

   (e) $\dfrac{3}{9} \times 2\tfrac{1}{3} =$

- -

(a) $\dfrac{2}{11}$, (b) $\dfrac{3}{32}$, (c) $\dfrac{3}{20}$, (d) $5\tfrac{1}{3}$, (e) $\dfrac{7}{9}$

Dividing Fractions

Procedure: Invert the divisor and proceed as in multiplication.

Examples: 1. $\dfrac{1}{5} \div \dfrac{1}{3} = \dfrac{1}{5} \times \dfrac{3}{1} = \dfrac{3}{5}.$

2. $\dfrac{9}{10} \div \dfrac{1}{3} = \dfrac{9}{10} \times \dfrac{3}{1} = \dfrac{27}{10} = 2\dfrac{7}{10}.$

3. $\dfrac{11}{12} \div \dfrac{7}{4} = \dfrac{11}{\cancel{12}_{3}} \times \dfrac{\cancel{4}^{1}}{7} = \dfrac{11}{21}.$

4. $16 \div \dfrac{86}{9} = \cancel{16}^{8} \times \dfrac{9}{\cancel{86}_{43}} = \dfrac{72}{43} = 1\dfrac{29}{43}.$

5. $21\dfrac{1}{2} \div 4 = \dfrac{43}{2} \times \dfrac{1}{4} = \dfrac{43}{8} = 5\dfrac{3}{8}.$

32. Any complex fraction may be written and solved as follows:

Examples: $\dfrac{5\frac{1}{2}}{6} = 5\dfrac{1}{2} \div 6 = \dfrac{11}{2} \times \dfrac{1}{6} = \dfrac{11}{12}$

$\dfrac{2\frac{1}{3}}{8\frac{1}{5}} = 2\dfrac{1}{3} \div 8\dfrac{1}{5} = \dfrac{7}{3} \times \dfrac{5}{41} = \dfrac{35}{123}$

Complete: (a) $\dfrac{2\frac{1}{2}}{15\frac{1}{2}} = 2\dfrac{1}{2} \div 15\dfrac{1}{2} =$

(b) $\dfrac{6\frac{1}{3}}{12} =$

(a) $2\dfrac{1}{2} \div 15\dfrac{1}{2} = \dfrac{5}{2} \times \dfrac{2}{31} = \dfrac{5}{31}$

(b) $\dfrac{6\frac{1}{3}}{12} = 6\dfrac{1}{3} \div 12 = \dfrac{19}{3} \times \dfrac{1}{12} = \dfrac{19}{36}$

In some cases a common multiple or denominator may be used to advantage as shown in the following examples:

Use of common multiple

Examples: $\dfrac{4\frac{1}{2}}{10} = \dfrac{4\frac{1}{2} \times 2}{10 \times 2} = \dfrac{9}{20}$

$\dfrac{5\frac{1}{4}}{108} = \dfrac{5\frac{1}{4} \times 4}{108 \times 4} = \dfrac{21}{432} = \dfrac{7}{144}$

Use of common denominator

Example: $\dfrac{14}{3\frac{1}{2}} = \dfrac{28}{2} \div \dfrac{7}{2} = 4$

Think of 14 as 28 ÷ 2. Since the denominators are the same, they will cancel out and 28 ÷ 7 = 4.

33. **Complete:** (a) $\dfrac{5\frac{1}{3}}{16} =$

(b) $\dfrac{8}{7\frac{1}{4}} =$

(a) $\dfrac{5\frac{1}{3}}{16} = \dfrac{5\frac{1}{3} \times 3}{16 \times 3} = \dfrac{16}{48} = \dfrac{1}{3}.$

(b) $\dfrac{8}{7\frac{1}{4}} = \dfrac{32}{4} \div 7\frac{1}{4} = \dfrac{32}{4} \times \dfrac{4}{29} = \dfrac{32}{29} = 1\dfrac{3}{29}.$

EXERCISE 4

Review of Fractions

Perform the following operations. Check your answers with those following this exercise. If you make more than one error in any section, review the appropriate section.

I. Addition
 1. $7\frac{1}{6} + 12\frac{1}{3} + 8\frac{5}{6}$ = _____.
 2. $36\frac{1}{3} + 3\frac{2}{3} + 27\frac{1}{4}$ = _____.
 3. $6 + 2\frac{3}{4} + 5\frac{3}{9} + 28\frac{3}{5}$ = _____.
 4. $2\frac{5}{8} + 5\frac{1}{2} + 7\frac{3}{8}$ = _____.
 5. $36\frac{1}{2} + 18\frac{3}{4} + 11\frac{2}{5} + 21\frac{1}{3}$ = _____.

II. Subtraction
 1. $28\frac{2}{3} - 8\frac{1}{6}$ = _____.
 2. $42\frac{7}{8} - 13\frac{3}{8}$ = _____.
 3. $14\frac{2}{3} - 3\frac{1}{6}$ = _____.
 4. $24\frac{3}{4} - 20\frac{1}{6}$ = _____.
 5. $120 - 101\frac{1}{6}$ = _____.

III. Multiplication
 1. $20\frac{1}{2} \times 15\frac{1}{2}$ = _____.
 2. $66 \times 4\frac{1}{3}$ = _____.
 3. $7\frac{1}{3} \times 81\frac{1}{2}$ = _____.
 4. $8\frac{1}{6} \times 5$ = _____.
 5. $1\frac{2}{3} \times 4\frac{1}{4}$ = _____.

IV. Division
 1. $95 \div 6\frac{1}{3}$ = _____.
 2. $28 \div \frac{2}{7}$ = _____.
 3. $12\frac{3}{4} \div 3$ = _____.
 4. $14\frac{1}{2} \div 3\frac{3}{4}$ = _____.
 5. $60\frac{1}{2} \div 16$ = _____.

Answers

I.   Addition: 1. $28\frac{1}{3}$ 2. $67\frac{1}{4}$ 3. $42\frac{41}{60}$ 4. $15\frac{1}{2}$ 5. $87\frac{59}{60}$

II. Subtraction: 1. $20\frac{1}{2}$ 2. $29\frac{1}{2}$ 3. $11\frac{1}{2}$ 4. $4\frac{7}{12}$ 5. $18\frac{5}{6}$

III. Multiplication: 1. $317\frac{3}{4}$ 2. 286 3. $597\frac{2}{3}$ 4. $40\frac{5}{6}$ 5. $7\frac{1}{12}$

IV. Division: 1. 15 2. 98 3. $4\frac{1}{4}$ 4. $3\frac{13}{15}$ 5. $3\frac{25}{32}$

UNIT 4. DECIMALS OR DECIMAL FRACTIONS

Changing a Common Fraction or Mixed Number to the Decimal Form

Procedure: Divide the numerator by the denominator to as many decimal places as desired. You may use a fraction at the end of a decimal instead of rounding off, as in example 3.

Examples:
1. $\frac{3}{8} = .375$.
2. $\frac{12}{5} = 2\frac{2}{5} = 2.4$.
3. $5\frac{1}{6} = 5.166\frac{2}{3}$ or 5.167 rounded to third decimal.

1. Find the decimal form of the following:

(a) $\frac{3}{4} = $ _____.   (b) $\frac{13}{4} = $ _____.

(c) $4\frac{1}{8} = $ _____. (d) $12\frac{1}{8} = $ _____.

(e) $\frac{26}{6} = $ _____. (f) $2\frac{2}{5} = $ _____.

- -

(a) $\frac{3}{4} = .75$.   (b) $\frac{13}{4} = 3\frac{1}{4} = 3.25$.
(c) $4\frac{1}{8} = 4.125$.   (d) $12\frac{1}{8} = 12.125$.
(e) $\frac{26}{6} = 4\frac{2}{6} = 4\frac{1}{3} = 4.33\frac{1}{3}$.   (f) $2\frac{2}{5} = 2.40$.

Changing a Decimal to a Common Fraction or a Mixed Number

To change a decimal to a common fraction or mixed number replace the decimal with the appropriate multiple of 10 and reduce to the lowest terms.

Examples: 1. $.25 = \dfrac{25}{100} = \dfrac{1}{4}$

2. $.375 = \dfrac{375}{1000} = \dfrac{3}{8}$

3. $.16\tfrac{2}{3} = \dfrac{16\tfrac{2}{3}}{100} = \dfrac{50}{3} \times \dfrac{1}{100} = \dfrac{1}{6}$

4. $2.08\tfrac{1}{3} = 2\dfrac{8\tfrac{1}{3}}{100} = 2\tfrac{1}{12}$

2. $.125 = \dfrac{}{1000} = \dfrac{}{8}$, $.02 = \dfrac{}{100} = \dfrac{}{50}$.

125, 1   2, 1

3. $.33\tfrac{1}{3} = \dfrac{33\tfrac{1}{3}}{100} = \dfrac{100}{3} \times \dfrac{1}{100} = \dfrac{100}{300} = \dfrac{}{3}$.

$.66\tfrac{2}{3} = \underline{} = \underline{} \times \underline{} = \underline{} = \underline{}$.

$\tfrac{1}{3}, \tfrac{2}{3}$

4. $3.83\tfrac{1}{3} = 3\dfrac{83\tfrac{1}{3}}{100} = 3 + \dfrac{83\tfrac{1}{3}}{100} = \underline{}$.

$3\tfrac{5}{6}$

5. $12.625 = \underline{}$.

$12\tfrac{5}{8}$

6. $.83\frac{1}{3}$ is equivalent (has the same value) to $\frac{5}{6}, \frac{5}{12}, \frac{7}{8}$? (change $.83\frac{1}{3}$ to a fraction to compare).

$$.83\frac{1}{3} = \frac{83\frac{1}{3}}{100} = \frac{250}{3} \times \frac{1}{100} = \frac{5}{6}.$$

7. Does $.125 = \frac{1}{8}$? yes ___ no ___ Verify your answer. _____.
   Does $.675 = \frac{7}{8}$? yes ___ no ___ Verify your answer. _____.

$.125 = \frac{1}{8}$. Proof: $.125 = \frac{125}{1000} = \frac{1}{8}$.

$.675$ does not equal $\frac{7}{8}$. Proof: $.675 = \frac{675}{1000} = \frac{27}{40}$.

8. Change .136 to a fraction and reduce to lowest terms.

$$.136 = \frac{136}{1000} = \frac{17}{125}.$$

Decimal Equivalents of Common Fractions (Aliquot Parts of 1 or $1.00)

An *aliquot* part is any number that can be divided evenly into another number. In business we are concerned primarily with those decimal equivalents of common fractions that are aliquot parts of 1 or $1.00. They are used so frequently that they should be memorized.

When decimal equivalents that are not even ($\frac{1}{3}, \frac{1}{6}$, etc.) are used, they should be carried to 4 or, in some cases, 5 decimal places to ensure the proper degree of accuracy unless the fraction part is used—$33\frac{1}{3}$ instead of .33333.

Decimal equivalents of common fractions are shown in Figure 1.1.

3rds		5ths		8ths		12ths	
$\frac{1}{3}$	$.33\frac{1}{3}$	$\frac{1}{5}$	.20	$\frac{1}{8}$	.125	$\frac{1}{12}$	$.08\frac{1}{3}$
$\frac{2}{3}$	$.66\frac{2}{3}$	$\frac{2}{5}$	.40	$\frac{2}{8}$	.25	$\frac{2}{12}$	$.16\frac{2}{3}$
		$\frac{3}{5}$	.60	$\frac{3}{8}$	.375	$\frac{3}{12}$	.25
4ths		$\frac{4}{5}$	.80	$\frac{4}{8}$	.50	$\frac{4}{12}$	$.33\frac{1}{3}$
$\frac{1}{4}$	.25			$\frac{5}{8}$	.625	$\frac{5}{12}$	$.41\frac{2}{3}$
$\frac{2}{4}$	.50	6ths		$\frac{6}{8}$	.75	$\frac{6}{12}$	.50
$\frac{3}{4}$	.75	$\frac{1}{6}$	$.16\frac{2}{3}$	$\frac{7}{8}$	.875	$\frac{7}{12}$	$.58\frac{1}{3}$
		$\frac{2}{6}$	$.33\frac{1}{3}$			$\frac{8}{12}$	$.66\frac{2}{3}$
		$\frac{3}{6}$	.50			$\frac{9}{12}$	.75
		$\frac{4}{6}$	$.66\frac{2}{3}$			$\frac{10}{12}$	$.83\frac{1}{3}$
		$\frac{5}{6}$	$.83\frac{1}{3}$			$\frac{11}{12}$	$.91\frac{2}{3}$

Tables for other decimal equivalents such as 16ths, 32nds, and 64ths are available or can be compiled. The 9ths are easy to remember since $\frac{1}{9} = .11\frac{1}{9}$, $\frac{2}{9} = .22\frac{2}{9}$, $\frac{3}{9} = .33\frac{3}{9}$ or $.33\frac{1}{3}$, and so on.

9. Any number that can be divided evenly into another number is an _____ part of that number.

  _____

  aliquot

10. $16\frac{2}{3}$ is an aliquot part of 1 because 1 can be divided evenly by $.16\frac{2}{3}$ _____ times.

  _____

  6

11. $.12\frac{1}{2}$, .50, and .20 are all _____ parts of _____.

  _____

  aliquot, 1

12. The aliquot parts of $1.00 in the following list are (underscore)

    $0.25, $0.17, $0.33⅓, $0.20, $0.23.

    _

    $0.25, $0.33⅓, $0.20

13. List the decimal equivalents of 9ths to 4 decimal places.

    ———, ———, ———, ———, ———, ———, ———, ———, ———.

    _

    .1111, .2222, .3333, .4444, .5556, .6667, .7778, .8889.

Using Aliquot Parts of $1.00 in Multiplication

If the decimal equivalents are known for the fractions being used, a great deal of time can be saved in many applications, particularly in invoice work. When values such as .33⅓ or .16⅔ are used, it is easier to divide by 3 or 6 than to multiply by the full decimal form. If .66⅔ is used, divide by 3 and multiply by 2, since this is equal to ⅔.

Example: 39 yd at $0.33⅓ a yd

Solution: $39 \times \frac{1}{3} = \$13.00$, since .33⅓ = ⅓ of $1.00

Example: 95 articles at 12½¢ each

Solution: $95 \times \frac{1}{8} = 11.875$ *or* $11.88

Example: 108 pieces at 41⅔¢ each

Solution: $108 \times \frac{5}{12} = \$45.00$

14. Complete the following as illustrated for the first problem.

(a) 32 yd at $12\frac{1}{2}$¢ a yd $32 \times \frac{1}{8} = \$4.00$ (answer).

(b) 85 lb at 60¢ a lb   _____.

(c) 120 yd at 0.37\frac{1}{2}$ a yd   _____.

(d) 25 pc at $33\frac{1}{3}$¢ each   _____.

(e) 120 yd at 0.41\frac{2}{3}$ a yd   _____.

(a) $4.00.
(b) $85 \times \frac{3}{5} = \$51.00$.
(c) $120 \times \frac{3}{8} = \$45.00$.
(d) $25 \times \frac{1}{3} = \$8.33$.
(e) $120 \times \frac{5}{12} = \$50.00$.

DECIMALS OR DECIMAL FRACTIONS

EXERCISE 5

I. Change to the decimal form. Record to 2 decimals and carry fractions; i.e., $\frac{2}{9} = .22\frac{2}{9}$. Check your answers with those listed at the end of this exercise.

1. $1\frac{3}{8} =$ _____. 2. $\frac{11}{9} =$ _____.
3. $\frac{1}{12} =$ _____. 4. $\frac{5}{11} =$ _____.
5. $\frac{3}{16} =$ _____. 6. $2\frac{5}{12} =$ _____.
7. $15\frac{1}{6} =$ _____. 8. $9\frac{1}{5} =$ _____.
9. $6\frac{5}{8} =$ _____. 10. $10\frac{3}{4} =$ _____.

II. Change to the fractional form; i.e., $3.91\frac{2}{3} = 3\frac{11}{12}$.

1. $.16\frac{2}{3} =$ _____. 2. $.222\frac{2}{9} =$ _____.
3. $1.875 =$ _____. 4. $.0625 =$ _____.
5. $.9025 =$ _____. 6. $.44\frac{4}{9} =$ _____.
7. $3.625 =$ _____. 8. $20.83\frac{1}{3} =$ _____.
9. $4.1875 =$ _____. 10. $.4375 =$ _____.

III. Find the cost of the following purchases. All prices are per unit.

1. 36 lb at $66\frac{2}{3}$¢ = _____. 2. 48 lb at $62\frac{1}{2}$¢ = _____.
3. 90 lb at 20¢ = _____. 4. 75 lb at $33\frac{1}{3}$¢ = _____.
5. 72 lb at $37\frac{1}{2}$¢ = _____. 6. 108 art* at $8\frac{1}{3}$¢ = _____.
7. 24 art* at $83\frac{1}{3}$¢ = _____. 8. 48 art* at $16\frac{2}{3}$¢ = _____.
9. 80 art* at $12\frac{1}{2}$¢ = _____. 10. 36 art* at $22\frac{2}{9}$¢ = _____.
11. 60 qt at $41\frac{2}{3}$¢ = _____. 12. 96 qt at $87\frac{1}{2}$¢ = _____.
13. 54 qt at $11\frac{1}{9}$¢ = _____. 14. 45 qt at 60¢ = _____.
15. 24 qt at $16\frac{2}{3}$¢ = _____. 16. 120 pc at 75¢ = _____.
17. 35 pc at 80¢ = _____. 18. 132 pc at 75¢ = _____.
19. 160 pc at 75¢ = _____. 20. 48 pc at $58\frac{1}{3}$¢ = _____.

*Articles

Answers

I. 1. $1.37\frac{1}{2}$ 2. $1.22\frac{2}{9}$
    3. $.08\frac{1}{3}$ 4. $.45\frac{5}{11}$
    5. $.18\frac{3}{1}$ 6. $2.41\frac{2}{3}$
    7. $15.16\frac{2}{3}$ 8. 9.20
    9. $6.62\frac{1}{2}$ 10. 10.75

II. 1. $\frac{1}{6}$ 2. $\frac{2}{9}$
    3. $1\frac{7}{8}$ 4. $\frac{1}{16}$
    5. $\frac{361}{400}$ 6. $\frac{4}{9}$
    7. $3\frac{5}{8}$ 8. $20\frac{5}{6}$
    9. $4\frac{3}{16}$ 10. $\frac{7}{16}$

III. 1. $36 \times \frac{2}{3} = \$24.00.$ 2. $48 \times \frac{5}{8} = \$30.00.$
     3. $90 \times \frac{1}{5} = \$18.00.$ 4. $75 \times \frac{1}{3} = \$25.00.$
     5. $72 \times \frac{3}{8} = \$27.00.$ 6. $108 \times \frac{1}{12} = \$\ 9.00.$
     7. $24 \times \frac{5}{6} = \$20.00.$ 8. $48 \times \frac{1}{6} = \$\ 8.00.$
     9. $80 \times \frac{1}{8} = \$10.00.$ 10. $36 \times \frac{2}{9} = \$\ 8.00.$
    11. $60 \times \frac{5}{12} = \$25.00.$ 12. $96 \times \frac{7}{8} = \$84.00.$
    13. $54 \times \frac{1}{9} = \$\ 6.00.$ 14. $45 \times \frac{3}{5} = \$27.00.$
    15. $24 \times \frac{1}{6} = \$\ 4.00.$ 16. $120 \times \frac{3}{4} = \$90.00.$
    17. $35 \times \frac{4}{5} = \$28.00.$ 18. $132 \times \frac{3}{4} = \$99.00.$
    19. $160 \times \frac{3}{4} = \$120.00.$ 20. $48 \times \frac{7}{12} = \$28.00.$

EXERCISE 6

Summary: Applications

Answers appear at the end of this exercise. If your answers do not agree with those shown, check your calculations before referring to the solutions that follow.

1. Mr. Whitman had a $\frac{2}{3}$ interest in a manufacturing concern. He sold $\frac{2}{5}$ of his interest for $6000. At the same rate, what was (a) the total amount of his interest and (b) the total worth of the manufacturing concern?

    (a) _____

    (b) _____

2. Mr. Bradshaw bought 200 used tires for $175 at an auction. He sold $\frac{1}{4}$ of them for $60.00, 16 at $7.50 each, 51 at $10.00 each, and junked the rest. How many tires did he throw away? What was his total profit if the cost of handling this transaction amounted to $65.00?

    Junked _____

    Profit _____

3. A man worked the following number of hours each day during a 5-day week; $6\frac{1}{2}$, $7\frac{3}{4}$, $8\frac{1}{2}$, 8 and $7\frac{2}{3}$, respectively. How many hours did he work and how much did he earn if he was paid at the rate of $6.20 an hour?

    Hours _____

    Earned _____

4. Mr. Eaton, Mr. Hayes, and Mr. Huff owned a business jointly and shared profits and losses in proportion to their investments which were $25,000, $15,000, and $30,000, respectively. What fractional part did each man own in the business? If profits amounted to $2682.50 for the current year, how much did each man receive as his share?

	Fraction	*Dollar*
Mr. Eaton	_____	$ _____
Mr. Hayes	_____	_____
Mr. Huff	_____	_____

82 UNIT 4

5. The following report represents rental receipts for the Bradford Equipment Rentals during the first 6 months of the current year and the same period during the preceding year. (a) Find the total receipts for each period. (b) Find the increase or decrease of this year as compared with the last year. (c) Find the average receipts per month for each period.

BRADFORD EQUIPMENT RENTALS

Month	This Year	Last Year	Increase	Decrease
January	$ 965.00	$ 926.50	$_____	$_____
February	1068.75	988.75	_____	_____
March	959.50	1001.50	_____	_____
April	1768.25	2100.50	_____	_____
May	1856.00	1962.00	_____	_____
June	1629.25	1598.75	_____	_____
Total	$	$	$	$

(c) $_____ and $_____

6. Visitors to the county museum during the first week after it opened were as follows: Sunday, 869; Monday, 456; Tuesday, 317; Wednesday, 725; Thursday, 294; Friday, 375; Saturday, 961. What was the average daily attendance?_____

7. Everett and Holt made the following purchases from the Evens Haines Co. during the month: $316.20, $216.25, and $190.50. Payments made during the same period amounted to $296.00, $395.00 and $150.00. There was a balance due at the beginning of the month amounting to $125.00. How much did Everett and Holt owe at the end of the month? $_____

8. Complete the following invoice. Record all answers (quantity × unit price) correct to the nearest cent.

SHIPLEY MERCANTILE COMPANY

Sold to J. E. Norman
Chester, New York

Invoice No. 10–563
Date June 6, 19__

Quantity	Description	Unit Price	Amount
23 yd	Linen	$ 1.25	$ _____
$16\frac{2}{3}$ yd	Plastic sheeting	.36	_____
100 yd	Cotton padding	$.02\frac{1}{2}$	_____
$8\frac{1}{3}$ yd	Wood (Baines)	12.48	_____
25 yd	Wool (W and F)	7.98	_____
65	Hooks #613	.16 cwt[a]	_____
$12\frac{1}{2}$ yd	Gingham	.96	_____
		Total	$ _____

[a] $0.16 per hundred

9. A profit of $3160 is to be divided among A, B, and C in the ratios of $\frac{1}{2}$, $\frac{1}{3}$, and $\frac{1}{6}$. How much should each receive?

A $ _____

B $ _____

C $ _____

10. Mr. Brown owned $\frac{3}{7}$ of a store. He sold $\frac{1}{3}$ of his share for $13,000. At the same rate, what was the value of the store? $ _____

Answers

1. (a) $15,000
   (b) $22,500

2. Junked 83
   Profit $450.00

3. Worked $38\frac{5}{12}$ hr
   Earned $238.18

4. Mr. Eaton $\frac{5}{14}$ $ 958.04
   Mr. Hayes $\frac{3}{14}$ $ 574.82
   Mr. Huff $\frac{6}{14}$ $1149.64

5. (a) This Year $8246.75
       Last Year $8578.00

   (b) | Month | Increase | Decrease |
       |---|---|---|
       | January | $ 38.50 | $ |
       | February | 80.00 | |
       | March | | 42.00 |
       | April | | 332.25 |
       | May | | 106.00 |
       | June | 30.50 | |
       | | $149.00 | $480.25 |
       | Total decrease | $331.25 | |

   (c) $1374.46 and $1429.67

6. 571

7. $ 6.95

8. $ 28.75
   6.00
   2.50
   104.00
   199.50
   0.10
   12.00
   $352.85

9. $1580.00
   1053.33
   526.67
   $3160.00

10. $91,000

Solutions

1. (a) $\frac{2}{5}$ = $ 6,000
       $\frac{1}{5}$ = $ 3,000   then
       $\frac{5}{5}$ = $15,000   (answer)
   (b) Therefore $\frac{2}{3}$ = $15,000,
       $\frac{1}{3}$ = $ 7,500,
       $\frac{3}{3}$ = $22,500 (answer).

2. $200 - (50 + 16 + 51) = 83$ tires junked.
    (a) $\frac{1}{4} \times 200 = 50$ tires \$ 60.00
     16 $\times$ \$7.50 $=$ 120.00
     51 $\times$ \$10.00 $=$ $\underline{510.00}$
     Total sales \$690.00

    Cost $=$ \$175.00 $+$ \$ 65.00 $=$ \$240.00.
    Profit $=$ \$690.00 $-$ \$240.00 $=$ \$450.00.

3. $38.4167 \times \$6.20 = \$238.183540$ or $\$238.18$

4. $\$25,000 + \$15,000 + \$30,000 = \$70,000$

    Mr. Eaton's share $= 25,000 \div 70,000 = \frac{5}{14}$.
    Mr. Hayes's share $= 15,000 \div 70,000 = \frac{3}{14}$.
    Mr. Huff's share $= 30,000 \div 70,000 = \frac{6}{14}$.

    Then

    Mr. Eaton received $\frac{5}{14} \times \$2682.50 =$ \$ 958.04
    Mr. Hayes received $\frac{3}{14} \times \$2682.50 =$ \$ 574.82
    Mr. Huff received $\frac{6}{14} \times \$2682.50 = $ 1149.64
     Total $= \$2682.50$

5. See answers.

6. $3997 \div 7 = 571$

7. Purchases $= \$316.20 + \$216.25 + \$190.50 = \$722.95$.
    Balance at the beginning of the month $= \$125.00$.
    Amount owed $= \$722.95 + 125.00 = \$847.95$.
    Payments made during month $= \$296 + \$395 + \$150 = \$841.00$.
    Balance due $= \$847.95 - \$841.00 = \$6.95$.

8. See answers.

9. $\frac{1}{2} + \frac{1}{3} + \frac{1}{6} = \$3160$.
    $\frac{3}{6} + \frac{2}{6} + \frac{1}{6} = \$3160$.

    $A = \frac{3}{6} \times \$3160 = \$1580.00$.
    $B = \frac{2}{6} \times \$3160 = \$1053.33$.
    $C = \frac{1}{6} \times \$3160 =$ \$ 526.67.

10. $\$13,000 \times 3 = \$39,000$ total value of share.
    If $\frac{3}{7} = \$39,000$, then $\frac{1}{7} = \$13,000$ and 100% or $\frac{7}{7} = 7 \times \$13,000 = \$91,000$

CHAPTER TWO
Percentage

OBJECTIVES

This chapter deals with the understanding and application of the basic formula for all percentage problems and the solution of problems in percentage.
When you have completed this study, you should be able to

(1) change any whole number, mixed number, decimal, fraction, or percent to any of the other forms.
(2) use aliquot parts instead of a percent, when possible, in multiplication work,
(3) find the percentage (amount) when the rate and base are known,
(4) find the rate (percent) when the percentage and base are known,
(5) find the base (100%) when the percentage and rate are known.

The first few frames discuss the meaning of percent and how percents may be converted to decimals or fractions and the converse. If you think that you are well acquainted with these relationships, test yourself by answering the following questions. If you choose *not* to answer the following questions, go to frame 1.

PRETEST

1. Express the following percents in the decimal form:

   $12\% = $ _____ , $21\frac{1}{2}\% = $ _____ , $\frac{2}{5}\% = $ _____ , $125.6\% = $ _____ ,

   $200\% = $ _____ , $.5\% = $ _____ , $\frac{1}{2}\% = $ _____ .

2. Express the following decimals in the percent form:

   $.06\frac{1}{3} = $ _____ %, $.22 = $ _____ %, $1.05 = $ _____ %, $.00\frac{1}{4}$ _____ %,

   $.0045 = $ _____ %, $.16\frac{1}{2} = $ _____ %, $3.00 = $ _____ %.

3. Express the following percents in the fractional form:

   $18\% = $ _____ , $8\frac{1}{3}\% = $ _____ , $16\frac{1}{2}\% = $ _____ .

   $6\frac{1}{4}\% = $ _____ , $210\% = $ _____ .

4. Express the following fractions in the decimal form and the percent form:

$\frac{3}{8}$ = .375   = $37\frac{1}{2}\%$. $\frac{3}{12}$ = _____ = _____.

$\frac{5}{6}$ = _____ = _____. $\frac{12}{92}$ = _____ = _____.

$\frac{2}{9}$ = _____ = _____. $\frac{2}{3}$ = _____ = _____.

5. Express each of the following percents as a decimal and as a fraction or mixed number:

25% = .25   = $\frac{1}{4}$. $\frac{1}{2}\%$ = _____ = _____.

16% = _____ = _____. $1\frac{1}{4}\%$ = _____ = _____.

$22\frac{1}{2}\%$ = _____ = _____. $15\frac{1}{2}\%$ = _____ = _____.

6. Show the decimal forms of the following. Note the relationships between them.

$\frac{1}{2}$ and $\frac{1}{2}\%$? $\frac{1}{2}$ = .50 , $\frac{1}{2}\%$ = .005 .

$\frac{1}{4}$ and $\frac{1}{4}\%$? $\frac{1}{4}$ = ____ , $\frac{1}{4}\%$ = ____ .

$\frac{1}{8}$ and $\frac{1}{8}\%$? $\frac{1}{8}$ = ____ , $\frac{1}{8}\%$ = ____ .

Now that you have completed this quiz compare your answers with those listed here. If you missed two or more in any section, go to frame 1. If you missed no more than one in any section, skip Unit 1 and begin with Unit 2, page 96.

1. 12% = .12, $21\frac{1}{2}\%$ = .215, $\frac{2}{5}\%$ = .004, 125.6% = 1.256, 200% = 2.00, .5% = .005, $\frac{1}{2}\%$ = .005.

2. $.06\frac{1}{3}$ = $6\frac{1}{3}\%$, .22 = 22%, 1.05 = 105%, $.00\frac{1}{4}$ = $\frac{1}{4}\%$, .0045 = .45%, $.16\frac{1}{2}$ = $16\frac{1}{2}\%$, 3.00 = 300%.

3. 18% = $\frac{18}{100}$ = $\frac{9}{50}$, $8\frac{1}{3}\%$ = $\frac{1}{12}$, $16\frac{1}{2}\%$ = $\frac{33}{200}$, $6\frac{1}{4}\%$ = $\frac{1}{16}$, 210% = $2\frac{1}{10}$.

4. $\frac{5}{6}$ = $83\frac{1}{3}$ = $83\frac{1}{3}\%$, $\frac{2}{9}$ = $.22\frac{2}{9}$ = $22\frac{2}{9}\%$, $\frac{3}{12}$ = .25 = 25%, $\frac{12}{92}$ = $\frac{3}{23}$ = .1304 = 13.04%, $\frac{2}{3}$ = $.66\frac{2}{3}$ = $66\frac{2}{3}\%$.

5. 16% = .16 = $\frac{4}{25}$, $22\frac{1}{2}\%$ = .225 = $\frac{9}{40}$, $\frac{1}{2}\%$ = .005 = $\frac{1}{200}$, $1\frac{1}{4}\%$ = .0125 = $\frac{1}{80}$, $15\frac{1}{2}\%$ = .155 = $\frac{31}{200}$.

6. $\frac{1}{4}$ = .25, $\frac{1}{4}\%$ = .0025, $\frac{1}{8}$ = .125, $\frac{1}{8}\%$ = .00125.

UNIT 1. CHANGING PERCENTS TO DECIMALS OR FRACTIONS AND CONVERSELY

Percentage

A common means of expressing relationships in business is essential. This becomes possible in the use of percentage by which the elements of a problem can be expressed in terms of a common unit of measure. Percentage is used to express relationships of many kinds, such as similarities or differences between groups, classes, fiscal periods, and increases or decreases. Percentage is also used to express rates in interest, discounts, taxes, fluctuations in prices, changes in the stock market, and many other measures too numerous to mention.

1. Any quantity may be divided into 100 equal parts, each of which represents a common unit of measure called a percent. Thus 2 percent represents two parts of 100 or 2 hundredths ($\frac{2}{100}$) of a whole unit. The fractional expression *hundredths* came to be replaced with the symbol %. Thus one hundredth ($\frac{1}{100}$) of a quantity may be expressed as 1%, $\frac{2}{100}$ as 2%, $\frac{3}{100}$ as 3%, and so on.

    4 percent is the same as $\frac{4}{100}$ or _____%.

    6 percent is the same as _____ or _____%.

    5 percent may be written as _____ or _____.

    -

    4 percent = $\frac{4}{100}$ = 4%.
    6 percent = $\frac{6}{100}$ = 6%.
    5 percent = $\frac{5}{100}$ = 5%.

2. Since hundredths may be written in the decimal form, any percent may be expressed in three ways: 1% = $\frac{1}{100}$ = .01, 3% = $\frac{3}{100}$ = .03, 20% = $\frac{20}{100}$ = .20, and so on. 14 percent may be written as _____, a _____, or a _____.
                                                                percent   fraction   decimal

    -

    14 percent = 14% = $\frac{14}{100}$ = .14.

3. The % sign takes the place of the two decimal places that denote hundredths: $1\% = \frac{1}{100} = .01$; conversely, $.01 = \frac{1}{100} = 1\%$. To change a percent to a decimal drop the % sign and move the decimal point two places to the left. Then $4\% = .04$, $125\% = 1.25$, $2.5\% = .025$, $\frac{1}{2}\% = .005$. The following percents written as decimals are

   $12\% =$ _____, $3\frac{1}{2}\% =$ _____, $106\% =$ _____.

   .12, .035, 1.06

4. To change a decimal to a percent move the decimal point two places to the right and use the % sign. Then $.16 = 16\%$, $.045 = 4.5\%$, $.12\frac{1}{2} = 12\frac{1}{2}\%$ or 12.5%, $.0056 = .56\%$. The following decimals written as percents are

   $.25 =$ _____%, $.20\frac{1}{2} =$ _____%, $2.26 =$ _____%, $.0025 =$ _____%.

   25%, $20\frac{1}{2}\%$, 226%, $.25\%$

5. Since percent denotes hundredths, all percents may be thought of automatically as fractions with a denominator of 100. To change a percent to a fraction drop the % sign, divide the percent quantity by 100, and reduce to lowest terms. Then

   $60\% = \frac{60}{100} = \frac{3}{5}$, $4\% = \frac{4}{100} = \frac{1}{25}$, $37\frac{1}{2}\% = \frac{37\frac{1}{2}}{100} = \frac{3}{8}$.

   Complete the following:

Problem	Fraction	Decimal
40%		
23%		
12.5%		

   $40\% = \frac{2}{5} = .40$, $23\% = \frac{23}{100} = .23$, $12.5\% = \frac{1}{8} = .125$.

6. If $16\frac{2}{3}\%$ were written as a fraction with a denominator of 100, it would be

$$\frac{16\frac{2}{3}}{100}.$$

In order to reduce it to a common fraction, study the following procedure.

(a) $\dfrac{16\frac{2}{3}}{100} = 16\frac{2}{3} \div 100 = \dfrac{50}{3} \times \dfrac{1}{100} = \dfrac{1}{6}$

OR

(b) $\dfrac{16\frac{2}{3}}{100} = \dfrac{16\frac{2}{3} \times 3}{100 \times 3} = \dfrac{50}{300} = \dfrac{1}{6}.$

Change $22\frac{2}{9}\%$ to a fraction. Reduce to lowest terms.

$22\frac{2}{9}\% =$ _____ .

- -

$\dfrac{22\frac{2}{9} \times 9}{100 \times 9} = \dfrac{200}{900} = \dfrac{2}{9}.$

7. If $12\% = \frac{12}{100} = \frac{3}{25}$, then the reverse is true. To change a fraction to a percent divide the numerator by the denominator to obtain the decimal form and then change the decimal form to a percent.

$\frac{3}{8} = .375 = 37.5\%$ or $37\frac{1}{2}\%.$

$\frac{5}{8} = .625 =$ _____%.

$\frac{11}{5} = 2.2 \;\;\; =$ _____%.

$\frac{3}{5} =$ ____ $=$ _____%.

- -

62.5% or $62\frac{1}{2}\%$, 220%, .60 = 60%

8. Any whole number such as 1 or 2 may be written as 1.00, 2.00. Then 1 = 1.00 = 100%, 2 = 2.00 = 200%, and so on. If .25 = 25% and 1.00 = 100%, then 1.25 = 125%. Express the following numbers in the percent form.

   3   = _____%.
   3.5 = _____%.
   4.25 = _____%.
   20   = _____%.

   _

   300%, 350%, 425%, 2000%

9. A mixed number such as $2\frac{1}{2}$ written as a decimal is 2.5 or 2.50, which is 250%. Study the following: $6\frac{1}{8} = 6.125 = 612.5\%$ or $612\frac{1}{2}\%$
   $$4\frac{1}{3} = 4.33\frac{1}{3} = 433\frac{1}{3}\%.$$

   Then $1\frac{2}{5} = $ _____ (decimal) = _____ (percent).

   $3\frac{1}{2} = $ _____ (decimal) = _____ (percent).

   $4\frac{2}{3} = $ _____ (decimal) = _____ (percent).

   _

   $1\frac{2}{5} = 1.40 = 140\%$.
   $3\frac{1}{2} = 3.50 = 350\%$.
   $4\frac{2}{3} = 4.66\frac{2}{3} = 466\frac{2}{3}\%$.

Aliquot Parts

Many percent values and their fractional equivalents that are used frequently should be memorized. It is often more convenient to use the fractional form than the decimal form in the solution of a problem.

Example: $8\frac{1}{3}\%$ of 144 = .083333 × 144 = 11.9995 or 12.

Procedure: This problem is a simple one if we know that $8\frac{1}{3}\% = \frac{1}{12}$, in which case 144 ÷ 12 = 12.

CHANGING PERCENTS TO DECIMALS AND FRACTIONS

Example: $12\frac{1}{2}\%$ of $96 = \frac{1}{8} \times 96 = 12$.

Procedure: This is less cumbersome than multiplying 96 by .125 (decimal equivalent of $12\frac{1}{2}\%$).

In Chapter 1, Unit 2, page 75, we talked about aliquot parts when we were multiplying with fractions. Since we can change any percent to a fraction, we can use this information and the table on page 76 when a percent is easier to use as a fraction. See examples above.

10. 25% of 324 is the same as $\frac{1}{4} \times 324 = 81$. Then 50% of 28 is the same as _____ $\times$ 28 = _____ and $16\frac{2}{3}\%$ of 360 is the same as _____ $\times$ 360 = _____ .

- -

$\frac{1}{2} \times 28 = 14, \frac{1}{6} \times 360 = 60$.

11. $41\frac{2}{3}\% = \frac{5}{12}$. If we neither remembered this fact nor had a table of reference, we would divide $41\frac{2}{3}$ by _____ and _____ to its lowest terms.

- -

100, reduce

12. $41\frac{2}{3}\% = \frac{41\frac{2}{3}}{100} = \frac{125}{3} \times \frac{1}{100} = \frac{5}{12}$.

Change $87\frac{1}{2}\%$ to a common fraction. _____

- -

$87\frac{1}{2}\% = \frac{87\frac{1}{2}}{100} = \frac{175}{2} \times \frac{1}{100} = \frac{7}{8}$.

94 UNIT 1

EXERCISE 7

By using what you have learned about percents and aliquot parts, you should be able to solve most of these problems mentally. You may wish to review the table of decimal equivalents, page 76, before you begin. Work out only those that give you difficulty.

I. Change each of the following numbers to the percent form:

1. .25 _25_ %   2. .33$\frac{1}{3}$ _____%   3. 1.65 _____%
4. .05 _____%   5. .005 _____%   6. 3 _____%
7. 1.06$\frac{1}{2}$ _____%   8. 1.25 _____%   9. 3$\frac{1}{2}$ _____%
10. .16 _____%   11. 2.05 _____%   12. .008 _____%
13. 10 _____%   14. .0036 _____%   15. 1$\frac{1}{4}$ _____%
16. .90 _____%   17. .00$\frac{1}{2}$ _____%   18. .7 _____%
19. .02$\frac{1}{2}$ _____%   20. 1$\frac{1}{2}$ _____%

II. Change each of the following percents to the decimal form:

21. 2% _.02_   22. 200% _____   23. .5% _____
24. $\frac{1}{4}$% _____   25. 1.6% _____   26. 1.5% _____
27. 16% _____   28. 25% _____   29. 300% _____
30. 16$\frac{1}{2}$% _____   31. .05% _____   32. 32$\frac{1}{2}$% _____
33. 9% _____   34. 4$\frac{1}{2}$% _____   35. 568% _____
36. $\frac{1}{2}$% _____   37. 23.2% _____   38. .56% _____
39. 1.7% _____   40. 115% _____

III. Change each of the following percents to a fraction or a mixed number:

41. 25% $\frac{1}{4}$ 42. 16$\frac{2}{3}$% _____   43. 12$\frac{1}{2}$% _____
44. 11$\frac{1}{9}$% _____   45. 108$\frac{1}{3}$% _____   46. 20% _____
47. 5% _____   48. 3$\frac{1}{2}$% _____   49. 30% _____
50. 125% _____   51. 15% _____   52. 83$\frac{1}{3}$% _____
53. 60% _____   54. 17% _____   55. .22% _____
56. 6% _____   57. $\frac{2}{5}$% _____   58. 38% _____
59. 46% _____   60. 375% _____

CHANGING PERCENTS TO DECIMALS AND FRACTIONS 95

IV. Change each of the following fractions or mixed numbers to the percent (%) form.

61. $\frac{3}{8}$ _____%   62. $\frac{5}{6}$ _____%   63. $\frac{1}{12}$ _____%

64. $\frac{3}{9}$ _____%   65. $\frac{2}{5}$ _____%   66. $\frac{5}{12}$ _____%

67. $\frac{1}{30}$ _____%   68. $\frac{1}{25}$ _____%   69. $\frac{1}{2}$ _____%

70. $\frac{3}{4}$ _____%   71. $1\frac{7}{8}$ _____%   72. $3\frac{3}{4}$ _____%

73. $\frac{1}{6}$ _____%   74. $\frac{2}{3}$ _____%   75. $\frac{2}{16}$ _____%

76. $\frac{4}{32}$ _____%   77. $1\frac{2}{5}$ _____%   78. $\frac{5}{9}$ _____%

79. $1\frac{1}{3}$ _____%   80. $20\frac{1}{2}$ _____%

Answers

Check your answers with those shown below. Review any section in which you feel you need extra study.

I.
1. 25%
2. $33\frac{1}{3}$%
3. 165%
4. 5%
5. .5 or $\frac{1}{2}$%
6. 300%
7. 106.5%
8. 125%
9. 350%
10. 16%
11. 205%
12. .8%
13. 1000%
14. .36%
15. 125%
16. 90%
17. $\frac{1}{2}$%
18. 70%
19. $2\frac{1}{2}$%
20. 150%

II.
21. .02
22. 2.00
23. .005
24. .0025
25. .016
26. .015
27. .16
28. .25
29. 3.00
30. .165
31. .0005
32. .325
33. .09
34. .045
35. 5.68
36. .005
37. .232
38. .0056
39. .017
40. 1.15

III.
41. $\frac{1}{4}$
42. $\frac{1}{6}$
43. $\frac{1}{8}$
44. $\frac{1}{9}$
45. $1\frac{1}{12}$
46. $\frac{1}{5}$
47. $\frac{1}{20}$
48. $\frac{7}{200}$
49. $\frac{3}{10}$
50. $1\frac{1}{4}$
51. $\frac{3}{20}$
52. $\frac{5}{6}$
53. $\frac{3}{5}$
54. $\frac{17}{100}$
55. $\frac{11}{5000}$
56. $\frac{3}{50}$
57. $\frac{1}{250}$
58. $\frac{19}{50}$
59. $\frac{23}{50}$
60. $3\frac{3}{4}$

96 UNIT 2

IV. 61. $37\frac{1}{2}\%$ 62. $83\frac{1}{3}\%$ 63. $8\frac{1}{3}\%$
 64. $33\frac{1}{3}\%$ 65. 40% 66. $41\frac{2}{3}\%$
 67. $3\frac{1}{3}\%$ 68. 4% 69. 50%
 70. 75% 71. $187\frac{1}{2}\%$ 72. 375%
 73. $16\frac{2}{3}\%$ 74. $66\frac{2}{3}\%$ 75. $12\frac{1}{2}\%$
 76. $12\frac{1}{2}\%$ 77. 140% 78. $55\frac{5}{9}\%$
 79. $133\frac{1}{3}\%$ 80. 2050%

UNIT 2. BASIC ELEMENTS OF PERCENT PROBLEMS

Before you proceed with this unit you may wish to test your understanding of the basic elements of percent problems and their application. The following test is designed for that purpose. If you take the test, results will indicate the areas, if any, that should be reviewed.

 If you *do not* take the test, go to frame 1, page 100.

PRETEST

Basic Elements of Percent Problems

Instructions

1. Carry answers correct to two decimals if they are not whole numbers.
2. Record rates such as $16\frac{2}{3}\%$ with the fraction, as in this case.
3. Record answers in the spaces provided.
4. When you have completed the test, check your answers with those that follow.

 I. 1. State the basic percentage formula. _____
  2. 26% of $930 = $241.80

   What is the base _____, rate _____, percentage _____?

  3. What is 23% of 96? _____

    2.6% of 300 _____

    $\frac{1}{2}$% of $150 _____

    .08% of 21.5 _____

    $112\frac{1}{2}$% of 144 _____

  4. 26 increased by 12% = _____.

    125 decreased by 15% = _____.

5. (a) If last year's school attendance of 3700 were increased by 12% this year, what would this year's attendance equal?

   _____

   (b) If Henry's earnings of $75.00 per week were reduced 6%, what would his new earnings be?

   _____

II. 1. What % is 15 of 45? _____

   27 of 86? _____

   152 of 64? _____

   5.43 of 36.2? _____

   $\frac{5}{6}$ of $\frac{2}{3}$? _____

2. (a) If the student enrollment of Haven's School were 3462 last year and 4085 this year, what percent increase does this represent?

   _____

   (b) Sales for Atlin Corp. dropped from $36,000,000 last year to $26,000,000 this year. What percent decrease does this represent?

   _____

III. 1. 156.50 is 125% of what number? _____

35 is $33\frac{1}{3}$% of what number? _____

$4\frac{1}{2}$% of _____ = $67\frac{1}{2}$. _____

250 is $2\frac{1}{2}$% of what number? _____

2. (a) The $2700 collected by the local charity drive last year represented 12% of its goal for the year. What is the goal?

_____

(b) Mary Haynes earned $36 more per month this year than last year. This was an increase of 25% over last year. How much did she earn per month last year?

_____

(c) If 40% or 1800 persons in a community were under 18 years of age, what was the total population?

_____

BASIC ELEMENTS OF PERCENT PROBLEMS

Answers

After you check your answers, follow the instructions below and review the frames covering the appropriate section.

I. Frames 1 to 4, page 100.   Frames 5 to 8, page 102.

1. Base × rate = percentage.
2. Base = 930.
   Rate = 26%.
   Percentage = $241.80.

3. .23 × 96 = 22.08.
   .026 × 300 = 7.80.
   .005 × $150 = $0.75.
   .0008 × 21.5 = .01720 = .02.
   1.125 × 144 = 162.

4. 26 × 1.12 = 29.12.
   125 × .85 = 106.25.

5. (a) 3700 × 1.12 = 4144.
   (b) $75 × .94 = $70.50.

II. 1. Frames 9 to 12, page 104.
   $15 \div 45 = .33\frac{1}{3} = 33\frac{1}{3}\%$.
   $27 \div 86 = .31395 = 31.40\%$.
   $152 \div 64 = 2.375 = 237.5\%$.
   $5.43 \div 36.2 = .15 = 15\%$.
   $\frac{5}{6} \div \frac{2}{3} = \frac{5}{4} = 1.25 = 125\%$.

2. Frames 17 to 21, pages 107 to 109.
   (a) $4085 \div 3462 = 1.179 = 1.18 = 118\%$.
   Increase = 118% − 100% = 18%.
   (b) $26,000,000 \div \$36,000,000 = 26 \div 36 = 72\frac{2}{9}\%$.
   Decrease = $100\% - 72\frac{2}{9}\% = 27\frac{7}{9}\%$ (28% would be acceptable).

III. Frames 13 and 14, page 107.

1. $156.50 \div 1.25 = 125\frac{1}{5}$ or 125.20.
   $35 \div .33\frac{1}{3}$ or $35 \times 3 = 105$.
   $67\frac{1}{2} \div .045 = 1500$.
   $250 \div .025 = 10,000$.

2. (a) $2700 ÷ .12 = $22,500.
   (b) $36 = 25% of last year, therefore 100% (last year) = $36 × 4 = $144.00.
   (c) $1800 \div .40 = 4500$ or $18 \div \frac{2}{5} = 4500$.

Instructions

1. If you made no more than one error in each Section (I, II, III), you may omit this unit and go to Exercise 9, page 112.
2. If you made more than one error in any section, study the frames that are indicated as reference for the answers shown above.
3. When all frames in which you need to review have been studied, go to Exercise 8, page 110.

Basic Elements of Percent Problems (the Percent Formula)

$$\text{Base} \times \text{rate} = \text{percentage}$$

OR

$$B \times R = P.$$

There are only three basic factors or elements in any percentage problem. These are the *base* (100% or the whole amount of anything), the *rate* (percent), and the *percentage* (amount).

The relationships of these factors is expressed as a formula, shown above. All percentage problems can be solved by using this formula. The secret to solving a problem successfully is the ability to identify the factors that are known and the factor that is to be found.

1. The three basic elements are the _____, _____, and _____.

   _____

   base, rate, percentage

2. 15% of 32 = .15 × 32 = 4.80. The rate is 15%, the base is 32, and the percentage is 4.80.

   In the problem 45% of 250 = 112.50, the rate is _____, the base is _____ and the percentage is _____.

   _____

   45%, 250, 112.50

3. The base always represents the whole amount of anything or _____%.

- -

100%

4. 12% of 620 = $74.40. The base is _____, the rate is _____.

- -

620, 12%

Finding the Percentage (Amount)

Base × rate = percentage

OR

B × R = P.

Example: Find 12% of 125.

Solution: 125 × .12 = 15 (answer)

What is wanted here is 12 parts (that is 12 hundredths) of 125 or $\frac{12}{100}$ × 125. The decimal form is generally used although the fractional form may be easier to use arithmetically in some cases.

Example: Mr. Smith earns $7900 a year. He saves 8% of this amount, which is how much?

Solution: $7900 × .08 = $632 (amount saved yearly)

5. To find the percentage (amount) all rates expressed as a percent must be changed to the decimal or fractional form before multiplying by any other number.

32% of 65 = .32 × 65 = _____.
rate base rate base percentage

25% of 220 = _____ × ____ = _____
                rate as   base percentage
                a decimal

OR

_____ × ____ = _____.
rate as   base percentage
a fraction

110% of 456 = 1.10 × 456 = _____.

- -

20.80,
25% of 220 = .25 × 220 = 55 or $\frac{1}{4}$ × 220 = 55,
501.6

6. The rate × base = _____.

Problem	Solution
4% of 86	_____ × _____ = _____.
130% of 540	_____ × _____ = _____.
125½% of 62	_____ × _____ = _____.

- -

.04   × 86 = 3.44,
1.30 × 540 = 702.00,
1.255 × 62 = 77.810.

7. Find the percentage if the base is $1200 and the rate is 20%.

- -

.20 or $\frac{1}{5}$ × 1200 = $240.

BASIC ELEMENTS OF PERCENT PROBLEMS 103

8. What is the percentage for the following problems? $37\frac{1}{2}\%$ of $480 = \frac{3}{8} \times 480 = 180$.

   (a) $12\frac{1}{2}\%$ of $360 = $ _____ .

   (b) $\frac{1}{4}\%$ of 96 $= $ _____ .

   (c)   113% of $240 $= $ _____ .

- -

   (a)   .125   × $360 = $45.
   (b)   .0025 ×   96 = .24.
   (c)   1.13   ×   240 = 271.20.

Finding the Rate (Percent)

Rate = percentage ÷ base

OR

$R = P \div B$.

Example: 30 is what percent of 180?

Solution: $30 \div 180 = \frac{1}{6} = .16\frac{2}{3} = 16\frac{2}{3}\%$.

In this case we wish to find out what fractional part 30 is of 180, expressed as a percent. We find that it is $16\frac{2}{3}$ parts (hundredths) or $16\frac{2}{3}\%$.

Example: In a class of 35 students 28 received passing grades. What percent did this represent?

Solution: $28 \div 35 = \frac{4}{5} = .80 = 80\%$.

Example: The sales for Benite Company amounted to $36,462 last week and $35,400 the week before. What percent increase does this represent?

Solution: This problem may be solved by two methods.
$36,462 − $35,400 = $1,062 increase in sales.
$1,062 ÷ $35,400 = .03 or 3% increase.

or

$36,462 ÷ $35,400 = 1.03 or 103%.

This means that last week's sales amounted to 103% of the preceding week's sales, or an increase of 3%.

9. What percent of the voters passed on a certain bond issue if, out of 870,000 voters, 713,400 voted in favor of the bonds?
   We know the base is 870,000 and the percentage is 713,400 but we don't know what the rate is.

   $$\frac{}{\text{percentage}} \div \frac{}{\text{base}} = \frac{}{\text{decimal rate}} = \frac{}{\text{percent rate}}.$$

   $713,400 \div 870,000 = .82 = 82\%$

10. Out of a class of 105 students 84 received passing grades. What percent does this represent?

    The base is ____, the percentage is ____.

    Rate is ____ ÷ ____ = ____%.

    105, 84
    Rate is $84 \div 105 = 80\%$.

11. The rate may be greater than 100%. Last week's sales for a store were $437,000. This week sales amounted to $489,440. What percent is this week's sales *of* last week's sales? What was the percent increase?

    In this problem the base is _____.

    _____ ÷ _____ = ____% % increase = ____.

    Keep the following two thoughts in mind when solving a problem of this sort.

    (a) Whenever you want to find a *rate*, you are going to *divide*.
    (b) The word "of," when used, precedes the *divisor (base)*.

    The base is last week's sales.
    $\$489,440 \div \$437,000 = 1.12$ or 112% $12\% =$ increase.

12. Find the rate (to 2 decimal places), given the percentage and base for the following. Show all remainders as a fraction, i.e., 16 is what % of 98? $16 \div 98 = .16\frac{16}{49}$ or $16\frac{16}{49}\%$.

    (a) What % of 96 is 24? ____ ÷ ____ = ____%.
    (b) 15 is what % of 300? ____ ÷ ____ = ____%.
    (c) 43 is what % of 344? ____ ÷ ____ = ____%.
    (d) What % of 16 is 64? ____ ÷ ____ = ____%.

(a) $24 \div 96 = 25\%$
(b) $15 \div 300 = 5\%$
(c) $43 \div 344 = 12\frac{1}{2}\%$
(d) $64 \div 16 = 400\%$

Finding the Base or 100%

Base = percentage ÷ rate

OR

$B = P \div R$.

Example: 54 is 15% of what number?

Solution: This is the same as saying that 15% (15 hundredths) of some number equals 54.

What is that number? If 15% = 54, then
1% = 54 ÷ 15 = 3.60,
100% = 3.60 × 100 = 360.

These steps can be completed at the same time, i.e., 54 ÷ .15 = 360.

Example: If the price of milk is now 22¢ a quart and represents an increase of 10% over the last month, what was the cost of milk at that time?

Solution: 22¢ = 110% of last month's price.
Therefore .22 ÷ 1.10 = .20 or 20¢.

Proof: 10% of 20¢ = 2¢ (amount of increase)

106 UNIT 2

Example: If 65%, or 468, of a school population were girls, how many boys were there?

Solution: 468 ÷ .65 = 720 school population.
720 − 468 = 252 boys.

Proof: If 65% were girls, then 100% − 65% or 35% = boys; 35% of 720 = 252.

13. Percentage ÷ rate = base; 26 is 32% of what number? Prove your answer.

$$\underset{\text{percentage}}{26} \div \underset{\text{rate}}{.32} = \underset{\text{base}}{81\tfrac{8}{32}} \text{ or } 81\tfrac{1}{4}$$

Proof: 81.25 × .32 = 26

648 is 120% of what number? $\underset{\text{percentage}}{\underline{}} \div \underset{\text{rate}}{\underline{}} = \underset{\text{base}}{\underline{}}$.

Proof: _____

----

648 ÷ 1.20 = 540.
Proof: 540 × 1.20 = 648.

14. When we want to find the base, the _____ is *always* the divisor.

Can the base be less than the percentage? Yes ___, no ___?

----

rate,   yes, when the rate is more than 100%.

15. Complete the following:
    (a) Percentage = __B__ × __R__.
    (b) Rate   = __P__ ÷ __B__.
    (c) Base   = __P__ ÷ __R__.

(a) Percentage = base × rate.
(b) Rate   = percentage ÷ base.
(c) Base   = percentage ÷ rate.

BASIC ELEMENTS OF PERCENT PROBLEMS 107

16. Solve the following:
    (a) Find $6\frac{1}{2}\%$ of 28 _____.
    (b) What % is 20 of 35? _____.
    (c) 45 is 18% of what number? _____.

    _

    (a) $.065 \times 28 = 1.820$.
    (b) $20 \div 35 = .57\frac{1}{7} = 57\frac{1}{7}\%$.
    (c) $45 \div .18 = 250$.

17. Mary Smith received an increase in salary from $475 per month last year to $570 this year. What percent increase does this represent? Since last year's figure was increased, it will have to be the divisor.

    Then $\$\_\_\_\_\_ \div \$\_\_\_\_\_ = \_\_\_\_\_\%$.

    Percent increase $= \_\_\_\_\_\%$.

    _

    $\$570 \div \$475 = 1.20 = 120\%$, percent increase $= 20\%$.

18. In the case of a decrease we will have something less than 100% when we divide by the older figure.

    Example: Suppose Harris' apple crop dropped from 92,000 tons last year to 68,000 tons this year. What percent decrease does this represent? Since last year's crop was decreased, it must be the divisor.

    Then $\$\_\_\_\_\_ \div \$\_\_\_\_\_ = \_\_\_\_\_\%$.

    Percent decrease $= 100\% - \_\_\_\_\_\% =$

    (record to nearest tenths of 1%).

    _

    $68,000 \div 92,000 = .739 = 73.9\%$.
    $100.0\% - 73.9\% = 26.1\%$ decrease.

19. M. Holman's salary was cut from $175 to $140 a week. What percent decrease does this represent?

_____

$140 ÷ $175 = .80 = 80%,   100% − 80% = 20% decrease.

20. John's salary was increased 12%. If he earns $890.40 a month now, what was his salary before the increase? What was the amount of increase?

This means that $890.40 = 112% of his former salary.
Then his salary before the increase (100%) = $890.40 ÷ 1.12 = $795.00.
Increase = $890.40 − $795.00 = $95.40.

Suppose John's salary were increased 8%. What was his salary before the increase and what was the amount of the increase?
Show solution here:

_____

$890.40 = 108% of his former salary.
His salary before the increase = $890.40 ÷ 1.08 = $824.44.
Increase = $890.40 − $824.44 = $65.96.

BASIC ELEMENTS OF PERCENT PROBLEMS 109

21. Receipts for this year at local football games decreased 16% over the year before. What were the receipts last year if this year's receipts amounted to $1629.60?

    In this case, since there was a decrease, $1629.60 = (100% − 16%) = 84% of last year's receipts.

    Then last year's receipts (100%) = _____.

    The amount of decrease = _____.

    -

    Last year's receipts = $1629.60 ÷ .84 = $1940.00.
    Amount of decrease = $1940.00 − $1629.60 = $310.40.

EXERCISE 8

I. Find the *percentage*, given the rate and base.

1. $16\frac{1}{2}\%$ of $350.00 \rule{2cm}{0.4pt}$
2. $\frac{1}{2}\%$ of 9260 \rule{2cm}{0.4pt}
3. 115% of $240 \rule{2cm}{0.4pt}
4. 200% of 82 \rule{2cm}{0.4pt}
5. .02% of 456 \rule{2cm}{0.4pt}
6. $16\frac{2}{3}\%$ of 960 \rule{2cm}{0.4pt}

II. Find the *rate*, given the percentage and base. Record whole number with any remainder shown as a fraction.

1. 32 is what % of 96? \rule{2cm}{0.4pt}
2. What % of 64 is 1.92? \rule{2cm}{0.4pt}
3. 300 is what % of 60? \rule{2cm}{0.4pt}
4. What % of 64 is 56? \rule{2cm}{0.4pt}
5. What % of 5000 is 2.5? \rule{2cm}{0.4pt}
6. $7.87\frac{1}{2}$ is what % of 63? \rule{2cm}{0.4pt}

III. Find the *base* (100%), given the rate and percentage. Record complete number with any remainder shown as a fraction.

1. 70 is 25% of what number? \rule{2cm}{0.4pt}
2. $16\frac{2}{3}\%$ of $ \rule{1cm}{0.4pt} = $264. \rule{2cm}{0.4pt}
3. If 272 = 34%, what is 100% \rule{2cm}{0.4pt}
4. $10.00 is $\frac{1}{2}\%$ of what amount? \rule{2cm}{0.4pt}
5. $39 is 75% of what amount? \rule{2cm}{0.4pt}
6. 125 is 110% of what number? \rule{2cm}{0.4pt}

IV. Record all amounts corrected to 2 decimals if uneven and all rates as whole numbers with any remainder shown as a fraction.

Examples: $22\frac{1}{2}\%$ of $961 = 216.225$. Record as 216.23.
15% of $\$2100 = \$1785$. Record as $\$1785.00$.
If rate is $33.333\ldots\%$ Record as $33\frac{1}{3}\%$.

1. Find $12\frac{1}{2}\%$ of 168. _____
2. $\frac{1}{2}$ is what % of $\frac{5}{6}$? _____
3. $\frac{1}{2}\%$ of 6200 is how much? _____
4. 92 increased by 5% is how much? _____
5. $21\frac{1}{2}$ decreased by 2% = ? _____
6. $37\frac{1}{2}$ is what % of $12\frac{1}{2}$? _____
7. 479.5 less 20% equals what amount? _____
8. 110% of 36 is how much? _____
9. .08% of 62 = ? _____
10. 59.07 is 22% of what number? _____

Answers

I.		II.		III.		IV.	
1.	$57.75	1.	$33\frac{1}{3}\%$	1.	280	1.	21
2.	46.30	2.	3%	2.	$1584	2.	60%
3.	$276.00	3.	500%	3.	800	3.	31.00
4.	164	4.	$87\frac{1}{2}\%$	4.	$2000	4.	96.60
5.	.0912	5.	.05%	5.	$52	5.	21.07
6.	160	6.	$12\frac{1}{2}\%$	6.	$113\frac{7}{11}$	6.	300%
						7.	383.60
						8.	39.60
						9.	.05
						10.	268.50

EXERCISE 9

Chapter Summary

Answers appear at the end of this exercise. If your answers do not agree with those shown, check your calculations before referring to the solutions that follow.

1. It has been estimated that the school population of Anderson County will increase by 25% during the next year. If the present enrollment is 3164, how many students will be enrolled next year?

2. Mr. Smith receives a 2% bonus on all sales he makes over $300 in any month. If his sales amounted to $450 during a certain month, what was the amount of his bonus?

3. Mrs. Jones' budget allows 12% of her income for entertainment and recreation. If she spent $320 for this purpose last year, what was her income?

4. A realtor purchased a house for $16,400. After spending $560 on improvements, he sold it for 120% of the purchase price. What was his profit?

5. If a town had a population of 3500 in 1940 and a population of 1200 in 1950, what was the percent of decrease (nearest tenth of 1%)?

6. S. J. Cain has 40% of his investments in common stock, 20% in savings and loan accounts, 15% in bonds, and the balance in real estate. The real estate investment amounts to $16,500. What is the total of his investments and how much is invested in stock, savings and loan accounts, and bonds, respectively?

Stock _____

Savings and
Loan _____

Bonds _____

Real
Estate _____

Total _____

7. Mrs. Haynes' salary was increased from $160 to $172 a week. What was the percent increase?

8. What number decreased by 37½% of itself equals 946?

9. The tax on Mr. Man's home was $500. This represented an increase of $300 over the year before. What was the rate of increase?

　　　　　　　　　　　　　　　　　　　　　　　　　　　　　　　　_____

10. Teachers in one district received an average annual salary of $9600 as compared with $6200 in another. How much more in terms of percent do the better paid teachers receive (nearest hundredth of 1%)?

　　　　　　　　　　　　　　　　　　　　　　　　　　　　　　　　_____

11. After making contributions to various charities an organization had $3562.50 left, which represented 95% of its total funds. How much did the organization give to charities?

　　　　　　　　　　　　　　　　　　　　　　　　　　　　　　　　_____

12. Mr. Ames spent 22% of his salary on rent, which amounted to $132. How much did he earn each month?

　　　　　　　　　　　　　　　　　　　　　　　　　　　　　　　　_____

13. Absenteeism for the Ajax Manufacturing Company amounted to 3% during May. This amount represented 45 persons. What was the total number of employees?

　　　　　　　　　　　　　　　　　　　　　　　　　　　　　　　　_____

14. Sales for the Javel Rug Co. increased from $7950 to $11,200 in a 2-month period. What rate of increase did this represent (nearest tenth of 1%)?

    _____

15. Mr. Haynes bought a house for $25,500 and made a down payment of 15%. What was the amount of the mortgage (balance due) on the house?

    _____

16. The sales for R & J Co. were $3500 more this year than last year—an increase of 16%. What did the sales total for last year? For this year?

    Last year _____

    This year _____

17. The American Wholesale Co. occupied 31,500 sq ft of floor space, of which the rug department used 1638 sq ft. What percent of the total floor space did this represent (nearest tenth of 1%)?

    _____

18. How much is $82.50 increased by $12\frac{1}{2}\%$ of itself?

    _____

19. M. Hurst, an apple grower, shipped 670 boxes of apples to the Central State Produce Company, commission merchants, to be sold on a commission of $16\frac{1}{2}\%$. The apples were sold at $3.50 a box. Insurance was $\frac{1}{2}\%$ of total (gross) sales. Transportation charges amounted to $92.05. Find the net proceeds. (Total sales *less* commissions, insurance, and transportation charges.)

20. Don Shipman asked an agent to make the following purchase for him: 73 crates of eggs, 12 dozen cartons to the crate at 37¢ a carton. The charges were commission, 12%; cartage, $42.50; and other expenses, $25.70. Find the total amount (gross cost) charged to Mr. Shipman.

Answers

1. 3955
2. $3.00
3. $2666.67
4. $2720
5. 65.7%
6. stock $26,400
7. $7\frac{1}{2}\%$
8. $1513\frac{3}{5}$
      s & l   13,200
9. 150%
10. 54.84%
      bonds   9,900
11. $187.50
12. $600
      real
13. 1500
14. 40.9%
      estate   16,500
15. $21,675
16. last year $21,875
                 $66,000
17. 5.2%
     this year $25,375
18. $92.81
19. $1854.29
20. $4424.37

Solutions

1. If 100% = 3164, then an increase of 25% = 1.25 × 3164 = 3955, or $\frac{1}{4}$ × 3164 = 791. 3164 + 791 = 3955.

2. $450 − $300 = $150; 2% of $150 = .02 × $150 = $3.00.

3. If 12% = $320, then 100% = $320 ÷ .12 = $2666.67.

4. Total price = $16,400 + $560 = $16,960;
120% of $16,400 = 1.20 × $16,400 = $19,680,
$19,680 − $16,960 = $2720 profit, OR $\frac{1}{5}$ of $16,400 = $3280,
$3280 − $560 = $2720.

5. Decrease = 3500 − 1200 = 2300; 2300 ÷ 3500 = .657 or 65.7%.

6. 40% + 20% + 15% = 75%; therefore 25% = $16,500 and 100% = 4 × $16,500 = $66,000.

    Stock   = 40% of $66,000 = $26,400
    Savings and loan = 20% of $66,000 = $13,200
    Bonds   = 15% of $66,000 = $ 9,900
    Real estate   = 25% of $66,000 = $16,500
    Total $66,000

7. $172 − $160 = $12 increase; therefore 12 ÷ 160 = .075, OR $7\frac{1}{2}\%$.

8. P = BR, P = 946, R = 100% − $37\frac{1}{2}\%$ = $62\frac{1}{2}\%$; $62\frac{1}{2}\%$ = $\frac{5}{8}$. Therefore $\frac{8}{8}$ or 100% must equal 946 ÷ $\frac{5}{8}$ = 1513.6 or $1513\frac{3}{5}$. The same result could, of course, be obtained by dividing 946 by $62\frac{1}{2}\%$.

9. $500 − $300 = $200 tax last year; $300 ÷ $200 = 1.50 or 150% increase.

10. $9600 − $6200 = $3400 difference; $3400 ÷ $6200 = .5484 or 54.84%.

11. 95% = $3562.50, 100% = $3562.50 ÷ .95 = $3750.00,
$3750.00 − $3562.50 = $187.50.

12. 22% = $132; therefore 100% = $132 ÷ .22 = $600 salary.

13. 3% = 45 persons; therefore 100% = 45 ÷ .03 = 1500.

14. $11,200 − $7,950 = $3250; $3,250 ÷ $7,950 = 40.9%.

15. 15% of $25,500 = $3,825; balance of mortgage = $25,500 − $3,825 = $21,675 OR 85% of $25,500 = $21,675.

16. If 16% = $3500, then 100% (last year) = $3500 ÷ .16 = $21,875; this year = $21,875 + $3,500 = $25,375.

17. 1638 ÷ 31,500 = .052 or 5.2%.

18. $82.50 × 1.125 = $92.8125 = $92.81, OR $\frac{1}{8}$ × $82.50 = $10.31, $10.31 + $82.50 = $92.81.

19.
670 × $3.50		$2345.00 total gross sales
less 16½% of $2345.00	$386.93	
½% of $2345.00	11.73	
transportation charges	92.05	490.71 total charges
		$1854.29 net proceeds

20.
Net cost (73 × 144 × .37)	$3889.44
Commission (12% of $3889.44)	466.73
Cartage	42.50
Other expenses	25.70
Total or gross cost	$4424.37

CHAPTER THREE
Trade and Cash Discounts

OBJECTIVES

In this chapter we apply our knowledge of percentages to trade and cash discounts. When you have completed the work in this chapter, you will be able to:

(1) calculate the amount of a single or chain (series) discount,
(2) calculate the net price of an item or the net balance of an invoice when a trade discount is allowed.
(3) calculate the rate of discount when the list and net prices are known,
(4) use a table for discounts in a series,
(5) calculate the decimal equivalent of a series of discounts,
(6) reduce any chain discount to a single discount,
(7) compute cash discounts and the amount paid, using all the terms of sale that are in common business usage,
(8) compute the balance due when a partial payment has been made on an account in which a cash discount is allowed.

UNIT I. MEANING OF TERMS

Trade Discount

Trade discount is a deduction from the *list* or *catalog* price of an article or from the total amount of an invoice. It is expressed as a percent (%) of the list price or the total of an invoice. It may consist of a single discount or a series of discounts (generally referred to as a chain discount).

Trade discounts are usually associated with sales made by manufacturers or wholesale commercial dealers and not by retail stores.

Use of Trade Discounts

A trade discount may be used for several reasons. Customers are classified by many companies and different discount rates are applied to each group; for example, schools are often granted a more generous discount than are other customers for the same item.

Additional discounts are often granted for purchases in large quantities to secure a desirable account or to meet competition.

Many industries that handle a wide assortment of merchandise provide prospective buyers with catalogs containing detailed descriptions of their sales items. The price quoted for each item is called the list price. The cost of these catalogs would be prohibitive if they were issued to keep current with changing prices. Consequently salesmen are furnished with inexpensive "discount" sheets that show the discounts allowed on catalog items. In this manner prices can be quoted to customers in keeping with fluctuating prices.

In any case, the list price quoted in the catalog is the same for all buyers. It is the discount allowed that provides the differences in the actual price paid for any item.

1. Before we solve any problems that deal with trade discounts we should be sure we know what we are talking about.

   Suppose Swanson Publishing Company purchase supplies from the Artman Paper Company in the amount of $127.50, less 30%: $127.50 is the *catalog* or *list* price of these supplies; 30% is the *trade discount*. It is a *single* trade discount. A and B Clothiers, a wholesale company, sells a certain dress that they carry for $78, less 35%, to the retail stores.

   The list price is $_____; the trade discount is _____%.

   _

   $78, 35%

2. The net price is the price actually paid by the buyer; it is the list price *less* the discount.

   If an item is marked $80, less 20%, then the *net price* equals $80 − (20% of $80) = $80 − $16 = $64; $80 is the _____ price.

   _

   list or catalog price

3. If an item is listed with a trade discount of 30%, the net price equals _____ % of the list price.

- -

70%

4. Trade discounts may be *single* or a *series*. So far we have just been talking about single discounts. If an article is listed at $85, less 10%, 5%, and 2%, the discount is a series and is referred to as a *chain* discount.

A discount of 25%, 10%, $2\frac{1}{2}$% is a _____ discount.

- -

chain

5. Maybelle Hardware lists one item at $15.60, less 45%, to one customer and the same item to another at $15.60, less 45% and 10%.

$15.60 is called the _____ or _____ price.

45% is a _____ discount.

45%, 10% is a _____ discount.

- -

list or catalog
single
chain or series

UNIT 2. SINGLE TRADE DISCOUNT

The next few frames deal only with problems in which single trade discounts are offered. Study the example given for each type of problem and then answer questions that follow.

Finding the Amount of Discount and Net Amount

Example: A typewriter is listed at $525.00 less 15%. Find the amount of discount and the net price.

Solution: $525.00 list or catalog price   100%
              78.75 discount ($525 × .15)   15%
              $446.25 net price (amount paid)   85%

6. In the example shown above, the list price is ____%, the discount = ____%, and the net price is ____%. The list price less the discount equals the _____.
Net price = $_____ − $_____ = $_____.

- -

100%, 15%, 85%   net price = $525.00 − $78.75 = $446.25

7. Find the amount of the discount and the net price on an article selling for $426.00, less 25%. What percent is the net price of the list price?

List price $_____   100%

Discount   _____   ____

Net price $_____   ____

- -

List price $426.00   100%
Discount   106.50   25
Net price $319.50   75%

8. Find the amount of discount and the net amount on the following articles:
    (a) $826.50, less 20%: Discount   = $_____ × ____ = $_____.
                                    Net amount = $_____ − $____ = $_____.
    (b) $119.20, less 25%: Discount   = $_____ × ____ = $_____.
                                    Net amount = $_____ − $____ = $_____.

- -

SINGLE TRADE DISCOUNT 123

(a) Discount   = $826.50 ×   .20 = $165.30.
    Net amount = $826.50 − $165.30 = $661.20.
(b) Discount   = $119.20 ×   .25 = $ 29.80.
    Net amount = $119.20 − $ 29.80 = $ 89.40.

9. In checking invoices (an invoice is a bill of sale), a clerk wanted to be sure the net prices were correct. She wished to do so without bothering to figure the discount.

   Example: $96 less 30% = $67.20 (net price). If 30% is taken off the list price, what % is left? ____ . (Remember that the list price is equal to 100%.) If you said 70%, you are correct. Then $96 × .70 = $67.20 (net price).

   Find the net price of a coat selling for $156.00, less 20%, without computing the discount.

   Net price = _____ × ____ = $_____ .

   70%   Net price = $156.00 × .80 = $124.80

10. A television set listed at $420.00, less 40% = $252.00. Prove $252.00 is the correct answer.

    List price $_____ _____%

    Discount   _____ _____

    Net price $_____ _____

    Proof: $420.00 × ____ = $252.00.

    List price $420, or 100%
    Discount $168, or 40%
    Net price $252, or 60%
    Proof: $420 × .60 = $252

11. Compute the net prices for the following problems without figuring the discount.

   Example: $ 82.00 less 40% $ 82.00 × .60 = $49.20.
   (a) $ 56.00 less 15% $ 56.00 × ____ = $_____.
   (b) $125.00 less 20% $125.00 × ____ = $_____.
   (c) $ 86.50 less 12% $_____ × ____ = $_____.
   (d) $526.28 less 50% $_____ × ____ = $_____.

   (a) $ 56.00 × .85 = $ 47.60.
   (b) $125.00 × .80 = $100.00.
   (c) $ 86.50 × .88 = $ 76.12.
   (d) $526.28 × .50 = $263.14.

12. Alen Mfg. Co. sells a certain coffee table for $65.00, less 15%. Calculate the net amount by two methods.

   Net amount = $65.00 × .85 = $55.25.
   Discount   = $65.00 × .15 = $ 9.75
   Net amount = $65.00 − $9.75 = $55.25.

SINGLE TRADE DISCOUNT

Finding the Rate of Discount
when the List Price and Net Price Are Known

Example: Mr. Howard bought a tractor listed at $985.00 for $861.87. What rate of discount was he allowed?

Solution: Since the list price is the base, or 100%, divide the discount by the list price for the rate.

$985.00 − $861.87 = $123.13 amount of discount
$123.13 ÷ $985.00 = .125 or $12\frac{1}{2}$% discount rate

Proof: If the discount equals $12\frac{1}{2}$%, the net price must equal $87\frac{1}{2}$%.
$985.00 × .875 = $861.87.

13. Mr. Jones purchased an automobile listed at $4290.00 for $3517.80. What discount rate was he allowed?

$\dfrac{\text{\$\_\_\_\_\_}}{\text{list price}} - \dfrac{\text{\$\_\_\_\_\_}}{\text{net price}} = \dfrac{\text{\$\_\_\_\_\_}}{\text{amount of discount}}.$

$\dfrac{\text{\$\_\_\_\_\_}}{\text{amount of discount}} \div \dfrac{\text{\$\_\_\_\_\_}}{\text{list price}} = \dfrac{\text{\_\_\_\_\_\%}}{\text{rate of discount}}.$

Proof: Net price = 100% − ____%/rate = ____%,
Net price = $4290.00 × _____ = $3517.80.

- -

$4290.00 − $3517.80 = $772.20.
$ 772.20 ÷ $4290.00 = .18 = 18%.
Net price = 100% − 18% = 82%.
Net price = $4290.00 × .82 = $3517.80.

14. What is the amount and rate of discount on an automobile tire listed at $35.00 if it is sold for $29.75?

Amount of discount = $_____ − $_____ = $_____.
Rate of discount   = $_____ ÷ $_____ = S_____.

- -

Amount of discount = $35.00 − $29.75 = $5.25.
Rate of discount   = $ 5.25 ÷ $35.00 = .15 = 15%.

EXERCISE 10

Answers appear at the end of this exercise. If your answers do not agree with those shown, check your calculations before referring to the solutions that follow.

1. Find the amount of discount and net or billing price on a piece of furniture listed at $1025.00, less 5%.

    Discount _____

    Net price _____

2. The catalog price quoted for silk yardage sold by Bourning Fabrics is $8.25 a yard, less 7%. What is the net price per yard?

    _____

3. Rollins and Company offered J. P. Point and Sons a 22% discount amounting to $56.75 on a piece of garden equipment. What were the list and net prices?

    List price _____

    Net price _____

4. If the list price of an article is $280.00 and the net price is $196.00, what is the discount rate?

    _____

5. Find the net price on a suit listed at $125.00 less 15%.

    _____

6. Grant Bros. offered a discount of 12½% amounting to $21.90 on their dinette tables. What were the list and net prices on these tables?

List price _____

Net price _____

7. If a washing machine sold for $416.00 less 7½%, what was the amount of discount?

_____

8. Which is the best price, a sewing machine selling for $275.00 net or one listed at $320.00 less 12½%? How much is the difference?

Best price _____

Difference _____

Answers

1. Discount $51.25
   Net price $973.75
2. $7.67
3. List price $257.95
   Net price $201.20
4. 30%
5. $106.25
6. List price $175.20
   Net price $153.30
7. $31.20
8. Best price $275.00
   Difference $5.00

Solutions

1. Discount = $1025 × .05 = $51.25.
   Net Price = $1025.00 − $51.25 = $973.75.

2. If the discount = 7%, then the net price = 93% of list price.
   Net price = $8.25 × .93 = $7.67.

3. Since 22% = $56.75, we want to find 100%, which is the list price.
   List price (100%) = $56.75 ÷ .22 = $257.95.
   Net price = $257.95 − $56.75 = $201.20.

4. Discount = $280 − $196 = $84.
   Discount rate = $84 ÷ $280 = .30 = 30%.

5. If 15% = discount, then 85% = net price. Therefore, net price = $125 × .85 = $106.25.

6. Since $12\frac{1}{2}\%$ = $21.90, the list price (100%) = $21.90 ÷ .125 = $175.20.
   However, since $12\frac{1}{2}\% = \frac{1}{8}$, the list price also = $21.90 × 8 = $175.20.
   Net price = $\frac{7}{8}$ × $21.90 = $153.30.
   Net price = $175.20 − $21.90 = $153.30.

7. Discount = $416 × .075 = $31.20.

8. Since $12\frac{1}{2}\% = \frac{1}{8}$, divide $320 by 8. Result is 40.
   Then $320 less $12\frac{1}{2}$ = $320 − $40 = $280.
   Best price is $275.00 by $5.00.

UNIT 3. TRADE DISCOUNT SERIES (CHAIN DISCOUNTS)

Example: Let us assume that the series 15%, 10%, and 5% is to be deducted from the total of an invoice amounting to $74.00. Find the net price and the amount of the discount.

Solution:
$74.00   total of invoice
 11.10   first discount (74 × .15)
$62.90   net amount after first discount
  6.29   second discount (62.90 × .10)
$56.61   net amount after second discount
  2.83   third discount (56.61 × .05)
$53.78   final net amount (answer)

$74.00 − $53.78 = $20.22 amount of discount.

1. As already mentioned, a trade discount may be a single discount or a series. The next frames discuss and present the solution to problems involving a series of discounts. These are also called chain discounts.

    10%, 5%, 5%, 2% is a _____ of discounts.

    Such a series is commonly referred to as a _____ discount.

    _

    series, chain

2. A chain discount, such as 10%, 5%, $2\frac{1}{2}$%, may also be written 10–5–$2\frac{1}{2}$%. 16%, 5%, 3% may be written _____.

    _

    16–5–3%.

3. The discounts in a series such as 5–10–15% may be taken in any order; the result will always be the same. Suppose a discount of 10–5% were taken on an invoice amounting to $560.00. We want to find the net amount and prove that 10–5% will give us the same answer as 5–10%.

(a) $560.00   less 10–5%

       $560.00   total of invoice

       _____   first discount (560 × .10)

       $_____   net amount after first discount

       _____   second discount (504 × .05)

       $_____   net amount (answer)

(b) $560.00   less 5–10%

       $560.00   total of invoice

       _____   first discount (560 × .05)

       $_____   net amount after first discount

       _____   second discount (532 × .10)

       $_____   net amount (answer)

(a) $560.00   total of invoice
           56.00   first discount (560 × .10)

       $504.00   net amount after first discount
           25.20   second discount (504 × .05)

       $478.80   net amount (answer)

(b) $560.00   total of invoice
           28.00   first discount (560 × .05)

       $532.00   net amount after first discount
           53.20   second discount (532 × .10)

       $478.80   net amount (answer)

TRADE DISCOUNT SERIES (CHAIN DISCOUNTS) 131

Another method of solving this problem (page 137) and to illustrate the fact that the series may be in any order is to use the complements of the discounts. Complements are discussed more fully in the next unit.

In this case the discounts are 10% and 5% and the complements are 90% and 95% (difference between 100% and the discounts).

In this series, when 10% is deducted, 90% is left; when 5% is deducted, 95% is left. The factors may be rearranged without changing the product; that is (in this case) .90 × .95 = .95 × .90 = .8550.

Solution: (.90 × .95) × $560 = .8550 × $560 = $478.80.
(.95 × .90) × $560 = .8550 × $560 = $478.80.

In other words, you are multiplying $560 by the same factor (.8550) regardless of the order of the complements.

4. What is $4500.00 less 20%, 15%, and $2\frac{1}{2}$%? Find the net amount by use of the complements, i.e., (100% − 20%), (100% − 15%), and (100% − $2\frac{1}{2}$%).

   $4500.00 × (_____ × _____ × _____) = $_____ net amount.

   Complements of 20%, 15%, and $2\frac{1}{2}$% are 80%, 85%, and $97\frac{1}{2}$%, respectively. Regardless of their order, .80 × .85 × .975 = .663.
   Then $4500 × .663 = $2983.50.

5. Sometimes students think that a series can be added together; that is, that 10–5% is the same as 15%. IT IS NOT because each discount is taken from a different amount or base. (If it were, it would have been quoted originally as 15%.)

   Example: $24.00 less 10–5%   **Example:** $24.00 less 15%

   Solution: $24.00   **Solution:** $24.00
                   2.40 (24 × .10)   3.60 (24 × .15)
                  ──────   ──────
                  $22.60 $20.40 net amount
                   1.13 (22.60 × .05)
                  ──────
                  $21.47 net amount

   Is 10–10–5% the same as 25%? Yes _____ no _____.

   ----

   no

6. Let us find the net amount when the series contains a discount that is not a whole number, i.e., $33\frac{1}{3}\%$, $12\frac{1}{2}\%$, $6\frac{1}{4}\%$.
   It is sometimes easier to take such discounts first in the series. If this is feasible or not depends on the problem.

   Example: $150 less 10–$33\frac{1}{3}\%$.

   Solution: $150.00
                     50.00   ($33\frac{1}{3}\%$ or $\frac{1}{3}$ × $150)
                 $100.00
                   10.00   (.10 × $100)
               $ 90.00   net amount

   Try these: (a) $63.60 less $16\frac{2}{3}\%$ and 10% (b) $126.00 less $66\frac{2}{3}\%$ and 2%
   Solution:

   ———————————————————

   (a) $63.60   (b) $126.00
        10.60 ($\frac{1}{6}$ of $63.60)   84.00 ($\frac{2}{3}$ × $126.00)
      $53.00 $ 42.00
       5.30 (.10 × $53.00)   .84 (.02 × $42.00)
      $47.70 net amount $ 41.16 net amount

7. Find the net price and amount of discount for the following:

   Example: $125.00   less 10–10–5%

   Solution: $125.00   list price

                   ———————— first discount

                 $———————— net amount after first discount

                   ———————— second discount

                 $———————— net amount after second discount

                   ———————— third discount

                 $ 96.19   net amount (answer)

   Amount of discount =   list price   —   net amount
                         = $————— – $————— = $—————.

   ———————————————————

$125.00
  12.50   first discount
$112.50
  11.25   second discount
$101.25
   5.06   third discount
$ 96.19   net amount
Amount of discount = $125.00 − $96.19 = $28.81.

8. Find the net price paid and the amount of discount for the following invoices:
(a) $98.20 less 10–5%   (b) $514.00 less $66\tfrac{2}{3}$–5%
(c) $9.20 less 10–5–$2\tfrac{1}{2}$%   (d) $460.00 less 50–10%

- -

Problem	Net price	Discount
(a)	$ 83.96	$ 14.24
(b)	162.76	351.24
(c)	7.67	1.53
(d)	207.00	253.00

Discount Tables

When the same series is to be used many times, tables of *net decimal equivalents* are referred to. These equivalents represent the net percent left of 100% (expressed as a decimal) or the net price left after the series of discounts has been deducted. The net amount is obtained by multiplying the dollar amount by the net decimal equivalent.

Example: Find the net amount and amount of discount if the series of 15%, 10%, and 5% were deducted from $30.00.

Procedure: Refer to the discount tables on pages 163 and 164. Look for the column headed 15. Find the number in the column that is in line with 10 and 5 in the left-hand column. It is .72675. This means that after the series 15%, 10%, and 5% has been deducted, approximately 73% or 73¢ is left out of every dollar. Therefore for $30.00 the net amount left is obtained by multiplying .72675 by 30. The result is 21.8025. Record as $21.80 net amount.

$30.00 − $21.80 = $8.20 *discount*.

Example: What is $65.00 less 25% and 5%?

Solution: Look for the column headed 25. Find the number in the column that is in line with 5 in the left-hand column. It is .7125. This means that after 25% and 5% have been deducted, 71.25% is left out of every dollar. Therefore for $65.00 the net amount = $65.00 × .7125 = $46.3125. Record as $46.31.

Discount = $65.00 − $46.31 = $18.69.

9. Notice that we must be able to read the discount tables accurately, so suppose we have some practice before we try to solve any problems. Turn to page 163 and find the net decimal equivalent (NDE) for the series 15–10–$7\frac{1}{2}$%. Look for the column headed by 15 in the tables. Find the number in the column that is in line with 10–$7\frac{1}{2}$ in the extreme left-hand column.

	Series	Net Decimal Equivalent (NDE)
Example:	15–10–$7\frac{1}{2}$%	.70763
(a)	$16\frac{2}{3}$–10–10%	_____
(b)	25–10%	_____
(c)	60–$7\frac{1}{2}$–5%	_____
(d)	35–10–10–5%	_____
(e)	35–10%	_____

- -

(a) .675, (b) .675, (c) .3515, (d) .50018, (e) .585

TRADE DISCOUNT SERIES (CHAIN DISCOUNTS)

10. When a series of discounts has been taken from 100%, what is left is called the *net decimal equivalent*, or the amount left in $1.00. According to the table, page 163, the net decimal equivalent for the series 10–10–5% is _____. This means that out of every dollar approximately _____¢, or _____%, is left when 10–10–5% has been deducted.

   _____ is called the _____ _____ _____ for the series 10–10–5%.

   .7695, 77¢ or 77%, .7695 is called the net decimal equivalent for the series 10–10–5%.

11. Find the net amount and amount of discount for an article selling for $520 less 20–10–5%.

   Solution: The net decimal equivalent for 20–10–5% (see page 163) is _____.

   Then $520.00 × _____ = $355.68   net amount.

   $520.00 − $355.68 = $_____ discount.

   .684, $520.00 × .684 = $355.68, $520.00 − $355.68 = $164.32 discount.

EXERCISE 11

Use of Discount Tables

Find the net amount and the amount of discount for the following problems. Use the discount tables.

	Problem		Solution
	Gross Amount	Discount (%)	
1.	$ 27.00	25–5	_____
2.	140.40	10–2½	_____
3.	300.25	12½–10–2½	_____
4.	35.66	50–10–10	_____
5.	803.50	35–10–5	_____
6.	600.90	40–5–5	_____
7.	30.50	50–10	_____
8.	286.00	30–7½	_____
9.	4.95	15–10–10–10	_____
10.	79.80	2½–10	_____

Answers

Check your answers with those shown below. Recalculate any that are different from those listed. Check the NDE first. If it is correct, the error should be in the multiplication.

	Net Price	Discount			Net Price	Discount
1.	$ 19.24	$ 7.76		2.	123.20	17.20
3.	230.54	69.71		4.	14.44	21.22
5.	446.55	356.95		6.	$325.39	$275.51
7.	13.73	16.77		8.	185.19	100.81
9.	3.07	1.88		10.	70.02	9.78

How to Compute Net Decimal Equivalents

Often a series that is not included in the discount tables is used, in which case it should be computed and added to the tables.

TRADE DISCOUNT SERIES (CHAIN DISCOUNTS) 137

Example: Find the net decimal equivalent for the series 12, 10, and 2%.

Solution: There are *two methods* that may be used to find the net decimal equivalent of any series.

Method 1. Discounts are deducted successively as follows:

100.00%	total or list price
12.00	first discount (12%)
88.00	percent left after first discount
8.80	second discount (10% of 88.00)
79.20	percent left after second discount
1.584	third discount (2% of 79.20)
77.616%	percent left after all discounts are deducted

Expressed as a decimal, 77.616% = .77616, which is the net decimal equivalent of the series.

Method 2. This method involves the use of complements.* The net decimal equivalent may be obtained by multiplying the complements of the series. The complements of 12, 10, and 2 are 88, 90, and 98, respectively.

.88 × .90 × .98 = .77616 net decimal equivalent.

Example: Find the net decimal equivalent for the series $12\frac{1}{2}$–$7\frac{1}{2}$–10%.

Solution: *Method 1.*

100.00%	
12.50	first discount (12.5%)
87.50	
6.5625	second discount (7.5%) (all digits are carried)
80.9375	
8.09375	third discount (10%) (all digits are carried)
72.84375%	.72844 as net decimal equivalent.

Round off to 5 decimals in the final answer only.

Method 2. Complements of the series are $87\frac{1}{2}$%, $92\frac{1}{2}$%, and 90%, respectively.

Then the net decimal equivalent = .875 × .925 × .90
= .7284375
= .72844 to 5 decimals.

---

*The complement of any number is the difference between it and the next highest power of 10. Thus the complement of 7 is 3 because 7 + 3 = 10; the complement of 18 is 82 because 18 + 82 = 100; the complement of 125 is 875 because 125 + 875 = 1000, and so on.

12. Find the NDE (net decimal equivalent) of the series 15–10–2% by both methods illustrated above.

Complete: *Method 1.* 100.00%   list or total
  15.00   first discount (.15 × 100)
  85.00   net amount after first discount
  _____   second discount (.10 × 85)
  _____   net amount after second discount
  _____   third discount (.02 × 76.5)
  _____% net amount after third discount (percent left after all discounts have been taken)
  _____   net decimal equivalent

Method 2. Use of complements

Complement of 15 is 100 − 15 = _____.

10 is 100 − 10 = _____.

2 is 100 − 2 = _____.

____ × ____ × ____ = _____ net decimal equivalent.

Method 1. 100.00%
  15.00
  85.00
  8.50
  76.50
  1.53
  74.97%
.7497 net decimal equivalent

Method 2.
.85 × .90 × .98 = .7497 net decimal equivalent

13. Find the net decimal equivalent for the series 25–10–3% by both methods.

Method 1. 100.00%
              25.00
              ―――――
              75.00
               7.50
              ―――――
              67.50
               2.025
              ―――――
              65.475%
         .65475 net decimal equivalent

Method 2. Complements of 25%, 10%, and 3% are 75%, 90%, and 97%, respectively. Then .75 × .90 × .97 = .65475 net decimal equivalent.

14. Calculate the net decimal equivalent for the series 45–10–10–5%. Show solution by both methods.

Method 1. 100.00%
  <u> 45.00</u>   first discount
    55.00
  <u>   5.50</u>   second discount
    49.50
  <u>   4.95</u>   third discount
    44.55
  <u> 2.2275</u>   fourth discount
    42.3225%
  or   .42323 as net decimal equivalent

Method 2. Complements of the series are 55%, 90%, 90%, and 95%, respectively.
Net decimal equivalent = .55 × .90 × .90 × .95 = .423225 = .42323 to five decimals.

15. Calculate the net decimal equivalent for the series $45-12\frac{1}{2}-2\frac{1}{2}\%$. Show the solution by both methods.

Method 1. 100.00%
  <u> 45.00</u>   first discount
    55.00
  <u>   6.875</u>   second discount
    48.125
  <u>   1.203125</u> third discount
    46.921875

.46922 = net decimal equivalent (to 5 decimals).

Method 2. The complements of the series are 55%, $87\frac{1}{2}\%$, and $97\frac{1}{2}\%$, respectively.

Net decimal equivalent = .55 × .875 × .975 = .46921875 = .46922 (to 5 decimals).

Single Discount Equivalent

A single discount equivalent of any series is the difference between 100% and the net decimal equivalent expressed as a percent.

Example: The net decimal equivalent for the series 10–10–5% is .7695. Expressed as a percent, .7695 = 76.95%. The single discount equivalent = 100% − 76.95% = 23.05%.

16. If the net decimal equivalent of the series 10% and 10% is .81, this means that 81% was left after the series was deducted. If 81% is left, the total discount (%) (amount taken way) = 100% − 81% = 19%. This means that 10% and 10% are equivalent to 19%. The series has been reduced to a single discount; 19% is called the single discount equivalent of the series 10%, 10%.

    $50.00 less 10% and 10% = $_____ and $50.00 less 19% = $_____.

$40.50 $40.50

17. Which of the following series are equivalent? 40–10–5%, 20–10–5–2½%, and 33⅓–10–10–5%   (*Hint.* Refer to the discount tables.)

    The net decimal equivalent for each of these series is _____, _____, _____, respectively.

    The two series that are equivalent are _____, _____.

    The single discount equivalents are _____, _____, _____, respectively.

NDE = .513, .6669, and .513
This means that the series 40–10–5% and 33⅓–10–10–5% are equivalent. The single discount equivalents are 48.7%, 33.31%, and 48.7%, respectively.

18. The NDE (net decimal equivalent) represents what is left (the NET amount) out of 100% after a series has been deducted. The single discount equivalent equals a series or chain discount reduced to a single discount. Find the net decimal equivalent and single discount equivalent for the series 15–10–5%.

Net decimal equivalent = _____ (5 decimals)

Single discount equivalent = _____%

NDE = .72675, single discount equivalent = 100.000% − 72.675% = 27.325%

19. One bicycle dealer offered a certain model for $67.50, less 15–10%; another offered the same model for $67.50, less 20–5%. Which is the best buy?

NDE for 15–10% = .765, for 20–5% = .76.
$67.50, less 20–5%, is the best offer, since the discount is greater.

EXERCISE 12

I. Compute the net decimal equivalents for the following series and compare with the tables on pages 163–164. Carry answers to 5 decimals.

1. 10–10–5% _____   2. 7½–5% _____
3. 50–10–5% _____   4. 12½–5–2½% _____
5. 7½–10–10–5% _____   6. 66⅔–10–10–5% _____
7. 37½–5% _____   8. 50–10–10–10% _____
9. 10–5–60% _____   10. 10–2½–15% _____

II. Using the tables of discounts, find the single discount equivalent for the following series (answers are shown at the end of this exercise):

1. 30–5–2½% _____   2. 7½–5–10% _____
3. 10–12½% _____   4. 35–10–10% _____
5. 50–10% _____   6. 37½–5–5% _____

III. Answers appear on the next page. If your answer does not agree with the one shown, check your calculations before referring to the solutions that follow.

1. A typewriter marked $135 was sold at a discount of 20%. What are the net price and the amount of discount?

    discount _____

    net price _____

2. Mr. Howard paid $96.25 for a chair that normally sells for $110.00. What rate of discount did he receive?

    _____

3. What was the list price of a lawn mower if it was sold for $106.50 and a discount of 13% was allowed?

    _____

4. Which is the best buy and by how much? (a) A stove listed at $560, less 20–10–5% or 40–10%, and (b) a refrigerator with discounts of 20–5–10% or 10–20–5%?

(a) _____

(b) _____

5. Discounts of 10% and 5% were allowed on ladies stockings listed at $18.00 a dozen. What was the net price of each pair of stockings?

_____

6. The Naylor Mercantile Company offered discounts of 10–10–2½% on all #625 items listed in their catalog. What do these amounts represent as a single discount?

_____

Answers

I. Answers will be found in the Tables.

II. 1. 35.162% 2. 20.912%
    3. 21.25%   4. 47.35%
    5. 55%   6. 43.594%

III. 1. Net price, $108.00
     Discount, $27.00
  2. 12½%
  3. $122.41
  4. (a) 40–10%, $80.64
     (b) same
  5. $1.28
  6. 21.025%

Solutions

III. 1. $135.00 × .20 = $27.00, discount; $135.00 − $27.00 = $108.00, net price.
2. $110.00 − $96.25 = $13.75, discount; $13.75 ÷ $110.00 = .125 or $12\frac{1}{2}\%$.
3. Since the discount is 13%, the list price = 100% − 13% = 87%.
   $106.50 ÷ .87 = $122.41.
4. (a) $560 less 20–10–5% = $383.04; $560 less 40–10% = $302.40.
      40–10% is best by $80.64 ($383.04 − $302.40).
   (b) 20–5–10% and 10–20–5% are equivalent; therefore the price would be the same.
5. ($18.00 ÷ 12) less 10–5% = $1.28.
6. The net decimal equivalent for 10–10–$2\frac{1}{2}\%$ is .78975.
   The single discount equivalent = 100.000% − 78.975% = 21.025%.

UNIT 4. CASH DISCOUNTS

Cash discount is a deduction allowed on an invoice or bill of goods to encourage payment in accordance with the terms of the sale. The manner in which terms are expressed varies with business concerns and invoice forms. They usually appear on the upper section of the invoice. Cash discounts represent a saving and are therefore taken advantage of whenever possible.

Terms of Sale

The next few frames deal with the terms of sale. If no terms are indicated on the bill of sale, it is usually due 30 days from the date of the invoice or on the first of the next month. No cash discount is involved in such cases.

Example: Mrs. Jones received a bill for $68.25 from the Fashion Shop, dated May 16. If no due date was given, Mrs. Jones should pay this obligation on June 1 or any day up to June 15 inclusive. (May has 31 days; therefore May 16 to June 15 is 30 days.)

1. Accordingly, an invoice or bill dated August 21 should be paid on _____ or any day up to _____ (August has 31 days).

September 1,   September 20

146   UNIT 4

2. *n/30* means that the bill must be paid within 30 days from the date of the invoice and may be subject to an interest charge if paid after that time. When the terms are n/30, no cash discount is granted; "n" stands for "net."

   Let us assume that terms for the following invoices are n/30. When are they due?

	Date of Invoice	Due Date
Example:	April 13	May 13
(a)	September 30	_____
(b)	March 2*	_____
(c)	July 21*	_____

   (a) October 30,   (b) April 1,   (c) August 20

   *March and July have 31 days.

3. *2/10, n/30* means that a 2% discount is allowed if the bill is paid within 10 days from the date of the invoice, but the total amount is due if paid on any day from the 11th to the 30th day from the date of the invoice. The discount and time allowed may be 1/10, n/30; 2/15, n/30; 2/15, n/60, and so on. The terms depend on company policy.

   Maine Bros. received a bill for $125.00 with terms of 2/10, n/30. If this bill is paid within 10 days from the date of the bill, Maine Bros. can save some money.

   (a) Suppose the bill were dated March 10. The latest date on which it could be paid and still receive a cash discount of 2% is _____.

   (b) 2% of $125.00 = _____ × _____ = _____.

   (c) n/30 means it is due within 30 days from the date of the invoice. In this case the latest day on which it should be paid is 30 days from March 10 or _____.

   (a) March 20,   (b) .02 × $125.00 = $2.50,   (c) April 9 (March has 31 days)

4. Mr. Holms owed $125.00 on an invoice, dated June 3 with terms of 1/15, n/60. He paid the bill on June 18. (a) What was the amount of the discount and how much did Mr. Holms pay?

Amount of discount = .01 × $125.00 = $_____.

Net amount paid   = $125.00 − $_____ = $_____.

(b) Suppose the bill was paid after June 18. What was the amount of payment?

(a) discount = $1.25, net amount paid = $123.75.

(b) amount of payment = $125.00 since no discount was allowed.

5. Mr. Smith received an invoice dated January 15, terms 2/10, n/30 amounting to $156.50. He paid this obligation on January 20.

(a) How much is the discount? _____.

(b) How much did Mr. Smith remit in payment? _____.

(a) .02 × $156.50 = $3.13,   (b) $156.50 − $3.13 = $153.37.

2/10, 1/15, n/30 means that a 2% discount is allowed if the invoice is paid within 10 days from the date of the invoice, a 1% discount is allowed if paid from the 11th to the 15th day, and the total amount is due if paid on any day from the 16th to the 30th day from the date of the invoice. Mary Bowen purchased some household fixtures for $67.50 on May 10 with terms of 2/10, 1/15, n/30. If she paid this bill on or before May 20, her discount would be 2% of $67.50. If she paid it after May 20 but not later than May 25, she would receive a cash discount of 1%. If she paid it after May 25, she would receive no cash discount and would have to pay the full amount in settlement of this obligation.

6. Mrs. Rucker received a bill with terms of 2/10, 1/15, n/30 dated April 22. She paid it on May 4. What percent discount did she receive? _____

1%. Ten days from April 22 is May 2, the last date in which a 2% discount would be granted.

7. What is the last date of payment for the following problems that would allow the buyer to receive the *best* discount?

Terms	Date of Invoice	Answer
2/10, n/30	March 20	_____
2/10, 1/15, n/30	February 26 (not a leap year)	_____
3/10, n/30	January 13	_____
1/15, n/30	October 15	_____

March 30, March 8, January 23, October 30

✓ *1%–10th EOM* (end of month) means that a 1% discount is allowed if the invoice is paid during the first 10 days of the next month following the date of the invoice.
2%–15th prox. means that a 2% discount is allowed if payment is made at any time during the first 15 days of the next month following the date of the invoice.
The terms "EOM" and "prox" mean the same thing.
1%–10th EOM means the same as 1%–10th prox.
2%–15th prox means the same as 2%–15th EOM.
It is a matter of usage.

8. What is the last date of payment in which a discount may be received if terms are

1% 10th EOM, dated May 31	_____
2% 10th EOM, dated July 5	_____
1% 10th EOM, dated December 31	_____
2% 15th prox, dated August 1	_____
1% 15th prox, dated October 15	_____
2% 15th prox, dated June 5	_____

June 10, August 10, January 10, September 15, November 15, July 15

9.

ALLEN PAPER COMPANY
Oakland, California

Sold to: Wohler Printing Co.   Invoice No. 00112

Cunningham, California   Date 10/25____

Terms: 1%–10th EOM

Item	Description	Unit	Price	Amount
600	sheets #175 tagboard $28\frac{1}{2}'' \times 45''$, 336 lb.	cwt	$20.75	$69.72

(a) Who is the buyer _____ and the seller _____ of these goods?

(b) What are the terms? _____

(c) How much did Allen Paper Co. receive if the discount was allowed? _____

(d) What is the latest date on which this bill may be paid in order to receive the discount? _____

(e) What is the latest date on which this bill should be paid if no discount is taken? _____

(a) Wohler Printing Co., Allen Paper Co.
(b) 1%–10th EOM
(c) $69.72 − $0.70 = $69.02
(d) November 10
(e) November 25

10. Find the cash discount received and the amount of payment for the following problems:

	Amount of Invoice	Terms	Date of Invoice	Date of Payment
(a)	$23.16	2/10, 1/15, n/30	January 5	January 20
(b)	44.65	1/10, n/30	August 27	September 1
(c)	58.95	1% 10th EOM	July 25	August 9
(d)	126.75	1% 15th prox	April 10	May 18

	Cash Discount	Amount of Payment
(a)	_____	_____
(b)	_____	_____
(c)	_____	_____
(d)	_____	_____

(a) $0.23 and $22.93
(b) $0.45 and $44.20
(c) $0.59 and $58.36
(d) none and $126.75

11. *Postdating* an invoice is common practice in some businesses; for example, a school may order textbooks in July for immediate shipment but request a September 1 billing. If a cash discount is allowed under such circumstances, the date of the invoice (not the date of the purchase order) is used.

Havenscourt Schools ordered 300 books, amounting to $1095, in July and asked for a November 1 billing. If the books were paid for on November 7 and the terms of the sale were 1/10, n/30, how much was remitted in payment?

_____

_____

Since the books were paid within 10 days of the billing date, the discount would be 1% of $1095. Amount of payment = $1095.00 − $10.95 = $1084.05.

12. *ROG* is an abbreviation for receipt of goods. This means that the terms of payment are computed from the day the goods are received, not the date of the invoice. This is advantageous to the buyer when shipment requires several days; for example, an invoice for merchandise is dated July 7 with terms 2/10 ROG but the shipment is not received until August 15. In this case the cash discount is allowed if payment is made any time up to and including August 25. When the net period is not indicated, it is generally understood to be 30 days from the receipt of the goods.

Meyers Bros. ordered some rugs amounting to $987.70 on June 3 from Dale Rug Manufacturers. The rugs were sent with an invoice dated June 10. Terms were n/30 ROG.

(a) If the rugs were received July 30, payment is due 30 days later or _____.
(b) If terms of 2/10, n/30 were offered and payment was made on August 4, what would the amount of payment be? _____

- -

(a) August 29 (Don't forget that July has 31 days.)
(b) Discount = .02 × $987.70 = $19.75.
    Net amount (payment) = $987.70 − $19.75 = $967.95.

Extra dating permits a longer period of time in which the purchaser may take advantage of a cash discount; for example, terms of 2/10-90X, 2/10-90 ex., or 2/10-90 extra (all mean the same thing) indicate that instead of 10 days an additional 90 days or a total of 100 days from the date of the invoice is the period of time during which the 2% cash discount may be taken.

Generally, extra dating terms are granted during the off-season for certain types of merchandise such as wet-weather clothing during the dry season and heating equipment during the summer months. This is done to encourage sales at those off-season times. An example taken from the cotton business serves as an illustration. If a mill can use 5000 bales of cotton over several months, it is to the advantage of the broker to induce the mill owner, with attractive terms, to take all the cotton at once if the broker is anxious to move his stock. In this way he not only equalizes a possible off-season market but also clears his warehouse, saves storage costs, or possibly makes room for new cotton.

13. Handley Bros. wanted to clear some of their woolen yardage. James Retail Store agreed to buy it with terms of 2/10-90 extra. These terms allow James Retail Store an extra 90 days in which to take advantage of the cash discount. Suppose the invoice were dated May 10.

    What would be the last day on which this bill could be paid and still receive the 2% discount? _____

    -

    May 10 + 100 days = August 18.

14. 2/10-60X means that 60 additional days are granted beyond the usual terms. In this case 70 days from the date of the invoice is granted in which the 2% discount may be taken.

    Jacob Mfgrs. disposed of some off-season garden equipment to Hale Nurseries. The invoice was dated September 12 with terms of 2/10-60X. What is the last day on which Hale Nurseries can take advantage of the cash discount? _____

    -

    September 12 + 70 days = November 21. (Remember, October has 31 days.)

15. When working in sales, the half cent is usually added to the net amount instead of to the discount. Try this problem.

    Mr. Green received an invoice dated June 14, terms 3/10, n/30, amounting to $37.50 less a trade discount of 5%. How much should be remitted in payment at the end of 10 days?

    Gross amount $37.50

    Trade discount   _____

    Net amount $_____

    Cash discount   _____

    Remittance $_____

Gross amount	$37.50	$37.50 × .95 = $35.625 (net amount).
Trade discount	1.87	$37.50 × .05 = $ 1.875 (discount).
Net amount	$35.63	
Cash discount	1.07	
Remittance	$34.56	

16. Mr. Allen received an invoice dated December 10, terms 2/10, n/30, amounting to $56.65 less a trade discount of 10%. He paid this bill on December 20. What was the amount of the payment?

   Gross amount $_____

   Trade discount _____

   Net amount $_____

   Cash discount _____

   Payment $_____

Gross amount	$56.65
Trade discount	5.66
Net amount	$50.99
Cash discount	1.02
Payment	$49.97

Partial Payment on Account

Sometimes a buyer makes a partial payment on an invoice during the cash-discount period. In such cases he is entitled to a discount on that portion of the bill that has been paid.

Example: Assume that an invoice dated May 21 amounts to $63.50 with terms of 2/15 prox. On June 13 a payment of $30 is made. Find the amount of the discount and the balance due on the invoice.

Solution: Since a 2% discount is allowed, any payment made within the discount period equals 98% of the sum to be credited to the account. This means that $30 = 98% of the sum to be credited. Therefore $30 ÷ .98 = 30.612 or $30.61 (amount to be credited).

$63.50   amount of invoice
30.61   amount credited as payment
$32.89   balance due
$30.61 − $30.00 = $0.61   cash discount

17. Now let us solve a similar problem together. Mr. Harper owed $250.00 with terms of 2/10, n/30. The bill was dated May 10. On May 18 Mr. Harper paid $125 on this account. What was the balance due?

Since a discount of 2% was allowed, $125.00 = 98% of the sum to be credited to the account. Then $125.00 ÷ _____ = $_____, the amount credited to the account. Mr. Harper received credit for $_____ instead of $125.00. The discount allowed is $_____ − $_____ = $2.55. The balance due equals the amount of the invoice ($_____) *less* the amount credited to the account ($_____) = $_____.

- -

$125.00 ÷ .98 = $127.55, the amount credited to the account.
Mr. Harper received credit for $127.55 instead of $125.00. The discount allowed is $127.55 − $125.00 = $2.55. The balance due = $250.00 − $127.55 = $122.45.

CASH DISCOUNTS

18. Find the amount of discount and balance due on the following:

Amount of invoice	$312.60	$200.00 = _____% of the sum to be credited.	
Date of invoice	January 1		
Terms	3/10, n/30	$200.00 ÷ _____ = $_____, the sum to be credited.	
Partial payment	January 8	$312.60 − $_____ = $_____ the balance due.	
Amount of payment	$200.00	$_____ − $_____ = $_____, the discount.	

$200.00 = 97\%$ of the sum to be credited.
$200.00 \div .97 = \$206.19$, the amount credited to the account.
$312.60 - \$206.19 = \$106.41$, the balance due.
$206.19 - \$200.00 = \$6.19$, the discount.

19. Find the amount of discount and the balance due on the following:

Amount of invoice $190.55
Date of invoice   August 24
Terms 2% 15th prox
Partial payment   September 2
Amount of payment $90.00

Balance due $_____.

Discount $_____.

$90.00 \div .98 = \$91.84$, the amount credited to the account.
$190.55 - \$91.84 = \$98.71$, the balance due.
$91.84 - \$90.00 = \$1.84$, the discount.

156 UNIT 4

EXERCISE 13

I. Find the last date of payment for the following problems that will allow the buyer to receive the best discount:

Invoice No.	Terms	Date of Invoice	Answer
1.	3/10, 1/30, n/90	July 22	_____
2.	2/10, 1/30, n/60	October 30	_____
3.	3/30, n/60	November 11	_____
4.	2/15, n/30	January 24	_____
5.	2% 10th EOM	May 31	_____
6.	1% 15th prox.	June 17	_____

II. Find the cash discount received and the amount of payment for the following problems:

No.	Amount of Invoice	Terms	Date of Invoice	Date of Payment	Cash Discount	Amount of Payment
1.	$ 32.81	2/10, n/30	May 15	May 26	$_____	$_____
2.	19.75	2/10, 1/30, n/60	Oct. 10	Oct. 20	_____	_____
3.	135.37	3/10, n/30	Jan. 21	Feb. 1	_____	_____
4.	346.90	3/10, 1/30, n/60	May 30	June 10	_____	_____
5.	78.60	1% 15th prox.	Dec. 19	Jan. 15	_____	_____
6.	402.96	2/10, 1/15, n/30	Dec. 31	Jan. 9	_____	_____

III. Find the amount of discount and balance due on the following:

No.	Amount of Invoice	Date of Invoice	Terms	Partial Date	Payment Amount	Amount of Discount	Balance Due
1.	$1079.50	May 31	1/15, n/60	June 10	$550.00	$_____	$_____
2.	445.00	Oct. 10	2/10, 1/30, n/60	Oct. 25	230.00	_____	_____
3.	86.75	Mar. 2	5/10	Mar. 12	56.00	_____	_____
4.	325.00	June 15	1% 10th EOM	July 9	175.00	_____	_____
5.	95.40	Dec. 15	3/30, n/30	Jan. 10	45.00	_____	_____
6.	38.75	Oct. 2	2/10, n/30	Oct. 8	25.00	_____	_____

Answers

I. 1. Aug. 1
   2. Nov. 9
   3. Dec. 11
   4. Feb. 8
   5. June 10
   6. July 15

II. 1. – & $32.81
   2. $0.39 & $19.36 or $0.40 & $19.35
   3. – & $135.37
   4. $3.47 & $343.43
   5. $0.79 & $ 77.81
   6. $8.06 & $394.90

III. 1. $5.55 & $523.95 or $5.56 & $523.94
   2. $2.32 & $212.68
   3. $2.95 & $ 27.80
   4. $1.77 & $148.23
   5. $1.39 & $ 49.01
   6. $0.51 & $ 13.24

Solutions

III. 1. 1% discount; therefore $550 = 99% of the sum to be credited to the account balance.

   Amount credited to the account = $550 ÷ .99 = $555.56.
   Balance due = $1079.50 − $555.56 = $523.94.
   Cash discount = $555.56 − $550.00 = $5.56.

2. 1% discount, therefore $230 = 99% of the sum to be credited to the account balance.

   Amount credited to the account = $230 ÷ .99 = $232.32.
   Balance due = $445.00 − $232.32 = $212.68.
   Cash discount = $232.32 − $230.00 = $2.32.

3. 5% discount; therefore $56 = 95% of the sum to be credited to the account balance.

   Amount credited to the account = $56 ÷ .95 = $58.95.
   Balance due = $86.75 − $58.95 = $27.80.
   Discount = $58.95 − $56.00 = $2.95.

4. 1% discount; therefore $175 = 99% of the sum to be credited to the account balance.

   Amount credited to the account = $175.00 ÷ .99 = $176.77.
   Balance due = $325.00 − $176.77 = $148.23.
   Discount = $176.77 − $175.00 = $1.77.

5. 3% discount; therefore $45.00 = 97% of the sum to be credited to the account balance.

   Amount credited to the account = $45.00 ÷ .97 = $46.39.
   Balance due = $95.40 − $46.39 = $49.01.
   Discount = $46.39 − $45.00 = $1.39.

6. 2% discount; therefore $25.00 = 98% of the sum to be credited to the account balance.

   Amount credited to the account = $25.00 ÷ .98 = $25.51.
   Balance due = $38.75 − $25.51 = $13.24.
   Discount = $25.51 − $25.00 = $0.51.

EXERCISE 14

Chapter Summary

Answers appear at the end of this exercise. If your answers do not agree with those shown, check your calculations before referring to the solutions that follow.

1. Find the net price on 25 pads of graph paper at 29¢ each and 50 pads of graph paper at 25¢ each if a 25% trade discount is granted.

2. What is the net selling price on an article listed at $805.70 less $25-16\frac{2}{3}-10\%$?

3. The Allan Manufacturing Co. in New York shipped merchandise amounting to $3175.00 to the Everen Stores in San Francisco. The invoice was dated June 3. The merchandise was received August 1. Terms of the sale were 2/10 ROG. What is the latest date that Everen Stores may pay this invoice and receive a cash discount? How much must be remitted in payment?

4. The Haight School District ordered 220 books from the Ever Ready Publishing Co. on December 15 with a request for a March 1 billing. The books sold for $3.75 each less a 20% trade discount. Shipping charges amounted to $4.50. A cash discount of 1% was allowed for payment within five days of the billing date. If the invoice was paid on March 2, what was the amount of the payment? (*Note:* The cash discount cannot be applied to shipping charges.)

5. Hale Services received the following items:
   6 bottles of correction fluid at $0.50 each, 6 bottles of correction thinner at $0.50 each, 2 lettering guides at $1.60 each, and 1 No. 5 stylus at $0.50. If a trade discount of 15% was allowed, what was the amount of the invoice?

   _____

6. How much will it cost the buyer if the manufacturer of an item sells it for $516.10 less $12\frac{1}{2}$% and 2%? (Solve directly as shown in frame 7, unit 3, page 132.)

   _____

7. Complete the following invoice. How much was remitted in payment if this bill was paid on January 16?

ANZEL PAPER COMPANY

Olympia, Washington

Date January 6, 19___
Sold to: Duncan Publishers
         Oakland, California

Invoice No. 1-0148

Terms: 1% 10 days, net 30 days

Quantity	Description	Unit	Price	Amount
50	Reams $8\frac{1}{2}$ × 11, 16# white mimeo paper	Ream	$2.62	$
			Less 50–10%	
			Total	$

_____

8. A retail store manager bought a bill of goods at a cost of $850.00 less 25% and 5%. If it was sold for $12\frac{1}{2}$% more than the net cost, what was the selling price? (Use tables.)

9. Zane bros. purchased a selection of floor lamps at a net price of $875.00 which were listed by the wholesaler at $1250.00. What was the rate of discount?

10. Which is the better discount for the buyer and by how much? (a) 30–10–$2\frac{1}{2}$% or 25–15–2%, (b) a single discount of 30% or 15–15%?

(a) _____

(b) _____

11. Shipley Publications received a bill for 50 reams of paper at $2.76 a ream less 50–10% discount. A 1% cash discount was granted if payment was received within 10 days from the date of the invoice. What was the amount of the payment if advantage was taken of the cash discount?

12. The Melody Music Co. listed a group of radios for $1650.00 less 25%. To meet competition the net price was dropped to $1113.75. What additional discount was added to meet this drop in price?

13. Hope Co. received a bill for $250.75 dated January 3 with terms 3/10, 1/15, n/30. The bill was paid on January 14. What was the amount remitted in payment?

_____

14. An invoice amounting to $517.50 less 50–10%, dated March 29 with terms of 2% 10 days, net 30 days was paid on April 3. What was the amount of payment? (Use tables.)

_____

DISCOUNT TABLE—Net Decimal Equivalents
(Net Value of $1.00 after Discounts Have Been Deducted)

Rate (%)	5	7½	10	12½	15
Net	.95	.925	.90	.875	.85
2½	.92625	.90188	.8775	.85313	.82875
5	.9025	.87875	.855	.83125	.8075
5, 2½	.87994	.85678	.83363	.81047	.78731
5, 5	.85738	.83481	.81225	.78969	.76713
5, 5, 2½	.83594	.81394	.79194	.76995	.74795
7½	.87875	.85563	.8325	.80938	.78625
7½, 2½	.85678	.83423	.81169	.78914	.76659
7½, 5	.83481	.81284	.79088	.76891	.74694
10	.855	.8325	.81	.7875	.765
10, 2½	.83363	.81169	.78975	.76781	.74588
10, 5	.81225	.79088	.7695	.74813	.72675
10, 5, 2½	.79194	.7711	.75026	.72942	.70858
10, 7½	.79088	.77006	.74925	.72844	.70763
10, 10	.7695	.74925	.729	.70875	.6885
10, 10, 5	.73103	.71179	.69255	.67331	.65408
10, 10, 5, 2½	.71275	.69399	.67524	.65648	.63772
10, 10, 10	.69255	.67433	.6561	.63788	.61965
10, 10, 10, 10	.62330	.60689	.59049	.57409	.55769

Rate %	16⅔	20	25	30	33⅓
Net	.83333	.80	.75	.70	.66667
2½	.8125	.78	.73125	.6825	.65
5	.79167	.76	.7125	.665	.63333
5, 2½	.77187	.741	.69469	.64838	.6175
5, 5	.75208	.722	.67688	.63175	.60167
5, 5, 2½	.73328	.70395	.65995	.61596	.58663
7½	.77083	.74	.69375	.6475	.61667
7½, 2½	.75156	.7215	.67641	.63131	.60125
7½, 5	.73229	.703	.65906	.61513	.58583
10	.75	.72	.675	.63	.6
10, 2½	.73125	.702	.65813	.61425	.585
10, 5	.7125	.684	.64125	.5985	.57
10, 5, 2½	.69469	.6669	.62522	.58354	.55575
10, 7½	.69375	.666	.62438	.58275	.555
10, 10	.675	.648	.6075	.567	.54
10, 10, 5	.64125	.6156	.57713	.53865	.513
10, 10, 5, 2½	.62522	.60021	.5627	.52518	.50018
10, 10, 10	.6075	.5382	.54675	.5103	.486
10, 10, 10, 10	.54675	.52488	.49208	.45927	.4374

DISCOUNT TABLE—Net Decimal Equivalents (*continued*)
(Net Value of $1.00 after Discounts Have Been Deducted)

Rate %	35	37½	40	45
Net	.65	.625	.60	.55
2½	.63375	.60938	.585	.53625
5	.6175	.59375	.57	.5225
5, 2½	.60206	.57891	.55575	.50944
5, 5	.58663	.56406	.5415	.49638
5, 5, 2½	.57196	.54996	.52796	.48397
7½	.60125	.57813	.555	.50875
7½, 2½	.58622	.56367	.54113	.49603
7½, 5	.57119	.54922	.52725	.48331
10	.585	.5625	.54	.495
10, 2½	.57038	.54844	.5265	.48263
10, 5	.55575	.53438	.513	.47025
10, 5, 2½	.54186	.52102	.50018	.45849
10, 7½	.54113	.52031	.4995	.45788
10, 10	.5265	.50625	.486	.4455
10, 10, 5	.50018	.48094	.4617	.42323
10, 10, 5, 2½	.48767	.46891	.45016	.41264
10, 10, 10	.47385	.45563	.4374	.40095
10, 10, 10, 10	.42647	.41006	.39366	.36086

Rate %	50	60	62½	66⅔
Net	.50	.40	.375	.33333
2½	.4875	.39	.36563	.325
5	.475	.38	.35625	.31666
5, 2½	.46313	.3705	.34734	.30875
5, 5	.45125	.361	.33844	.30083
5, 5, 2½	.43997	.35198	.32998	.29331
7½	.4625	.37	.34688	.30833
7½, 2½	.45094	.36075	.3382	.30062
7½, 5	.43938	.3515	.32953	.29292
10	.45	.36	.3375	.3
10, 2½	.43875	.351	.32906	.2925
10, 5	.4275	.342	.32063	.285
10, 5, 2½	.41681	.33345	.31261	.27788
10, 7½	.41625	.333	.31219	.2775
10, 10	.405	.324	.30375	.27
10, 10, 5	.38473	.3078	.28856	.2565
10, 10, 5, 2½	.37513	.30011	.28135	.25009
10, 10, 10	.3645	.2916	.27338	.243
10, 10, 10, 10	.32805	.26244	.24604	.2187

Answers

1. 14.81
2. $453.21
3. August 11
   $3111.50
4. $657.90
5. $8.25 or $8.24
6. $442.56
7. $58.36
8. $681.33
9. 30%
10. (a) 30–10–2½% by 1.05%
    (b) 30% by 2.25%
11. $61.48
12. 10%
13. $248.24
14. $228.22

Solutions

1. $25 \times 29¢ = \$\ 7.25$
   $50 \times 25¢ = \underline{\ 12.50}$
   $\$19.75$
   less 25% $\underline{\ \ 4.94}$
   $\$14.81$

2. $\$805.70$ gross amount
   $\underline{\ 134.28}$ 1/6 (16⅔%)
   671.42
   $\underline{\ 167.855}$ 1/4 (25%)
   503.565
   $\underline{\ \ 50.3565}$ 10%
   $453.2085 = \$453.21$

3. August 1 plus 10 days = August 11
   $3175.00 gross amount
   $\underline{\ \ \ 63.50}$ 2% discount
   $3111.50 net amount

4. $220 \times \$3.75 = \$825.00$ gross
   less $\underline{\ 165.00}$ 20% trade discount
   $\$660.00$ net amount
   $\underline{\ \ \ \ 6.60}$ 1% cash discount
   $\$653.40$
   plus $\underline{\ \ \ \ 4.50}$ shipping charges
   $\$657.90$ amount paid

5. $6 \times \$0.50 = \$3.00$
   $6 \times\ \ 0.50 = \ \ 3.00$
   $2 \times\ \ 1.60 = \ \ 3.20$
   $1 \times\ \ 0.50 = \underline{\ \ 0.50}$
   $\$9.70$ gross amount
   less $\underline{\ \ 1.45}$ 15% trade discount
   $\$8.25$ net amount

6. $\$516.10$
   $\underline{\ \ 64.51}$ 12½% (⅛)
   $\$451.59$
   $\underline{\ \ \ 9.03}$ 2%
   $\$442.56$ net amount

7. $50 \times \$2.62 = \$131.00$
   NDE 50–10% = .45
   $131 \times .45 = \$58.95$ net amount
   1% of $58.95 = \$0.59$
   $\$58.95 - \$0.59 = \$58.36$ amount paid

8. NDE for 25–5% = .7125
   $\$850.00 \times .7125 = \$605.63$ cost
   $\$605.63 \times .125 = \$75.70$
   $\$605.63 + \$75.70 = \$681.33$ selling price

9. $1250 − $875 = $375
    $375 ÷ $1250 = .30 or 30%

10. (a) NDE for 30–10–2½% = .61425
        NDE for 25–15–2% = .62475
        Difference = .62475 − .61425
                   = .0105 or 1.05%
        30–10–2½% is best

    (b) NDE for 15–15% = .7225
        NDE for 30% = .70
        Difference = .7225 − .70
                   = .0225 or 2.25%
        30% is best

11. 50 × $2.76 = $138.00 gross amount
    NDE for 50–10% = .45
    $138 × .45 = $62.10 net amount
        less 1%   .62 cash discount
                 $61.48 amount paid

12. $1650 less 25% = $1237.50 net
    $1237.50 − $1113.75 = $123.75
    $123.75 ÷ $1237.50 = .10 or 10%

13. Paid after 10 days, therefore
    $250.75 less 1% = $248.24

14. NDE for 50–10% = .45
    $517.50 × .45 = $232.88 net amount
    2% of $232.88 = $4.66
    $232.88 − $4.66 = $228.22 paid

CHAPTER FOUR
Merchandising

OBJECTIVES

Merchants buy and sell goods for a profit. This chapter deals with the manner in which *gross profit* or *markup* and *markdown* are computed. In addition, operating costs and net profit are discussed.

When you have completed the work in this chapter, you will be able to

(1) compute the amount and rate of markup based on (a) cost and (b) selling price,
(2) compute the selling price when the cost price and markup rate are known,
(3) compute the cost price when the selling price, and markup rate are known,
(4) compute the markdown and rate of markdown if the original and actual selling prices are known,
(5) compute the original sales price if the reduced sales price and rate of markdown are known,
(6) compute the original sales price and actual sales price if the markdown and rate of markdown are known.
(7) compute operating costs, gross profit (or loss), and net profit (or loss) if the rates, selling price or cost price, rate of markup, and the base are known.

UNIT 1. MARKUP

Merchants are in the business of buying and selling goods at a profit. The difference between the cost and the selling price must be sufficient to cover all operating expenses with an amount remaining, called net profit, that will justify the operation of the business. This difference is referred to as *gross profit* or *markup*. [Cost equals the net cost (price of goods bought) plus buying expenses such as transportation and other handling charges.]

1. The *markup* or *gross profit* is the difference between the selling price and cost price of an article.

   If Jackson Bros. pay $57.50 for a coat and sell it for $98.00, what is the markup?

   Selling price   _____

   Cost price   _____

   Markup   _____

   Selling price $98.00
   Cost price   57.50
   Markup $40.50

2. What is the markup on an article that sells for $25.00 and cost $11.30? _____

   $25.00 − $11.30 = $13.70 (markup).

Finding the Amount and Rate of Markup

By definition the *markup* is the difference between the selling price and the cost price, based on the assumption, of course, that the selling price is greater than the cost price:

$$\text{markup} = \text{selling Price} - \text{cost Price}.$$

The *markup* may be computed on the *cost* or the *selling price*. There is no uniform or standard rule. The method used depends on many factors such as tradition or precedent, accounting system, method used for inventory records, type of merchandise, certain unique characteristics of a business, and size of the business.

In general, manufacturers, wholesalers, and jobbers use the cost price as the basis for computing markup. Furniture stores, as a rule, also figure markup on cost price. It is common practice for the larger retail stores to use the selling price as a base for computing markup. Many retail stores (usually small ones) however, use the wholesale or cost price.

The markup may be based on the *cost* or *selling* price.
An article costs $25.00 and sells for $37.50.
The markup = $37.50 − $25.00 = $12.50.
Find the rate when the markup is as follows:

(a) *Based on cost*

We are asking ourselves, "What percent of the cost is the markup?"

Markup rate = markup ÷ cost = $12.50 ÷ $25.00 = .50 or 50%.

(b) *Based on selling price*

In this case we want to know what percent of the selling price is the markup?

Markup rate = markup ÷ selling price
= $12.50 ÷ $37.50 = $.33\frac{1}{3}$ or $33\frac{1}{3}\%$.

3. Johnsons paid $56.00 for an article and sold it for $70.00.

   (a)   Markup = $_____?

   (b)   Markup = _____% of cost?

   (c)   Markup = _____% of selling price?

- -

(a)   Markup = $70.00 − $56.00 = $14.00.
(b)   Markup rate (% of cost) = $14.00 ÷ $56.00 = .25 or 25%.
(c)   Markup rate (% of selling price) = $14.00 ÷ $70.00 = .20 or 20%.

EXERCISE 15

Markup—Amount and Rate

General Instructions. Record all money amounts correct to the nearest cent. Record all percent figures correct to the nearest tenth of 1% unless they are even (25%, 62%, etc.) or have a common fraction remainder ($33\frac{1}{3}\%$, $40\frac{3}{4}\%$, etc.)

If your answers do not agree with those shown, check your calculations before referring to the solutions that follow.

I. Find the *amount* of markup and the *rate* of markup for the following examples, based on the cost price and based on the selling price (see example).

				Percent Markup	
No.	Cost Price	Selling Price	Markup	On Cost	On Selling Price
Example	$125.30	$160.80	$35.50	28.3	22.1
1.	60.00	80.00	———	———	———
2.	75.50	105.70	———	———	———
3.	32.00	48.00	———	———	———
4.	56.00	63.00	———	———	———
5.	24.95	32.00	———	———	———

II. Applications
   1. A retail clothier paid $15.00 for a suit and sold it for $22.50. What were the amount and rate of markup based on cost?

2. The Starr Furniture Co. bought a table for $40.00. Transportation charges were $5.00. If the table sells for $60.00, find the markup and % markup on cost. (*Note*. Transportation charges are considered a part of cost.)

3. What is the rate of markup on an article that cost $44.00 and sells for $65.00 if it is based on the selling price?

4. James Bros. bought one dozen hampers from a wholesaler for $12.50 each less 10% and 5%. If they were sold at retail for $15.00 each, what were the markup for the dozen and the percent markup based on the retail price?

5. Hoffman fixes his selling price at a set rate on the sales price. What markup rate does he use if the sells an article for $64.00 that cost him $40.00?

Answers

		Markup	% on Cost	% on Selling Price
I.	1.	$20.00	$33\frac{1}{3}$	25
	2.	30.20	40	28.6
	3.	16.00	50	$33\frac{1}{3}$
	4.	7.00	$12\frac{1}{2}$	$11\frac{1}{9}$
	5.	7.05	28.3	22.0

II. 1. $7.50, 50%
    2. $15.00, $33\frac{1}{3}$%
    3. 32.3%
    4. $51.75, $28\frac{3}{4}$%
    5. $37\frac{1}{2}$%

Solutions

I. 1.   Markup = $80.00 − $60.00 = $20.00
        Percent markup on cost = $20.00 ÷ $60.00 = .$33\frac{1}{3}$ or $33\frac{1}{3}$%.
        Percent markup on selling price = $20.00 ÷ $80.00 = .25 or 25%.
  2.–5. All solved in the same manner as No. 1.

II. 1. Markup = $22.50 − $15.00 = $7.50.
      Percent markup on cost = $7.50 ÷ $15.00 = .50 or 50%.

    2. Markup = $60.00 − ($40.00 + $5.00) = $15.00.
      Percent markup on cost = $15.00 ÷ $45.00 = .$33\frac{1}{3}$ or $33\frac{1}{3}$%.

    3. Markup = $65.00 − $44.00 = $21.00.
      Percent markup on selling price = $21.00 ÷ $65.00 = .323 or 32.3%.

    4. List price = $12.50 × 12 = $150.00.
      Cost price = $150.00 less 10% and 5% = $150.00 × .855 = $128.25.
      Selling price = $15.00 × 12 = $180.00.
      Markup = $180.00 − $128.25 = $51.75.
      Percent markup on selling price = $51.75 ÷ $180.00 = .2875 or $28\frac{3}{4}$%.

    5. Markup = $64.00 − $40.00 = $24.00.
      Percent markup on selling price = $24.00 ÷ $64.00 = .375 or $37\frac{1}{2}$%.

MARKUP 173

Finding the Selling Price when the Cost and Markup Rate Are Known

4. A radio cost a dealer $25.00. How much must he sell it for if the markup is 15% of the cost?

   Cost = $25.00.

   Markup = 15% of $25.00 = $3.75.

   Selling price = cost + markup = $25.00 + $3.75 = $28.75.

   Find the selling price on a coat that cost the dealer $45.00 if the markup is 55% of the cost.

   Cost = $_____

   Markup = _____% of $_____ = $_____ .

   Selling price = $_____ + $_____ = $_____ .

   -

   Cost = $45.00; markup = 55% of $45.00 = $24.75.
   Selling price = $45.00 + $24.75 = $69.75.

5. A dealer paid $190.00 for a stove. What is the selling price if the markup is 40% of the cost?

   -

   Markup = .40 × $190.00 = $76.00.
   Selling price = $190.00 + $76.00 = $266.00.

6. A merchant paid $80.00 for an electric grill and wishes to sell it with a markup of 35%, based on the selling price. What is the selling price?

The base (selling price in this case) = 100%.
Cost price = selling price − markup = 100% − 35% = 65%.

But the cost price also = $80.00. Therefore 65% = $80.00. If 65% = $80.00, our problem is to find 100%.

Selling price (100%) = $80.00 ÷ .65 = $123.08.

Proof: markup = 35% of selling price = .35 × $123.08 = $43.08.
        markup = selling price − cost price = $123.08 − $80.00 = $43.08.

7. Jacob Bros. paid $56.00 for a coat that they wish to sell at a markup of 60% of the selling price. What is the selling price?

Selling price is base. Cost = 100% − _____ = _____%.

Selling price (100%) = _____.

Proof: _____.

- -

Cost = 100% − 60% = 40%.
Selling price (100%) = $56.00 ÷ .40 = $140.00.
Markup = 60% of $140.00 = .60 × $140.00 = $84.00.
Markup = selling price − cost = $140.00 − $56.00 = $84.00.

8. Manning Co. buys a certain coffee table for $11.20. What does it sell for if the markup is (a) 80% of cost, (b) 80% of the selling price?

(a) Markup   = _____.
     Selling price = _____.

(b) Selling price = _____%.
     Cost   = _____% − _____% = _____%.
     Cost also   = $_____.
     Selling price = $_____ ÷ _____ = $_____.

- -

(a) Markup = .80 × $11.20 = $8.96.
      Selling price = $11.20 + $8.96 = $20.16.
(b) Selling price = 100%.
      Cost = 100% − 80% = 20%.
      Cost also = $11.20.
      Selling price (100%) = $11.20 ÷ .20 = $56.00.

9. Harper & Co. buys hampers for $6.70. What do they sell for if the markup is (a) 90% of cost, (b) 60% of the selling price?

    (a)   (b)

_____

(a) Cost = $6.70.   (b) Selling price = 100%.
      Markup = 90% of $6.70 = $6.03.   Markup = 60% of selling price.
      Selling price = $6.70 + $6.03 =   Cost = 40% of selling price.
      $12.73.   Cost also = $6.70.
                                                  Selling price (100%) =
                                                      $6.70 ÷ .40 = $16.75
                                                  OR
                                                      $6.70 ÷ $\frac{2}{5}$ = $16.75.

EXERCISE 16

Finding the Selling Price

Answers appear at the end of this exercise. If your answers do not agree with those shown, check your calculations before referring to the solutions that follow.

I. Find the selling price for the following articles (see example).

				Selling Price	
No.	Article	Cost Price	Markup Rate	Based on Cost	Based on Selling Price
Example	Table	$35.00	40%	$49.00	$58.33
1.	Highchair	9.40	25%	————	————
2.	Desk	100.50	50%	————	————
3.	Sofa	400.00	20%	————	————
4.	Table	120.00	$12\frac{1}{2}\%$	————	————
5.	Radio	45.00	15%	————	————
6.	Picture	75.00	$33\frac{1}{3}\%$	————	————

II. Solve the following problems. Until you are sure of yourself, it is best to work out each step fully.

1. L. Dakin & Co. purchased 2 doz. chairs for $360.00. Freight charges totaled $115.00. Find the selling price if a 30% gross profit (markup) on cost is to be realized. (Cost price includes freight charges.)

2. Wohler bought some purses for $4.50. At what price must they be sold if a markup of 40% is based on the selling price?

3. A hi-fi set cost $320.00 less 25% and 10%. What must it sell for to gain $37\frac{1}{2}$% of the selling price?

   _____

4. A dealer pays $22.80 for an article that he sells at a markup of 20% on the selling price. What is his selling price?

   _____

5. A hardware dealer used a markup of $16\frac{2}{3}$% on cost on some merchandise for which he paid $4.50. What was the selling price?

   _____

6. A retailer purchases suits for $35.00 on which he uses a markup of 25%. What would the selling price be if the markup is based on (a) cost, (b) selling price?

   (a)_____,

   (b)_____.

Answers

	Selling Price	
	Based on Cost	Based on Selling Price
I. 1.	$ 11.75	$ 12.53
2.	150.75	201.00
3.	480.00	500.00
4.	135.00	137.14
5.	51.75	52.94
6.	100.00	112.50

II. 1. $617.50
   2. $7.50
   3. $345.60
   4. $28.50
   5. $5.25
   6. (a) $43.75
      (b) $46.67

Solutions

I. 1. Based on cost:

    Markup $9.40 × .25 = $2.35.
    Selling price $9.40 + $2.35 = $11.75.

    Based on selling price:

    Selling price = 100%, markup = 25%.
    Cost price = 100% − 25% = 75%.
    Cost price also = $9.40.
    Selling price (100%) = $9.40 ÷ .75 = $12.53
              OR
                  = $9.40 ÷ $\frac{3}{4}$ = $12.53.

  2.–6. All solved in the same manner as No. 1.

II. 1. Cost = $360.00 + $115.00 = $475.00.
    Markup = $475.00 × .30 = $142.50.
    Selling price = cost + markup = $475.00 + $142.50 = $617.50.

  2. Selling price = 100%, markup = 40%, cost price = 100% − 40% = 60%.
    Cost price also = $4.50.
    Selling price (100%) = $4.50 ÷ .60 = $7.50
              OR
                  = $4.50 ÷ $\frac{3}{5}$ = $7.50.

3. Cost = $320.00 less 25% and 10% = $320.00 × .675 = $216.00.
   Selling price = 100%, markup = $37\frac{1}{2}$%, cost price = 100% − $37\frac{1}{2}$% = $62\frac{1}{2}$%.
   Selling price (100%) = $216.00 ÷ .625 = $345.60
       OR
         = $216.00 ÷ $\frac{5}{8}$ = $345.60.

4. Selling price = 100%, cost price = 100% − 20% = 80%.
   Cost price also = $22.80.
   Selling price (100%) = $22.80 ÷ .80 = $28.50
       OR
         = $22.80 ÷ $\frac{4}{5}$ = $28.50.

5. Cost price = $4.50 ÷ $16\frac{2}{3}$% = $\frac{1}{6}$.
   Markup = $4.50 × $\frac{1}{6}$ = $0.75.
   Selling price = $4.50 + $0.75 = $5.25.

6. (a) Cost price = $35.00.
     Markup = $35.00 × .25 = $8.75 OR = $35.00 × $\frac{1}{4}$ = $8.75.
     Selling price = $35.00 + $8.75 = $43.75.
   (b) Selling price = 100%, cost price = 100% − 25% = 75% or $\frac{3}{4}$.
     Cost price also = $35.00.
     Selling price (100%) = $35.00 ÷ .75 = $46.67
       OR
         = $35.00 ÷ $\frac{3}{4}$ = $46.67.

Finding the Cost Price
When the Selling Price and Markup Rate Are Known

10. The markup may be based on the _____ or _____.
    If the markup is based on the cost, the _____ equals _____%.
    If the markup is based on the selling price, the_____ equals
    _____%.

- -

cost or selling price, cost equals 100%, selling price equals 100%.

11. A suit sold in a local store for $50.00. What was the cost if the markup of 30% was based on the *selling price*?

    Selling price = $_____.

    Markup = 30% of selling price = _____.

    Cost price = selling price − markup = _____.

    Selling price = $50.00.
    Markup = 30% of selling price = .30 × $50.00 = $15.00.
    Cost price = selling price − markup = $50.00 − $15.00 = $35.00.

12. A local store sold an electric iron for $14.95. What was the cost if the markup of 40% was based on the selling price? The solution is shown here in tabular form.

Selling price (base)	$14.95	100%
Markup	5.98	40
Cost price	$ 8.97	60%

    (selling price − markup)

    Markup = $14.95 × .40 = $5.98.
    Cost price = $14.95 × .60 = $8.97
        OR
          = $14.95 − $5.98 = $8.97.

13. If the selling price is the base, it equals _____%.

    If the markup equals 30%, the cost price = _____%.

    Prove the cost price in frame 11 ($35.00) is correct by filling in the following statement.

    Cost price = _____% of $_____ = $35.00.

    Cost price = 70% of $50.00 = $35.00.

14. The Unruh Shop marks up all goods on the *selling price*. If it sold a coat for $150.00, what was the cost price if the markup was 40%?

    Markup = _____.

    Cost price = _____.

Markup = .40 × $150.00 = $60.00
Cost price = $150.00 − $60.00 = $90.00

15. Marks Furniture Co. sells one of its lounge chairs for $99.50. If the markup is 50%, based on the cost, how much did it cost?

    In this case the cost is the base and therefore equals 100%.
    Selling price = cost + markup = 100% + 50% = 150%.
    The selling price also equals $99.50.
    If 150% = $99.50, then the cost price = $99.50 ÷ 1.50 = $66.33.
    Proof: 150% of $66.33 = $99.50 (selling price)

    If the selling price of a chair was $102.50 and the markup was 60%, based on cost, how much did the chair cost?

    Cost = _____%.

    Selling price = cost + markup = _____% + _____% = _____%.

    Selling price also = $_____.

    Cost price (100%) = $_____ ÷ _____ = $_____.

    Proof: _____% of $_____ = $102.50 (selling price).

    Cost = 100%.
    Selling price = cost + markup = 100% + 60% = 160%.
    Selling price also = $102.50.
    Cost price = $102.50 ÷ 1.60 = $64.06.
    Proof: 160% of $64.06 = $102.496 = $102.50 (selling price).

16. Peterson's carry a lamp that they sell for $75.00. What is the cost if the markup is 70% of (a) the cost, (b) the selling price?

    (a) Cost = base (100%).
        Selling price $75.00   ―%
        Markup   _____   70
        Cost   _____   100%

    (b) Selling price = base (100%).
        Selling price $75.00   100%
        Markup   _____   70
        Cost price $_____   _____%

(a) Cost = base (100%).
Selling price $75.00   170%
Markup   30.88   70
────────────────────────────
Cost price $44.12   100%
Cost price (100%) = $75.00 ÷ 1.70
                  = $44.12.

(b) Selling price = base (100%).
Selling price $75.00   100%
Markup   52.50   70
────────────────────────────
Cost price $22.50   30%
Markup = .70 × $75.00 = $52.50.
Cost price = $75.00 − $52.50 =
           = $22.50
           OR
         = $75.00 × .30 =
         = $22.50.

Dollar markup was not requested nor needed but is shown to complete the form.

EXERCISE 17

Finding the Cost Price

Answers appear at the end of this exercise. If your answers do not agree with those shown, check your calculations before referring to the solutions that follow.

I. Find the cost for the following items (see example).

Item	Selling Price	Markup Rate	Cost Price When Markup is Based on Selling Price	Cost Price When Markup is Based on Cost Price
Example	$95.00	22%	$74.10	$77.87
1.	102.00	10%	———	———
2.	63.00	$16\frac{2}{3}\%$	———	———
3.	9.26	$33\frac{1}{3}\%$	———	———
4.	18.25	25%	———	———
5.	302.20	$12\frac{1}{2}\%$	———	———

II. Solve the following problems. Indicate all steps in your solution.

1. Mr. Dixon priced his electric coffee pots to sell for $21.75. If he used a 20% markup on cost, what did he pay for them?

2. Hemp Bros. sold their TV tables at $25.00 less 10%. What was the purchase price of these tables if a markup of 40% on the net selling price was used?

3. A druggist sells a face cream for $2.50 a jar on which he realizes a 30% markup of the selling price. What is his cost price?

_____

4. A gift shop sells a crystal vase for $10.00 at a markup of $66\frac{2}{3}\%$ on cost. What is the cost?

_____

5. The Hammer Manufacturing Co. makes gunstocks that sell for $37.50. What is the cost if the markup on cost is 50%?

_____

Answers

		Cost Price When Markup is Based on	
		Selling Price	Cost Price
I.	1.	$ 91.80	$ 92.73
	2.	52.50	54.00
	3.	6.17	6.95
	4.	13.69	14.60
	5.	264.42 or 264.43	268.62
II.	1.	$18.13	
	2.	$13.50	
	3.	$ 1.75	
	4.	$ 6.00	
	5.	$25.00	

Solutions

I. 1. *Markup based on selling price*

   Selling price = 100%.
   Markup = $102.00 × .10 = $10.20.
   Cost = $102.00 − $10.20 = $91.80.

   Markup based on cost

   Cost = 100%.
   Selling price = cost price + markup = 100% + 10% = 110%.
   Selling price also = $102.00.
   Cost price (100%) = $102.00 ÷ 1.10 = $92.73.

   2–5 solved in the same manner.

II. 1. The cost price = the base; therefore it = 100%.
   Selling price = cost price + markup = 100% + 20% = 120%
   Selling price also = $21.75.
   Cost price = $21.75 ÷ 1.20 = $18.13.

   2. Selling price = $25.00 less 10% = $25.00 − $2.50 = $22.50.
   Markup = .40 × $22.50 = $9.00.
   Cost price = $22.50 − $9.00 = $13.50.

   3. Markup = $2.50 × .30 = $0.75.
   Cost price = $2.50 − $0.75 = $1.75.

   4. Cost price = 100% since it is the base.
   Selling price = cost price + markup = 100% + $66\frac{2}{3}$% = $166\frac{2}{3}$% (same as $\frac{5}{3}$).
   Selling price also = $10.00.
   Cost price (100%) = $10.00 ÷ $\frac{5}{3}$ = $6.00.

   5. Cost price = 100% since it is the base.
   Selling price = 100% + 50% = 150%.
   Selling price also = $37.50.
   Cost price (100%) = $37.50 ÷ 1.50 = $25.00.

UNIT 2. MARKDOWN

A *markdown* is a reduction in the selling price. It is a particular kind of discount and refers only to a reduction in a previously established selling price. Such a reduction is made for one or more reasons. It is a means, for example, of moving old merchandise, stimulating sales, disposing of hard-to-sell goods or damaged merchandise.

Markdown = original selling price − actual selling price.
Percent Markdown = amount of markdown ÷ original selling price.

1. If a coat that originally sold for $100 was marked down to $75, $100 is the original selling price or previous marked price, and $75 is the actual selling price. The markdown = $100 − $75 = $25.

    What is the actual selling price of a dress that was marked down from $56 to $35? $_____ What is the original selling price? $_____ What is the markdown? $_____

    Actual selling price, $35,   original selling price, $56,   markdown, $21.

2. A coat that originally sold for $80 was marked down on a storewide sale to $54. The amount of markdown = $80 − $54 = $26.

    What would have been the amount of markdown if the coat were reduced to $57.50? $_____? To $39.90? $_____

    $80.00 − $57.50 = $22.50, $80.00 − $39.90 = $40.10.

3. If a dress that originally sold for $15.00 was reduced to $7.50, the percent (%) markdown = $7.50 ÷ $15.00 = .50 = 50%.

    What would be the percent markdown if it had been reduced to $10.00? _____%, To $5.00? _____% To $8.00? _____%

    $66\tfrac{2}{3}\%$, $33\tfrac{1}{3}\%$, $53\tfrac{1}{3}\%$

4. A lady's suit, which had sold for $110.00, is marked down to $85.00 as part of a promotional sale. What were the markdown and the rate of markdown?

    Markdown = _____.

    Percent markdown = _____.

Markdown = $110.00 − $85.00 = $25.00.
Percent markdown = $25.00 ÷ $110.00 = .227 = 22.7%.

5. A local store advertized a $33\frac{1}{3}\%$ markdown on some of its dresses that originally sold for $27.50. What was the new price?

   Markdown = $33\frac{1}{3}\%$ of $27.50 = $9.17 OR $\frac{1}{3}$ × $27.50 = $9.17.
   New selling price = $27.50 − $9.17 = $18.33.

   Haines Bros. decided to mark down some of their suits that sold for $59.60. If the markdown was 25%, what was the new sales price?

   Markdown = _____.

   New sales price = _____.

   -

   Markdown = .25 × $59.60 = $14.90.
   New sales price = $59.60 − $14.90 = $44.70.

6. Jacobs wanted to clear some hampers that were marked $34.50. If they were reduced 20%, what is the new sales price?

   -

   Markdown = .20 × $34.50 = $6.90
   New sales price = $34.50 − $6.90 = $27.60

7. What would be the new sales price for the hampers in frame 6 if they had been marked down 25%? _____ 40%? _____ $33\frac{1}{3}\%$? _____

   -

Markdown = .25 × $34.50 = $8.62.
New selling price = $34.50 − $8.62 = $25.88.
Markdown = .40 × $34.50 = $13.80.
New selling price = $34.50 − $13.80 = $20.70.
Markdown = .33⅓ × $34.50 = $11.50.
   OR
        = ⅓ × $34.50 = $11.50.
New selling price = $34.50 − $11.50 = $23.00.

8. "Fashions" marked down some of their coats $30.00, which was $37\frac{1}{2}\%$ of the original selling price. What was the original selling price and the reduced selling price?

The original selling price was reduced by $37\frac{1}{2}\%$. It is the base or 100%.
Then $30.00 ÷ .375 = $80.00 or $30.00 ÷ ⅜ = $80.00 *original selling price*
    $80.00 − $30.00 = $50.00   *new (reduced) selling price*

What is the original and new selling price on a dress that was reduced $4.50, or 18%?

Original selling price (100%) = _____.

Reduced (new) selling price = _____.

Original selling price (100%) = $4.50 ÷ .18 = $25.00.
Reduced selling price   = $25.00 − $4.50 = $20.50.

EXERCISE 18

Markdown

Answers appear at the end of this exercise. If your answers do not agree with those shown, check your calculations before referring to the solutions which follow.

I. Find the missing factors in the following list. Show full percent for markdown rates. Answers for this section are shown below.

No.	Original Selling Price	Actual Selling Price	Markdown	% Markdown
1.	$125.00	$_____	$25.00	_____
2.	37.50	_____	_____	$33\frac{1}{3}$
3.	132.00	121.00	_____	_____
4.	_____	86.25	_____	25
5.	_____	_____	58.00	$16\frac{2}{3}\%$

II. 1. What is the markdown rate on a table that normally sells for $95.00 if the price is reduced to $60.00?

2. An article costs $25.00. It was marked up 25% of cost and later reduced by $6\frac{1}{2}\%$ for a clearance sale. What were the markdown and the reduced selling price?

Markdown _____
Reduced selling price _____

3. Ott's Drug Store reduced some of its Christmas cards 50% after the holidays. If the original markup was $66\frac{2}{3}\%$ of the selling price and the cost of the cards was $2.00 a box, what was the reduced selling price?

4. The Fairprice Market sold all of its jump ropes in a January sale for $0.76 each. The markdown was 20%. What were the amount of the original sales price and the markdown?

Original sales price _____

Markdown _____

Answers

No.	Original Selling Price	Actual Selling Price	Markdown	% Markdown
I. 1.	$	$100.00		20
2.		25.00	$12.50	
3.			11.00	$8\frac{1}{3}$
4.	115.00		28.75	
5.	348.00	290.00		

II. 1. 36.8%
   2. Markdown = $2.03.
      Reduced selling price = $29.22.
   3. $3.00.
   4. Markdown = $0.19.
      Original sales price = $0.95.

Solutions

I. 1. Actual selling price = $125.00 − $25.00 = $100.00.
     Percent markdown = $25.00 ÷ $125.00 = .20 = 20%.

  2. Markdown = $37.50 × $.33\frac{1}{3}$ OR $37.50 × $\frac{1}{3}$ = $12.50.
     Actual selling price = $37.50 − $12.50 = $25.00.

  3. Markdown = $132.00 − $121.00 = $11.00.
     Percent markdown = $11.00 ÷ $132.00 = $.08\frac{1}{3}$ = $8\frac{1}{3}$%.

  4. Markdown = 25%.
     Actual selling price = 75% of original selling price.
     Actual selling price = $86.25.
     Original selling price (100%) = $86.25 ÷ .75 = $115.00.
                  OR
                      = $86.25 ÷ $\frac{3}{4}$ = $115.00.
     Markdown = $115.00 − $86.25 = $28.75.

5. Markdown = $58.00. It also = $16\frac{2}{3}\%$ or $\frac{1}{6}$ of original selling price.
Since the original selling price is the base or 100%, it equals $58.00 ÷ $\frac{1}{6}$ = $348.00.
Actual selling price = $348.00 − $58.00 = $290.00.

II. 1. Markdown = $95.00 − $60.00 = $35.00.
Percent markdown = $35.00 ÷ $95.00 = .368 = 36.8%.

2. Cost = $25.00.
Markup = .25 × $25.00 = $6.25.
Original selling price = $25.00 + $6.25 = $31.25.
Markdown = $6\frac{1}{2}\%$ of $31.25 = .065 × $31.25 = $2.03.
Reduced selling price = $31.25 − $2.03 = $29.22.

3. Cost = $2.00.
Markup = $66\frac{2}{3}\%$ of selling price.
Selling price is the base or 100%.
Cost price = 100% − $66\frac{2}{3}\%$ = $33\frac{1}{3}\%$ or $\frac{1}{3}$ of the selling price.
Since the cost price = $2.00, the selling price = $2.00 × 3 = $6.00.
Markdown = 50% of $6.00 = $3.00.
Reduced selling price = $3.00.

4. If the markdown = 20%, the January sale price of $0.76 = 80% of the original selling price.
Original selling price = $0.76 ÷ .80 = $0.95.
Markdown = $0.95 − $0.76 = $0.19.

UNIT 3. PROFIT AND LOSS

As stated in the introduction to this chapter, merchants are in the business of buying and selling goods for profit. The difference between the selling price and cost price is called the *markup* or *gross profit*. The gross profit can also be thought of as the total of net profit plus all operating expenses (expenses of conducting the business).

Operating expenses in turn may be broken down into overhead expenses (general and administrative expenses such as salaries, rent, lights, and repairs) and selling expenses (advertising, salesmen's expenses, promotion, commissions, etc.). When the gross profit is insufficient to meet the costs of operating the business, a net loss occurs. These relationships can be summarized in equation form as follows:

gross profit = selling price − cost price
gross profit = operating expenses + net profit
net profit or loss = gross profit − operating expenses

1. We have learned that the difference between the selling price and the cost price of an article is the markup. *Markup is also the gross profit.*

   A coat that cost $56 sold for $127.
   The markup = $127 − $56 = $71.
   $71 is also the *gross profit*.

   What is the gross profit on a desk selling for $375 that cost $196? $_____

   Gross profit = $375.00 − $196.00 = $179.00.

2. Gross profit = operating expenses + net profit.

   If a company earned a net profit of $376,490 and operating expenses amounted to $2,015,950, the gross profit = $2,015,950 + $376,490 = $2,392,440.

   Complete the following: Operating Expenses (1) $320.02   (2) $995,060
                                      Net profit   56.48   15,990
                                      Gross profit $_____ $_____

   ----

   (1) $376.50,   (2) $1,011,050

3. Complete the following statements:

   Gross profit = selling price − _____.
   Gross profit = net profit   + _____.

   Gross profit = selling price − cost price.
   Gross profit = net profit + operating expenses.

4. Johnson Bros. sold floor furnaces for $130 for which they paid $84.50. They realized a net profit of 8% on sales. What were their gross profit and operating expenses on one furnace? (Net profit is computed on sales.)

Gross profit   = selling price − cost price

= _____ − _____ = _____ .

Net profit   = 8% of selling price

= .08 × _____ = _____ .

Operating expenses = gross profit − net profit.

= _____ − _____ = _____ .

Gross profit = $130.00 − $84.50 = $45.50.
Net profit = .08 × $130.00 = $10.40.
Operating expenses = $45.50 − $10.40 = $35.10.

5. An article sells for $25.00. The net profit is 7%; operating expenses are 39%. Gross profit is based on the selling price. Find the amount of net profit, operating expenses, and gross profit.

Net profit   = .07 × $25.00 = $_____ .

Operating expenses = _____ × $25.00 = $_____ .

Gross profit   = net profit + operating expenses =

= _____ + _____ = _____ .

Net profit   = .07 × $25.00 = $1.75.
Operating expenses = .39 × $25.00 = $9.75.
Gross profit   = $1.75 + $9.75 = $11.50.
        OR
= (.07 + .39) × $25.00 = .46 × $25.00 = $11.50.

194 UNIT 3

6. What is the cost price in terms of dollars and cents, and percent of the selling price for the article in frame 5?

   Cost price ($) = _____.

   Cost price (%) = _____.

   -

   Cost price = selling price − gross profit = $25.00 − $11.50 = $13.50.
   Cost price = selling price − gross profit = 100% − 46% = 54%.

7. O'Brian Merchants wish to realize a 15% net profit on rugs that were purchased for $130.00. Operating expenses equaled 20%. Assuming that profit is based on the selling price, what selling price is required? How much are the net profit, operating expenses, and the gross profit?

   Gross profit = _____% + _____% = _____%.

   Selling price = _____% because it is the base.

   Cost price = 100% − gross profit = _____%.

   Cost price also = $130.00.

   Selling price (100%) = _____ ÷ _____ = $_____.

   Net profit = .15 × $_____ = $_____.

   Operating expenses = .20 × $_____ = $_____.

   Gross profit = _____ = $_____.

   -

   Gross profit = 15% + 20% = 35%.
   Selling price = 100% because it is the base.
   Cost price = 100% − 35% = 65%.
   Selling price = $130 ÷ .65 = $200.00.
   Net profit = .15 × $200.00 = $30.00.
   Operating expenses = .20 × $200.00 = $40.00.
   Gross profit = .35 × $200.00 = $70.00 OR $30.00 + $40.00 = $70.00.

PROFIT AND LOSS 195

8. The information given and obtained in frame 7 presented in tabular form is as follows: Study and then go on to the example.

Selling price	$200.00	100%	base
Cost price	130.00	65	(100% − 35%)
Gross profit	$ 70.00	35	(15% + 20%)
Operating expenses	40.00	20	
Net profit	$ 30.00	15	

Hampton Co. made a net profit of 10% on rugs that were bought for $120.00 each. Operating expenses were 24%. If profit is based on the selling price, what was the selling price of these rugs? How much were the net profit, operating expenses, and gross profit? Record answers in tabular form. (Use formulas from frame 7 to answer these questions.)

Selling price $_____   _____ %

Cost price   _____   _____

Gross profit $_____   _____

Operating expenses   _____   _____

Net profit   _____   _____

- -

Selling price	$181.82	100%	$120 ÷ .66 = $181.82
Cost price	120.00	66	$181.82 − $120.00 = $61.82
Gross profit	$ 61.82	34	.24 × $181.82 = $43.64
Operating expenses	43.64	24	.10 × $181.82 = $18.18
Net profit	18.18	10	

EXERCISE 19

Profit and Loss

Answers appear at the end of this exercise. If your answers do not agree with those shown, check your calculations before referring to the solutions that follow.

1. Mrs. Romine bought some ladies suits at $30.00 each. At what price must she sell them to make a gross profit of 40%? (Profit is based on the selling price.)

    _____

2. The A-C Furniture Co. buys coffee tables for $27.50. What is the selling price if the gross profit is 45% of the selling price?

    _____

3. A gas stove sells for $260.00. If operating expenses are 30% of sales and net profit is 10% of sales, what is the cost of the stove?

    _____

4. Edwards Jewelers earned a net profit on sales of 22% on watches that were bought for $55.00 each. Operating expenses were $32\frac{1}{2}$% of sales. If all watches were sold, what were the net profit, operating expenses, and gross profit?

    Net profit _____

    Operating expenses _____

    Gross profit _____

Answers

1. $ 50.00
3. $156.00

2. $50.00
4. Net profit $26.59
   Operating expenses $39.29
   Gross profit $65.88

Solutions

1. Selling price = 100%.
   Gross profit = 40%; therefore cost price = 60%.
   Selling price = $30.00 ÷ .60 = $50.00.
2. Gross profit = 45% of sales; cost price = 100% − 45% = 55%.
   Selling price = $27.50 ÷ .55 = $50.00.
3. Selling price = $260.00.
   Overhead expenses = .30 × $260.00 = $78.00.
   Net profit = .10 × $260.00 = $26.00.
   Gross profit = $78.00 + $26.00 = $104.00.
   Cost price = $260.00 − $104.00 = $156.00.
4.

Selling price	$120.88	100%
Cost price	55.00	$45\frac{1}{2}$
Gross profit	$ 65.88	$54\frac{1}{2}$
Overhead expenses	39.29	$32\frac{1}{2}$
Net profit	26.59	22

EXERCISE 20

Chapter Summary

Answers appear at the end of this exercise. If your answers do not agree with those shown, check your calculations before referring to the solutions which follow.

1. Find the selling price of a dress costing $19.50 if the markup is 20% (a) based on cost, and (b) based on selling price.

    (a) _____

    (b) _____

2. The cost of a suit, which sold for $95.00, was $66.50. What was the percent markup based on the selling price?

    _____

3. Find the percent markup, based on cost, on an article costing $128.00 and selling for $160.00.

    _____

4. A merchant bought goods for $760.00 less 20% and 10%. He sold the goods at a markup of 15% of the cost. Find the markup and the retail price.

    Markup _____

    Retail price _____

5. The original selling price of an article was $35.00. It was reduced to $30.25 for clearance. What was the markdown rate (nearest tenth of 1%)?

_____

6. A store sold a chest for $27.50 less 10%. If a gross profit of 30% was made, based on the selling price, what was the cost?

_____

7. The Sonoma Music Co. purchased some radios for $19.00 each on which they used a markup of 40%, based on the selling price. (a) What was the selling price for each radio? (b) How much was the gross profit?

(a) _____

(b) _____

8. The Fashion Shop reduced their fall coats in a postholiday sale by $8\frac{1}{3}\%$ of the marked price. These coats originally sold for $65.00. What was the actual selling price?

_____

9. The Remond Furniture Co. makes a net profit of $6.40, or 8%, based on cost, on a table that sells for $110.00. What are (a) the cost and (b) the operating expenses?

(a) _____

(b) _____

10. Home Bros. mark an article to earn a net profit of 10% on sales. Operating expenses are 22%. What are (a) the selling price if the cost is $74.80, (b) the net profit, and (c) gross profit?

(a) ──────

(b) ──────

(c) ──────

Answers

1. (a) $23.40
   (b) $24.38
2. 30%
3. 25%
4. Markup $ 82.08
   Retail $629.28
5. 13.6%
6. $17.32
7. (a) $31.67
   (b) $12.67
8. $59.58
9. (a) $80.00
   (b) $23.60
10. (a) $110.00
    (b) $ 11.00
    (c) $ 35.20

Solutions

1. (a) markup based on the cost.
   Markup = $19.50 × .20 = $3.90.
   Selling price = $19.50 + $3.90 = $23.40.
   (b) Markup based on the selling price.
   Cost price = 100% − 20% = 80%.
   Cost price also = $19.50.
   Selling price = $19.50 ÷ .80 = $24.38.
2. Markup = $95.00 − $66.50 = $28.50.
   Percent markup = $28.50 ÷ $95.00 = .30 = 30%.
3. Markup = $160.00 − $128.00 = $32.00.
   Percent markup = $32.00 ÷ $128.00 = .25 = 25%.
4. Cost = $760.00 less 20% and 10% = $760.00 × .72 = $547.20.
   Markup = $547.20 × .15 = $82.08.
   Selling price = $547.20 + $82.08 = $629.28.
5. Markup = $35.40 − $30.25 = $4.75.
   Percent markup = $4.75 ÷ $35.00 = .136 = 13.6%.
6. Selling price = $27.50 less 10% = $27.50 − $2.75 = $24.75.
   Gross profit = $24.75 × .30 = $7.43.
   Cost price = $24.75 − $7.43 = $17.32.
7. Selling price = 100%, therefore cost price = 100% − 40% = 60%.
   Cost price also = $19.00.
   Selling price = $19.00 ÷ .60 = $31.67.
   Gross profit = $31.67 − $19.00 = $12.67.
8. $8\frac{1}{3}\% = \frac{1}{12}$ Then the markdown = $\frac{1}{12}$ × $65.00 = $5.42.
   Actual selling price = $65.00 − $5.42 = $59.58.
9. Cost = 100%, then cost = $6.40 ÷ .08 = $80.00.
   Gross profit = $110.00 − $80.00 = $30.00.
   Operating expense = $30.00 − $6.40 = $23.60.
10. Gross profit = 10% + 22% = 32%.
    Selling price = 100%, therefore cost price = 100% − 32% = 68%.
    Cost price also = $74.80.
    (a) Selling price = $74.80 ÷ .68 = $110.00.
    (b) Net profit = 10% of $110.00 = $11.00.
    (c) Gross profit = .32 × $110.00 = $35.20.

CHAPTER FIVE
Depreciation

OBJECTIVES

The means by which depreciation is computed is of special importance to the accountant, the income tax man, and individuals who maintain their own business records and prepare their own income tax returns when several assets are to be considered.

The three most common methods of figuring depreciation are discussed here. Upon completion of this chapter, you will be able to

(1) compute the depreciation and book value for any year in the life of an asset by the straight-line method and sum-of-the-years-digits methods if the original cost, salvage value, and estimated life of the asset are known,
(2) compute the depreciation and book value for any year in the life of an asset by the declining balance method if the cost and life expectancy of the asset are known,
(3) compute the additional first-year depreciation when the original cost is known.
(4) compute the ordinary depreciation for the first year by the straight line, sum-of-digits, and declining balance methods when an additional first-year depreciation is taken if the original cost and salvage value are known,
(5) prepare depreciation schedules by the straight-line, sum-of-the-digits, and declining balance methods.

UNIT 1. INTRODUCTION TO DEPRECIATION

By definition, *depreciation* is a *decrease* in the value of property because of wear, deterioration, or obsolescence. In any business enterprise it is the loss in value of fixed assets such as buildings and equipment.

Good business practice requires a means in the accounting system of providing funds for the replacement of these assets when necessary. How this is done depends on the method used, the type of asset, and the business practice. There are several methods of handling depreciation expense. Any reasonable method may be used and different ones may be used for different assets. The Federal Government, however,

INTRODUCTION TO DEPRECIATION 203

limits the amount that can be claimed for tax purposes. The Federal Government also limits the use of certain methods which are explained in subsequent pages.

The value of any asset at the end of its useful life is called junk, scrap, or salvage value. The following quote is from the Internal Revenue Service, Publication No. 17: "The determination of salvage value depends upon your policy. If it is your policy to dispose of assets which are still in good operating condition, the salvage value may represent a large part of the original cost of the asset. However, if you customarily use an asset until its inherent useful life has been substantially exhausted, salvage value may represent no more than junk value."

1. Assume that an automobile that was bought for $3500 last year is now worth $2200. $3500 − $2200 = $_____ = _____ for the first year.

   H. Spoon bought a typewriter for $465 two years ago. It is now worth $240. The depreciation during the two years is $_____.

   $1300 = depreciation, $465 − $240 = $225

2. If a typewriter that was originally purchased for $470 was worth $60 after a useful life of 5 years, the total depreciation = $_____.

   $470 − $60 = $410

3. The book value of an asset at any time is the difference between the original cost and the total depreciation charges to that date.

   Book value = original cost *less* depreciation to date.

   A desk that originally cost $560 depreciated $300 during a 3-year period. The book value at the end of this period is $_____.

   $560 − $300 = $260.

4. The value of any asset at the end of its useful life is called junk, scrap, or salvage value.

   An adding machine is worth $25 after a useful life of 10 years; $25 is called the _____ of the machine.

   _

   junk, scrap, or salvage value

5. The book value equals the salvage value at the end of the useful life of an asset. A building that cost $35,000 was considered to have a salvage value of $7500 at the end of 30 years.
   Complete the following statements:

   Salvage value = $_____.

   Book value at the end of 30 years = $_____.

   _

   Salvage value = $7500.
   Book value at the end of 30 years = $7500.

The Straight-Line Method

6. The straight-line method of computing depreciation is the simplest. When this method is used, the annual depreciation (amount written off) is the same throughout the useful life of the asset. Assume that a typewriter that cost $560.00 when new will have a useful life of 5 years. Scrap value is estimated to be $63.00.

   Complete the following statements (straight-line method):

   Total depreciation = cost less scrap value = $_____ − $_____ = $_____.

   Annual depreciation = total depreciation ÷ 5 = $_____.

   Depreciation for 2 years = 2 × annual depreciation = 2 × $_____ = $_____.

   for 3 years = 3 × annual depreciation = 3 × $_____ = $_____.

   for 4 years = 4 × annual depreciation = 4 × $_____ = $_____.

   Book value at the end of 3 years = original cost *less* depreciation for 3 years
   = $_____ − $_____ = $_____.

   Book value at the end of 4 years = original cost *less* depreciation for 4 years.
   = $_____ − $_____ = $_____.

   Book value at the end of 5 years = $_____.

   _

   $560.00 − $63.00 = $497.00.
   $497.00 ÷ 5 = $ 99.40.
   2 × $99.40 = $198.80.
   3 × $99.40 = $298.20.
   4 × $99.40 = $397.60.
   $560.00 − $298.20 = $261.80.
   $560.00 − $397.60 = $162.40.
   Book value at the end of 5 years = scrap value or $63.00.

7. Depreciation schedule for example in frame 6.

End of Year	Annual Depreciation	Depreciation to Date	Book Value End of Year
0	$ –	$ –	$560.00
1	99.40	99.40	460.60
2	99.40	198.80	361.20
3	99.40	298.20	261.80
4	99.40	397.60	162.40
5	99.40	497.00	63.00

$497.00 + $63.00 = $560.00.   (scrap value)
Total depreciation + scrap value = original cost.

(a) What is the book value after 3 years? _____.

(b) What is the total depreciation at the end of 2 years? _____.

(a) $261.80, (b) $198.80

8. Adams Co. bought an adding machine for $325.00. It was to be written off (depreciated) in 5 years with a scrap value of $25.00 at the end of that time.

Total depreciation = $_____; annual depreciation = $_____.

Total depreciation = $300.00; annual depreciation = $60.00.

9. Prepare a depreciation schedule for the problem in frame 8.

End of Year	Annual Depreciation	Depreciation to Date	Book Value End of Year
___	$_____	$_____	$_____
___	_____	_____	_____
___	_____	_____	_____
___	_____	_____	_____
___	_____	_____	_____
___	_____	_____	_____

End of Year	Annual Depreciation	Depreciation to Date	Book Value End of Year
0	$ –	$ –	$325.00
1	60.00	60.00	265.00
2	60.00	120.00	205.00
3	60.00	180.00	145.00
4	60.00	240.00	85.00
5	60.00	300.00	25.00

EXERCISE 21

Solve these problems by the straight-line method of depreciation. Answers appear at the end of this exercise. If your answers do not agree with those shown, check your calculations before referring to the solutions that follow.

1. A machine costing $4500.00 is to be written off in 10 years. If it has a scrap value of $250.00 at the end of that time, what are (a) the annual depreciation charge and (b) the book value at the end of 5 years?

    (a) _____

    (b) _____

2. If a machine costing $2700.00 is worth $300.00 at the end of 5 years, find the annual depreciation charge.

    _____

3. An automobile bought for $4600.00 has an estimated life of 5 years, at which time it will have a scrap value of $650.00. What will it be worth at the end of 3 years?

    _____

4. An asset that cost $3000.00 has an estimated life of 5 years and a scrap value of $100.00. Prepare a schedule to show the depreciation to date and the book value for each year.

End of Year	Annual Depreciation	Depreciation to Date	Book Value End of Year
0	...	...	$3000.00
1	$ _____	$ _____	_____
2	_____	_____	_____
3	_____	_____	_____
4	_____	_____	_____
5	_____	_____	_____

5. Furniture purchased for $1750.00 is depreciated over a 10-year period. The estimated scrap value is $300.00. What are (a) the annual depreciation charge and (b) the book value at the end of 6 years?

(a) _____

(b) _____

6. A shop costing $19,200.00 has a life of 30 years. It has no scrap value. (a) What is the annual depreciation charge? (b) What is the book value at the end of 10 years?

(a) _____

(b) _____

Answers

1. (a) $425.00
   (b) $2375.00
2. $480.00
3. $2230.00
4. See solutions.
5. (a) $145.00
   (b) $880.00
6. (a) $640.00
   $12,800.00

Solutions

1. $4500.00 − $250.00 = $4250.00 (total depreciation).
   (a) $4250.00 ÷ 10 = $425.00 (annual depreciation).
   (b) $4500 − (5 × $425.00) = $4500 − $2125.00 = $2375.00.
2. $2700.00 − $300.00 = $2400.00 (total depreciation).
   $2400.00 ÷ 5 = $480.00.
3. $4600.00 − $650.00 = $3950.00 (total depreciation).
   $3950.00 ÷ 5 = $790.00 (annual depreciation).
   $4600.00 − (3 × $790.00) = $4600.00 − $2370.00 = $2230.00.
4.

End of Year	Annual Depreciation	Depreciation to Date	Book Value End of Year
0	–	–	$3000.00
1	$580.00	$ 580.00	2420.00
2	580.00	1160.00	1840.00
3	580.00	1740.00	1260.00
4	580.00	2320.00	680.00
5	580.00	2900.00	100.00

5. $1750.00 − $300.00 = $1450.00 (total depreciation).
   (a) $1450.00 ÷ 10 = $145.00.
   (b) $1750.00 − (6 × $145.00) = $1750.00 − $870.00 = $880.00.
6. (a) $19,200.00 ÷ 30 = $640.00.
   (b) $19,200.00 − (10 × $640.00) = $19,200.00 − $6400.00 = $12,800.00.

UNIT 2. ACCELERATED METHODS OF DEPRECIATION

When the straight-line method of depreciation is used, the annual depreciation is the same for each year. Sometimes, however, a businessman may wish to charge off more to depreciation in the early life of an asset and lesser amounts as it gets older. The sum-of-the-years-digits and the declining-balance methods make this possible.

In many cases these methods are considered advantageous because a quicker recovery of the investment is realized. Also, savings in income taxes are made at a time when it may be most desirable. In addition, there tends to be less disparity between the book value and actual market value when these methods are applied to "style" merchandise such as the automobile on which the reduction in market value is often high during the first years of life.

For tax purposes either of these methods may be used if it meets the requirements of the Internal Revenue Service. Limitations are discussed for each method under its own heading.

10. When an accelerated method of depreciation is used, more is charged off to depreciation in the early life of an asset and lesser amounts as it gets older. When the straight-line method is used, the depreciation is always (the same/not the same) for each year of its useful life.

----

same

11. The declining balance and sum-of-the years-digits methods of depreciation are accelerated methods. With them we would charge off (more/less) depreciation in the early life of the asset and (more/less) as it gets older.

When accelerated methods of depreciation are used, the depreciation for the first year will be (more than/less than/equal to) any other year?

In which year will the amount of depreciation be the least amount? _____

----

more, less, more than, last year

The Sum-of-the-Years-Digits Method

Internal Revenue Service limitations. This method of depreciation may be used only if the property has a useful life of 3 or more years and was acquired new after December 31, 1953, or constructed, reconstructed, or erected after December 31, 1953.

12. If an asset is to be written off in 5 years by the sum-of-the-years-digits method, the digits, i.e., 1, 2, 3, 4, and 5 add to 15; 15 is the sum of the years digits (1 + 2 + 3 + 4 + 5). The first year's depreciation will be the *greatest* or $\frac{5}{15}$ of the total depreciation; the second year's depreciation will be $\frac{4}{15}$, and so on. What fraction of the total depreciation will equal the depreciation for the third, fourth, and fifth years, respectively? _____, _____, _____ .

$\frac{3}{15}, \frac{2}{15}, \frac{1}{15}$.

13. Suppose we bought a bookcase for $95.00 to be depreciated by the sum-of-the-years-digits method for 5 years. The scrap or salvage value was estimated to be $20.00.
Total depreciation = $95.00 − $20.00 = $75.00.
Sum of digits = 15 (see frame 12).
Depreciation for the first year = $\frac{5}{15}$ × $75.00 = $_____ .

second year = $\frac{4}{15}$ × $75.00 = _____ .

third year = $\frac{3}{15}$ × $75.00 = _____ .

fourth year = $\frac{2}{15}$ × $75.00 = _____ .

fifth year = $\frac{1}{15}$ × $75.00 = _____ .

$25.00
 20.00
 15.00
 10.00
  5.00
―――――
$75.00

14. What is the sum of the digits for 4, 6, and 8 years? ____, ____, ____ .

10,   21,   36

15. When an asset is written off in 5 years, it is a simple matter to add the digits 1 to 5 inclusive, but it becomes cumbersome if the life expectancy is, for example, 20 years. The sum of any series of this kind may be found quickly by applying the formula

$$S = \frac{n^2 + n}{2},$$

where n represents the number of years in which the asset is depreciated:

$n^2 = n \times n$. If $n = 3$, then $n^2 = 3 \times 3$.
　　　　　　　If $n = 7$, then $n^2 = 7 \times 7$, and so on.

Examples: Life expectancy

　　5 years　　$S = \dfrac{5^2 + 5}{2} = \dfrac{(5 \times 5) + 5}{2} = 15.$

　　6 years　　$S = \dfrac{6^2 + 6}{2} = 21.$

　　15 years　　$S = \dfrac{15^2 + 15}{2} = 120.$

Complete:　20 years　　$S =$ 　　　　　$=$ _____.

　　　　　　　30 years　　$S =$ 　　　　　$=$ _____.

_____

20 years, $S = \dfrac{20^2 + 20}{2} = 210.$

30 years, $S = \dfrac{30^2 + 30}{2} = 465.$

16. If the sum-of-the-years-digits for 15 years is 120, the depreciation for the first year $= \frac{15}{120} \times$ total depreciation.

Second year　　$=$ _____ $\times$ total depreciation.

Third year　　　$=$ _____ $\times$ total depreciation.

Fourteenth year $=$ _____ $\times$ total depreciation.

Last year　　　$=$ _____ $\times$ total depreciation.

_____

Second year　　$= \frac{14}{120} \times$ total depreciation.
Third year　　　$= \frac{13}{120} \times$ total depreciation.
Fourteenth year $= \frac{2}{120} \times$ total depreciation.
Last year　　　$= \frac{1}{120} \times$ total depreciation.

17. If an asset was depreciated $3680.00 in 8 years by the sum-of-the-years-digits, what was the depreciation for the third year? The fifth year?

   $n = 8$ $S = $ _____ $=$ ___.

   Depreciation for third year = ___ × _____ = $_____.

   Depreciation for fifth year = ___ × $_____ = $_____.

   $S = \dfrac{8^2 + 8}{2} = \dfrac{64 + 8}{2} = 36$

   Third year depreciation = $\frac{6}{36}$ × $3680.00 = $613.33.
   Fifth year depreciation = $\frac{4}{36}$ × $3680.00 = $408.89.

18. A typewriter cost $650.00. It is to be written off in 5 years with a scrap value of $50.00. Prepare a depreciation schedule by the sum-of-the-years-digits method.

DEPRECIATION SCHEDULE

End of Year	Annual Depreciation	Depreciation to Date	Book Value End of Year
0	–	–	$650.00
1	$200.00	$200.00	450.00
2	160.00	360.00	290.00
3	120.00	480.00	170.00
4	80.00	560.00	90.00
5	40.00	600.00	50.00 scrap value

Solution: $S = \dfrac{5^2 + 5}{2} = 15.$

Total depreciation = $650.00 − $50.00 = $600.00.

Annual depreciation:

First year $\frac{5}{15}$ × $600 = $200
Second year $\frac{4}{15}$ × $600 = $160
Third year $\frac{3}{15}$ × $600 = $120
Fourth year $\frac{2}{15}$ × $600 = $ 80
Fifth year $\frac{1}{15}$ × $600 = $ 40

Total depreciation: $600

Complete the following schedule for a typewriter that cost $525.00 to be written off in 5 years with a scrap value of $75.00. Use the sum-of-the-years-digits method of depreciation.

DEPRECIATION SCHEDULE

End of Year	Annual Depreciation	Depreciation to Date	Book Value End of Year
0	$ _____	$ _____	$ _____
1	_____	_____	_____
2	_____	_____	_____
3	_____	_____	_____
4	_____	_____	_____
5	_____	_____	75.00

Total depreciation = _____ . S (sum of digits) = _____ .

Yearly depreciation, first   year _____ × _____ = _____ .

Yearly depreciation, second year _____ × _____ = _____ .

Yearly depreciation, third   year _____ × _____ = _____ .

Yearly depreciation, fourth year _____ × _____ = _____ .

Yearly depreciation, fifth   year _____ × _____ = _____ .

End of Year	Annual Depreciation	Depreciation to Date	Book Value End of Year
0	–	–	$525.00
1	$150.00	$150.00	375.00
2	120.00	270.00	255.00
3	90.00	360.00	165.00
4	60.00	420.00	105.00
5	30.00	450.00	75.00

19. Refer to frame 18.

Notice that the depreciation for the first year $= \frac{5}{15} \times \$600.00 = \$200.00$.

and the depreciation for the second year $= \frac{4}{15} \times \$600.00 = \$160.00$.

Total depreciation for the *first 2 years* $= \frac{9}{15} \times \$600.00 = \$360.00$.

Total depreciation for the *first 3 years* $= \frac{12}{15} \times \$600.00 = \$\rule{1cm}{0.15mm}$.

Total depreciation for the *first 4 years* $= \rule{1cm}{0.15mm} \times \$600.00 = \$\rule{1cm}{0.15mm}$.

Book value = original cost less depreciation to date.

Book value, end of 2 years = $\rule{2cm}{0.15mm}$ − $\rule{2cm}{0.15mm}$ = $\rule{2cm}{0.15mm}$.

Book value, end of 3 years = $\rule{2cm}{0.15mm}$ − $\rule{2cm}{0.15mm}$ = $\rule{2cm}{0.15mm}$.

Book value, end of 4 years = $\rule{2cm}{0.15mm}$ − $\rule{2cm}{0.15mm}$ = $\rule{2cm}{0.15mm}$.

- -

Total depreciation for the first 3 years $= \$480.00$.
Total depreciation for the first 4 years $= \frac{14}{15} \times \$600.00 = \$560.00$.
Book value, end of 2 years = $\$650.00 - \$360.00 = \$290.00$
Book value, end of 3 years = $\$650.00 - \$480.00 = \$170.00$.
Book value, end of 4 years = $\$650.00 - \$560.00 = \$90.00$.

20. A piece of furniture costing $725.00 has an estimated salvage value of $25.00 at the end of 10 years. Find (a) the depreciation for the fourth year and (b) the book value at the end of 4 years.

S (sum of digits) = $\rule{1cm}{0.15mm}$.

Total depreciation = $\rule{2cm}{0.15mm}$.

(a) Depreciation for the fourth year = $\rule{2cm}{0.15mm}$.

[Depreciation for first 4 years (expressed as fractional part of total depreciation) = 10/ + 9/ + 8/ + 7/ = $\rule{1cm}{0.15mm}$.]

(b) Book value, end of 4 years = $725.00 − depreciation for first 4 years

$= \$725.00 - (\rule{1cm}{0.15mm} \times \$\rule{2cm}{0.15mm})$

$= \$725.00 - \$\rule{2cm}{0.15mm} = \$\rule{2cm}{0.15mm}$

- -

$$S = \frac{10^2 + 10}{2} = 55.$$

Total depreciation = $725.00 − $25.00 = $700.00.
(a) Depreciation for the fourth year = $\frac{7}{55}$ × $700.00 = $89.09.
Depreciation for the first 4 years = $\frac{34}{55}$.
(b) Book value, end of 4 years = $725.00 − ($\frac{34}{55}$ × $700.00) = $725.00 − $432.73 = $292.27.

EXERCISE 22

Solve the following problems by the sum-of-the-years-digits method of depreciation. Answers appear at the end of this exercise. If your answers do not agree with those shown, check your calculations before referring to the solutions that follow.

1. A jeep costing $2730.00 has an estimated salvage value of $250.00 at the end of 5 years. Find the depreciation for the (a) second year and (b) fourth year.

    (a) _____

    (b) _____

2. An adding machine costing $420.00 has an estimated life of 6 years. At the end of that time its scrap value equaled 12% of its original cost. (a) How much was the depreciation for the third year? (b) What was the book value at the end of the second year?

    (a) _____

    (b) _____

3. Set up a depreciation schedule for a $900.00 asset whose life is 4 years. Scrap value is estimated at $75.00.

End of Year	Annual Depreciation	Depreciation to Date	Book Value End of Year
0	$ —	$ —	$900.00
1	_____	_____	_____
2	_____	_____	_____
3	_____	_____	_____
4	_____	_____	_____
5	_____	_____	_____
Total	$_____	xxxx	xxxx

4. A merchant buys $8000.00 worth of store fixtures which he estimates will last 20 years. At the end of this time they will be worthless. (a) What is the amount charged to depreciation at the end of the first year? (b) What is the book value at the end of the first year?

(a) _____

(b) _____

5. Find the book value of the store fixtures in problem 4 at the end of 15 years (*Hint*. Depreciation = 1 + 2 + 3 + 4 + 5 or 15 parts for last 5 years.)

_____

Answers

1. (a) $661.33
   (b) $330.67
3. See solutions.
5. $571.43

2. (a) $ 70.40
   (b) $ 226.40
4. (a) $ 761.90
   (b) $7238.10

Solutions

1. Total depreciation = $2730.00 − $250.00 = $2480.00.

   Sum of years digits = $\dfrac{5^2 + 5}{2} = 15$.

   (a) Depreciation for the second year = $\frac{4}{15}$ ths of the total
   Depreciation = $\frac{4}{15} \times \$2480 = \$661.33$.
   (b) Depreciation for the fourth year = $\frac{2}{15}$ ths of the total depreciation = $\frac{2}{15} \times \$2480 = \$330.67$

2. Scrap value = 12% of cost = .12 × $420 = $50.40.
   Total depreciation = $420.00 − $50.40 = $369.60.

   Sum of years digits = $\dfrac{6^2 + 6}{2} = 21$.

   (a) Depreciation for the third year = $\frac{4}{21} \times \$369.60 = \$70.40$.
   (b) Book value at the end of the second year = cost − depreciation to date
   = $420.00 − ($\frac{11}{21}$* × $369.60) = $420.00 − $193.60 = $226.40.

3.
End of Year	Annual Depreciation	Depreciation to Date	Book Value End of Year
0	$ –	$ –	$900.00
1	330.00	330.00	570.00
2	247.50	577.50	322.50
3	165.00	742.50	157.50
4	82.50	825.00	75.00
Total	$825.00		

4. $S = \dfrac{20^2 + 20}{2} = 210$.

   Depreciation for the first year = $\frac{20}{210} \times \$8000.00 = \$761.90$.
   Book value end of first year = $8000.00 − $761.90 = $7238.10.

5. At the end of 15 years $\frac{195}{210}$ ths will have been depreciated. This leaves $\frac{15}{210}$ ths at the end of the 15th year. Therefore the book value at the end of the 15th year = $\frac{15}{210} \times \$8000 = \$571.43$.

---

*First year = $\frac{6}{21}$, second year = $\frac{5}{21}$.

UNIT 3. ACCELERATED METHODS OF DEPRECIATION

The Declining-Balance Method

Internal Revenue Service Limitations. The maximum rate that may be used in computing depreciation by this method is *twice* the straight-line rate, provided that the property has a useful life of three or more years and was acquired new after December 31, 1953, or constructed, reconstructed, or erected after December 31, 1953. One and one-half times the straight-line rate is the maximum rate that may be used on tangible property that does not meet the above requirements if this method results in a reasonable allowance for depreciation. This includes new or used property acquired before January 1, 1954, and used property acquired after December 31, 1953.

21. The maximum rate of depreciation by this method is twice the annual rate by the straight-line method.

Suppose the life of an asset	=	5 years	30 years	20 years
The straight-line rate	=	$\frac{1}{5}$ or 20%	$\frac{1}{30}$ or $3\frac{1}{3}$%	$\frac{1}{20}$ or 5%
The maximum declining-balance rate	=	$\frac{2}{5}$ or 40%	$\frac{2}{30}$ or $6\frac{2}{3}$%	$\frac{2}{20}$ or 10%

    What is the maximum declining-balance rate, expressed as a fraction and percent, for an asset that is written off in 25 years? 50 years? 10 years? 8 years?

    Fraction ____ ____%; Fraction ____ ____%; Fraction ____ ____%

    _____

    $\frac{2}{25}$ or 8%, $\frac{2}{50}$ or 4%, $\frac{2}{10}$ or 20%, $\frac{2}{8}$ or 25%

22. In the declining-balance method of depreciation salvage value is ignored when the depreciation for any year is calculated.

    Example: Suppose a machine that cost $750.00 were depreciated by this method for 10 years? Salvage value is estimated to be $50.00.

    Straight-line rate = 10%.
    Declining balance rate = 20%.
    Depreciation for first year = .20 × $750.00 = $150.00.

    What would the depreciation be for the first year on a machine that cost $600.00 for 10 years with a salvage value of $75.00? (Use 2 × the straight-line rate.)

    ____ × _____ = _____ .

    _____

    .20 × $600 = $120.

23. The depreciation for each year *after* the first is calculated on the book value at the end of the preceding year.

An asset that cost $450.00 was to be written off in 5 years. Salvage value was estimated at $50.00. Find the depreciation and book value for each year, using the declining balance method.

Straight-line rate = 20%;   2 × straight-line rate = 40%.

Cost of asset	$450.00	
Depreciation, first year	180.00	(40% of $450.00)
Book value, end of first year	$270.00	
Depreciation, second year	108.00	(40% of $270.00)
Book value, end of second year	$162.00	
Depreciation, third year	_____	(40% of _____)
Book value, end of third year	$	
Depreciation, fourth year	_____	(40% of _____)
Book value, end of fourth year	$ 58.32	
Depreciation, fifth year	8.32*	
Book value, end of fifth year	$ 50.00	salvage value

- -

Depreciation, third year	$64.80	(40% of $162.00)
Book value, end of third year	$97.20	
Depreciation, fourth year	38.88	(40% of $97.20)
Book value, end of fourth year	$58.32	

---

*40% of $58.32 = $23.33. If this figure were used, however, it would reduce the book value at the end of 5 years to less than the estimated salvage value. Therefore, no more than $8.32 may be charged off in the fifth year.

24. Complete the schedule below, using the information in frame 23.

Depreciation Schedule for Problem in Frame 23

End of Year	Annual Depreciation	Depreciation to Date	Book Value End of Year
0	—	—	$450.00
1	_____	_____	_____
2	_____	_____	_____
3	_____	_____	_____
4	_____	_____	_____
5	_____	_____	50.00 (salvage value)

- -

End of Year	Annual Depreciation	Depreciation to Date	Book Value End of Year
0	—	—	$450.00
1	$180.00	$180.00	270.00
2	108.00	288.00	162.00
3	64.80	352.80	97.20
4	38.88	391.68	58.32
5	8.32	400.00	50.00 (salvage value)

25. A piece of machinery that cost $1500 is to be depreciated by the declining-balance method for 20 years with a salvage value of $150 at the end of that time (use 2 × the straight-line rate). Find the depreciation and book value for the first two years.

   Straight-line rate of depreciation = ____%.
   Declining-balance rate of depreciation = ____%.
   Original cost $_____
   Depreciation, first year   _____   (____% of $_____)
   Book value, end of first year $_____   (original cost less depreciation)

   Depreciation, second year   _____   (____% of $_____)
   Book value, end of second year $_____   (book value end of first year less depreciation for second year)

Straight-line rate = 5%.
Declining balance rate = 10%.
Original cost $1500.00
Depreciation, first year   150.00   (10% of $1500.00)
Book value, end of first year $1350.00
Depreciation, second year   135.00   (10% of $1350.00)
Book value, end of second year $1215.00

ACCELERATED METHODS OF DEPRECIATION

26. Prepare a depreciation schedule by the declining-balance method for a calculating machine that cost $1200 with a salvage value of $150 at the end of 5 years of useful life. Use twice the straight-line rate.

Depreciation Schedule

End of Year	Annual Depreciation	Depreciation to Date	Book Value End of Year
0	—	—	$1200.00
1	_____	_____	_____
2	_____	_____	_____
3	_____	_____	_____
4	_____	_____	_____
5	_____	_____	_____

Rate = _____%

End of Year	Annual Depreciation	Depreciation to Date	Book Value End of Year
0	—	—	$1200.00
1	$480.00	$ 480.00	720.00
2	288.00	768.00	432.00
3	172.80	940.80	259.20
4	103.68	1044.48	155.52
5	5.52*	1050.00	150.00

Rate = 40%

*If more than this amount was taken, the salvage value would be less than $150.00.

EXERCISE 23

Solve the following problems using the declining-balance method of depreciation. Use twice the straight-line rate for all of these problems. Answers appear at the end of this exercise. If your answers do not agree with those shown, check your calculations before referring to the solutions that follow.

1. A piece of furniture was acquired for $450.00. It is to be written off in 10 years. The salvage value is estimated at $50.00. Find the book value at the end of 4 years.

   _____

2. A machine costing $677.50 will last 10 years and have a scrap value of $50.00 (a) Find the book value at the end of 3 years. (b) How much would the book value be if the straight-line method was used?

   (a) _____

   (b) _____

3. An asset costing $3000 has a life of 5 years. What is the depreciation for the third year?

   _____

4. Using a rate of 20%, prepare a depreciation schedule for the first 5 years for a machine that cost $6000.

End of Year	Annual Depreciation	Depreciation to Date	Book Value End of Year
0	$ —	$ —	$6000.00
1	_____	_____	_____
2	_____	_____	_____
3	_____	_____	_____
4	_____	_____	_____
5	_____	_____	_____

5. What rate should be used for assets that are to be written off in 8 years? 15 years? 30 years? 12 years?

_____

_____

_____

_____

6. Calculate the depreciation for the third year on an asset worth $500 if its life is estimated to be 8 years?

_____

Answers

1. $184.32   2. (a) $346.88   3. $432.00
4. See solutions   (b) $489.25   5. 25%
6. $70.31 $13\frac{1}{3}$

                                                                                                                                                $6\frac{2}{3}$

                                                                                                                                                $16\frac{2}{3}$

Solutions

1. Since the straight-line rate is 10%, the declining-balance rate is 20%.

    Cost $450.00
    less   90.00   depreciation first year (20% of $450.00)
             $360.00   book value at end of first year
    less   72.00   depreciation second year (20% of $360.00)
             $288.00   book value at end of second year
    less   57.60   depreciation third year (20% of $288.00)
             $230.40   book value at end of third year
    less   46.08   depreciation fourth year (20% of $230.40)
             $184.32   book value at end of fourth year

2. Straight-line rate of depreciation = 10%.
   Declining-balance rate of depreciation = 20%.

   (a) Cost $677.50
       less   135.50   depreciation first year (20% of $677.50)
              $542.00   book value at end of first year
       less   108.40   depreciation second year (20% of $542.00)
              $433.60   book value at end of second year
       less   86.72   depreciation third year (20% of $433.60)
              $346.88   book value at end of third year

   (b) Total depreciation = $677.50 − $50.00 = $627.50.
       depreciation for 3 years = 30% of $627.50 = $188.25.
       book value by straight-line method = $677.50 − $188.25 = $489.25.

3. Straight-line rate = 20%; therefore declining-balance rate = 40%.

   Cost $3000.00
   less   1200.00   depreciation for first year (40% of $3000.00)
         $1800.00   book value at end of first year
   less   720.00   depreciation for second year (40% of $1800.00)
         $1080.00   book value at end of second year
            432.00   depreciation for third year (40% of $1080.00)

4.

End of Year	Annual Depreciation	Depreciation to Date	Book Value End of Year
0	$ —	$ —	$6000.00
1	1200.00	1200.00	4800.00
2	960.00	2160.00	3840.00
3	768.00	2928.00	3072.00
4	614.40	3542.40	2457.60
5	491.52	4033.92	1966.08

5. If the rate for the declining-balance method is twice the straight-line rate, the rate for 8 years = 25%, for 15 years = $13\frac{1}{3}$%, for 30 years = $6\frac{2}{3}$%, and for 12 years = $16\frac{2}{3}$%.

6. The rate for 8 years on a straight-line basis = $12\frac{1}{2}$%. Therefore the declining-balance rate = 25%.

   Cost $500.00
   less   125.00   depreciation for first year (25% of $500.00)
           $375.00   book value at end of first year
   less   93.75   depreciation for second year (25% of $375.00)
           $281.25   book value at end of second year
             70.31   depreciation for third year

UNIT 4. ADDITIONAL FIRST-YEAR DEPRECIATION

1. The Internal Revenue Service permits an additional first-year allowance for depreciation on tangible personal property if it has a life of more than six years. *This amounts to 20% of the original cost.* The allowance may be applied to any method of depreciation but must be claimed during the first year of ownership.

   What would the additional first-year depreciation be on a truck that cost $4700.00? $_____. On a piece of machine purchased for $8900.00? $_____.

   _

   20% or $\frac{1}{5}$ of $4700.00 = $940.00.
   20% or $\frac{1}{5}$ of $8900.00 = $1780.00.

A desk calculator that cost $1205.00 is to be written off in 10 years. The salvage value is estimated at $100.00. An additional first-year depreciation is to be taken. A depreciation schedule for the three methods discussed in this chapter is shown on page 230.

Under the straight-line method the annual ordinary depreciation shown above is $86.40, computed as follows:

(a) Deduct the salvage value and additional first-year depreciation allowance from the cost; i.e., $1205.00 − ($100.00 + $241.00) = $864.00.
(b) Divide $864.00 by 10 (years of useful life); i.e., $864.00 ÷ 10 = $86.40.

Under the sum-of-the-years-digits method the sum of the years digits is 55. The annual ordinary depreciation shown in the schedule is computed as follows:

(a) Deduct the salvage value and additional first-year depreciation allowance from the cost; i.e., $1205.00 − ($100.00 + $241.00) = $864.00.
(b) The ordinary annual depreciation for the first year would $= \frac{10}{55} \times $864.00 = 157.09; for the second year would $= \frac{9}{55} \times $864.00 = 141.38, and so on.

Under the declining-balance method the annual ordinary depreciation rate equals 20% (twice the straight-line rate) for this example. The salvage value is ignored. The ordinary depreciation for the first year is 20% of the cost *after* the additional first-year depreciation is deducted; i.e.,

First-year ordinary depreciation $= .20 \times$ (cost − additional first year depreciation)
$= .20 \times ($1205.00 − $241.00)$
$= .20 \times $964.00 = $192.80;$
Second-year ordinary depreciation $= .20 \times ($964.00 − $192.80)$
$= .20 \times $771.20 = $154.24,$ and so on.

ANNUAL DEPRECIATION

Year	Straight-Line	Declining-Balance	Sum-of-the-Years-Digits
First-yr additional depreciation (20% of original cost)	$ 241.00	$ 241.00	$ 241.00
First-yr ordinary depreciation	86.40	192.80	157.09
Total first-yr depreciation	$ 327.40	$ 433.80	$ 398.09
Second-yr depreciation	86.40	154.24	141.38
Third-yr depreciation	86.40	123.39	125.67
Fourth-yr depreciation	86.40	98.71	109.96
Fifth-yr depreciation	86.40	78.97	94.26
Sixth-yr depreciation	86.40	63.18	78.55
Seventh-yr depreciation	86.40	50.54	62.83
Eighth-yr depreciation	86.40	40.43	47.13
Ninth-yr depreciation	86.40	32.35	31.42
Tenth-yr depreciation	86.40	25.88	15.71
Total depreciation	$1105.00	$1101.49	$1105.00
Salvage value	$100.00	$103.51	$100.00

2. (a) Under the straight-line method the ordinary depreciation is based on the [original cost less salvage value/original cost less (additional first-year depreciation + salvage value)].

   (b) Under the sum-of-the-digits method the ordinary depreciation is based on the [original cost less salvage value/original cost less (additional first-year depreciation + salvage value)].

   (c) Under the declining-balance method the ordinary depreciation is based on the [original cost/original cost less (additional first-year depreciation)].

(a) original cost less (additional first-year depreciation + salvage value)
(b) original cost less (additional first-year depreciation + salvage value)
(c) original cost less additional first-year depreciation

ADDITIONAL FIRST-YEAR DEPRECIATION 231

3. Mr. Johns purchased a truck for $4300 with a salvage value of $500 at the end of 10 years. If the owner took an additional first-year depreciation, what would the ordinary annual depreciation be by (a) the straight-line method (b) the sum-of-the-digits method for the first year?

Original cost = $_____.
Additional first-year depreciation = ____% of $_____ = $_____.
Original cost − (additional first-year depreciation + salvage value) = $_____.

(a) Ordinary annual depreciation = $_____ ÷ 10 = $_____.
(b) $S = 55$.
   Ordinary annual depreciation (first year) = $\frac{10}{55}$ × $_____ = $_____.

- -

Original cost = $4300.
Additional first-year depreciation = 20% of $4300 = $860.
Original cost − (additional first-year depreciation + salvage value) = $2940.
(a) $2940 ÷ 10 = $294.00.
(b) $\frac{10}{55}$ × $2940.00 = $534.55.

4. Suppose a desk that cost $600 had a useful life of 8 years and a salvage value of $100.00. What would the amount of the additional first-year depreciation be if it were taken, and what would the ordinary annual depreciation for the first year be if the declining-balance method were used?

Straight-line rate = _____%.
Declining-balance rate = _____% (use 2 × the straight-line rate).
Additional first-year depreciation = _____.
Ordinary depreciation first year = _____% of (original cost − additional first-year depreciation).
   = _____ × $_____ = $_____.

- -

Straight-line rate = $12\frac{1}{2}$%.
Declining-balance rate = 25%.
Additional first-year depreciation = 20% of $600 = $120.
Ordinary depreciation first year = 25% of ($600 − $120) = .25 × $480 = $120.

EXERCISE 24

Chapter Summary

Answers appear at the end of this exercise. If your answers do not agree with those shown, check your calculations before referring to the solutions that follow.

1. (a) What is the annual depreciation, using the straight-line method, on a building worth $65,000 if it is built to last 40 years and has an estimated salvage value of $12,000? (b) What would the accumulated depreciation be after 10 years? (c) What would the book value equal after 25 years?

    (a) _____

    (b) _____

    (c) _____

2. In problem 1, if an additional first-year depreciation is taken, how much is the regular annual depreciation?

    _____

3. Property acquired for $40,000 has an estimated life of 10 years. If the scrap value is $2000, find (a) the depreciation for the second year and (b) the book value at the end of 8 years. Use the sum-of-the-years-digits method.

    (a) _____

    (b) _____

4. An asset cost $6000 and has an estimated life of 8 years. It has no salvage value. Find the depreciation for the first year by using (a) the straight-line method, (b) the declining-balance method, and (c) the sum-of-the-years-digits method.

    (a) _____

    (b) _____

    (c) _____

5. A truck cost $5600 and has an estimated trade-in value of $800 at the end of 5 years. Find the book value at the end of 3 years by using the declining-balance method.

_____

6. Prepare a depreciation schedule for 5 years by each of the methods discussed in this chapter for the following example.

Mr. Haines bought a tractor for $2895.00. The estimated salvage value at the end of the 10 years is $495.00. Use the schedule forms that follow.

(a) Straight-line

Year	Annual Depreciation	Depreciation to Date	Book Value
			$2895.00
1	$_____	$_____	_____
2	_____	_____	_____
3	_____	_____	_____
4	_____	_____	_____
5	_____	_____	_____

(b) Sum-of-the-digits

Year	Annual Depreciation	Depreciation to Date	Book Value
			$2895.00
1	$_____	$_____	_____
2	_____	_____	_____
3	_____	_____	_____
4	_____	_____	_____
5	_____	_____	_____

(c) Declining-balance

Year	Annual Depreciation	Depreciation to Date	Book Value
			$2895.00
1	$_____	$_____	_____
2	_____	_____	_____
3	_____	_____	_____
4	_____	_____	_____
5	_____	_____	_____

Answers

1. (a) $1325.00
   (b) $13,250.00
   (c) $31,875.00
2. $1000.00
3. (a) $6218.18
   (b) $4072.73
4. (a) $750.00
   (b) $1500.00
   (c) $1333.33
5. $1209.60
6. See solutions

Solutions

1. Total depreciation = $65,000 − $12,000 = $53,000.
   Annual depreciation = $53,000 ÷ 40 = $1325.
   Depreciation for 10 years = 10 × $1325 = $13,250.
   Depreciation for 25 years = 25 × $1325 = $33,125.
   Book value at the end of 25 years = $65,000 − $33,125 = $31,875.

2. Additional first-year depreciation = 20% of cost = 20% of $65,000 = $13,000.
   Total depreciation to be written off exclusive of additional first-year depreciation = $65,000 − [$13,000 + $12,000 (scrap value)] = $40,000.
   Annual depreciation = $40,000 ÷ 40 = $1000.

3. $S = \dfrac{10^2 + 10}{2} = 55.$

   (a) Second-year depreciation = $\frac{9}{55}$ × $38,000 = $6218.18.
   (b) Depreciation for 8 years leaves a book value of $\frac{3}{55}$ths of cost plus the scrap value; i.e., book value at the end of 8 years = ($\frac{3}{55}$ × $38,000) + $2000 = $4072.73.

CHAPTER SUMMARY   235

4. Cost of asset = $6000. Estimated life is 8 years.
   (a) Annual depreciation (straight-line method) = $6000 ÷ 8 = $750.00.
   (b) Depreciation for the first year (declining-balance method) = $6000 ÷ 4 = $1500.00.
   (c) $S = \dfrac{8^2 + 8}{2} = 36$. The first year = $\frac{8}{36}$ or $\frac{2}{9}$ of $6000 = $1333.33.

5. Cost $5600.00. Rate = 40%.
   Book value, end of first year = $5600 − (40% of $5600) = $3360.
   Book value, end of second year = $3360 − (40% of $3360) = $2016.
   Book value, end of third year = $2016 − (40% of $2016) = $1209.60.

6. (a) Straight-line

		Year	Annual Depreciation	Depreciation to Date	Book Value
Cost	$2895.00				$2895.00
Salvage value	495.00	1	$240.00	$ 240.00	2655.00
Total depreciation	$2400.00	2	240.00	480.00	2415.00
Annual depreciation =		3	240.00	720.00	2175.00
$2400.00 ÷ 10 = $240		4	240.00	960.00	1935.00
		5	240.00	1200.00	1695.00

(b) Sum-of-the-digits

$S = \dfrac{10^2 + 10}{2} = 55$

Total depreciation = $2400.00
First-year depreciation = $\frac{10}{55}$ × $2400
Second-year depreciation = $\frac{9}{55}$ × $2400
Third-year depreciation = $\frac{8}{55}$ × $2400
Fourth-year depreciation = $\frac{7}{55}$ × $2400
Fifth-year depreciation = $\frac{6}{55}$ × $2400

Year	Annual Depreciation	Depreciation to Date	Book Value
			$2895.00
1	$436.36	436.36	2458.64
2	392.73	829.09	2065.91
3	349.09	1178.18	1716.82
4	305.45	1483.63	1411.37
5	261.82	1745.45	1149.55

(c) Declining-balance
   Since the time is 10 years, the rate = 2 × straight-line rate = 2 × 10% = 20%.

Year	Annual Depreciation	Depreciation to Date	Book Value	
			$2895.00	
1	$579.00	$ 579.00	2316.00	20% of $2895.00
2	463.20	1042.20	1852.80	20% of $2316.00
3	370.56	1412.76	1482.24	20% of $1852.80
4	296.45	1709.21	1185.79	20% of $1482.24
5	237.16	1946.37	948.63	20% of $1185.79

CHAPTER SIX
Payroll

OBJECTIVES

Before 1935 the preparation and maintenance of payroll records were fairly simple, but, with the passage of the Social Security Act of August 14, 1935, the Fair Labor Standards Act of 1938, and the Current Tax Payment Act of 1943, as well as state unemployment compensation laws, the problem of handling payroll records became increasingly complex.

Many records are necessary to satisfy the requirements of these Federal and state laws. Consequently, the work of the payroll clerk has expanded greatly. Payroll records are maintained in accordance with the kind and size of the business.

When you have completed this chapter, you will be able to

(1) compute regular, overtime, and gross earnings on an hourly basis,
(2) compute hourly rates for employees paid on a weekly or monthly basis,
(3) compute earnings on a weekly or monthly basis for regular and overtime pay,
(4) compute payroll deductions required by Federal law (FICA taxes—Social Security taxes), and Federal Income Tax Withholding,
(5) compute net earnings for any specified period of time on an hourly, weekly, or monthly basis,
(6) compute earnings based on a piece-rate payroll system,
(7) compute earnings based on commissions,
(8) prepare a cash sheet for a payroll paid in cash,
(9) prepare a change memorandum,
(10) prepare a payroll or (a) an hourly rate and (b) a piece-rate basis.

UNIT 1. TIME PAYMENT PAYROLL SYSTEM

When an employee is paid on a time basis, he may be paid by the hour, the week, every 2 weeks, the month, or the year. The term *salary* is usually applied to compensation based on a monthly, semimonthly, or yearly basis, whereas the term *wages* is applied to shorter periods.

Regular Earnings

1. *Regular* earnings are based on a rate per hour; for example, if a man works a total of 30 hours in a week and is paid at the rate of $4.90 an hour, his regular earnings are 30 × $4.90 or $147.00.

   (a) What would the regular earnings be of a man who works a total of 35 hours in a week at $4.25 an hour? _____

   (b) A. Johnson worked $36\frac{1}{2}$ hours during the week at $6.55 an hour. How much were his regular earnings for the week? _____

   (a) 35 × $4.25 = $148.75, (b) 36.5 × $6.55 = 239.075 = $239.08

Overtime Earnings

Overtime represents the number of hours worked beyond the normal time prescribed by law or agreement; for example, if the working day consists of 8 hours, then any time worked in excess of 8 hours is overtime.

Assume that Mr. Jones worked for the A & R Company. When employed, he was told that the working day began at 8:30 A.M. and stopped at 5:30 P.M., with one hour for lunch, 5 days a week. This represents an 8-hour day and a 40-hour week. If he works more than 8 hours in any day or more than 40 hours during any week, he is working over time.

If Mr. Jones worked 10 hours on Monday, 9 hours on Wednesday and 8 hours on all other days during a certain week; he worked 3 hours overtime.

2. Mary Hopkins was employed as a clerk. Her working day was 7 hours, 5 days a week. If she worked 8 hours on Monday, 9 hours on Tuesday, $7\frac{1}{2}$ hours on Thursday, and 7 hours each on Wednesday and Friday, she worked _____ total hours during the week and _____ hours overtime.

   Total hours worked = $8 + 9 + 7 + 7\frac{1}{2} + 7 = 38\frac{1}{2}$.
   Total hours overtime = $38\frac{1}{2} - 35 = 3\frac{1}{2}$.

The rate for overtime is always greater than the regular pay rate. It may be $1\frac{1}{2}$ or 2 times the regular rate or some other factor determined by company policy. The number of decimal places (degree of accuracy) to which the overtime rate is carried, as well as the manner in which payroll records are compiled and maintained, also depends on company policy.

Let us assume that *overtime** is paid at the rate of $1\frac{1}{2}$ times the regular rate.

Example A: Regular rate = $4.90.
Overtime rate = $1\frac{1}{2}$ × $4.90 = $7.35.

Example B: Regular rate = $4.15.
Overtime rate = $1\frac{1}{2}$ × $4.15 = $6.225 (do not round off to the nearest cent).

3. What are the overtime hourly rates for the following? (Overtime is $1\frac{1}{2}$ × the regular rate.)
   (a) Regular rate = $5.05.

   Overtime rate = _____.
   (b) Regular rate = $3.50.

   Overtime rate = _____.

- -

(a) $1\frac{1}{2}$ × $5.05 = $7.575, (b) $1\frac{1}{2}$ × $3.50 = $5.25.

---

*In some cases double the regular rate applies for work on Sundays and holidays or for night work. The manner in which overtime is computed, if it is paid at all, depends on the law as it applies to some employees and businesses.

4. Mr. Jackson worked in a mill at $5.50 an hour. The regular working week (Monday through Friday) was 40 hours. He was paid $1\frac{1}{2}$ times the regular rate for any overtime during the work week. If, however, he worked on Saturday or Sunday, he was paid double the regular rate.

Regular rate = $5.50
Overtime rate at $1\frac{1}{2}$ × regular rate = 1.5 × $5.50 = $8.25
Overtime rate at 2 × regular rate = 2 × $5.50 = $11.00

What are the overtime hourly rates for the following?

(a) Regular rate = $5.07.

    Overtime rate ($1\frac{1}{2}$ × regular rate) = $_____ (carry all decimals).

    Overtime rate (2 × regular rate) = $_____.

(b) Regular rate = $7.35.

    Overtime rate ($1\frac{1}{2}$ × regular rate) = $_____ (carry all decimals).

    Overtime rate (2 × regular rate) = $_____.

(a) Overtime rate ($1\frac{1}{2}$ × $5.07) = $7.605.
    Overtime rate (2 × $5.07) = $10.14.
(b) Overtime rate ($1\frac{1}{2}$ × $7.35) = $11.025.
    Overtime rate (2 × $7.35) = $14.70.

5. Total of *gross* earnings is the sum of regular and overtime earnings.

If Miss Jones received regular earnings of $70.25 and overtime earnings of $20.75, her total or gross earnings were $_____ + $_____ = $_____.

$70.25 + $20.75 = $91.00

6. Mr. Smith worked 45 hours in a week at the rate of $7.90 per hour. Overtime is paid for all hours in excess of 40 at $1\frac{1}{2}$ times the regular rate. What were his regular earnings, his overtime earnings, and his total or gross earnings?

Regular earnings   40 × $7.90 = $316.00
Overtime earnings   5 × $11.85 = $ 59.25
Total earnings   = $375.25

The number of hours per week at the regular pay rate could easily be 35. The examples in this text, however, are based on the most common practice of 40 hours a week with time and a half for overtime unless stated otherwise.

If Mr. Smith in this example had worked 48 hours during the week at the same rate, find his regular, overtime, and total earnings.

Regular earnings $_____   Show work here:

Overtime earnings $_____

Total earnings $_____

Regular earnings $316.00   (40 × $7.90)
Overtime earnings $ 94.80   (8 × $11.85)
Total earnings $410.80   ($316.00 + $94.80)

7. Mrs. Otts worked 43 hours in a week at the rate of $4.15 an hour. What was the total amount of her earnings?

Regular earnings   40 × $ 4.15   = $166.00
Overtime earnings   3 × $ 6.225 = $ 18.68
Total earnings $166.00 + $18.68 = $184.68

If Mrs. Otts had worked for 46 hours instead of 43, what would her earnings have been?

Regular earnings $_____   Show work here:

Overtime earnings $_____

Total earnings $_____

Regular earnings $166.00   (40 × $4.15)
Overtime earnings $ 37.35   (6 × $6.225)
Total earnings $203.35   ($166.00 + $37.35)

8. Mary Haines worked 45 hours during the week at $3.75 an hour. If she is paid overtime for all hours over 40 at $1\frac{1}{2}$ times the regular rate, what were her regular, overtime, and gross earnings for the week?

Regular rate = $_____.

Overtime rate = $_____.

Regular earnings $_____

Overtime earnings $_____

Total earnings $_____

- -

Regular rate = $3.75
Overtime rate = $1\frac{1}{2}$ × $3.75 = $5.625
Regular earnings $150.00 (40 × $3.75)
Overtime earnings $ 28.13 (5 × $5.625)
Total earnings $178.13 ($150.00 + $28.13)

Hourly Rates for Employees Paid on a Weekly or Monthly Basis

The hourly rate is often needed for personnel paid by the week or month, for many employees are paid overtime for work exceeding a 40-hour week. Hourly rates are also needed when an employee is hired at an odd time during the week or day or to figure sick leave without pay, vacation without pay, or termination of employment.

9. Changing *weekly* pay rate to *hourly* rate. Divide the weekly rate by the number of hours in the week.

   If Mr. Smith earns $98.00 for a 40-hour week, compute his hourly and overtime rate.

   Hourly rate = $98.00 ÷ 40 = $2.45.
   Overtime rate = $1\frac{1}{2}$ × $2.45 = $3.675.

   Compute the hourly and overtime rate ($1\frac{1}{2}$ × regular rate) for a person who earns $125.00 for a 40-hour week.

   Hourly rate = $_____ ÷ 40 = $_____ (carry full decimal).

   Overtime rate = _____ = $_____ (carry full decimal).

   -

   Hourly rate = $125.00 ÷ 40 = $3.125.
   Overtime rate = $1\frac{1}{2}$ × $3.125 = $4.6875.

10. (a) Mr. Haynes earns $180.00 per week. What are his hourly rate and overtime rate if overtime is 1½ times the regular rate? (40-hour week)

Hourly rate $_____ ÷ _____ = $_____.

Overtime rate 1½ × $_____ = $_____.

(b) If Mr. Haynes in (a) worked five hours overtime during a week, how much were his gross earnings?

Regular earnings $_____

Overtime earnings $_____

Gross earnings $_____

- -

(a) Hourly rate $180.00 ÷ 40 = $4.50
    Overtime rate   1½ × $ 4.50 = $6.75
(b) Regular earnings $180.00
    Overtime earnings $ 33.75   (5 × $6.75)
    Gross earnings $213.75   ($180.00 + $33.75)

11. Miss Brown earns $150.00 a week (40-hour week). During one week she took off six hours without pay. What were her earnings?

- -

Hourly rate = $150.00 ÷ 40 = $3.75
6 × $3.75 = $22.50
Earnings for week = $150.00 − $22.50 = $127.50

Changing *monthly* rate to *hourly* rate. The hourly rate is needed to determine what allowance should be made (if any) for overtime work and leave without pay (absences in which no salary is paid). (Sick leave and annual leave are not taken into account. In some cases the time allowed for these benefits may be deducted from the total number of weeks for the year when computing the weekly pay rate. Tables available for this purpose are generally found in the payroll offices of all large business enterprises.)

To change a monthly rate to an hourly rate, proceed as follows:

(a) Find the weekly rate. This may be computed in one of two ways; i.e., multiply the monthly salary by 12 to obtain the yearly rate and then divide by 52 (number of weeks in a year) or divide the monthly salary by $4\frac{1}{3}$ (average number of weeks in a month).

(b) Find the hourly rate (divide the weekly rate by number of hours in week).

Example: Mann Products pays its stenographers $600.00 a month. What are the weekly and hourly rates?

Weekly rate $600.00 \div 4\frac{1}{3} = \$138.46$ or $\frac{\$600 \times 12}{52} = \$138.46$

Hourly rate $\$138.46 \div 40 = \$ 3.46$ (degree of accuracy depends on company policy; two decimals are used here for convenience.)

12. Miss Smith earns $520 a month. What are her (a) weekly, (b) hourly, and (c) overtime rates?

   (a) Weekly rate = _____.

   (b) Hourly rate = _____.

   (c) Overtime rate = _____.

   -

   (a) Weekly rate = $520.00 \div 4\frac{1}{3} = \$120.00$.
   (b) Hourly rate = $\$120.00 \div 40 = \$ 3.00$.
   (c) Overtime rate = $\$ 3.00 \times 1\frac{1}{2} = \$ 4.50$.

13. If Miss Smith in frame 12 worked 15 hours overtime during the month, what were her gross earnings? $_____

   -

   Regular pay   = $520.00.
   Overtime pay   = 15 × $4.50 = $67.50.
   Gross earnings = $67.50 + $520.00 = $587.50.

14. Harry Edwards earns $750 a month. During one month he took a week's vacation without pay. How much did he earn that month? $_____

- -

Weekly rate = $750 ÷ $4\frac{1}{3}$ = $173.08.
Earnings $750.00 − $173.08 = $576.92.

EXERCISE 25

Answers appear at the end of this exercise. If your answers do not agree with those shown, check your calculations before referring to the solutions that follow. (Use a 40-hour week and time and a half for overtime unless stated otherwise.)

1. Mr. Jenkins worked 43 hours during the week at the rate of $5.35 an hour. What was his gross earnings?

   _____

2. Mr. Sawyer worked 39 hours regular time, 15 hours overtime at time and a half, and 9 hours at double time. If his regular rate was $4.60 an hour, how much did he earn?

   _____

3. A man worked 7 hours on Tuesday, $5\frac{1}{2}$ hours on Saturday, and 8 hours on other days except Sunday. At 5.12\frac{1}{2}$ an hour, what did he earn for the week?

   _____

4. Howard Butler receives $165.00 a week. Compute his earnings for a week in which he worked 48 hours.

   _____

5. Mrs. Hynes receives $670.00 a month as an office clerk. She is paid time and a half for overtime. If she works 15 hours overtime during the month, how much are her total earnings? Compute hourly and overtime rates correct to 3 decimals. _____

6. James Jason earned $650.00 a month as a stock clerk. During the month he took off 6 hours to which he was not entitled (leave without pay). What did he receive for the month? (Leave without pay is computed on the regular hourly rate.) Compute hourly rate correct to 2 decimals. _____

7. Find the hourly rate for the following pay schedules: (a) $900.00 a month, (b) $630.00 a month, (c) $135.00 a week, and (d) $336.00 biweekly (every two weeks). Record final answer to 3 decimals.

(a) _____
(b) _____
(c) _____
(d) _____

Answers

1. $238.08
2. $407.10
3. $239.59
4. $214.50
5. $727.98
6. $627.50
7. (a) $5.192, (b) $3.635, (c) $3.375, (d) $4.20

Solutions

1. $1\frac{1}{2} \times \$5.35 = \$8.025$
   Overtime = $3 \times \$8.025 = \$24.075 = \$24.08$
   Regular pay = $40 \times \$5.35 = \$214.00$
   Total or gross earnings = $\$24.08 + \$214.00 = \$238.08$
2. Overtime rate = $1\frac{1}{2} \times \$4.60 = \$6.90$
   Double time rate = $2 \times \$4.60 = \$9.20$
   Overtime pay = $15 \times \$6.90 = \$103.50$
   Double time pay = $9 \times \$9.20 = \$82.80$
   Regular pay = $39 \times \$4.60 = \$179.40$
   Total earnings = $\$103.50 + \$82.80 + \$179.40 = \$365.70$
3. Total hours = $44\frac{1}{2}$
   Overtime hours = $44\frac{1}{2} - 40 = 4\frac{1}{2}$
   Overtime rate = $1\frac{1}{2} + \$5.125 = \$7.6875$
   Regular earnings = $40 \times \$5.125 = \$205.00$
   Overtime earnings = $4\frac{1}{2} \times \$7.6875 = \$34.59$
   Total earnings = $\$205.00 + \$34.59 = \$239.59$
4. Hourly rate = $\$165.00 + 40 = \$4.125$
   Overtime rate = $\$4.125 \times 1\frac{1}{2} = \$6.1875$
   Overtime earnings = $8 \times \$6.1875 = \$49.50$
   Total earnings = $\$165.00 + \$49.50 = \$214.50$
5. Hourly rate = $\dfrac{\$670 \times 12}{52} \times \dfrac{1}{40} = \$3.865$
   OR
   (a) $\$670 \div 4\frac{1}{3} = \$154.617$ weekly rate, (b) $\$154.617 \div 40 = \$3.865$
   Overtime rate = $1\frac{1}{2} \times \$3.865 = \$5.798$
   Overtime earnings = $15 \times \$5.798 = \$86.97$
   Total earnings = $\$670.00 + \$86.97 = \$756.97$
6. Hourly rate = $\dfrac{\$650 \times 12}{52} \times \dfrac{1}{40} = \$3.75$ or $\dfrac{(\$650 + 4\frac{1}{3})}{40} = \$3.75$
   Time off = $6 \times \$3.75 = \$22.50$
   Earnings = $\$650.00 - \$22.50 = \$627.50$

7. (a) $\dfrac{\$900 \times 12}{52} \times \dfrac{1}{40} = \$5.192$ or $\dfrac{(\$900 \div 4\frac{1}{3})}{40} = \$5.192$

(b) $\dfrac{\$630 \times 12}{52} \times \dfrac{1}{40} = \$3.635$ or $\dfrac{(\$630 \div 4\frac{1}{3})}{40} = \$3.635$

(c) $\$135.00 \div 40 = \$3.375$

(d) $\$336.00 \div 2 = \$168.00$

$\$168.00 \div 40 = \$4.20$ hourly rate

UNIT 2. PAYROLL DEDUCTIONS

Payroll deductions fall into two categories, those required by law and those of a voluntary nature. The second group includes such deductions as employees association dues, credit union payments, pension plans, government bonds, and stock purchases. It is not uncommon to have 12 or more deductions listed on a paycheck voucher. The number of such deductions depends on the company and the individual employee.

Deductions required by law affect all employees. To meet the requirements established for such deductions it is important that the employer and those responsible for the preparation and maintenance of the payroll be thoroughly acquainted with the provisions of the law.

All states and the District of Columbia have unemployment insurance laws. Some states and local districts have income tax withholding laws. In some cases benefits are paid to employees who are absent from their jobs because of disability. Because these laws are not uniform, only those deductions required by Federal law and affecting all employees are discussed and applied in this chapter.

Federal Insurance Contribution Act Tax (FICA)

This tax is commonly referred to as the *Social Security tax*. For those who meet the requirements of the law it provides for their retirement and other benefits as well as benefits for their dependents and survivors.

Taxes for this purpose are withheld from the employee's earnings. The employer also pays an amount equal to that withheld from each employee's earnings. The rate has increased several times since enactment of the law. As of January 1, 1977 this **tax applies only to the first $16,500 paid to any employee in the calendar year. This equals 5.85% of $16,500 or $965.25**

The FICA rate, as of January 1, 1978 is 5.85% which has been in effect since 1973.

PAYROLL DEDUCTIONS 249

The Internal Revenue Service provides Social Security tax tables for the purpose of determining the amount to be withheld on gross earnings. Sections of two pages of these tables are shown on page 274.

Note: The base on which the maximum tax paid is computed for any employee has been increased several times since 1951, when it was $3600.00. As of Jan. 1, 1977 it was increased to $16,500. During this period both current and projected rates have changed several times. In addition, the Federal income tax withholding tables are also subject to change. For these reasons the answers to all payroll problems involving taxes withheld are based on the year 1977, the most complete information available at the time of this printing.

1. Find the FICA tax (taxes withheld for Social Security) on wages amounting to (a) $250.65 and (b) $335.00.

   Solution: 5.85% rates—(a) $250.65 × .0585 = $14.66
   (b) $335.00 × .0585 = $19.60

   Find the FICA tax on the following earnings:

   (a) $516.90 _____

   (b) $276.00 _____

   (a) $516.90 × .0585 = $30.24
   (b) $276.00 × .0585 = $16.15

2. An employer pays the Federal Government the same amount of FICA taxes that is paid by the employee. If Mr. Richards pays $11.03 in FICA taxes each month, his employer also pays $_____ each month.

   Allen Smith earns $175.00 per week. How much of this amount does he pay in FICA taxes? $_____. How much does his employer pay? $_____.

   Mr. Richard's employer pays $11.03 each month.
   Allen Smith pays $175.00 × .0585 = $10.24

3. The maximum FICA tax that can be paid by any employee for the year 1975 is 5.85% of $16,500 or $965.25. If Mr. Hope earns $17,000 a year, his total FICA tax is $_____.

$965.25

4. Mr. Haynes earned $16,100 during the first eleven months of the year 1977. If his earnings for December amounted to $1180, how much did he pay in FICA taxes during that month? $_____

Since Mr. Haynes cannot pay on more than $16,500 during 1977 he can pay only on the difference or $400, ($16,500-16,100). His tax = $400 x .0585 = $23.40.

5. If tables are available (see section of the tables shown on page 274), it is a simple matter to determine the FICA tax.

   Example: Determine the FICA tax on earnings of $250.50.

   Solution: Turn to the table on pages 274-275; $250.50 is at least $250.35 but less than $250.52. The FICA tax is applied to any amount between these two amounts, i.e., $14.65.

   The FICA tax on $263.00 is $_____; on $69.50 it is $_____.
   The FICA tax on $56.16 is $_____; on $249.15 it is $_____.

$15.39, $4.07
$ 3.29, $14.58

Federal Income Tax Withholding

The Current Tax Payment Act of 1943 requires all employers to withhold a certain percent of wages paid (after exemption) to their employees for income tax purposes. (There are certain classifications of wage earners to whom this does not apply.) Since 1943 the rates and the amounts to be withheld have been changed frequently.

   Two methods may be used to determine the amount of income taxes to be withheld. These are called the *percentage method* and the *wage bracket method*. Employers may use either one; the results are essentially the same.

The percentage method: Employers who use this method must make a percent computation based on the income tax withholding table for one exemption for various payroll periods (weekly, biweekly, semimonthly, monthly, quarterly, semi-annually, annually, and daily or miscellaneous), together with a rate table for the corresponding payroll period and the marital status of the employee. Computers are often used for this method and are especially valuable for payroll periods that are longer than a month. Because this method can be complex, many employers prefer the wage bracket method used in this book.

The wage bracket method: The Federal Government provides income tax withholding tables for single and married taxpayers for the following payroll periods: weekly, biweekly, semimonthly, monthly, and daily or miscellaneous. The table to be used is determined by the marital status and payroll period of the taxpayer. (The tables provided date from the most recent revision of the tax law—1970.)

The amount of tax withheld is determined by the number of *exemptions* and the amount of *gross earnings*. An exemption represents the number of persons supported by the taxpayer plus any additional number allowed by law. Persons 65 years of age or older may claim 2 exemptions.

The principles involved in the use of all these tables are the same. For this reason tables in this book are for weekly and monthly payroll periods for married taxpayers.

6. The number of exemptions depends on how many persons the taxpayer supports. A worker who supports his wife and 3 children may claim ____ exemptions.

   A single person may claim more than one exemption if he supports persons in addition to himself. A single person who supports his mother may claim ____ exemptions.

   5, 2

7. The income tax withholding table used is determined by (a) the marital status, (b) the payroll period, and (c) the gross earnings of the taxpayer.

Example: Find the income tax withheld (ITW) on a weekly salary of $82.50 for a married person with 2 exemptions.

Solution: Refer to the weekly payroll table on page 276. Since $82.50 is at least $82.00 but less than $84.00, the amount to be withheld is $1.00, as shown under the column headed "2 exemptions."

What is the income tax withheld for (a) a married person with a weekly salary of $212.50 and 3 exemptions; (b) a married person with a weekly salary of $360.00 and 2 exemptions? (a) $_____ (b) $_____.

(a) $23.30, (b) $57.00   Note that the columns on the left read "at least but less than."

8. **Example:** Mr. Smith earns $875.00 a month. He has 3 children and claims 5 exemptions which include himself and his wife. Find the amount of tax withheld.

   Solution: See monthly payroll table on page 278. Since $875.00 is more than $840.00 but less than $880.00, the amount of tax is $61.60 for 5 exemptions.

What is the income tax withheld for (a) a married person with a monthly salary of $960.00 and 2 exemptions; (b) a married person with a weekly salary of $125.00 and 3 exemptions? (a) $_____ (b) $_____.

(a) $119.90, (b) $6.10

9. Net pay or earnings (sometimes called take home pay) equals gross earnings *less* all deductions.

Mr. Frick (a married man) earned $625.00 regular pay, $56.00 overtime during a certain month. Complete the following. He claimed 2 exemptions.

Regular earnings $_____

Overtime earnings _____

Gross earnings $_____

FICA tax (5.85%) $_____

ITW _____

Total deductions $_____

Net earnings (gross pay less deductions) $_____

Regular earnings	$625.00	
Overtime earnings	56.00	
Gross earnings		$681.00
FICA tax (5.85%)	$ 39.84	
ITW	67.10	
Total deductions		$106.94
Net earnings		$574.06

10. Mr. Manning worked 8½, 7, 6¼, 10, 15 hours during a week at $6.25 an hour (40 hour week). He is married and claims 4 exemptions. Complete the following:

Regular earnings, _____ (hr) × $6.25 = $_____

Overtime earnings _____

Gross earnings $_____

FICA taxes (5.85%) $_____

ITW _____

Total deductions $_____

Net earnings $_____

Regular earnings, 40 × $6.25 = $250.00
Overtime earnings, $6\frac{3}{4}$ × $9.375 = 63.28

Gross earnings	$313.28
FICA taxes (5.85%)	$ 18.33
ITW	37.90
Total deductions	$ 56.23
Net earnings	$257.05

11. Compute the income tax withheld for a married employee with 2 dependents who earns $910 a *week*.

    Solution: (a) Notice at the bottom of the weekly payroll period schedule that the amount of tax withheld for any wage of $870 or more equals a stated sum *plus* 36% of the amount in excess of $870.
    (b) The amount in excess of $870 is $910 − $870 = $40. The amount for 2 dependents (bottom line) = $228.10.
    (c) The total tax withheld = $228.10 + (36% of $40) = $228.10 + $14.40 = $242.50.

    How much is the income tax withheld for a married employee with 4 dependents who earns $3700 a *month*?

$3700 − $3640 = $60
Income tax withheld = $896.70 + (36% of $60) =
$896.70 + $21.60 = $918.30

EXERCISE 26

Instructions: Use the FICA rate for 5.85% and the tax withholding tables on pages 276–279. Answers appear at the end of this exercise. If your answers do not agree with those shown, check your calculations before referring to the solutions.

1. Find the FICA tax on the following wages: (a) $270.00, (b) $436.10, (c) $60.50, (d) $112.48, and (e) $234.21.

2. Find the amount of income taxes withheld for the following. Assume that all are married employees.

	No. of Exemptions	Payroll Period	Wages Earned	Taxes Withheld
(a)	2	week	$ 228.00	_____
(b)	4	month	3840.00	_____
(c)	none	month	965.00	_____
(d)	5	week	195.00	_____
(e)	3	week	595.00	_____

3. Complete the following partial payroll. The overtime rate ($1\frac{1}{2}$ times the regular rate) applies to all time over 40 hours during the week.

PAYROLL

For Week Ending January 23, 19___

Employee No.	Hours					Total Hours	Hourly Rate	Earnings		
	Mon.	Tue.	Wed.	Thu.	Fri.			Regular	Overtime	Total
32	8	7½	10	8	8	41½	$4.30	$172.00	$9.68	$181.68
33	7	8	8	7½	9		4.00			
34	8	8	9	8½	8		3.50			
35	10	8	8	7½	8		3.25			
36	6	9½	8	8	8		2.75			
37	9	10	10	7	7		2.80			
Total							XXXX			

Note: See section on crossfooting, page 17, if needed.

4. Compute the FICA and withholding taxes and complete the following partial payroll. Assume that all employees are married and that none has earned $16,500 to date for the year.

PAYROLL

For Week Ending May 11, 19___

Employee No.	Exemptions	Total Earnings	Deductions				Net Earnings
			F.I.C.A.	Tax Withheld	Other	Total	
260	2	$205.00			$5.20		
217	1	321.50			3.00		
284	3	187.25			4.50		
296	2	290.84			4.50		
300	0	275.00			5.20		
301	4	167.55			5.20		
Total							

5. Mrs. J. Carroll earns $600.00 a month as a clerk for the Sabin Realty Co. She worked 4 hours overtime during the month. If she is paid time and a half for all overtime, what were her total gross earnings for the month? (Use a 40-hour week.) (Compute hourly and overtime rates corrected (or rounded) to four decimals.)

_____

6. Mr. Smith was employed by the Frick Iron Works at a salary of $460.00 for a 40-hour week. (a) Compute his hourly rate and his overtime rate at time and a half. (b) In how many weeks will he have paid in the maximum allowed for FICA taxes at the regular rate? [Maximum amount = $965.25 (1977).]

(a) _____
(b) _____

EXERCISE 26

Answers and Solutions

1. (a) $15.80 (b) $25.51 (c) $3.54 (d) $6.58 (e) $13.70
2. (a) $27.50 (b) $968.70 (c) $141.20 (d) $13.50 (e) $123.90
3.

PAYROLL

For Week Ending January 23, 19____

Employee No.	Hours M.	T.	W.	Th.	F.	Total Hours	Hourly Rate	Earnings Regular	Overtime	Total
32	8	7½	10	8	8	41½	$4.30	$172.00	$9.68	$181.68
33	7	8	8	7½	9	39½	4.00	158.00	–	158.00
34	8	8	9	8½	8	41½	3.50	140.00	7.88	147.88
35	10	8	8	7½	8	41½	3.25	130.00	7.31	137.31
36	6	9½	8	8	8	39½	2.75	108.63	—	108.63
37	9	10	10	7	7	43	2.80	112.00	12.60	124.60
Total	48	51	53	46½	48	246½	XXXX	$820.63	$37.47	$858.10

4.

PAYROLL

For Week Ending May 11, 19____

Employee No.	Exemptions	Total Earnings	FICA	Deductions Tax Withheld	Other	Total	Net Earnings
260	2	$ 205.00	$11.99	$ 24.10	$5.20	$ 41.29	$ 163.71
217	1	321.50	18.81	50.60	3.00	72.41	249.09
284	3	187.25	10.95	17.30	4.50	32.75	154.50
296	2	290.84	17.01	39.50	4.50	61.01	229.83
300	0	275.00	16.09	41.70	5.20	62.99	212.01
301	4	167.55	9.80	10.40	5.20	25.40	142.15
Total		$1447.14	$84.65	$183.60	$27.60	$295.85	$1151.29

5. Hourly rate = $\dfrac{\$600 \times 12}{52} \times \dfrac{1}{40} = \$3.4615$

   Overtime rate = $3.4615 × 1½ = $5.1923
   Overtime = 4 × $5.1923 = $20.77
   Total earnings = $600.00 + $20.77 = $620.77

6. (a) Hourly rate, $11.50
      Overtime rate, $17.25
   (b) $460 x .0585 = $26.91
      $965.25 ÷ $26.91 = 36 weeks

UNIT 3. PIECE-RATE PAYROLL SYSTEM, COMMISSIONS

Piece-Rate Payroll System

1. The *piece-rate* payroll system is one in which the employee is paid on a unit production basis. For straight piecework the amount earned equals the number of articles or units of work produced, multiplied by the unit price. If an employee produces 375 articles in a day at 12¢ each, his earnings for the day equals 375 × .12 or $45.00.

   Mrs. Johnson packs apples for the local apple growers association for which she receives 21¢ a box. If she packs 120 boxes in a day, how much were her gross earnings? _____

   _____

   120 × .21 = $25.20

2. (a) If Mrs. Johnson (frame 1) averaged 140 boxes a day for 5 days, how much did she earn for the week? _____
   (b) J. Smith receives $4.00 for each unit completed in an assembly plant. He completed 24 units during a certain week. What were his gross earnings? _____

   _____

   (a) 140 × 5 × .21 = $147.00.
   (b) 24 × $4.00 = $96.00.

3. Compute the gross earnings for the partial payroll shown here.

PAYROLL

For week ending May 10, 19____

Employee No.	Units Produced						Piece Rate	Gross Earnings
	M	T	W	Th	F	Total		
21	120	98	101	96	110	525	$0.425	$223.13
23	87	85	90	91	89	____	0.3725	_____
24	111	109	110	112	108	____	0.36	_____
26	90	92	89	91	93	____	0.425	_____
28	99	96	98	100	101	____	0.3925	_____
Total							xxxx	

Employes No.	Units Produced						Piece Rate	Gross Earnings
	M	T	W	Th	F	Total		
21	120	98	101	96	110	525	$0.425	$223.13
23	87	85	90	91	89	442	0.3725	164.65
24	111	109	110	112	108	550	0.36	198.00
26	90	92	89	91	93	455	0.425	193.38
28	99	96	98	100	101	494	0.3925	193.90
Total	507	480	488	490	501	2466	xxxx	$973.06

Commissions

Many businesses pay their employees wholly or in part on a commission basis. The commission is a fee, generally a percent of money received in a transaction; for example, real estate salesmen receive a certain percent of their sales. Store sales personnel may, in addition to their salaries, receive a special commission or bonus for selling hard-to-move merchandise. As an added inducement to stimulate business, sales clerks may be paid a percent of the dollar volume of sales made above a certain amount within a specified period of time. In every instance the commission serves as an incentive to the salesman to increase sales and as a reward for his efforts.

Example: Mr. A Hyatt sells real estate. His sales for 4 months amounted to $117,500. If he received a 6% commission, how much did he earn during that time?

Solution: Commission = 6% of $117,500 = .06 × $117,500 = $7050.

4. Mr. Hopkins sells vacuum cleaners at $95.00 each. He receives a 30% commission on each cleaner. How much does he earn in a week in which he sells 12 machines?

   Gross sales = _____ .

   Commission = _____ .

Gross sales = 12 × $ 95.00 = $1140.00.
Commission = .30 × $1140.00 = $ 342.00.

5. Mrs. Clark receives a salary of $152.00 a week as a sales clerk for the Comfy Shoe Store. Her sales during 1 week were $350.00. If she received a 5% commission on all sales over $300 during any week, what were her total earnings for the week?

   Solution: Salary $152.00
       Commission (5% of $50)   2.50
       Total earnings $154.50

Mary Oliver received a salary of $115 a week as a sales clerk for the High Fashion Shop. Her sales for one week amounted to $865.00. If she received a 6% commission on all sales over $500 a week, what were her total earnings for the week?

$865.00 − $500.00 = $365.00 (excess of $500 in sales for the week)
Commission = .06 × $365.00 = $21.90
Total earnings = $115.00 + $21.90 = $136.90

6. A. Jeffers received $130.00 a week as a sales clerk. In addition, he was paid a 5% commission for all sales over $900 plus an additional 2% on all sales over $1200 in any one week. How much were his earnings for a week in which his sales were $1625.00?

Sales over $900 = $1625 − $900 = $725
Sales over $1200 = $1625 − $1200 = $425
Commission = (.05 × $725) + (.02 × $425) = $36.25 + $8.50 = $44.75
Total earnings = $44.75 + $130.00 = $174.75
Commission = (.05 × $300) + (.07 × $425) = $15.00 + $29.75 = $44.75.

OR

5% on sales over $900 but less than $1200 (i.e. $725 − $425 = $300) + 7% on sales over $1200.
Commission = (.05 × $300) + (.07 × $425) = $15.00 + $29.75 = $44.75.

EXERCISE 27

Answers appear at the end of this exercise. If your answers do not agree with those shown, check your calculations before referring to the solutions that follow.

1. Mrs. James packs apples for the Local Apple Growers Association for which she receives 17¢ a box. How much does she earn in a week if she averages 160 boxes per day for 5 days?

2. H. Harvey assembles plastic facemasks for oxygen therapy and receives $2.06 for each unit. If he assembles 18 on Monday, 23 on Tuesday, 17 on Wednesday, 20 on Thursday, and 20 on Friday, how much does he earn for the week?

3. Mr. Remick, a married man with three exemptions, sells real estate and receives a commission of $3\frac{1}{2}\%$ on all sales. If his sales amounted to $256,225 for the month, find his gross earnings, standard deductions, and net earnings. Assume that he has paid no FICA taxes for the year.

4. Mr. Swartz received a commission of $2\frac{1}{2}\%$ on all sales made above $300 in any single day. If his sales for Monday through Saturday amounted to $350, $475, $500, $310, $671, and $392, respectively, how much did he earn in commissions for the week?

5. The Empire Department store gave the sales personnel a 3% commission on certain speciality items that did not sell readily. The sales for these items amounted to $936 in a particular month. If this sum was divided among 8 sales clerks, how much did each receive?

_____

6. The Home Beauty Shop pays all operators $12 for an 8-hour day, plus 50% of all business over $24 received during the day. If Miss Heenan does $75 worth of business during a certain day, how much does she earn?

_____

Answers

1. $136.00   2. $201.88   3. $6425.88 net
4. $22.45   5. $3.51   6. $37.50

Solutions

1. $160 × 5 × .17 = $136.00.
2. 18 + 23 + 17 + 20 + 20 = 98 masks assembled in a week.
   98 × $2.06 = $201.88.
3. Commission = .035 × $256,225 = $8967.875 = $8967.88.
   FICA taxes = $8967.88 × .0585 = $524.62
   ITW (from table) = [$919.20 + 36% of ($8967.88 − $3640.00) = $2837.24
        Deductions = $524.62 + $2837.24 = $3361.86
        Net earnings = $8967.88 − $3361.86 = $5606.02
4. Excess for the week of any amount more than $300 a day = ($350 − $300) + ($475 − $300) + ($500 − $300) + ($310 − $300) + ($671 − $300) + ($392 − $300) = $898.
   $898 × .025 = $22.45.
5. $926 × .03 = $28.08 total commission.
   $28.08 ÷ 8 = $3.51 per sales person.
6. $75 − $24 = $51.
   $51 × .50 = $25.50 commission.
   $25.50 + $12.00 + $37.50 total earnings.

UNIT 4. CASH PAYROLLS

Payment of Payrolls in Cash

Many employers prefer to pay their employees in cash. When this is done, it is necessary to have the exact currency for each employee's pay envelope. A payroll cash sheet is prepared for this purpose. After the number of bills and coins required has been determined, a *change memorandum* is prepared. The bank, on presentation of this memorandum and a check for the total amount of the payroll, will provide the denominations required.

1. Mr. Kopper earned $55.00 and was paid in cash. His employer pays him in the least number of bills or currency possible. The largest denominations in bills in common business usage for this purpose is $20.00. Check the most appropriate answer below:

    (a) Two $20 bills and three $5 bills. _____

    (b) Two $20 bills, one $10 bill, and one $5.00 bill. _____

    (b)

2. Mr. Adams earned $23.62 on a certain day. If he is paid in cash, he will receive ___ $20 bills, ___ $1 bills, ___ half dollars, ___ dimes, and ___ pennies.

    ----

    1 $20 bill, 3 $1 bills, 1 half dollar, 1 dime, and 2 pennies.

3. List the bills and currency needed to pay $37.57 in cash.

   $20 bills   No. ___
   10 bills   ___
   5 bills   ___
   1 bills   ___
   half dollars   ___
   quarters   ___
   dimes   ___
   nickels   ___
   pennies   ___

   $20 bills   No. 1
   10 bills   1
   5 bills   1
   1 bills   2
   half dollars   1
   quarters   –
   dimes   –
   nickels   1
   pennies   2

4. The currency breakdown for a cash payroll is prepared on a *cash sheet*. From the *cash sheet* a *change memorandum* or *memorandum of cash* for *pay roll* is prepared. These forms are illustrated on the facing page.

CASH SHEET

Payroll Week Ending July 3, 19____

		Bills				Coins			
Employee	Net Pay	20	10	5	1	.50	.25	.10	.05	.01
113	$ 68.32	3		1	3		1		1	2
114	61.45	3			1		1	2		
117	82.60	4			2	1		1		
120	71.12	3	1		1			1		2
125	88.70	4		1	3	1		2		
126	55.81	2	1	1		1	1		1	1
Totals	$428.00	19	2	3	10	3	3	6	2	5

MEMORANDUM OF
CASH FOR PAY ROLL
FOR

A B C Company

July 3 ____, 19____

NUMBER		AMOUNT	
19	Twenties	380	00
2	Tens	20	00
3	Fives	15	00
	Twos		
10	Ones	10	00
	Silver Dollars		
3	Halves	1	50
3	Quarters		75
6	Dimes		60
2	Nickels		10
5	Pennies		05
	TOTAL	428	00

P & S FORM 96

5. Complete the Cash Sheet and Memorandum of Cash for Payroll shown here:

CASH SHEET

Payroll   Week ending October 16, 19__

		Bills				Coins				
Employee	Net Pay	20	10	5	1	.50	.25	.10	.05	.01
200	$ 98.00	4	1	1	3					
201	102.50	5			2	1				
204	96.25	4	1	1	1		1			
206	152.75	7	1		2	1	1			
210	146.97	7		1	1	1	1	2		2
Total	$596.47	27	3	3	9	3	3	2		2

Memorandum of
CASH FOR PAY ROLL
for

Johnson & Abbot Company
October 16 , 19__

Number	Amount
Twenties 27	$540.00
Tens 3	30.00
Fives 3	15.00
Ones 9	9.00
Halves 3	1.50
Quarters 3	.75
Dimes 2	.20
Nickels 0	.00
Pennies 2	.02
Total	$596.47

Cash Sheet

Employee	Net Pay	Bills				Coins				
		20	10	5	1	.50	.25	.10	.05	.01
200	$ 98.00	4	1	1	3					
201	102.50	5			2	1				
204	96.25	4	1	1	1		1			
206	152.75	7	1		2	1	1			
210	146.97	7		1	1	1	1	2		2
Total	$596.47	27	3	3	9	3	3	2		2

Change Memorandum

27	Twenties	$540.00
3	Tens	30.00
3	Fives	15.00
9	Ones	9.00
3	Halves	1.50
3	Quarters	.75
2	Dimes	.20
—	Nickels	—
2	Pennies	.02
	Total	$596.47

EXERCISE 28

Chapter Summary

Answers with solutions appear at the end of this exercise. If your answers do not agree with those shown, check your calculations before referring to the solution.

1. Complete Payroll A. Use a 40-hour week. Overtime is figured at time and a half.
2. Complete Payroll B.
3. Prepare a cash sheet and change memorandum for Payroll A. (See page 266.)

4. Miss Smith worked for the Amber Company as a stenographer for $750 a month. She was absent without leave for 5 days (one week). What was the amount of her gross earnings for the month if she worked 40 hours per week and an 8-hour day? (Carry weekly rate to 2 decimals.)

5. Mr. Ames is a salesman for the Manning Mercantile Company. In addition to a regular monthly salary of $875, he received a commission of 5% on all sales in excess of $500 during the month. If his sales amounted to $1875 during a certain month, what were his (a) gross earnings, (b) FICA taxes, (c) income taxes withheld, and (d) net earnings? Mr. Ames is married and claims 2 exemptions. (Use 1977 FICA rate and income tax withholding.)

(a) _____
(b) _____
(c) _____

A. PAYROLL SUMMARY

Work Week Ending June 14, 19___ Date of Payment _____ Sheet No. _____

Employee	Marital Status	Exemptions	Hours of Work M	T	W	Th	F	Total Hours	Hourly Rate	Earnings Regular	Over-time	Total Wages	Deductions FICA (5.85%)	With-holding Tax	Other Deductions	Total Deductions	Net Earnings
Ames, J.	M	2	8	7	8	8½	9		$4.20						$2.50		
Bell, S.	M	3	7½	8	8	10	10		3.95						5.00		
Ellis, A.	M	1	8	8	8	8	8		3.20						5.00		
King, M.	M	3	9	8	8½	9	8		4.50						2.50		
Moore, R.	M	2	7	7	9	9	8		3.65						2.50		
Wells, H.	M	2	8	8	7½	7½	10		5.20						2.50		
Total	X	X							XXXX								

B. PAYROLL SUMMARY

Work Week Ending August 1, 19___ Date of Payment _____ Sheet No. _____

Employee	Marital Status	Exempt.	Units Produced M	T	W	Th	F	Total Pieces	Piece Rate	Gross Pay	Deductions FICA (5.85%)	With-holding Tax	Other Deductions	Total Deductions	Net Pay
Bens, L.	M	0	800	850	700	920	910		.0192				$1.25		
Cain, C.	M	1	250	220	300	315	275		.061				1.25		
Dietz, F.	M	1	415	430	420	450	462		.025				1.25		
Hale, D.	M	4	300	322	360	410	390		.1025				1.25		
Hope, C.	M	3	950	990	975	998	950		.03				1.25		
Main, H.	M	2	150	165	170	167	182		.202				1.25		
Total	X	X							XXXX						

Answers and Solutions

1.

A. PAYROLL SUMMARY

Work Week Ending June 14, 19___ Date of Payment ___ Sheet No. ___

Employee	Marital Status	Exemptions	Hours of Work M	T	W	Th	F	Total Hours	Hourly Rate	Earnings Regular	Overtime	Total Wages	Deductions FICA (5.85%)	Withholding Tax	Other Deductions	Total Deductions	Net Earnings
Ames, J.	M	2	8	7	8	8½	9	40½	$4.20	$168.00	$3.15	$171.15	$10.01	$18.20	$2.50	$30.71	$140.44
Bell, S.	M	3	7½	8	8	10	10	43½	3.95	158.00	20.74	178.74	10.46	15.30	5.00	30.76	147.98
Ellis, A.	M	1	8	8	8	8	8	40	3.20	128.00	—	128.00	7.49	11.60	5.00	24.09	103.91
King, M.	M	3	9	8	8½	9	8	42½	4.50	180.00	16.88	196.88	11.52	19.30	2.50	33.32	163.56
Moore, R.	M	2	7	7	8	9	8	39	3.65	142.35	—	142.35	8.33	11.70	2.50	22.53	119.82
Wells, H.	M	2	8	8	7½	7½	10	41	5.20	208.00	7.80	215.80	12.62	25.80	2.50	40.92	174.88
Total	X	X	47½	46	48	52	53	246½	XXXX	$984.35	$48.57	$1032.92	$60.43	$101.90	$20.00	$182.33	$850.59

B. PAYROLL SUMMARY

Work Week Ending August 1, 19___ Date of Payment ___ Sheet No. ___

Employee	Marital Status	Exempt.	Units Produced M	T	W	Th	F	Total Pieces	Piece Rate	Gross Pay	Deductions FICA (5.85%)	Withholding Tax	Other Deductions	Total Deductions	Net Pay
Bens, L.	M	0	800	850	700	920	910	4,180	.0192	$ 80.26	$ 4.70	$ 5.60	$1.25	$11.55	$ 68.71
Cain, C.	M	1	250	220	300	315	275	1,360	.061	82.96	4.85	3.50	1.25	9.60	73.36
Dietz, F.	M	1	415	430	420	450	462	2,177	.025	54.43	3.18	—	1.25	4.43	50.00
Hale, D.	M	4	300	322	360	410	390	1,782	.1025	182.66	10.69	14.40	1.25	26.34	156.32
Hope, C.	M	3	950	990	975	998	950	4,863	.03	145.89	8.53	9.80	1.25	19.58	126.31
Main, H.	M	2	150	165	170	167	182	834	.202	168.47	9.86	16.20	1.25	27.31	141.16
Total	X	X	2865	2977	2925	3260	3169	15,196	XXXX	$714.67	$41.81	$49.50	$7.50	$98.81	$615.86

2. **CASH SHEET, PAYROLL A**

Employee	Net Earnings	Bills				Coins				
		20	10	5	1	.50	.25	.10	.05	.01
Ames	$140.44	7					1	1	1	4
Bell	147.98	7		1	2	1	1	2		3
Ellis	103.91	5			3	1	1	1	1	1
King	163.56	8			3	1			1	1
Moore	119.82	5	1	1	4	1	1		1	2
Wells	174.88	8	1		4	1	1	1		3
Total	$850.59	40	2	2	16	5	5	5	4	14

3. **CHANGE MEMORANDUM, PAYROLL A**

Number	Amount
40 twenties	$800.00
2 tens	20.00
2 fives	10.00
16 ones	16.00
5 halves	2.50
5 quarters	1.25
5 dimes	.50
4 nickels	.20
14 pennies	.14
	$850.59

4. 5 days = 1 week; then $\dfrac{\$750 \times 12}{52} = \$173.08$.

    $750.00 − $173.08 = $576.92

5. $1875.00 − $500 = $1375.00 sales in excess of $500.
    $1375.00 × .05 = $68.75 commission.
    $68.75 + $875.00 = $943.75 gross earnings.
    FICA tax = $943.75 × .0585 = $55.21.
    Income Tax Withheld = $113.10 (from tables).
    Net earnings = $943.75 − ($113.10 + $55.21) = $775.44

SOCIAL SECURITY EMPLOYEE TAX TABLE

5.85 percent employee tax deductions

Wages		Tax to be withheld	Wages		Tax to be withheld	Wages		Tax to be withheld	Wages		Tax to be withheld
At least	But less than		At least	But less than		At least	But less than		At least	But less than	
$44.36	$44.53	$2.60	$55.48	$55.65	$3.25	$66.59	$66.76	$3.90	$77.70	$77.87	$4.55
44.53	44.71	2.61	55.65	55.82	3.26	66.76	66.93	3.91	77.87	78.04	4.56
44.71	44.88	2.62	55.82	55.99	3.27	66.93	67.10	3.92	78.04	78.21	4.57
44.88	45.05	2.63	55.99	56.16	3.28	67.10	67.27	3.93	78.21	78.38	4.58
45.05	45.22	2.64	56.16	56.33	3.29	67.27	67.44	3.94	78.38	78.55	4.59
45.22	45.39	2.65	56.33	56.50	3.30	67.44	67.61	3.95	78.55	78.72	4.60
45.39	45.56	2.66	56.50	56.67	3.31	67.61	67.78	3.96	78.72	78.89	4.61
45.56	45.73	2.67	56.67	56.84	3.32	67.78	67.95	3.97	78.89	79.06	4.62
45.73	45.90	2.68	56.84	57.01	3.33	67.95	68.12	3.98	79.06	79.24	4.63
45.90	46.07	2.69	57.01	57.18	3.34	68.12	68.30	3.99	79.24	79.41	4.64
46.07	46.24	2.70	57.18	57.36	3.35	68.30	68.47	4.00	79.41	79.58	4.65
46.24	46.42	2.71	57.36	57.53	3.36	68.47	68.64	4.01	79.58	79.75	4.66
46.42	46.59	2.72	57.53	57.70	3.37	68.64	68.81	4.02	79.75	79.92	4.67
46.59	46.76	2.73	57.70	57.87	3.38	68.81	68.98	4.03	79.92	80.09	4.68
46.76	46.93	2.74	57.87	58.04	3.39	68.98	69.15	4.04	80.09	80.26	4.69
46.93	47.10	2.75	58.04	58.21	3.40	69.15	69.32	4.05	80.26	80.43	4.70
47.10	47.27	2.76	58.21	58.38	3.41	69.32	69.49	4.06	80.43	80.60	4.71
47.27	47.44	2.77	58.38	58.55	3.42	69.49	69.66	4.07	80.60	80.77	4.72
47.44	47.61	2.78	58.55	58.72	3.43	69.66	69.83	4.08	80.77	80.95	4.73
47.61	47.78	2.79	58.72	58.89	3.44	69.83	70.00	4.09	80.95	81.12	4.74
47.78	47.95	2.80	58.89	59.06	3.45	70.00	70.18	4.10	81.12	81.29	4.75
47.95	48.12	2.81	59.06	59.24	3.46	70.18	70.35	4.11	81.29	81.46	4.76
48.12	48.30	2.82	59.24	59.41	3.47	70.35	70.52	4.12	81.46	81.63	4.77
48.30	48.47	2.83	59.41	59.58	3.48	70.52	70.69	4.13	81.63	81.80	4.78
48.47	48.64	2.84	59.58	59.75	3.49	70.69	70.86	4.14	81.80	81.97	4.79

226.42	226.59	13.25	237.53	237.70	13.90	248.64	248.81	14.55	259.75	259.92	15.20
226.59	226.76	13.26	237.70	237.87	13.91	248.81	248.98	14.56	259.92	260.09	15.21
226.76	226.93	13.27	237.87	238.04	13.92	248.98	249.15	14.57	260.09	260.26	15.22
226.93	227.10	13.28	238.04	238.21	13.93	249.15	249.32	14.58	260.26	260.43	15.23
227.10	227.27	13.29	238.21	238.38	13.94	249.32	249.49	14.59	260.43	260.60	15.24
227.27	227.44	13.30	238.38	238.55	13.95	249.49	249.66	14.60	260.60	260.77	15.25
227.44	227.61	13.31	238.55	238.72	13.96	249.66	249.83	14.61	260.77	260.95	15.26
227.61	227.78	13.32	238.72	238.89	13.97	249.83	250.00	14.62	260.95	261.12	15.27
227.78	227.95	13.33	238.89	239.06	13.98	250.00	250.18	14.63	261.12	261.29	15.28
227.95	228.12	13.34	239.06	239.24	13.99	250.18	250.35	14.64	261.29	261.46	15.29
228.12	228.30	13.35	239.24	239.41	14.00	250.35	250.52	14.65	261.46	261.63	15.30
228.30	228.47	13.36	239.41	239.58	14.01	250.52	250.69	14.66	261.63	261.80	15.31
228.47	228.64	13.37	239.58	239.75	14.02	250.69	250.86	14.67	261.80	261.97	15.32
228.64	228.81	13.38	239.75	239.92	14.03	250.86	251.03	14.68	261.97	262.14	15.33
228.81	228.98	13.39	239.92	240.09	14.04	251.03	251.20	14.69	262.14	262.31	15.34
228.98	229.15	13.40	240.09	240.26	14.05	251.20	251.37	14.70	262.31	262.48	15.35
229.15	229.32	13.41	240.26	240.43	14.06	251.37	251.54	14.71	262.48	262.65	15.36
229.32	229.49	13.42	240.43	240.60	14.07	251.54	251.71	14.72	262.65	262.83	15.37
229.49	229.66	13.43	240.60	240.77	14.08	251.71	251.89	14.73	262.83	263.00	15.38
229.66	229.83	13.44	240.77	240.95	14.09	251.89	252.06	14.74	263.00	263.17	15.39
229.83	230.00	13.45	240.95	241.12	14.10	252.06	252.23	14.75	263.17	263.34	15.40
230.00	230.18	13.46	241.12	241.29	14.11	252.23	252.40	14.76	263.34	263.51	15.41
230.18	230.35	13.47	241.29	241.46	14.12	252.40	252.57	14.77	263.51	263.68	15.42
230.35	230.52	13.48	241.46	241.63	14.13	252.57	252.74	14.78	263.68	263.85	15.43
230.52	230.69	13.49	241.63	241.80	14.14	252.74	252.91	14.79	263.85	264.02	15.44

CHAPTER SUMMARY

INCOME TAX WITHHOLDING*

MARRIED Persons — **WEEKLY** Payroll Period

And the wages are—		And the number of withholding allowances claimed is—										
At least	But less than	0	1	2	3	4	5	6	7	8	9	10 or more
		The amount of income tax to be withheld shall be—										
$0	$48	$0	$0	$0	$0	$0	$0	$0	$0	$0	$0	$0
48	49	.10	0	0	0	0	0	0	0	0	0	0
49	50	.20	0	0	0	0	0	0	0	0	0	0
50	51	.40	0	0	0	0	0	0	0	0	0	0
51	52	.60	0	0	0	0	0	0	0	0	0	0
52	53	.80	0	0	0	0	0	0	0	0	0	0
53	54	.90	0	0	0	0	0	0	0	0	0	0
54	55	1.10	0	0	0	0	0	0	0	0	0	0
55	56	1.30	0	0	0	0	0	0	0	0	0	0
56	57	1.40	0	0	0	0	0	0	0	0	0	0
57	58	1.60	0	0	0	0	0	0	0	0	0	0
58	59	1.80	0	0	0	0	0	0	0	0	0	0
59	60	1.90	0	0	0	0	0	0	0	0	0	0
60	62	2.20	0	0	0	0	0	0	0	0	0	0
62	64	2.50	.10	0	0	0	0	0	0	0	0	0
64	66	2.90	.40	0	0	0	0	0	0	0	0	0
66	68	3.20	.80	0	0	0	0	0	0	0	0	0
68	70	3.60	1.10	0	0	0	0	0	0	0	0	0
70	72	3.90	1.40	0	0	0	0	0	0	0	0	0
72	74	4.20	1.80	0	0	0	0	0	0	0	0	0
74	76	4.60	2.10	0	0	0	0	0	0	0	0	0
76	78	4.90	2.50	0	0	0	0	0	0	0	0	0
78	80	5.30	2.80	.40	0	0	0	0	0	0	0	0
80	82	5.60	3.10	.70	0	0	0	0	0	0	0	0
82	84	5.90	3.50	1.00	0	0	0	0	0	0	0	0
84	86	6.30	3.80	1.40	0	0	0	0	0	0	0	0
86	88	6.60	4.20	1.70	0	0	0	0	0	0	0	0
88	90	7.00	4.50	2.10	0	0	0	0	0	0	0	0
90	92	7.30	4.80	2.40	0	0	0	0	0	0	0	0
92	94	7.60	5.20	2.70	.30	0	0	0	0	0	0	0
94	96	8.00	5.50	3.10	.60	0	0	0	0	0	0	0
96	98	8.30	5.90	3.40	1.00	0	0	0	0	0	0	0
98	100	8.70	6.20	3.80	1.30	0	0	0	0	0	0	0
100	105	9.40	6.80	4.30	1.90	0	0	0	0	0	0	0
105	110	10.40	7.70	5.20	2.70	.30	0	0	0	0	0	0
110	115	11.40	8.60	6.00	3.60	1.10	0	0	0	0	0	0
115	120	12.40	9.60	6.90	4.40	2.00	0	0	0	0	0	0
120	125	13.40	10.60	7.70	5.30	2.80	.40	0	0	0	0	0
125	130	14.40	11.60	8.70	6.10	3.70	1.20	0	0	0	0	0
130	135	15.40	12.60	9.70	7.00	4.50	2.10	0	0	0	0	0
135	140	16.40	13.60	10.70	7.80	5.40	2.90	.50	0	0	0	0
140	145	17.40	14.60	11.70	8.80	6.20	3.80	1.30	0	0	0	0
145	150	18.40	15.60	12.70	9.80	7.10	4.60	2.20	0	0	0	0
150	160	19.90	17.10	14.20	11.30	8.40	5.90	3.50	1.00	0	0	0
160	170	21.90	19.10	16.20	13.30	10.40	7.60	5.20	2.70	.30	0	0
170	180	23.90	21.10	18.20	15.30	12.40	9.50	6.90	4.40	2.00	0	0
180	190	25.60	23.10	20.20	17.30	14.40	11.50	8.60	6.10	3.70	1.20	0
190	200	27.30	24.80	22.20	19.30	16.40	13.50	10.60	7.80	5.40	2.90	.50
200	210	29.00	26.50	24.10	21.30	18.40	15.50	12.60	9.80	7.10	4.60	2.20
210	220	30.70	28.20	25.80	23.30	20.40	17.50	14.60	11.80	8.90	6.30	3.90
220	230	32.40	29.90	27.50	25.00	22.40	19.50	16.60	13.80	10.90	8.00	5.60
230	240	34.10	31.60	29.20	26.70	24.30	21.50	18.60	15.80	12.90	10.00	7.30
240	250	35.80	33.30	30.90	28.40	26.00	23.50	20.60	17.80	14.90	12.00	9.10
250	260	37.50	35.00	32.60	30.10	27.70	25.20	22.60	19.80	16.90	14.00	11.10
260	270	39.20	36.70	34.30	31.80	29.40	26.90	24.50	21.80	18.90	16.00	13.10
270	280	41.70	38.40	36.00	33.50	31.10	28.60	26.20	23.70	20.90	18.00	15.10
280	290	44.20	40.60	37.70	35.20	32.80	30.30	27.90	25.40	22.90	20.00	17.10
290	300	46.70	43.10	39.50	36.90	34.50	32.00	29.60	27.10	24.70	22.00	19.10
300	310	49.20	45.60	42.00	38.60	36.20	33.70	31.30	28.80	26.40	23.90	21.10
310	320	51.70	48.10	44.50	40.90	37.90	35.40	33.00	30.50	28.10	25.60	23.10

*From IRS Publication 15 (Rev. November 1977)

MARRIED Persons — WEEKLY Payroll Period

And the wages are—		And the number of withholding allowances claimed is—										
At least	But less than	0	1	2	3	4	5	6	7	8	9	10 or more
		The amount of income tax to be withheld shall be—										
$320	$330	$54.20	$50.60	$47.00	$43.40	$39.80	$37.10	$34.70	$32.20	$29.80	$27.30	$24.90
330	340	56.70	53.10	49.50	45.90	42.30	38.80	36.40	33.90	31.50	29.00	26.60
340	350	59.20	55.60	52.00	48.40	44.80	41.20	38.10	35.60	33.20	30.70	28.30
350	360	62.00	58.10	54.50	50.90	47.30	43.70	40.10	37.30	34.90	32.40	30.00
360	370	64.80	60.80	57.00	53.40	49.80	46.20	42.60	39.00	36.60	34.10	31.70
370	380	67.60	63.60	59.50	55.90	52.30	48.70	45.10	41.50	38.30	35.80	33.40
380	390	70.40	66.40	62.30	58.40	54.80	51.20	47.60	44.00	40.40	37.50	35.10
390	400	73.20	69.20	65.10	61.10	57.30	53.70	50.10	46.50	42.90	39.30	36.80
400	410	76.00	72.00	67.90	63.90	59.80	56.20	52.60	49.00	45.40	41.80	38.50
410	420	78.80	74.80	70.70	66.70	62.60	58.70	55.10	51.50	47.90	44.30	40.70
420	430	81.60	77.60	73.50	69.50	65.40	61.40	57.60	54.00	50.40	46.80	43.20
430	440	84.50	80.40	76.30	72.30	68.20	64.20	60.20	56.50	52.90	49.30	45.70
440	450	87.70	83.20	79.10	75.10	71.00	67.00	63.00	59.00	55.40	51.80	48.20
450	460	90.90	86.30	81.90	77.90	73.80	69.80	65.80	61.70	57.90	54.30	50.70
460	470	94.10	89.50	84.90	80.70	76.60	72.60	68.60	64.50	60.50	56.80	53.20
470	480	97.30	92.70	88.10	83.50	79.40	75.40	71.40	67.30	63.30	59.30	55.70
480	490	100.50	95.90	91.30	86.60	82.20	78.20	74.20	70.10	66.10	62.10	58.20
490	500	103.70	99.10	94.50	89.80	85.20	81.00	77.00	72.90	68.90	64.90	60.80
500	510	107.10	102.30	97.70	93.00	88.40	83.80	79.80	75.70	71.70	67.70	63.60
510	520	110.70	105.50	100.90	96.20	91.60	87.00	82.60	78.50	74.50	70.50	66.40
520	530	114.30	109.10	104.10	99.40	94.80	90.20	85.60	81.30	77.30	73.30	69.20
530	540	117.90	112.70	107.50	102.60	98.00	93.40	88.80	84.20	80.10	76.10	72.00
540	550	121.50	116.30	111.10	105.90	101.20	96.60	92.00	87.40	82.90	78.90	74.80
550	560	125.10	119.90	114.70	109.50	104.40	99.80	95.20	90.60	86.00	81.70	77.60
560	570	128.70	123.50	118.30	113.10	107.90	103.00	98.40	93.80	89.20	84.60	80.40
570	580	132.30	127.10	121.90	116.70	111.50	106.30	101.60	97.00	92.40	87.80	83.20
580	590	135.90	130.70	125.50	120.30	115.10	109.90	104.80	100.20	95.60	91.00	86.30
590	600	139.50	134.30	129.10	123.90	118.70	113.50	108.30	103.40	98.80	94.20	89.50
600	610	143.10	137.90	132.70	127.50	122.30	117.10	111.90	106.70	102.00	97.40	92.70
610	620	146.70	141.50	136.30	131.10	125.90	120.70	115.50	110.30	105.20	100.60	95.90
620	630	150.30	145.10	139.90	134.70	129.50	124.30	119.10	113.90	108.80	103.80	99.10
630	640	153.90	148.70	143.50	138.30	133.10	127.90	122.70	117.50	112.40	107.20	102.30
640	650	157.50	152.30	147.10	141.90	136.70	131.50	126.30	121.10	116.00	110.80	105.60
650	660	161.10	155.90	150.70	145.50	140.30	135.10	129.90	124.70	119.60	114.40	109.20
660	670	164.70	159.50	154.30	149.10	143.90	138.70	133.50	128.30	123.20	118.00	112.80
670	680	168.30	163.10	157.90	152.70	147.50	142.30	137.10	131.90	126.80	121.60	116.40
680	690	171.90	166.70	161.50	156.30	151.10	145.90	140.70	135.50	130.40	125.20	120.00
690	700	175.50	170.30	165.10	159.90	154.70	149.50	144.30	139.10	134.00	128.80	123.60
700	710	179.10	173.90	168.70	163.50	158.30	153.10	147.90	142.70	137.60	132.40	127.20
710	720	182.70	177.50	172.30	167.10	161.90	156.70	151.50	146.30	141.20	136.00	130.80
720	730	186.30	181.10	175.90	170.70	165.50	160.30	155.10	149.90	144.80	139.60	134.40
730	740	189.90	184.70	179.50	174.30	169.10	163.90	158.70	153.50	148.40	143.20	138.00
740	750	193.50	188.30	183.10	177.90	172.70	167.50	162.30	157.10	152.00	146.80	141.60
750	760	197.10	191.90	186.70	181.50	176.30	171.10	165.90	160.70	155.60	150.40	145.20
760	770	200.70	195.50	190.30	185.10	179.90	174.70	169.50	164.30	159.20	154.00	148.80
770	780	204.30	199.10	193.90	188.70	183.50	178.30	173.10	167.90	162.80	157.60	152.40
780	790	207.90	202.70	197.50	192.30	187.10	181.90	176.70	171.50	166.40	161.20	156.00
790	800	211.50	206.30	201.10	195.90	190.70	185.50	180.30	175.10	170.00	164.80	159.60
800	810	215.10	209.90	204.70	199.50	194.30	189.10	183.90	178.70	173.60	168.40	163.20
810	820	218.70	213.50	208.30	203.10	197.90	192.70	187.50	182.30	177.20	172.00	166.80
820	830	222.30	217.10	211.90	206.70	201.50	196.30	191.10	185.90	180.80	175.60	170.40
830	840	225.90	220.70	215.50	210.30	205.10	199.90	194.70	189.50	184.40	179.20	174.00
840	850	229.50	224.30	219.10	213.90	208.70	203.50	198.30	193.10	188.00	182.80	177.60
850	860	233.10	227.90	222.70	217.50	212.30	207.10	201.90	196.70	191.60	186.40	181.20
860	870	236.70	231.50	226.30	221.10	215.90	210.70	205.50	200.30	195.20	190.00	184.80
		36 percent of the excess over $870 plus—										
$870 and over		238.50	233.30	228.10	222.90	217.70	212.50	207.30	202.10	197.00	191.80	186.60

INCOME TAX WITHHOLDING*
MARRIED Persons — **MONTHLY** Payroll Period

And the wages are—		And the number of withholding allowances claimed is—									
At least	But less than	0	1	2	3	4	5	6	7	8	9	10 or more
		The amount of income tax to be withheld shall be—									
$0	$208	$0	$0	$0	$0	$0	$0	$0	$0	$0	$0	$0
208	212	.30	0	0	0	0	0	0	0	0	0	0
212	216	1.00	0	0	0	0	0	0	0	0	0	0
216	220	1.60	0	0	0	0	0	0	0	0	0	0
220	224	2.30	0	0	0	0	0	0	0	0	0	0
224	228	3.00	0	0	0	0	0	0	0	0	0	0
228	232	3.70	0	0	0	0	0	0	0	0	0	0
232	236	4.40	0	0	0	0	0	0	0	0	0	0
236	240	5.00	0	0	0	0	0	0	0	0	0	0
240	248	6.10	0	0	0	0	0	0	0	0	0	0
248	256	7.40	0	0	0	0	0	0	0	0	0	0
256	264	8.80	0	0	0	0	0	0	0	0	0	0
264	272	10.10	0	0	0	0	0	0	0	0	0	0
272	280	11.50	.90	0	0	0	0	0	0	0	0	0
280	288	12.90	2.20	0	0	0	0	0	0	0	0	0
288	296	14.20	3.60	0	0	0	0	0	0	0	0	0
296	304	15.60	5.00	0	0	0	0	0	0	0	0	0
304	312	16.90	6.30	0	0	0	0	0	0	0	0	0
312	320	18.30	7.70	0	0	0	0	0	0	0	0	0
320	328	19.70	9.00	0	0	0	0	0	0	0	0	0
328	336	21.00	10.40	0	0	0	0	0	0	0	0	0
336	344	22.40	11.80	1.10	0	0	0	0	0	0	0	0
344	352	23.70	13.10	2.50	0	0	0	0	0	0	0	0
352	360	25.10	14.50	3.90	0	0	0	0	0	0	0	0
360	368	26.50	15.80	5.20	0	0	0	0	0	0	0	0
368	376	27.80	17.20	6.60	0	0	0	0	0	0	0	0
376	384	29.20	18.60	7.90	0	0	0	0	0	0	0	0
384	392	30.50	19.90	9.30	0	0	0	0	0	0	0	0
392	400	31.90	21.30	10.70	0	0	0	0	0	0	0	0
400	420	34.30	23.70	13.00	2.40	0	0	0	0	0	0	0
420	440	38.10	27.10	16.40	5.80	0	0	0	0	0	0	0
440	460	42.10	30.50	19.80	9.20	0	0	0	0	0	0	0
460	480	46.10	33.90	23.20	12.60	2.00	0	0	0	0	0	0
480	500	50.10	37.60	26.60	16.00	5.40	0	0	0	0	0	0
500	520	54.10	41.60	30.00	19.40	8.80	0	0	0	0	0	0
520	540	58.10	45.60	33.40	22.80	12.20	1.60	0	0	0	0	0
540	560	62.10	49.60	37.10	26.20	15.60	5.00	0	0	0	0	0
560	580	66.10	53.60	41.10	29.60	19.00	8.40	0	0	0	0	0
580	600	70.10	57.60	45.10	33.00	22.40	11.80	1.10	0	0	0	0
600	640	76.10	63.60	51.10	38.60	27.50	16.90	6.20	0	0	0	0
640	680	84.10	71.60	59.10	46.60	34.30	23.70	13.00	2.40	0	0	0
680	720	92.10	79.60	67.10	54.60	42.10	30.50	19.80	9.20	0	0	0
720	760	100.10	87.60	75.10	62.60	50.10	37.60	26.60	16.00	5.40	0	0
760	800	107.20	95.60	83.10	70.60	58.10	45.60	33.40	22.80	12.20	1.60	0
800	840	114.00	103.40	91.10	78.60	66.10	53.60	41.10	29.60	19.00	8.40	0
840	880	120.80	110.20	99.10	86.60	74.10	61.60	49.10	36.60	25.80	15.20	4.50
880	920	127.60	117.00	106.30	94.60	82.10	69.60	57.10	44.60	32.60	22.00	11.30
920	960	134.40	123.80	113.10	102.50	90.10	77.60	65.10	52.60	40.10	28.80	18.10
960	1,000	141.20	130.60	119.90	109.30	98.10	85.60	73.10	60.60	48.10	35.60	24.90
1,000	1,040	148.00	137.40	126.70	116.10	105.50	93.60	81.10	68.60	56.10	43.60	31.70
1,040	1,080	154.80	144.20	133.50	122.90	112.30	101.60	89.10	76.60	64.10	51.60	39.10
1,080	1,120	161.60	151.00	140.30	129.70	119.10	108.50	97.10	84.60	72.10	59.60	47.10
1,120	1,160	168.40	157.80	147.10	136.50	125.90	115.30	104.60	92.60	80.10	67.60	55.10
1,160	1,200	177.90	164.60	153.90	143.30	132.70	122.10	111.40	100.60	88.10	75.60	63.10
1,200	1,240	187.90	172.30	160.70	150.10	139.50	128.90	118.20	107.60	96.10	83.60	71.10
1,240	1,280	197.90	182.30	167.50	156.90	146.30	135.70	125.00	114.40	103.80	91.60	79.10
1,280	1,320	207.90	192.30	176.70	163.70	153.10	142.50	131.80	121.20	110.60	99.60	87.10
1,320	1,360	217.90	202.30	186.70	171.00	159.90	149.30	138.60	128.00	117.40	106.80	95.10
1,360	1,400	227.90	212.30	196.70	181.00	166.70	156.10	145.40	134.80	124.20	113.60	102.90
1,400	1,440	237.90	222.30	206.70	191.00	175.40	162.90	152.20	141.60	131.00	120.40	109.70

*From IRS Publication 15 (Rev. November 1977)

MARRIED Persons — MONTHLY Payroll Period

And the wages are—		And the number of withholding allowances claimed is—										
At least	But less than	0	1	2	3	4	5	6	7	8	9	10 or more
		The amount of income tax to be withheld shall be—										
$1,440	$1,480	$247.90	$232.30	$216.70	$201.00	$185.40	$169.80	$159.00	$148.40	$137.80	$127.20	$116.50
1,480	1,520	257.90	242.30	226.70	211.00	195.40	179.80	165.80	155.20	144.60	134.00	123.30
1,520	1,560	269.10	252.30	236.70	221.00	205.40	189.80	174.20	162.00	151.40	140.80	130.10
1,560	1,600	280.30	262.80	246.70	231.00	215.40	199.80	184.20	168.80	158.20	147.60	136.90
1,600	1,640	291.50	274.00	256.70	241.00	225.40	209.80	194.20	178.50	165.00	154.40	143.70
1,640	1,680	302.70	285.20	267.70	251.00	235.40	219.80	204.20	188.50	172.90	161.20	150.50
1,680	1,720	313.90	296.40	278.90	261.40	245.40	229.80	214.20	198.50	182.90	168.00	157.30
1,720	1,760	325.10	307.60	290.10	272.60	255.40	239.80	224.20	208.50	192.90	177.30	164.10
1,760	1,800	336.30	318.80	301.30	283.80	266.30	249.80	234.20	218.50	202.90	187.30	171.70
1,800	1,840	347.50	330.00	312.50	295.00	277.50	260.00	244.20	228.50	212.90	197.30	181.70
1,840	1,880	358.70	341.20	323.70	306.20	288.70	271.20	254.20	238.50	222.90	207.30	191.70
1,880	1,920	370.90	352.40	334.90	317.40	299.90	282.40	264.90	248.50	232.90	217.30	201.70
1,920	1,960	383.70	363.70	346.10	328.60	311.10	293.60	276.10	258.60	242.90	227.30	211.70
1,960	2,000	396.50	376.50	357.30	339.80	322.30	304.80	287.30	269.80	252.90	237.30	221.70
2,000	2,040	409.30	389.30	369.30	351.00	333.50	316.00	298.50	281.00	263.50	247.30	231.70
2,040	2,080	422.10	402.10	382.10	362.20	344.70	327.20	309.70	292.20	274.70	257.30	241.70
2,080	2,120	434.90	414.90	394.90	374.90	355.90	338.40	320.90	303.40	285.90	268.40	251.70
2,120	2,160	447.70	427.70	407.70	387.70	367.70	349.60	332.10	314.60	297.10	279.60	262.10
2,160	2,200	461.10	440.50	420.50	400.50	380.50	360.80	343.30	325.80	308.30	290.80	273.30
2,200	2,240	475.50	453.30	433.30	413.30	393.30	373.30	354.50	337.00	319.50	302.00	284.50
2,240	2,280	489.90	467.40	446.10	426.10	406.10	386.10	366.10	348.20	330.70	313.20	295.70
2,280	2,320	504.30	481.80	459.30	438.90	418.90	398.90	378.90	359.40	341.90	324.40	306.90
2,320	2,360	518.70	496.20	473.70	451.70	431.70	411.70	391.70	371.70	353.10	335.60	318.10
2,360	2,400	533.10	510.60	488.10	465.60	444.50	424.50	404.50	384.50	364.50	346.80	329.30
2,400	2,440	547.50	525.00	502.50	480.00	457.50	437.30	417.30	397.30	377.30	358.00	340.50
2,440	2,480	561.90	539.40	516.90	494.40	471.90	450.10	430.10	410.10	390.10	370.10	351.70
2,480	2,520	576.30	553.80	531.30	508.80	486.30	463.80	442.90	422.90	402.90	382.90	362.90
2,520	2,560	590.70	568.20	545.70	523.20	500.70	478.20	455.70	435.70	415.70	395.70	375.70
2,560	2,600	605.10	582.60	560.10	537.60	515.10	492.60	470.10	448.50	428.50	408.50	388.50
2,600	2,640	619.50	597.00	574.50	552.00	529.50	507.00	484.50	462.00	441.30	421.30	401.30
2,640	2,680	633.90	611.40	588.90	566.40	543.90	521.40	498.90	476.40	454.10	434.10	414.10
2,680	2,720	648.30	625.80	603.30	580.80	558.30	535.80	513.30	490.80	468.30	446.90	426.90
2,720	2,760	662.70	640.20	617.70	595.20	572.70	550.20	527.70	505.20	482.70	460.20	439.70
2,760	2,800	677.10	654.60	632.10	609.60	587.10	564.60	542.10	519.60	497.10	474.60	452.50
2,800	2,840	691.50	669.00	646.50	624.00	601.50	579.00	556.50	534.00	511.50	489.00	466.50
2,840	2,880	705.90	683.40	660.90	638.40	615.90	593.40	570.90	548.40	525.90	503.40	480.90
2,880	2,920	720.30	697.80	675.30	652.80	630.30	607.80	585.30	562.80	540.30	517.80	495.30
2,920	2,960	734.70	712.20	689.70	667.20	644.70	622.20	599.70	577.20	554.70	532.20	509.70
2,960	3,000	749.10	726.60	704.10	681.60	659.10	636.60	614.10	591.60	569.10	546.60	524.10
3,000	3,040	763.50	741.00	718.50	696.00	673.50	651.00	628.50	606.00	583.50	561.00	538.50
3,040	3,080	777.90	755.40	732.90	710.40	687.90	665.40	642.90	620.40	597.90	575.40	552.90
3,080	3,120	792.30	769.80	747.30	724.80	702.30	679.80	657.30	634.80	612.30	589.80	567.30
3,120	3,160	806.70	784.20	761.70	739.20	716.70	694.20	671.70	649.20	626.70	604.20	581.70
3,160	3,200	821.10	798.60	776.10	753.60	731.10	708.60	686.10	663.60	641.10	618.60	596.10
3,200	3,240	835.50	813.00	790.50	768.00	745.50	723.00	700.50	678.00	655.50	633.00	610.50
3,240	3,280	849.90	827.40	804.90	782.40	759.90	737.40	714.90	692.40	669.90	647.40	624.90
3,280	3,320	864.30	841.80	819.30	796.80	774.30	751.80	729.30	706.80	684.30	661.80	639.30
3,320	3,360	878.70	856.20	833.70	811.20	788.70	766.20	743.70	721.20	698.70	676.20	653.70
3,360	3,400	893.10	870.60	848.10	825.60	803.10	780.60	758.10	735.60	713.10	690.60	668.10
3,400	3,440	907.50	885.00	862.50	840.00	817.50	795.00	772.50	750.00	727.50	705.00	682.50
3,440	3,480	921.90	899.40	876.90	854.40	831.90	809.40	786.90	764.40	741.90	719.40	696.90
3,480	3,520	936.30	913.80	891.30	868.80	846.30	823.80	801.30	778.80	756.30	733.80	711.30
3,520	3,560	950.70	928.20	905.70	883.20	860.70	838.20	815.70	793.20	770.70	748.20	725.70
3,560	3,600	965.10	942.60	920.10	897.60	875.10	852.60	830.10	807.60	785.10	762.60	740.10
3,600	3,640	979.50	957.00	934.50	912.00	889.50	867.00	844.50	822.00	799.50	777.00	754.50
		36 percent of the excess over $3,640 plus—										
$3,640 and over		986.70	964.20	941.70	919.20	896.70	874.20	851.70	829.20	806.70	784.20	761.70

CHAPTER SEVEN
Property and Sales Taxes

OBJECTIVES

This chapter deals with property taxes and those factors that determine the amount paid, such as assessment rates and tax rates. Problems involving the use of sales taxes are also included.

Upon completion of this chapter, you should be able to
(1) compute the assessed valuation if the assessment rate and market price are known,
(2) compute the market price if the assessed valuation and assessment rate are known,
(3) compute the tax rate on property,
(4) compute property taxes if the assessed valuation and tax rate are known,
(5) compute the tax if the tax rate, assessment rate, and market price are known,
(6) compute the amount of sales tax and gross cost for any given item if the selling price and sales tax rate are known,
(7) compute sales tax on an item in which an excise tax is included,
(8) compute the list price if the cost (including the sales tax) and the sales tax rate are known.

UNIT 1. PROPERTY TAXES

Although property taxes vary from state to state, the method of computation is the same. The tax rate is based on the *assessed valuation* of the property; valuation is determined by individuals called assessors who are elected or appointed. It represents a certain percent or fractional part of the current market price. Some states may have an assessment rate of 20%; others may have a rate as high as 60%.

Each state provides means, within its governing framework, of periodically adjusting assessment rates in keeping with changing fair market values. This is done by the legislature or some body such as a county board of assessment or state board of equalization. Valuations must be at the fair market value.

1. When a piece of property is offered for sale, the price set by the owner is the *asking price*. The seller tries to get the best price he can and the buyer tries to get the lowest price he can. The final price agreed on is the *market price*.

   Mr. Lind offered his home for sale at $27,500. It sold for $26,500; $26,500 is the _____.

   -

   market price

2. The assessed value placed on a piece of property for tax purposes is determined by individuals called *assessors*. The assessed value is based on a given percent of the market price.

   A home worth $56,000 is assessed at 20% of its value or $11,200; $11,200 is called the _____.

   -

   assessed value

3. The market price of a piece of property is usually (more than/less than) the asking price. The assessed value of a piece of property is (more than/less than) the market price. The person who determines what a piece of property is worth for tax purposes is called an _____.

   -

   less than, less than, assessor

4. Mr. Allen owns an apartment house worth $175,000. It is assessed at 25% of its value. The assessed valuation is _____.

   -

   $43,750

5. Mrs. Smith's home was assessed at $2700. What was the market price if the assessment rate was 20%? 22%? (Since the assessed valuation = market price × assessment rate, the market price = assessed valuation ÷ assessment rate.)

   20% _____   22% _____

   $13,500, $12,272.73

Finding the Tax Rate

In order to determine the total funds needed, the usual procedure is to prepare a *budget* based on the requirements of the county, district, or municipality. After it has been accepted and all other sources of income taken into account, the tax rate is determined as follows:

$$\text{Tax rate}^* = \frac{\text{total funds needed}}{\text{total assessed valuation}}$$

$$\text{OR} = \frac{\text{taxes to be collected}}{\text{total assessed valuation}}.$$

6. The tax rate depends on how much money is required and the assessed valuation. Hemp City prepared a budget and found that it needed $2,165,000 to operate. Income *other* than property taxes amounted to $975,000. The amount to be collected as property taxes is _____.

   $2,165,000 − $975,000 = $1,190,000

7. If the funds needed are $1,190,000 and the assessed valuation of the property is $23,110,000, the tax rate is $1,190,000 ÷ $23,110,000 = .051492 = 5.15%.

   Let us assume that a town needs $465,000 to meet its requirements. If the assessed valuation is $10,000,000, the tax rate equals $_____ ÷ $_____ = _____%.

   ----

   tax rate equals $465,000 ÷ $10,000,000 = .0465 = 4.65%

---

*Tax rates can and usually do vary from district to district within a state, county, or city. These variations are due to the amount of bonded indebtedness, type of improvements or services, etc.

PROPERTY TAXES 283

8. Complete the following statements:

Assessed valuation = _____ × _____.

Tax rate = _____ ÷ _____.

- -

Assessed valuation = assessment rate × market price.
Tax rate = total funds needed or taxes to be collected ÷ total assessed valuation.

9. A tax rate of 7.85% expressed as a decimal = .0785. This means that $0.0785 is the tax rate per dollar of assessed valuation. This rate may also be expressed in cents per dollar of assessed valuation; $0.0785 = 7.85 cents.

Express a tax rate of 11.94% as $_____ per dollar of assessed valuation;

as _____ cents per dollar of assessed valuation.

- -

$0.1194
11.94 cents

10. Tax rates may be expressed as mills. A *mill* is a tenth of a cent.

   1 mill = .001
   2 mills = .002
  10 mills = .010
  $1\frac{1}{2}$ mills = .0015, etc.

Then $0.024 = 2 cents + 4 mills or 24 mills,
      0.0245 = 2 cents + 4.5 mills or 24.5 mills.
A tax rate of 7.85% (frame 9) = .0785 = 7.85 cents = 78.5 mills.

Express 3.06% as mills per dollar of assessed valuation. _____

       6.85% as mills per dollar of assessed valuation. _____

- -

30.6 mills
68.5 mills

11. Tax rates are also expressed as "dollars per $100 or $1000 of assessed valuation." A tax rate of 12.45% = .1245 or $0.1245 per dollar of assessed valuation. For $100 of assessed valuation, multiply this rate by 100. Then, $0.1245 per *dollar* of assessed valuation = $12.45 per *$100* of assessed valuation. For $1000 of assessed valuation, multiply the rate by 1000. Then, $0.1245 per *dollar* of assessed valuation = $124.50 per *$1000* of assessed valuation.

    Change the following rates per dollar of assessed valuation as indicated.

    (a) $0.1168 = $_____ per $100 of assessed valuation.

    (b) $0.09667 = $_____ per $1000 of assessed valuation.

    (c) 10.45%   = $_____ per $100 of assessed valuation.

    (d) 6.93%   = $_____ per $1000 of assessed valuation.

    (a) $11.68
    (b) $96.67
    (c) $10.45
    (d) $69.30

12. To summarize, we have found that tax rates may be expressed in several ways—as a percent, in mills (tenth of a cent), or in dollars and cents. A rate of 4.65% may be expressed as

    (a) $0.0465 or 4.65 cents per dollar of assessed valuation
    (b) 46.5 mills per dollar of assessed valuation
    (c) $4.65 per $100 of assessed valuation
    (d) $46.50 per $1000 of assessed valuation

    (a) Express 5.62% as $_____ per $100 of assessed valuation and $_____ per $1000 of assessed valuation.

    (b) Express $11.96 per $100 of assessed valuation as _____% and $_____ per dollar of assessed valuation.

    (a) $5.62, $56.20,   (b) 11.96%, $0.1196

PROPERTY TAXES

13. When there is a fractional remainder, the rate is rounded to the next higher digit. (The number of decimals used depends on local practice.) Therefore .0432712 recorded to 3 decimals would equal .044, not. 043.

    Record the following rates correct to 4 decimals.

    .05634 _____   .06822 _____

    .10626 _____   .09914 _____

    _____

    .0564   .0683
    .1063   .0992

14. The tax rate is actually the total of several rates applied to special purposes; for example, a total tax rate of $10.39 per $100 of assessed valuation may be made up of rates as follows: county, $2.86; city, $2.34; school, $4.84; special district, $0.35. In some cases there may be a water district, transit district, mosquito abatement district, and others.

    What is the total tax rate per $100 of assessed valuation if it is made up of the following rates: county, $3.10; city, $2.98; school, $6.54; special district, $0.98; transit, $1.09? $_____

    _____

    $14.69

Finding the Tax

The following formulas are used to find the tax:

Assessed valuation = assessment rate × market value.
Taxes = assessed valuation × tax rate.

15. The market price of a building is $75,600. If the assessment rate is 20%, what is the assessed valuation?

    Assessed valuation = _____ × _____ = $_____.

    If the tax rate is $11.42 per $100 assessed valuation, the taxes will

    equal _____ × _____ = $_____.

    _____

Assessed valuation = .20 × $75,600 = $15,120.

Taxes = $\frac{$15,120}{100}$ × 11.42 = $1726.70 OR $151.20 × 11.42 = $1726.70.

16. Mrs. Cecil Jones owned a home worth $17,500. The assessment rate was 28%. What tax did she pay if the tax rate was $9.16667 per $100 assessed valuation?

    Assessed valuation = _____.

    Tax = _____.

    _

    Assessed valuation = $17,500 × .28 = $4900.
    Tax = $49.00 × 9.16667 = $449.17.

17. Mr. Riedell lives in the country and therefore has no city tax. His land is assessed at $1320, improvements at $2750. Tax rates per $100 of assessed valuation are the following: county, $2.95; school, $5.04; special district, $0.53. Find the amount of tax for each purpose, the total tax rate, and the total taxes to be paid.

    Total assessed valuation = $_____ + $_____ = $_____.

    County tax = $_____ × $_____ = $_____
    (carry to 3 decimals).

    School tax = $_____ × $_____ = $_____
    (carry to 3 decimals).

    Special district = $_____ × $_____ = $_____
    (carry to 3 decimals).

    Total taxes = $_____ (round answer to nearest cent)

    Total tax rate = $_____ per $100 of assessed valuation.

    Total tax = $_____ × $_____ = $_____.

    _

    Total assessed valuation = $1320 + $2750 = $4070.
    County tax = $40.70 × $2.95 = $120.065.
    School tax = $40.70 × $5.04 = $205.128.
    Special district = $40.70 × $0.53 = $21.571.
    Total taxes = $346.764 or $346.76.
    Total tax rate = $8.52 per $100 of assessed valuation.
    Total tax = $40.70 × $8.52 = $346.76.

EXERCISE 29

Instructions: Complete Sections I, II, and III as indicated. Record answers in the spaces provided. Compare your results with those shown at the end of this exercise. *Section IV:* Answers appear at the end of this exercise. If your answers do not agree with those shown, check your calculations before referring to the solutions which follow.

I. Change the given rate to the new rate:

1. 67 mills to percent _____

2. $1.68 per $100 to $1000 _____

3. $10.667 per $100 to per dollar _____

4. 4.012¢ per dollar to dollars per $100 _____

5. 11.916% to dollars per $100 _____

6. $3\frac{1}{2}$% to dollars per $1000 _____

7. $2\frac{1}{2}$ mills to dollars per $100 _____

8. $12.8125 per $100 to nearest whole mills _____

9. $3.02 per $100 to cents per $1.00 _____

10. $0.52 per $1000 to percent _____

II. Find the amount of tax for the following:

No.	Assessed Value	Tax Rate	Amount of Tax
1.	$ 3,000	$6\frac{1}{2}$%	_____
2.	45,500	$11.06 per $100	_____
3.	309,060	$0.035 per $1.00	_____
4.	65,450	$0.04 per $1.00	_____
5.	80,000	$15.168 per $1000	_____
6.	17,500	$12.86 per $100	_____

III. Find the assessed valuation and amount of tax paid for the following:

No.	Market Value	Assessment Rate	Tax Rate	Assessed Value	Taxes
1.	$ 20,000	26%	$12.50 per $100	_____	_____
2.	19,800	25%	$ 8.33 per $100	_____	_____
3.	35,750	20%	$10.06 per $100	_____	_____
4.	64,900	28%	$6\frac{1}{2}\%$	_____	_____
5.	125,600	25%	$8\frac{1}{3}\%$	_____	_____
6.	22,450	30%	$ 0.25 per dollar	_____	_____

IV. Word problems:

1. How much does Mrs. James pay in taxes if her home is assessed at $25,000 and the tax rate is $11.9167 per $100?

2. Find the assessed value of property worth $16,500 if the assessment rate is 27%.

3. Taxes amounting to $5000 were paid on a piece of property in a district in which the tax rate is $12\frac{1}{2}\%$. At this rate what would the expected market value of the property be if the assessment rate is 30% (nearest dollar)?

4. The tax rate in Middletown is $6.15 per $100. The budget is established at $4,750,000. What is the total assessed valuation of property in Middletown (nearest dollar)?

5. The total budget of a certain city is $136,845,000, of which 75% must be raised by property taxes. If the tax rate is $11.00 per $1000, what is the total assessed valuation of property in the city?

6. H. Howen owns a piece of property worth $16,500 which is assessed at 22% of its value. He pays $0.41 per $100 for a special junior college fund, $0.02 per $100 for education of mentally retarded, $0.001 per $100 for education of institutionalized pupils (countrywide), and $0.089 mandatory countywide tax in place of state equalization aid. These are additional educational levies to the school district rates. How much did Mr. Howen pay for each of these needs? What was the total tax?

 _____

 _____

 _____

 _____

 Total

7. What is the current market value of a house if current taxes amount to $350, the tax rate is $5.00 per $100, and the assessment rate is 25%?

290 UNIT 1

8. John Bradshaw purchased a house for $35,750 in a town which has an assessment rate of 30%. The tax rate is $8.35 per $100. How much of his total tax is spent on education if 62% of the district taxes are spent for that purpose?

_____

9. What is the tax rate per $100 (corrected to two decimals) for a community where property is assessed at $43,460,000 if the budget requirements total $6,000,000?

_____

10. Mr. Mulliken owns a home in a city which he rents for $160 a month. The assessed value of this property is $1300 for the land, $1850 for the improvements, and $50 for personal property. (a) If the tax rate is $11.53 per $100, find the taxes paid for the year. (b) If repairs and depreciation amounted to $256 in a year, what was the net income realized?

(a) _____

(b) _____

Answers

Section I

1. 6.7%
2. $16.80 per $1000
3. $0.10667 per dollar
4. $4.012 per $100
5. $11.916 per $100
6. $35.00 per $1000
7. $0.25 per $100
8. 128 mills
9. $0.0302 or 3.02 cents
10. .052%

Section II

1. $195.00
2. $5032.30
3. $10,817.10
4. $2618.00
5. $1213.44
6. $2250.50

PROPERTY TAXES

Section III

	Assessed Valuation	Taxes Paid
1.	$5,200.00	$ 650.00
2.	4,950.00	412.34
3.	7,150.00	719.29
4.	18,172.00	1181.18
5.	31,400.00	2616.67
6.	6,735.00	1683.75

Section IV

1. $2979.18
2. $4455.00
3. $133,333
4. $77,235,772
5. $9,330,340,909
6. $14.88
      0.73
      0.04
      3.23
   $18.88
7. $28,000
8. $555.23
9. $13.81
10. (a) $368.96
    (b) $1295.04

Solutions

III. 1. $.26 \times \$20,000 = \$5,200.00$.
      $52.00 \times \$12.50 = \$650.00$.
  2.–6. are solved in the same manner.

IV. 1. Taxes paid $= \$250.00 \times \$11.9167 = \$2979.18$.
    2. Assessed valuation $= \$16,500 \times .27 = \$4455.00$.
    3. Assessed valuation $= \$5000 \div .125 = \$40,000$ OR $\$5000 \times 8 = \$40,000$. Market value $= \$40,0000 \div .30 = \$133,333$.
    4. Total assessed valuation $= \$4,750,000 \div .0615 = \$77,235,772$. (\$6.15 per \$100 expressed as a decimal $= .0615$).
    5. Amount to be raised by taxes $= \$136,845,000 \times .75 = \$102,633,750$.
       Assessed valuation $= \$102,633,750 \div .011 = \$9,330,340,909$.
    6. Assessed valuation $= \$16,500 \times .22 = \$3630.00$.
       Special junior college fund $= \$36.30 \times .41 = \$14.88$
       Mentally retarded fund $= \$36.30 \times .02 = $ .73
       Institutionalized pupils $= \$36.30 \times .001 = $ .04
       Mandatory countywide tax $= \$36.30 \times .089 = $ 3.23
                                                                                $18.88
       Total tax $= \$36.30 \times .52 = \$18.88$ (check).
    7. Assessed value $= \$ 350 \div .05 = \$7000$.
       Market value $= \$7000 \div .25 = \$28,000$ OR $\$7000 \times 4 = \$28,000$.
    8. Assessed value $= \$35,750 \times .30 = \$10.725$.
       Taxes paid $= \$107.25 \times 8.35 = \$895.54$.
       Education tax $= \$895.54 \times .62 = \$555.23$.

9. Tax rate = $6,000,000 ÷ $43,460,000 = $13.81 per $100.
10. Total assessed valuation = $1300 + $1850 + $50 = $3200.
    (a) Taxes paid   = $32.00 × $11.53 = $368.96.
    (b) Total expenses = $368.96 + $256.00 = $624.96.
        Gross income = $160 × 12 = $1920.
        Net income   = $1920.00 − $624.96 = $1295.04.

UNIT 2. SALES TAXES

The general sales tax has become an increasingly important and popular source of revenue for most states as well as many counties and municipalities. The seller acts as an agent because he collects the tax directly from the buyer at the time of the sale. The amount collected is then remitted periodically to the city, county, or state as required by law.

Tax rates are expressed as a percent and vary between states from 2 to 5% or more. City and county taxes are generally much lower—$\frac{1}{4}, \frac{1}{2}$, and 1%. Although there are a few exceptions to the rule, in general a sales tax is levied only on purchases made and delivered within a tax area.

To ensure a high degree of accuracy in filling out sales slips or invoices and to save time, tax schedules are used by most sales clerks.

1. If you can answer the following questions accurately, skip to frame 8. If you do not get a perfect score or choose not to answer these questions, go to frame 2.

   (a) A sales tax is based on the (retail/wholesale) price of an article?
   (b) If the sales tax is 5%, what is the amount of the sales tax for an article that sells for $165.00? _____
   (c) The sales tax rate for a certain state is 5%. What is the total sales tax rate in a city of the state in which there is a 1% city tax and a $\frac{1}{2}$% transportation tax? _____
   (d) What is the total cost of a dress that sells for $39.50 plus a 4% sales tax? _____
   (e) M. Pratt purchased a table for $135 less 10% trade discount. If a sales tax of $3\frac{1}{2}$% is added, what is the total cost of the purchase? _____

- -

(a) retail, (b) $8.25, (c) $6\frac{1}{2}$%, (d) $41.08,
(e) $135 less 10% = $121.50.
    $121.50 × .035 = $4.25.
    total cost   = $125.75.

2. Mary Hynes bought a coat for $95.00. What sales tax did she pay if the rate was 5%?

   Solution: Sales tax = $95.00 × .05 = $4.75.

   What tax would she have paid if the rate was $4\frac{1}{2}$%? 5.4%? _____ , _____

   -

   $95.00 × .045 = $4.275 = $4.28, $95.00 × .054 = $5.13

3. Mr. Haynes bought a desk that was listed at $190.00. If the sales tax rate is 4%, how much did the desk cost?

   Tax   = _____ × $190.00 = $_____ .

   Total cost = $190.00 + $_____ = $_____ .

   -

   Tax = .04 × $190.00 = $7.60.
   Total cost = $190.00 + $7.60 = $197.60.

4. In a city in which the sales tax is $5\frac{1}{2}$%, compute the total cost of

   $3\frac{1}{2}$ yd gingham at 1.97\frac{1}{2}$ a yd $_____

   16 yd linen at $4.12 a yd   _____

   3 spools thread at .20 each   _____

                       Total $_____

               Plus sales tax   _____

                  Total cost $_____

   -

$ 6.91
 65.92
  0.60

$73.43
  4.04

$77.47

5. In a community in which $\frac{1}{4}$% tax for a transit system is added to the sales tax of 4%, what is the total cost of a garment selling for $112.50?

   Total tax = _____.

   Total cost = _____.

   -

   Total tax = $112.50 × .0425 = $4.78
   Total cost = $112.50 + $4.78 = $117.28

6. J. E. Jensen ordered a lawn mower priced at $69.75. He was allowed a discount of 5%. The sales tax equaled 3% for the state and $\frac{1}{2}$% for the city. How much did the lawn mower cost?

   Discount = _____.

   Net price = _____.

   Sales tax ($3\frac{1}{2}$%) = _____ (always based on the net price).

   Total cost = _____.

   -

   Discount = .05 × $69.75 = $3.49.
   Net price = $69.75 − $3.49 = $66.26.
   Sales tax ($3\frac{1}{2}$%) = .035 × $66.26 = $2.32.
   Total cost = $66.26 + $2.32 = $68.58.

7. J. Brown bought a hedge cutter marked $110.00 less 15%. If the sales tax is $5\frac{1}{2}$%, what is the total cost of the purchase?

   Net price = $_____.

   Sales tax = $_____.

   Total cost = $_____.

   -

   Net price = $110.00 less 15% = $110 − $16.50 = $93.50.
   Sales tax = .055 × $93.50 = $5.14.
   Total cost = $93.50 + $5.14 = $98.64.

The *excise tax*, by definition, is a Federal tax levied on the manufacture, sale, or consumption of a commodity within a country. Since it represents part of the cost, it is passed on to the consumer or buyer as part of the purchase price. If, however, this tax appears on an invoice distinct from other costs of an item, it must be added to the retail price before the sales tax is computed. There are only a few commodities on which an excise tax is so applied.

In addition to automobile tires, excise taxes are imposed on foreign automobiles coming into this country and domestic cars, guns, and alcoholic beverages. At this time, however, the automobile tire seems to be the only commodity listed on which the excise tax is publicized.

Example: George Mann bought 2 automobile tires at $15.95 each. The excise tax on each tire was $2.08. What is the total amount of the purchase if a sales tax of 3% is included?

Solution: Basic sales price (2 × $15.95)   = $31.90
　　　　　　Excise tax (2 × $2.08)　　　　　 =   4.16
　　　　　　Total sales price ($31.90 + $4.16) = $36.06
　　　　　　Sales tax (.03 × $36.06)　　　　 =   1.08
　　　　　　Total amount of purchase ($36.06 + $1.08) = $37.14

8. Mr. Guthrie bought 2 automobile tires, size 8.85 × 15, for $19.95 each. The excise tax on each tire was $2.86. Find the sales tax if the state tax rate is $2\frac{1}{2}\%$. Complete the following:

　　Basic sales price　　　　　$_____

　　Excise tax　　　　　　　　_____

　　Total sales price　　　　　$_____

　　Sales tax　　　　　　　　 _____

　　Total amount of purchase　_____

- -

　　Basic sales price　　　　　$39.90　(2 × $19.95)
　　Excise tax　　　　　　　　 5.72　(2 × $ 2.86)
　　Total sales price　　　　　$45.62
　　Sales tax ($2\frac{1}{2}\%$)　　　　　 1.14　($45.62 × .025)
　　Total amount of purchase　$46.76

UNIT 2

9. If Miss Hass bought a coat for $107.10, which included a sales tax of 2%, what is the list price?

   Solution: The list price = 100%.
   Since $107.10 is 2% more than the list price, it equals 102% of the list price.
   The list price (100%) = $107.10 ÷ 1.02 = $105.00.

   Find the list price on a garment that sold for $91.00, 4% sales tax included.

   $91.00 = _____ % of the list price.

   List price (100%) = $91.00 ÷ _____ = $_____.

   -

   $91.00 = 104% of the list price
   List price (100%) = $91.00 ÷ 1.04 = $87.50.

Cash discounts cannot be applied against sales taxes. The following example serves as an illustration.

Mrs. Moffit bought some furniture for $950.00 plus a sales tax of 4%. The invoice was dated November 2 with terms of 1%—10th EOM. This bill was paid on December 3. What is the total amount of the remittance?

Solution: Sales tax = $950.00 × .04 = $38.00.
Total amount due = $38.00 + $950.00 = $988.00.
Cash discount = 1% of $950.00 = $9.50.
Amount of remittance = $988.00 − $9.50 = $978.50.

10. J. Taylor owed $42.60 plus a 3% sales tax. Terms were 2/10, n/30. If the cash discount is allowed, how much is required to pay this obligation in full?

    Sales tax   = _____.

    Total amount due   = _____.

    Cash discount   = _____.

    Amount of payment   = _____.

    -

    Sales tax = $42.60 × .03 = $1.278 = $1.28.
    Total amount due = $42.60 + $1.28 = $43.88.
    Cash discount = .02 × $42.60 = $0.85.
    Amount of payment = $43.88 − $0.85 = $43.03.

EXERCISE 30

Answers appear at the end of this exercise. If your answers do not agree with those shown, check your calculations before referring to the solutions that follow.

1. If the sales tax in a state is 4%, what tax is collected on the following purchases: (a) $48.20, (b) $36.01?

    (a) _____

    (b) _____

2. Mrs. O'Neil had a suit cleaned for $2.25. What was the total charge if she paid a tax of 4.2% for the service?

3. What was the marked price for an article that cost $66.63, a $2\frac{1}{2}$% sales tax included?

4. J. Fleming bought a piece of machinery for $125 less 5%. What was the total amount paid if he was charged a $4\frac{1}{2}$% sales tax and an additional $\frac{1}{4}$% city tax?

5. M. Howard owed $420.00 plus a 3% sales tax with terms of 2/10, n/30. If he paid this bill within 10 days, how much was his remittance?

Answers

1. (a) $1.93
   (b) $1.44
2. $2.34
3. $65.00
4. $124.39
5. $424.20

Solutions

1. (a) $48.20 × .04 = $1.928 = $1.93.
   (b) $36.01 × .04 = $1.4404 = $1.44.
2. Tax = $2.25 × .042 = $0.0945 = $0.09.
   Total charge = $2.25 + $0.09 = $2.34.
3. $66.63 ÷ 1.025 = $65.00.
4. 5% of $125 = $6.25.
   Net price = $125.00 − $6.25 = $118.75.
   Sales tax = $118.75 × .0475 = $ 5.64.
   Total cost = $118.75 + $5.64 = $124.39.
5. Sales tax = .03 × $420 = $12.60.
   Cash discount = .02 × $420 = $8.40.
   Payment = ($420.00 + $12.60) − $8.40 = $432.60 − $8.40 = $424.20.

EXERCISE 31

Chapter Summary

Answers appear at the end of this exercise. If your answers do not agree with those shown, check your calculations before referring to the solutions that follow.

1. The budget for a town is $5,650,000; 85% of this amount must be raised by property taxes. What is the tax rate per $100 if the total assessed valuation of property in the town is $25,360,000? (Carry answer to three decimals.)

    _____

2. Find the tax paid for the following:

	Market Value	Assessment Rate	Tax Rate
(a)	$30,000	25%	$11.50 per $100
(b)	15,750	22.4%	$0.096 per $1
(c)	52,500	27%	$9\frac{1}{2}\%$

   (a) _____

   (b) _____

   (c) _____

3. Taxes amounting to $1794 were paid on a piece of property in a district in which the tax rate is $11\frac{1}{2}\%$. At this rate what would the expected market value of the property be if the assessment rate is 30%?

    _____

4. A sewing machine was bought for $240.00. If a sales tax of $5\frac{1}{2}\%$ is added, what is the amount of the tax and the total cost of the machine?

    tax _____

    cost _____

CHAPTER SUMMARY

5. The Home Apts. bought some new carpet at a cost of $895.00 and were granted a 5% trade discount. Sales taxes amounted to 5.4%. Terms 1%–10 EOM. If they took advantage of the cash discount, what was the total payment for this purchase?

6. J. Hawks ordered 3 tires for his car at a cost of $17.95 each. The excise tax on each tire was $2.86. What is the total amount of this purchase if a 4.2% sales tax was added?

Answers

1. $18.937
3. $52,000
5. $887.66

2. (a) $ 862.50
   (b) $ 338.69
   (c) $1346.63
4. Tax $ 13.20
   Cost $253.20
6. $65.05

Solutions

1. Taxes to be raised = $5,650,000 × .85 = $4,802,500.
   Tax rate = (amount of taxes to be raised) ÷ (assessed valuation)
   = $4,802,500 ÷ $25,360,000 = .189373 = $18.937 per $100 of assessed valuation.
2. (a) Assessed valuation = $30,000 × .25 = $7500.
      Taxes = $75.00 × 11.50 = $862.50.
   (b) Assessed valuation = $15,750 × .224 = $3528.
      Taxes = $3528 × 0.096 = $338.69.
   (c) Assessed valuation = $52,500 × .27 = $14,175.
      Taxes = $14,175 × .095 = $1346.63.
3. Assessed valuation = taxes collected ÷ rate = $1794 ÷ .115 = $15,600.
   Market value = assessed valuation ÷ assessment rate
   = $15,600 ÷ .30 = $52,000.
4. Sales tax = $240 × .055 = $13.20.
   Total cost = $240.00 + $13.20 = $253.20.
5. Net cost = $895.00 − ($895.00 × .05) = $895.00 − $44.75 = $850.25.
   Sales tax = $850.25 × .054 = $45.91.
   Total cost = $850.25 + $45.91 = $896.16.
   Cash discount = 1% of $850.25 = $8.50.
   Payment for purchase = $896.16 − $8.50 = $887.66.
6. 3 × $17.95 = $53.85.
   Excise tax = 3 × $2.86 = $8.58.
   Cost = $53.85 + $8.58 = $62.43.
   Sales tax = $62.43 × .042 = $2.62.
   Total cost = $62.43 + $2.62 = $65.05.

CHAPTER EIGHT
Insurance

This chapter deals with some of the mathematical problems and the means of solving them that are common to the fire, automobile, and life insurance businesses.

When you have completed this chapter, you will be able to
(1) Recognize and apply terms in insurance such as policy, premium, indemnity, coinsurance, beneficiary, liability, and risk,
(2) compute the annual premium, and premium for more than a year on a fire insurance policy if the rate and amount of insurance are known,
(3) determine the maximum amount of indemnity paid by an insurance company in case of loss,
(4) compute the premiums and the amount paid in case of loss when they are divided between two or more insurance companies (called multiple carriers),
(5) compute losses paid, in case of fire, by an insurance company when a coinsurance clause is involved,
(6) compute premiums for short-term (less than one year) insurance policies,
(7) compute the cost and refund on a short-term insurance policy when canceled by (a) the insured and (b) the insurer (insurance company),
(8) compute the amount of refund on an automobile insurance policy when canceled by (a) the insured and (b) the insurance company,
(9) compare life insurance policies as to types of coverage and costs,
(10) compute the annual premium on life insurance policies on an annual, semi-annual, and quarterly basis,
(11) compute total cost of life insurance and compare between age groups and types of coverage.

UNIT 1. FIRE INSURANCE

Fire insurance provides for protection against fire losses or losses that may be directly related to a fire as a primary cause of the damage sustained, such as water damage. The cost of such insurance depends on many factors: the type of structure, location, proximity of fire departments and type of equipment used, fire hazards, and water supply. When a commercial building is concerned, the character of its contents and the kind and size of the business are important considerations. A building with an inside sprinkler system may realize a saving of 70 to 90% credit.

1. In which of the following groups would the fire insurance be the least expensive?
    (a) A concrete or wooden building? _____
    (b) A building with a sprinkler system or one without? _____
    (c) A structure two miles from a fire station or one located six miles away?
    _____

- -

(a) concrete,   (b) with a sprinkler system,   (c) 2 miles from the fire station.

2. The person, organization, or business that buys the insurance is called the *insured*; the company that sells the insurance is called the *insurer* (sometimes called "carrier"). The written agreement between the two parties is called the *insurance policy*. The *face* amount of the policy represents the amount of insurance carried (insurance coverage).

    Mr. Hemp insured his home for $15,000 with the Fairprice Insurance Company. Complete the following:

    Insured _____

    Insurer or carrier _____

    Face of policy _____

- -

Mr. Hemp
Fairprice Insurance Company
Face of policy $15,000

The *premium* is the annual or periodic cost of the insurance policy.

Most fire insurance policies are written for 1 or 3 years. Under some circumstances, however, policies are written for 2, 4, or 5 years. (Periods of less than 1 year are discussed later in this unit.)

Policies are generally written in multiples of $100 or $1000, e.g., $15,000. Usually a policy is not written for a sum that includes a fraction of a dollar.

The fire rate is based on a unit of insurance and is quoted on $100 increments, i.e., $0.04 per $100 for a term of 1 year. Typical rates in a protected fire area are $0.10

per $100 for fire, $0.04 for extended coverage,* and $0.05 for an all-risk clause on a private residence or noncommercial property. In unprotected areas the rates may be as much as 200% to 500% more than in protected areas.

Few fires result in a total loss. In well-protected areas it is estimated that many losses are less than 10% of the total value of the property. In unprotected or poorly protected areas the percent of total losses is higher.

Finding the Annual Premium

Annual premium = rate × amount of insurance.

Example: A building is insured for $28,000 for 1 year at a rate of $0.40 per $100 of coverage. Find the annual premium.

Solution: ($28,000 ÷ 100) × $0.40 = $112 annual premium
OR
280.00 × $0.40 = $112.

Example: If a home is insured for $30,000 at $1.56 per $1000, what is the annual premium?

Solution: In this case, the rate is per $1000 therefore divide $30,000 by 1000 and then multiply by $1.56.
Then 30.00 × $1.56 = $46.80 annual premium.

3. Find the annual premium for
   (a) a home insured for $17,500 at $0.28 per $100,
   (b) a building insured for $45,000 at $2.07 per $1000.

_____

(a) 175 × $0.28 = $49.00.
(b) 45 × $2.07 = $93.15.

Extended coverage covers insurance against losses due to windstorm, hail, explosion, riot and civil commotion, damage by aircraft or by vehicle, and smoke damage.

Finding the Premium for More than a Year

Policies written for a year are called "annual policies" and use a basic rate, whereas policies for more than a year are called "term policies" and are written at a discount rate. These discount rates vary throughout the United States, but the following schedule is representative. Some states write only annual and 3-year policies. Some companies write term policies with no discount offered to protect the insured against possible increases in rates after the first year.

Term (Years)	Annual Rate Factor
2	1.85
3	2.7

Reference: Insurance Service Office, San Francisco, 1977.

Example: A building is insured for $30,000. If the rate is $0.40 per $100 of coverage, what is the premium for 3 years?

Solution: Annual premium = 300 × $0.40 = $120.
Instead of multiplying the annual premium by 3, use the appropriate rate factor shown above.
Then the 3-year premium = $120 × 2.7 = $324
OR
the 3-year premium = 300 × $0.40 × 2.7 = $324.

4. A building is insured for $750,000. If the rate is $3.50 per $1000, what are the premiums for (a) 2 years? (b) 3 years?

(a) _____.

(b) _____.

- -

(a) 750 × $3.50 × 1.85 = $4856.25.
(b) 750 × $3.50 × 2.7 = $7087.50.

5. H. Ames Co. insured one of its buildings for $30,000 for 3 years at $2.50 per $1000 of coverage. (a) What was the premium for 3 years? (b) What was the cost difference in buying a 3-year premium instead of 3 one-year premiums?

Solution: (a) Three-year premium = 30 × $2.50 × 2.7 = $202.50.

(b) Annual premium = 30 × $2.50 = $75.00.
Premium for 3 years on annual basis = $75 × 3 = $225.00.
Cost difference = $225.00 − $202.50 = $22.50.

Notice that the factor for 3 years is 2.7. This is equal to 3.00 − 2.70 = .30 or 30% saving on the annual premium for 1 year. Saving = .30 × $75 = $22.50.

Johnson Bros. carried $22,000 on a building for 3 years at $1.19 per $1000. What was the difference in cost if he bought a 3-year policy instead of 3 one-year policies?

Annual premium = 22 × $1.19 = $26.18.
Premium for 3 years on annual basis = $26.18 × 3 = $78.54.
Premium for 3-year policy = $26.18 × 2.7 = $70.69.
Difference in cost = $78.54 − $70.69 = $7.85 OR $26.18 × .30 = $7.85.

6. Find the premium on the following?

	Amount of Insurance	Rate	Terms (Years)	Premium
(a)	$12,500	$0.18 per $ 100	1	_____
(b)	36,000	1.65 per $1000	3	_____
(c)	4,200	0.52 per $ 100	2	_____
(d)	15,000	1.863 per $1000	3	_____
(e)	7,500	2.86 per $1000	2	_____

(a) 125 × $0.18 = $22.50.
(b) 36 × $1.65 × 2.7 = $160.38.
(c) 42 × $0.52 × 1.85 = $40.40.
(d) 15 × $1.863 × 2.7 = $75.45
(e) 7.5 × $2.86 × 1.85 = $39.68

7. How much did the insured "save" in problems (d) and (e) over a straight annual rate basis?

(d) _____.
(e) _____.

(d) Rate for 3 years = 2.7 or a savings of 30% of the annual premium for one year. The annual premium = 15 × $1.863 = $27.95; saving = $27.95 × .30 = $8.39.
(e) Rate for 2 years = 1.85 or a saving of 15% of the annual premium for one year. The annual premium = 7.5 × $2.86 = $21.45; saving = $21.45 × .15 = $3.22.

8. Insurance companies pay only the amount of insurance carried (face of policy) or the amount of the loss, whichever is the lower, but never more than the property is worth.

Examples:

Amount of Insurance	Amount of Loss	Amount Paid
$20,000	$ 5,000	$ 5,000
26,000	30,000	26,000
10,000	10,000	10,000

What would be the amount paid at most on the following losses?

	Amount of Insurance	Amount of Loss	Amount Paid
(a)	$36,000	$37,000	$_____
(b)	42,000	10,500	_____
(c)	15,000	15,000	_____
(d)	5,000	6,000	_____

(a) $36,000
(b) $10,500
(c) $15,000
(d) $ 5,000

Multiple Carriers

Insurance on a particular piece of property may be divided between 2 or more companies. This may be done for several reasons. When it is done, each insurance company must bear any losses in the same proportion that its coverage is to the total insurance carried. (Policies of this type must read exactly alike or there may be a penalty in case of loss.)

Examples: A warehouse and its contents, worth $125,000, were insured in Company A for $50,000 at 69¢ per $100, Company B for $30,000 at 45¢ per $100, and Company C for $20,000 at 75¢ per $100. (a) Find the premium paid to each company and the total premium. (b) If a fire caused a 50% loss ($62,500), how much must each company pay the insured?

Solution: (a) Annual premium, Company A = 500 × $0.69 = $345
Company B = 300 × $0.45 = $135
Company C = 200 × $0.75 = $150

Total annual premium = $630

(b) The total insurance carried is $50,000 + $30,000 + $20,000 = $100,000.
The percent of total insurance carried by each company is

Company A $50,000 ÷ $100,000 = 0.50 or 50%.
Company B $30,000 ÷ $100,000 = 0.30 or 30%.
Company C $20,000 ÷ $100,000 = 0.20 or 20%.

Therefore the amount of the loss paid by each company is as follows:

Company A, 50% of $62,500 or .50 × $62,500 = $31,250
Company B, 30% of $62,500 or .30 × $62,500 = $18,750
Company C, 20% of $62,500 or .20 × $62,500 = $12,500

Total loss = $62,500

9. A building was insured for $90,000. The insurance was distributed among 3 companies as follows: Company A $45,000, Company B $30,000, and Company C $15,000. What percent of the total insurance did each company carry?

Company A _____

B _____

C _____

Company A $45,000 ÷ $90,000 = .50 = 50%.
Company B $30,000 ÷ $90,000 = $.33\frac{1}{3}$ = $33\frac{1}{3}$%.
Company C $15,000 ÷ $90,000 = $.16\frac{2}{3}$ = $16\frac{2}{3}$%.

10. A & C Manufacturing Company suffered a fire loss of $45,000. Their insurance was distributed between 2 companies. Company A carried $50,000 and Company B carried $30,000. How much of the loss did each company pay the A & C Manufacturing Company?

Percent of total insurance carried by each company:

Company A _____

Company B _____

Amount of loss paid by each company:

Company A _____

Company B _____

Percent of total insurance carried by each company:

Company A = $50,000 ÷ $80,000 = $\frac{5}{8}$ = .625 = $62\frac{1}{2}$%.
Company B = $30,000 ÷ $80,000 = $\frac{3}{8}$ = .375 = $37\frac{1}{2}$%.

Amount of loss paid by each company:

Company A, .625 × $45,000 = $28,125 OR $\frac{5}{8}$ × $45,000 = $28,125.
Company B, .375 × $45,000 = $16,875 OR $\frac{3}{8}$ × $45,000 = $16,875.

11. Bowen and Company insured their building for $125,000 which was divided among 3 companies: Company A $50,000, Company B $37,500, and Company C $37,500. A fire caused damage amounting to $6500. How much did each company pay on the loss?

Percent of insurance carried by each company:

Company A = $50,000 ÷ $125,000 = .40 = 40%.
Company B = $37,500 ÷ $125,000 = .30 = 30%.
Company C = $37,500 ÷ $125,000 = .30 = 30%.

Amount of loss paid by each company:

Company A = .40 × $6500 = $2600
Company B = .30 × $6500 = $1950
Company C = .30 × $6500 = $1950
$\qquad$ Total loss = $6500

EXERCISE 32

Answers appear at the end of this exercise. If your answers do not agree with those shown, check your calculations before referring to the solutions that follow.

1. A home valued at $30,000 is insured for $24,000. (a) If fire caused damages of $16,500, how much did the insurance company pay? (b) If the damages amounted to $25,000, how much did the insurance company pay?

    (a) _____

    (b) _____

2. A building worth $75,000 was insured for $60,000 at $0.2065 per $100. (a) What was the annual premium? (b) How much did the insurance company pay on a loss of $61,000 due to fire and water damage?

    (a) _____

    (b) _____

3. A building was insured for $75,000. The insurance was distributed as follows: Company A, $15,000; Company B, $10,000; Company C, $12,500; and Company D, $37,500. If the building was damaged by fire to the extend of $52,000, how much did each company pay?

    A _____

    B _____

    C _____

    D _____

4. In problem 3, if the damages amounted to $78,000, how much did each company pay?

    A _____

    B _____

    C _____

    D _____

Answers

1. (a) $16,500
   (b) $24,000

2. (a) $123.90
   (b) $60,000

3. A $10,400.00
   B   6,933.33
   C   8,666.67
   D 26,000.00
   $52,000.00

4. A $15,000
   B   10,000
   C   12,500
   D   37,500
   $75,000

Solutions

1. (a) $16,500, since it is less than coverage.
   (b) $24,000, not $25,000, since $24,000 was the limit of insurance carried.
2. (a) Annual premium = $600 × 0.2065 = $123.90
   (b) Insurance paid = $60,000, since that was the limit of coverage.
3. Each company paid according to the ratio its coverage was to the total:

   Company A = $15,000 ÷ $75,000 or $\frac{15}{75}$ × $52,000 = $10,400.00

   Company B = $10,000 ÷ $75,000 or $\frac{10}{75}$ × $52,000 = 6,933.33

   Company C = $12,500 ÷ $75,000 or $\frac{12\frac{1}{2}}{75}$ × $52,000 = 8,666.67

   Company D = $37,500 ÷ $75,000 or $\frac{37\frac{1}{2}}{75}$ × $52,000 = 26,000.00

   Total = $52,000.00

4. If the damages were $78,000, then the payments amounted to

   Company A = $\frac{15}{75}$ × $75,000 = $15,000,

   Company B = $\frac{10}{75}$ × $75,000 = $10,000,

   Company C = $\frac{12\frac{1}{2}}{75}$ × $75,000 = $12,500,

   Company D = $\frac{37\frac{1}{2}}{75}$ × $75,000 = $37,500,

   OR

   since $78,000 exceeds the amount of insurance, each company will pay just the amount it carries, i.e.,

   Company A $15,000, Company B $10,000,
   Company C $12,500, Company D $37,500.

   The total insurance coverage carried was $75,000; therefore the owner would have to bear the difference or $3000.

Coinsurance

Most fires result in partial losses. Consequently property owners are inclined to carry no more insurance than they think is necessary. To encourage policy holders to carry more insurance the insurance companies offer (at reduced rates) policies with a *coinsurance* clause.

When a policy contains a coinsurance clause, the insured must carry a specified percent (80% is common) of the replacement cost value or actual cash value of the property insured in order to be reimbursed for the loss or the amount of insurance carried, whichever is the lowest figure.

Coinsurance clauses are common in commercial insurance but not in private or noncommercial insurance except in some states. The 80% or 90% clauses are common, although many policies contain 100% clauses and some may be less than 80%.

The amount paid on losses by the insurance companies when coinsurance clauses are involved is

$$\frac{\text{amount of insurance carried}}{(\text{coinsurance}\%)(\text{value of property})} \times \text{loss}.$$

The value of the property may be the actual cash value or the replacement cost, depending on how the policy is written.

Example: Property valued at $75,000 with an 80% coinsurance clause is insured for $60,000. Fire damages amounted to $42,500. Find the amount of payment by the insurance company.

Solution: $\dfrac{\$60,000}{80\% \text{ of } \$75,000} \times \$42,500 = \dfrac{\$60,000}{\$60,000} \times \$42,500 = \$42,500.$

12. H. Mann & Co. owned a warehouse worth $450,000. It was insured for $360,000. Fire caused damage amounting to $25,000. If the policy contained an 80% coinsurance clause, what was the amount of the indemnity (amount paid by the insurance company)?

Solution:

$\dfrac{\$360,000}{.80 \times \$450,000} \times \$25,000 = \dfrac{\$360,000}{\$360,000} \times \$25,000 = \$25,000.$

Property worth $16,000 is insured for $12,800. If the loss due to fire amounted to $14,400 and the policy contained an 80% coinsurance clause, what is the amount of indemnity (amount paid by the insurance company for the loss)?

Solution: $\dfrac{\$12,800}{80\% \text{ of } \$16,000} \times \$14,400 = \dfrac{\$12,800}{\$12,800} \times \$14,400 = \$14,400;$

but $14,400 is greater than the insurance carried. The insurance company will pay no more than the face of the policy, i.e., $12,800. Therefore the amount of indemnity is $12,800.

13. A building worth $25,000 is insured for $20,000. Loss due to fire amounted to $26,500. If the policy contained an 80% coinsurance clause, what was the amount of indemnity?

    Solution:

- -

$\dfrac{\$20,000}{.80 \times \$25,000} \times \$26,500 = \dfrac{\$20,000}{\$20,000} \times \$26,500 = \$26,500;$

but $26,500 is greater than the amount of insurance carried. Therefore the amount paid = $20,000.

An apartment house valued at $150,000 is insured for $100,000. Loss due to fire was $62,500. If the policy contained an 80% coinsurance clause, what was the amount of indemnity?

Solution: $\dfrac{\$100,000}{80\% \text{ of } \$150,000} \times \$62,500 = \dfrac{\$100,000}{\$120,000} \times \$62,500$

$= \dfrac{5}{6} \times \$62,500 = \$52,083.33.$

In this case the property owner bears the remainder of the loss, i.e., $62,500 − $52,083.33 = $10,416.67.

14. Find the amount of payment by the insurance company for the following: A building valued at $200,000 with a 90% coinsurance clause is insured for $140,000. Fire caused damage amounting to $2650.

   Solution:

   $$\frac{\$140{,}000}{.90 \times \$200{,}000} \times \$2650 = \frac{\$140{,}000}{\$180{,}000} \times \$2650 = \frac{7}{9} \times \$2650 = \$2061.11 \text{ amount paid.}$$

EXERCISE 33

Answers appear at the end of this exercise. If your answers do not agree with those shown, check your calculations before referring to the solutions that follow.

I. Find the amount paid to the insured in each of the following examples under a policy with a coinsurance clause as stated:

No.	Value of Property	Insurance	Fire Loss	Coinsurance Percent	Amount Paid
1.	$57,000	$40,000	$15,000	100	
2.	14,000	8,000	6,500	80	
3.	37,500	30,000	27,000	90	
4.	12,000	9,000	12,000	80	
5.	7,000	5,000	4,000	90	
	8,500	6,200	6,800	100	

II. Applications

1. A motel valued at $125,000 was insured for $90,000. Fire caused damage amounting to $95,000. If the insurance contained a 90% coinsurance clause, how much did the insurance company pay on the loss?

2. A building worth $60,000 was insured for $\frac{4}{5}$ of its value. A fire loss amounted to $15,000. What was the amount of indemnity if the policy contained a 90% coinsurance clause?

FIRE INSURANCE

3. The A. C. Electric Company insured its warehouse worth $90,000 for $50,000 and the contents worth $200,000 for $150,000. The insurance policy contained an 80% coinsurance clause. If fire destroyed $\frac{2}{3}$ of the building and $\frac{1}{2}$ of the contents, (a) what was the amount of settlement and (b) what was the total loss to the property owner?

(a) _____

(b) _____

4. A hotel worth $90,000 was completely destroyed by fire. Insurance with a 90% coinsurance clause was carried by three companies: Company A, $36,000; Company B, $18,000; and Company C, $9000. (a) Find the amount of the claim paid by each company; (b) what part of the loss did the property owner share?

(a) A _____

B _____

C _____

(b) _____

5. Hipple Canvas Company insured their shop for $55,000 with an 80% coinsurance clause. Fire caused damages amounting to $30,000. If the shop was worth $75,000, how much was the insurance settlement?

_____

6. A piece of property was insured for $4000 with a 70% coinsurance clause. The property was worth $8000. If damages, due to fire, amounted to $6000, what did the insurance company pay?

_____

Answers

Section I

1. $10,526.32
2. $4,642.86
3. $24,000.00
4. $ 9,000.00
5. $3,174.60
6. $ 4,960.00

Section II

1. $76,000.00
2. $13,333.33
3. (a) $135,416.67
   (b) $ 24,583.33
4. (a) A $36,000
       B $18,000
       C $ 9,000
   (b) $27,000
5. $27,500
6. $4,000

Solutions

I. 1. $\dfrac{\$40,000}{100\% \text{ of } \$57,000} \times \$15,000 = \$10,526.32.$

2. $\dfrac{\$8,000}{80\% \text{ of } \$14,000} \times \$ 6,500 = \$ 4,642.86.$

3. $\dfrac{\$30,000}{90\% \text{ of } \$37,500} \times \$27,000 = \$24,000.$

4. $\dfrac{\$ 9,000}{80\% \text{ of } \$12,000} \times \$12,000 = \$11,250.$ This amount is more than the coverage; therefore the answer is $9,000.

5. $\dfrac{\$ 5,000}{90\% \text{ of } \$ 7,000} \times \$ 4,000 = \$3,174.60.$

6. $\dfrac{\$ 6,200}{100\% \text{ of } \$ 8,500} \times \$ 6,800 = \$4,960.00.$

II. 1. Amount of insurance paid $= \dfrac{\$90,000}{.90 \times \$125,000} \times \$95,000 = \$76,000.$

2. Insured for $\frac{4}{5}$ of $60,000 or $48,000

   Indemnity $= \dfrac{\$48,000}{.90 \times \$60,000} \times \$15,000 = \$13,333.33.$

FIRE INSURANCE

3. Destruction of building $= \frac{2}{3} \times \$90{,}000 = \$60{,}000$
   Destruction of contents $= \frac{1}{2} \times \$200{,}000 = \underline{\$100{,}000}$
   $\hspace{8em}$ Total loss $= \$160{,}000$

   (a) Payment on contents
   $$\frac{\$150{,}000}{.80 \times \$200{,}000} \times \$100{,}000 = \$93{,}750.00.$$
   Payment on building
   $$\frac{\$50{,}000}{.80 \times \$90{,}000} \times \$60{,}000 = \$41{,}666.67.$$
   Total settlement $= \$93{,}750.00 + \$41{,}666.67 = \$135{,}416.67$.

   (b) Total loss to owner $= \$160{,}000 - \$135{,}416.67 = \$24{,}583.33$.

4. (a) Amount of claim paid by each company will be the amount of insurance carried since the building was completely destroyed.
   $$\text{Company A} = \frac{\$36{,}000}{.90 \times \$90{,}000} \times \$90{,}000 = \$40{,}000.*$$
   $$\text{Company B} = \frac{\$18{,}000}{.90 \times \$90{,}000} \times \$90{,}000 = \$20{,}000.*$$
   $$\text{Company C} = \frac{\$9{,}000}{.90 \times \$90{,}000} \times \$90{,}000 = \$10{,}000.*$$

   (b) Loss to the owner $= \$90{,}000 - \$63{,}000 = \$27{,}000$.

5. Insurance settlement $= \dfrac{\$55{,}000}{.80 \times \$75{,}000} \times \$30{,}000 = \$27{,}500$.

6. Insurance payment $= \dfrac{\$4{,}000}{.70 \times \$8{,}000} \times \$6{,}000 = \$4285.71.\dagger$

Short-Term Policies and Cancellation

Short-term policies (less than 1 year) for fire and casualty insurance, with the exception of the automobile, are written at a higher rate than those for annual policies; for example, a short-term policy for 4 months costs 44% of the annual premium and a 6-month policy costs 60% of the annual premium. The daily charges increase as the periods become shorter.

The standard short-rate table shown on page 320 is used to determine the premium charge for short-term policies. It is also used when the insured party cancels a policy.

---

*These amounts exceed the amount of coverage carried by each company. Therefore the amount of claim paid by each company is $36,000, $18,000 and $9000, respectively, or a total of $63,000.
†This amount exceeds amount of coverage; therefore the payment is only $4000.

SHORT-RATE TABLE

Days Policy in Force	Percent of 1-Year Premium	Days Policy in Force	Percent of 1-Year Premium	Days Policy in Force	Percent of 1-Year Premium
1	5	95–98	37	219–223	69
2	6	99–102	38	224–228	70
3– 4	7	103–105	39	229–232	71
5– 6	8	106–109	40	233–237	72
7– 8	9	110–113	41	238–241	73
9–10	10	114–116	42	242–246 (8 months)	74
11–12	11	117–120	43	247–250	75
13–14	12	121–124 (4 months)	44	251–255	76
15–16	13	125–127	45	256–260	77
17–18	14	128–131	46	261–264	78
19–20	15	132–135	47	265–269	79
21–22	16	136–138	48	270–273 (9 months)	80
23–25	17	139–142	49	274–278	81
26–29	18	143–146	50	279–282	82
30–32 (1 month)	19	147–149	51	283–287	83
33–36	20	150–153 (5 months)	52	288–291	84
37–40	21	154–156	53	292–296	85
41–43	22	157–160	54	297–301	86
44–47	23	161–164	55	302–305 (10 months)	87
48–51	24	165–167	56	306–310	88
52–54	25	168–171	57	311–314	89
55–58	26	172–175	58	315–319	90
59–62 (2 months)	27	176–178	59	320–323	91
63–65	28	179–182 (6 months)	60	324–328	92
66–69	29	183–187	61	329–332	93
70–73	30	188–191	62	333–337 (11 months)	94
74–76	31	192–196	63	338–342	95
77–80	32	197–200	64	343–346	96
81–83	33	201–205	65	347–351	97
84–87	34	206–209	66	352–355	98
88–91 (3 months)	35	210–214 (7 months)	67	356–360	99
92–94	36	215–218	68	361–365 (12 months)	100

†Many automobile insurance policies are written for 3 to 6 months with rates quoted on a 3- and 6-month basis.

Finding the Premium on Short-Term Policies

Mr. Easton, while on a new assignment, lived in temporary quarters for 3 months before moving to a permanent residence. During that time he insured his household furnishings for $20,000 at a rate of $0.207 per $100. What was the cost of the insurance?

Solution: Annual premium = 200 × $0.27 = $41.40.
Rate for 3 months (Short-Rate Table) = 35%.
Cost of insurance = 35% of $41.40 = .35 × $41.40 = $14.49.

If the time had been 2 months, the cost would equal 27% of the annual premium.
If the time was 168 days, the cost would equal 57% of the annual premium.
If the time was 169, 170, 171 days, the cost would equal 57% of the annual premium.

15. What percent of the annual premium should be charged to cover insurance carried for (a) 41 days ____% (b) 5 months ____%
 (c) 289 days ____% (d) 10 months ____%
 (e) 204 days ____% (f) 14 days ____%

- -

(a) 22% (b) 52%
(c) 84% (d) 87%
(e) 65% (f) 12%

16. Mr. and Mrs. Thomas insured a piano valued at $1500 for the full amount for 15 days. What was the cost of the insurance if the rate was $1.25 per $100?

 Annual premium _____

 Rate for 15 days (Short-Rate Table) _____%

 Cost of insurance _____

- -

Annual premium = 15 × $1.25 = $18.75.
Rate for 15 days = 13%.
Cost of insurance = .13 × $18.75 = $2.44.

17. B. Howen insured some merchandise for $15,000 at a rate of $0.75 per $100. What was the cost if the coverage was for (a) 5 months? (b) 225 days?
 (a)
 (b)

- -

Annual premium = 150.00 × $0.75 = $112.50.
(a) Cost for 5 months = $112.50 × .52 = $58.50.
(b) Cost of insurance for 225 days = $112.50 × .70 = $78.75.

Cancellation of Short-Term Policies

The cancellation clause in a standard fire insurance policy specifies that the policy holder may cancel at any time. The insurance company may also cancel the policy but must give the insured 5 days notice (10 days to mortgagee) in writing so that other insurance may be obtained and become effective on the date of cancellation. The manner in which refunds are handled is explained as follows.

If the insured cancels: If the insured cancels a fire insurance policy, he receives a refund in accordance with rates shown on the standard short-rate table. The number of days in force must equal the *exact* number from the date the policy was written up to and including the day it was canceled.

Example: Mr. Axtel canceled a 1-year policy, costing $37.00, 33 days after it had been purchased. What was the amount of the refund?

Solution: According to the short-rate table, the charge for 33 days is 20% of the annual premium: .20 × $37.00 = $7.40.
The refund amounts to the difference between this charge and the annual premium: $37.00 − $7.40 = $29.60.
Since the charge for 33 days is 20%, the refund is equal to 80% of the annual premium: .80 × $37.00 = $29.60.

Example: Mr. Hynes purchased a 1-year policy, dated July 17, for his home, on which he paid a premium of $32.00. On September 22 he sold his home and notified his insurance agent that he wished to cancel his policy. (a) What did the insurance cost Mr. Hynes? (b) What was the refund paid by the insurance company?

Solution: Annual premium = $32.00.
Exact days (July 17–Sept. 22) = 67.
Rate for 67 days = 29% of annual premium.

(a) The premium charge for 67 days is .29 × $32.00 = $9.28.
(b) The refund is $32.00 − $9.28 = $22.72 OR, since the charge for 67 days is 29%, 71% of the annual premium = .71 × $32.00 = $22.72.

18. Mr. Brown paid $35.00 for a 1-year fire insurance policy on his home. Four months later he sold his home, at which time he canceled the insurance. What was the amount of the insurance refund?

Insurance for 4 months (short-rate table) = 44%.
Insurance charge = $35 × .44 = $15.40.
Refund = $35.00 − $15.40 = $19.60 OR $35.00 × .56 = $19.60.

19. A Chatman purchased a 1-year policy, dated August 15, for his home, on which he paid a premium of $42.00. On October 12 he canceled the insurance. (a) How much did the insurance cost the buyer? (b) What was the refund?

Annual premium = $42.00.
Exact days (August 15 to October 12) = 58.
Insurance for 58 days (short-rate table) = 26%.
(a) Cost of insurance = $42.00 × .26 = $10.92.
(b) Amount of refund = $42.00 − $10.92 = $31.08 OR $42.00 × .74 = $31.08.

If the insurer (insurance company) cancels: Sometimes a policy is canceled by the insurance company. When this is done, the amount retained by the insurance company is based on a direct prorata basis, using *exact* days and a 365-day year. It is the ratio of the time the policy was in force to the total time for which the policy was written and paid for. (This ruling also applies to any term of a year or more.)

Example: Baines & Co. insured its factory on March 3 for a year. The policy was canceled by the carrier the following October 15. If the annual premium was $130.00, what was the cost of the insurance and the amount of the refund?

Solution: Days in force (March 3–Oct. 15) = 226.
Amount of premium retained by the carrier = $130.00 × 226/365 = $80.49.
Amount refunded to Baines & Co. = $130.00 − $80.49 = $49.51.

20. Hemp Manufacturer Co. insured a newly acquired building on April 12 for 1 year at a cost of $95.00. The policy was canceled by the insurance company on November 22. What were (a) the cost of the insurance to Hemp Manufacturer Co. and (b) the amount of the refund?

Days in force (April 12 to November 22) = _____.
Amount of premium retained by the insurance company (cost of the insurance to Hemp Manufacturer Co.) = _____.

Amount of refund = _____.

Days in force (April 12 to November 22) = 224.
Cost of insurance = $95.00 × 224/365 = $58.30.
Amount of refund = $95.00 − $58.30 = $36.70.

EXERCISE 34

Answers appear at the end of this exercise. If your answers do not agree with those shown, check your calculations before referring to the solutions that follow.

1. What percent of the annual premium would be charged to the policy holder to cover insurance for 39 days? 16 days? 201 days? 90 days?

2. If Maynard & Co. insured merchandise in a warehouse for 90 days, what would be the premium charge on a policy worth $35,000 at $1.16 per $100 per year?

3. Mrs. Hazelton insured her home for a year, effective March 14. On October 3 the home was sold, at which time the owner canceled the insurance. If the premium was $32.50, what was the net premium charge? What was the amount of the refund?

　　　　　　　　　　Net premium charge _____

　　　　　　　　　　Refund _____

4. Mr. Urton insured his housetrailer and contents for $26,000 at a rate of $1.065 per $100 on June 10 for a year. On December 15 the insurance company canceled the policy. Find the refund due Mr. Urton.

5. The Hoffman Manufacturing Co. insured a building for $750,000 on September 2 for a 1-year term at $0.1075 per $100. On the following February 15 the policy was canceled by the carrier. What was the amount of the refund?

Answers

1. 21%, 13%, 65%, 35%.
2. $142.10
3. Net premium charge $21.13
   Refund $11.37
4. $134.28
5. $439.57

Solutions

1. Obtain answers from the short-rate table.
2. Annual premium = $350.00 × 1.16 = $406.00.
   The rate for 90 days (from table) = 35%.
   Therefore the premium charge = $406.00 × .35 = $142.10.
3. March 14 to October 3 = 203 days.
   The rate for 203 days = 65% (from table).
   Net premium = $32.50 × .65 = $21.13.
   Refund = $32.50 − $21.13 = $11.37.
4. Annual premium = $260.00 × 1.065 = $276.90.
   June 10 to December 15 = 188 days.
   Premium charge for 188 days = $276.90 × $\frac{188}{365}$ = $142.62.
   Refund = $276.90 − $142.62 = $134.28.
5. Annual premium = $7500.00 × .1075 = $806.25.
   September 2 to February 15 = 166 days.
   Premium charge = $806.25 × $\frac{166}{365}$ = $366.68.
   Refund = $806.25 − $366.68 = $439.57.

UNIT 2. AUTOMOBILE INSURANCE

Automobile insurance is one of the most common types of casualty insurance. Insurance is often required in the public interest to cover the many hazards of ownership, in repairs, and in the use of an automobile.

Types of Automobile Insurance

Liability insurance: There are 2 kinds of liability insurance.
(a) *Property damage* protects owner against damages to another person's car or property.
(b) *Bodily injury* or *public liability* protects owner against the cost of injuries to other people due to negligence in the operation of his car.

Other insurance: Insurance may be purchased to cover charges for such services as towing, road service, disability, death benefits, use of other cars, medical payments, and uninsured motorists.

1. If the driver of a car damages another car by his own negligence, what type of liability insurance will protect him? _____.

   Liability insurance is classified as either _____ or _____.

   As the result of an accident due to his own negligence, Mr. Howard caused injury to another person. What type of insurance would protect him in this case? _____.

   _

   Property damage
   Property damage, bodily injury or public liability
   Bodily injury

2. Maximum and minimum limits of insurance carried varies among the states. Bodily injury coverage of $5000/$10,000 (5/10) means that the owner of a motor vehicle is protected to a maximum payment of $5000 for any one person and to a maximum payment of $10,000 in any one accident in which the owner of the automobile may have injured more than one person.

   A coverage of 15/30 means _____
   _____
   _____

   _

   Maximum payment of $15,000 to any one person in an accident and maximum payment of $30,000 in any one accident in which more than 1 person has been injured

Premiums

3. The 3 primary classifications used to determine rates are (a) use of car (business or pleasure), age, marital status, and sex of driver, (b) territorial area of state in which the car is located, and (c) value of car. The classifications are then applied to rate charts for comprehensive (fire and theft), collision, bodily injury, medical payments, and property damage.

Rates are primarily determined by _____

_____ ,

_____ ,

_____ .

- -

use of car, age, marital status, and sex of driver,
territorial area of state in which the car is located,
value of car.

Canceling Policies

Automobile insurance may be canceled by the insured or insurer. The same rules apply as those used for fire insurance.

If the insured cancels: A short-rate table is used to compute the refund and the amount retained by the insurer by most, but not all, carriers. The table is used for problems presented in this text.

Example: Assume that Mr. Hale canceled his automobile insurance policy after it has been in effect for 3 months. (a) How much did the insurance company retain and (b) how much was Mr. Hale's refund? The premium paid for 1 year was $125.00.

Solution: (a) Refer to the short-rate table, page 320. The charge for 3 months is 35% of the annual premium. Amount retained by the insurance company = $125.00 × .35 = $43.75.
(b) Refund to Mr. Hale = $125.00 − $43.75 = $81.25.

4. The owner of an automobile paid a premium of $140 and then canceled the policy 42 days later. Compute the (a) cost of the insurance and (b) the refund.

Annual premium = $140.00; charge for 42 days (short-rate table) = 22%.
Cost of insurance (amount retained by insurance company) = $140.00 × .22 = $30.80.
Refund = $140.00 − $30.80 = $109.20.

If the insurer cancels: The law permits the insurance company to retain no more than the exact prorata amount of the premium for the number of days the policy has been in force, based on a 365-day year.

Example: Mr. Wilson insured his automobile for 1 year. After it had been in effect 135 days the insurance company canceled the policy. If the premium paid was $160.50, (a) how much was retained by the insurance company and (b) how much was refunded to Mr. Wilson?

Solution: (a) $\dfrac{135}{365} \times \$160.50 = \$59.36$, amount retained by insurance company.

(b) $160.50 − $59.36 = $101.14, amount refunded to Mr. Wilson.

5. A. Hicks's insurance on his car was $110 for the year. He paid his insurance on March 10. The following June 23 the insurance company canceled his policy. (a) How much did the insurance company retain and (b) how much was refunded to A. Hicks?

Days in force = _____.

(a)

(b)

Days in force (March 10 to June 23) = 105 days.
(a) Amount retained by insurance company = 105/365 × $110.00 = $31.64.
(b) Amount of refund = $110.00 − $31.64 = $78.36.

6. Mr. Pepper's annual insurance cost on his automobile was $173.50. If the policy was canceled 115 days after it was in force, how much was refunded to him if (a) he canceled the policy or (b) if the insurance company canceled the policy?

(a)

(b)

(a) Annual premium = $173.50, 115 days = 42% charge (see table).
Premium charge = $173.50 × .42 = $72.87.
Refund = $173.50 − $72.87 = $100.63.
(b) Premium charge = $173.50 × $\frac{115}{365}$ = $54.66.
Refund = $173.50 − $54.66 = $118.84.

7. Mr. Johnson purchased automobile insurance that cost $155.00 on March 10 and canceled it on September 6 when he sold the car. How much was his refund?

March 10 to September 6 = 180 days.
Charge for 180 days = 60% (from table).
Premium charge = $155.00 × .60 = $93.00.
Refund = $155.00 − $93.00 = $62.00
OR, since 60% was charged, the refund was 40%: $155 × .40 = $62.

UNIT 3. LIFE INSURANCE

In general, the purpose of life insurance is to provide financial assistance to the dependents of the insured in the event of his death. The kind of insurance program purchased depends on the income, indebtedness, amount of security desired for dependents, number of dependents, and the age of the insured.

The first life insurance policies on record were written for very short periods of time—6 months or a year. Today almost any kind of life insurance desired may be purchased.

Life Insurance Policies

Term insurance policies provide protection for the survivors (beneficiaries) of the insured for a limited time only, such as 1, 2, 3, 4, 5, or 10 years. It is therefore temporary. If death of the insured occurs during the term, the full amount of insurance carried (face of policy) is paid to the beneficiaries. If the insured is still living when the insurance expires, he is no longer insured, but before the insurance is terminated it may, under certain conditions, be converted to another form of life insurance.

1. Mrs. Owen bought a 10-year term insurance policy in the amount of $3000 to be paid to her daughter in the event of her death.

    (a) What is the face of the policy? _____

    (b) Who is the beneficiary? _____

    If Mrs. Owens should die 3 years after buying this insurance, how much would her beneficiary receive? _____
    If Mrs. Owens lived more than 10 years and did not convert the insurance to some other form, is she still insured? ____

    (a) $3000
    (b) Her daughter
    $3000, No

Straight life insurance policies offer permanent insurance protection during the life of the insured. This type of insurance requires payment of a specified premium each year until the death of the insured when the face of the policy is paid to the beneficiary. This insurance has an advantage over term insurance because it can be borrowed against and usually has a cash surrender value after the second year.

2. John Mainland bought a $5000 life insurance policy on which he paid $80 a year, payable to his wife on his death.

    (a) What is the annual premium? _____

    (b) How much did he pay on this insurance during 40 years? _____

    (c) How much will the beneficiary receive at his death? _____

    (a) $80.00
    (b) $80 × 40 = $3200
    (c) $5000

Limited-payment life insurance policies require that premiums be paid for a fixed number of years. If the policy is a 20-year payment policy, the insured pays premiums for 20 years or until his death, whichever occurs first. If the insured is living at the end of 20 years, no more payments are made but he is insured for the rest of his life. At his death the face of the policy is paid to his beneficiary. A policy of this kind may also be written to mature at a specified age such as 65. An advantage of this coverage is that premiums are paid during a person's most productive years.

3. Mr. Jackson bought a 20-year payment policy for $10,000 at age 25. (a) How old will he be (assuming that he is still living) when no more payments will be required? _____ (b) If Mr. Jackson died at age 30, how much would his beneficiary receive? _____

(a) 45 years
(b) $10,000

Endowment life insurance policies provide some savings in addition to the protection covered by life insurance. It is the most expensive form of life insurance. Such policies are usually purchased for an anticipated need at some future time, such as a supplement to retirement income. Like the limited-payment life insurance policy, the endowment policy is written for a specified number of years or to mature at some designated age such as 60 or 65.

In the event of the insured's death, the face of the policy is paid to the beneficiary. If however, the insured lives beyond his endowment, he has one of several options when the policy matures. He may choose to receive the face amount of the policy in a lump sum or in periodic equal payments, with any balance remaining at his death to be paid to his beneficiary or estate. The money may also become income for minor children to be paid monthly or annually.

Both the limited payment and endowment life insurance policies may be borrowed against after a specified period of time.

4. If Mrs. Nelson bought a 20-year endowment, would she have to pay anything more on the policy after that time? _____ If she died before 20 years had passed, how much would be paid to her beneficiary? _____

No
Face of the policy

Differences between *limited-payment life* insurance and *endowment life* insurance: endowment life insurance is more expensive because the insurance company must build a reserve in order to pay the face of the policy at the end of the payment period. In a limited-payment life insurance policy the insurance company makes no payment until the death of the insured, which may be several years after he has made the last payment.

An endowment policy is payable (if requested by the insured) at the end of the payment period. A limited-payment policy is payable *only* at the death of the insured.

5. Mr. Haines bought a limited-payment life insurance policy in the amount of $30,000 for 20 years; Mr. Jackson bought an endowment for the same amount for 20 years.

  (a) Which policy was the most expensive? _____
  (b) If both of the insured parties died before 20 years, would the beneficiaries receive the same amount? _____
  (c) If both men lived beyond 20 years, what is the earliest date on which the endowment policy could be paid? _____.
  The limited-payment policy? _____.
  (d) After 20 years how much do the insured pay in premiums? _____

  (a) Endowment
  (b) Yes
  (c) At the end of 20 years. At the death of the insured.
  (d) None

Cost of Insurance—Premiums

The cost of insurance depends on the kind of policy, the amount of coverage desired, and the age and sex of the insured. The policy bought depends, in turn, on the kind of coverage that also fits the buyer's budget.

Rates are based on tables of *life expectancy*. Obviously life expectancy decreases with age, which, in turn, increases the cost of insurance. Rates are slightly higher for males, since females have a greater life expectancy. Rates also depend on whether the insurance company is participating or nonparticipating. A participating company is one in which the policy holder shares in the earnings of the company by way of yearly dividends. A nonparticipating insurance company does not share its earnings with policy holders. For this reason net costs, not gross costs, should be the basis of comparison of rates between companies.

The following table is representative of rates for males of a nonparticipating life insurance company for the four kinds of insurance policy discussed. Since females have a longer life expectancy, their rates are slightly lower than those shown. The rates listed below the table for periods other than annual may differ slightly between companies.

ANNUAL PREMIUMS PER $1000 INSURANCE*

Age	5-Year Term	10-Year Term	Straight Life	20-Payment Life	20-Year Endowment
20	4.94	4.95	11.58	19.35	41.47
25	4.99	5.00	13.40	21.95	41.64
30	5.09	5.18	16.02	24.81	42.00
35	5.62	6.08	19.20	28.14	42.70
40	7.07	7.95	23.11	32.14	43.97
45	9.51	11.08	28.05	37.28	46.02
50	13.50	15.91	34.16	42.80	48.62
55	19.41	—	42.46	49.69	—
60	28.98	—	53.76	58.77	—

*Semiannual rate is 51% of annual rate, quarterly rate is 26% of annual rate, and monthly rate is 9% of annual rate.

6. The cost of life insurance depends on

(a) _____,

(b) _____,

(c) _____,

(d) _____.

Life expectancy (decreases/increases) with age.
As we get older, the cost of insurance (increases/decreases).

The least expensive life insurance discussed here is _____.

The most expensive life insurance is _____.
Which three types of life insurance are purchased for a fixed number of years?

_____, _____, and _____.

(a) to (d), inclusive, are *amount of insurance coverage, age, sex, kind of policy*.
decreases
increases
term
endowment
Term, limited-payment life and endowment

Find the annual premium on a $3000 straight life insurance policy that was purchased at age 30.

Solution: (a) Locate 30 under "age" column in table. Follow this line across to column headed "Straight Life."
(b) The number shown, $16.02, is the annual premium on a $1000 policy.
(c) Premium for $3000 = 3 × $16.02 = $48.06.

7. Find the annual premium on a $5000 20-payment life insurance policy that is issued at age 20? At 25?

Age 20, $19.35 × 5 = $96.75. Age 25, $21.95 × 5 = $109.75.

8. How much less would a policy for 20-payment life insurance cost than a 20-year endowment at age 45?

Solution: Annual premium for 20-year endowment = $46.02 per $1000
Annual premium for 20-payment life = $37.28 per $1000
Difference $ 8.74

Compare the total premium paid on a $15,000 life insurance policy for a 10-year term over a 10-year period for a straight-life policy purchased at age 20.

Ten-year term insurance:
    Annual premium on $15,000 = _____.
    Total premiums paid in 10 years = _____.

Straight life:
    Annual premium on $15,000 = _____.
    Total premiums paid in 10 years = _____.

Difference = _____.

Ten-year annual premium = 15 × $4.95 = $74.25; for 10 years = $742.50.
Straight-life annual premium = 15 × $11.58 = $173.70; for 10 years = $1737.00.
Difference = $1737.00 − $742.50 = $994.50.

How much more are the premiums for a year on a $1000, 20-year endowment at age 25 if paid quarterly instead of annually?

Solution: Rates for semiannual, quarterly, and monthly premium payments are listed under the premium tables.

Annual premium = $41.64.
Quarterly premium = $41.64 × .26 = $10.83.

Premium for 1 year on quarterly basis = $10.83 × 4 = $43.32.
Amount saved if paid annually = $43.32 − $41.64 = $1.68.

9. J. Hampton, age 25, wished to buy a 20-payment life insurance policy for $4000. What would his total yearly premium payments be for a year if they were made (a) quarterly (b) semiannually (c) annually?

(a) _____ .

(b) _____ .

(c) _____ .

The rate for a 25-year old person on a 20-payment life insurance policy is $21.95 per thousand. The premium on a $4000 policy, if paid on an annual basis, is $21.95 × 4 = $87.80. (a) If the premium is paid on a quarterly basis, the amount paid each quarter = $87.80 × .26 = $22.828, or $22.83. For the year this would amount to $22.83 × 4 = $91.32. (b) If paid semiannually, each payment would equal $87.80 × .51 = $44.78, which amounts to $89.56 for the year ($44.78 × 2). (c) The annual premium = $21.95 × 4 = $87.80.

EXERCISE 35

Chapter Summary

Answers appear at the end of this exercise. If your answers do not agree with those shown, check your calculations before referring to the solutions that follow.

1. Find the premium for each of the following fire insurance policies.

	Amount of Insurance	Rate	Term* (Years)	Premium
(a)	$ 16,500	$0.72 per $100	1	$ _____
(b)	32,000	0.55 per $1000	3	_____
(c)	154,500	0.96 per $100	3	_____
(d)	94,000	0.24 per $100	2	_____
(e)	540,000	0.19 per $100	2	_____

   *Discount rates on page 305.

   (a) _____
   (b) _____
   (c) _____
   (d) _____
   (e) _____

2. Moore and Sons insured an apartment building against fire for $350,000. It was distributed as follows: Company A carried $\frac{1}{4}$ of this amount at $0.21 per $100, Company B carried $\frac{1}{3}$ of the remainder at $0.19 per $100, and Company C carried the balance at $0.175 per $100. What was the premium paid to each company and what was the total premium cost for 1 year?

   A _____
   B _____
   C _____
   T _____

3. If, in problem 2, a fire caused damages amounting to 10% of the total insurance carried, what was the payment made by each carrier? Assume that there were no coinsurance requirements.

A _____

B _____

C _____

T _____

4. Find the payment made by the insurance company for each of the following.

	Value of Property	Amount of Insurance	Fire Loss	Coinsurance Clause	Payment
(a)	$215,000	$150,000	$86,000	80%	$_____
(b)	80,000	70,000	72,000	90%	_____
(c)	67,500	50,000	7,100	100%	_____
(d)	34,000	25,000	13,600	80%	_____

(a) _____

(b) _____

(c) _____

(d) _____

5. Johnson Bros. insured the contents of its warehouse against fire for 60 days. If the annual premium was $32.50, what was the net cost of the insurance?

_____

6. A store was insured against fire loss for $350,000 at $0.95 per $100; the contents were insured for $500,000 at $0.86 per $100. The effective date of the policy was January 3. On July 6 of the same year the store owners canceled the policy. Find the refund paid by the insurance company. (Assume that this was not a leap year.)

_____

7. Mr. Hopkins bought fire insurance on his home on October 14 and canceled it on December 19 of the same year. The policy was written for $22,000 at $0.12 per $100. What was the premium charge for the period that the policy was in effect?

8. Mr. Hayley insured his shop, valued at $40,000, for $\frac{4}{5}$ of its value. How much would the insurance company pay if damages resulting from a fire amounted to $33,000? To $22,500? (No coinsurance clause was included.)

(a) _____

(b) _____

9. The Fox Realty Co. carries $20,000 fire insurance on a piece of property worth $30,000. The policy contains an 80% coinsurance clause. How much would the insurance company pay for loss from fire amounting to $10,800?

10. If the annual premium on a fire insurance policy was $40.00, how much of the premium was returned to the insured if (a) the insurance was canceled by the policy holder after 90 days or (b) the insurance was canceled by the carrier after 90 days?

(a) _____

(b) _____

11. An automobile policy with an annual premium of $155.00 was canceled by the insured 105 days after it had been in force. How much was refunded to the insured?

12. After 96 days the carrier canceled an automobile insurance policy costing $178.00. How much did the carrier retain?

    _____

13. Find the annual premium on a $5000 life insurance policy for ages 25, 40, and 60 for (a) 5-year term, (b) straight life, and (c) 20-year endowment.

	(a)	(b)	(c)
25 yr	_____	_____	_____
40 yr	_____	_____	_____
60 yr	_____	_____	_____

14. How much more would a man 35 years of age pay for $1000 of insurance on a 20-payment life policy if premiums were paid (a) quarterly, (b) monthly, or (c) semiannually than if paid annually?

    (a) _____

    (b) _____

    (c) _____

15. B. Burns, who is 20, carries a 10-year term life insurance policy for $4000. If he is living at the end of that time, how much would he have paid in annual premiums during that time?

    _____

16. Compare the cost of a 20-payment life insurance policy for $5000 for a young man 25 years of age with one 45 years of age. How much in total premiums would each pay compared with the face of the policy if he lived for the term of the policy?

    _____

CHAPTER SUMMARY 341

17. Mr. Mason, 45 years old, wishes to have additional insurance protection for his 15-year-old daughter for 10 years to cover her education expenses in the event of his death. What would term insurance cost on $5000 for that time if he paid premiums annually and semiannually?

            Annually _____

            Semiannually _____

Answers

1. (a) $ 118.80
   (b) $ 47.52
   (c) $4004.64
   (d) $ 417.36
   (e) $1898.10
2. A $183.75
   B $ 99.75
   C $367.50
   T $651.00
3. A $ 8,750
   B $ 5,250
   C $21,000
   T $35,000
4. (a) $75,000.00
   (b) $70,000.00
   (c) $ 5,259.26
   (d) $12,500.00
5. $8.78
6. $2,973.75
7. $7.66
8. (a) $32,000
   (b) $22,500
9. $9000
10. (a) $26.00
    (b) $30.14
11. $94.55
12. $46.82
13.   (a) (b) (c)
    25 yr $ 24.95 $ 67.00 $208.20
    40 yr $ 35.35 $115.55 $219.85
    60 yr $144.90 $268.80 none offered
14. (a) $1.14
    (b) $2.22
    (c) $0.56
15. $198.00
16. $2195, $3728
17. Annually $554.00
    Semiannually $565.00

Solutions

1. (a) $ 165.00 × .72 = $118.80.
   (b) $ 32.000 × .55 × 2.7 = $47.52.
   (c) $1545.00 × .96 × 2.7 = $4004.64
   (d) $ 940.00 × .24 × 1.85 = $417.36.
   (e) $5400.00 × .19 × 1.85 = $1898.10

CHAPTER SUMMARY

2. Amounts carried by each company

   A $\frac{1}{4} \times \$350,000 = \$87,500.$
   B $\frac{1}{5} \times \frac{3}{4} \times \$350,000 = \$52,500$ OR $\frac{1}{5} \times (\$350,000 - \$87,500) = \$52,500.$
   C $\$350,000 - (\$87,500 + \$52,500) = \$210,000.$

   Premium paid by each company

   A $\$ 875.00 \times .21 = \$183.75.$
   B $\$ 525.00 \times .19 = \$ 99.75.$
   C $\$2100.00 \times .175 = \$367.50.$
   Total $= \$651.00.$

3. Total insurance $350,000, damage = 10% of $350,000 or $35,000

   Payments made by each carrier

   A $\frac{1}{4} \times \$35,000 = \$ 8,750.$
   B $\frac{3}{20} \times \$35,000 = 5,250.$
   C $\frac{3}{5} \times \$35,000 = 21,000.$
   Total $= \$35,000.$

4. (a) $\dfrac{\$150,000}{.80 \times \$215,000} \times \$86,000 = \$75,000,$

   (b) $\dfrac{\$70,000}{.90 \times \$80,000} \times \$72,000 = \$70,000,$

   (c) $\dfrac{\$50,000}{1.00 \times \$67,500} \times \$ 7,100 = \$5,259.26,$

   (d) $\dfrac{\$25,000}{.80 \times \$34,000} \times \$13,600 = \$12,500.$

5. Insurance for 60 days = 27% of annual premium (short rate table).
   Therefore the net cost of the insurance = $32.50 × .27 = $8.78.

6. Total premium = ($3500 × .95) + ($5000 × .86) = $3325 + $4300 = $7625.

   January 3 to July 6 = 184 days
   184 days = 61% of annual premium; therefore the refund = 39% of the annual premium or $7625 × .39 = $2973.75.

7. Annual premium = $220.00 × .12 = $26.40.
   October 14 to December 19 = 66 days.
   66 days = 29% of annual premium.
   Premium charge for 66 days = $26.40 × .29 = $7.66.

8. Total insurance carried = $\frac{4}{5} \times \$40,000 = \$32,000.$

   (a) $32,000 because it is the face of the policy.
   (b) $22,500 since it is the amount of damages.

9. $\dfrac{\$20,000}{.80 \times \$30,000} \times \$10,800 = \$9,000.$

10. Charge for 90 days = 35% of annual premium (short rate table).

   (a) If 35% was charged, then 65% was refunded.
   Therefore the refund = .65 × $40.00 = $26.00.
   (b) $\frac{90}{365}$ × $40.00 = $9.86, refund = $40.00 − $9.86 = $30.14.

11. Charge for 105 days = 39% of annual premium; therefore 61% = refund.
   Refund = $155 × .61 = $94.55.

12. Amount retained by carrier = $178 × $\frac{96}{365}$ = $46.82.

13.
Years	(a)	(b)	(c)
25	$ 24.95	$ 67.00	$208.20
40	35.35	115.55	219.85
60	144.90	268.80	none offered

   This information is read directly from the table on page 334 and multiplied by 5, since the rates are quoted per $1000.

14. Annual premium = $28.14.

   (a) $28.14 × .26 × 4 = $29.28; additional cost = $1.14.
   (b) $28.14 × .09 × 12 = $30.36; additional cost = $2.22.
   (c) $28.14 × .51 × 2 = $28.70; additional cost = $0.56.

15. Annual premium = $4.95 per $1000.
   Annual premium on $4000 = $4.95 × 4 = $19.80.
   Paid in premium during 10 years = $19.80 × 10 = $198.00.

16. Amount paid in 20 years

   25-year old = $21.95 × 5.000 × 20 = $2195.00,
   45-year old = $37.28 × 5.000 × 20 = $3728.00.

17. Annual premium = $11.08 × 5.000 = $55.40.
   Total premiums paid for 10 years on an annual basis = $55.40 × 10 = $554.00.

   On a semiannual basis

   (a) premium every 6 months = $55.40 × .51 = $ 28.25,
   (b) premium per year   = $28.25 × 2 = $ 56.50,
   (c) premium for 10 years   = $56.50 × 10 = $565.00.

CHAPTER NINE
Interest

OBJECTIVES

Interest is the price paid for the use of money. The amount paid depends on the amount borrowed or loaned, the rate charged (expressed as a percent), and the time for which the money is used. Time may be expressed in days, months, or years. The rate (percent) is the charge per annum unless otherwise stated.

Banks and many other financial agencies are in the business of lending money. The rates they charge are dependent on many factors. The supply of money, legal restrictions, credit rating of the borrower, type of security, and purpose of the loan all affect the interest rate.

When you have completed this chapter, you will be able to

(1) recognize and apply simple interest (ordinary, commercial, and accurate) and compound interest (principal, rate, time, maturity value, and conversion periods),
(2) compute time (number of days or years) in which a loan is made on (a) a 30-day basis, (b) exact number of days,
(3) compute exact time (number of days) in which a loan is made by use of a table,
(4) compute simple interest by use of the basic formula, $I = Prt$,
(5) compute ordinary and banker's interest by the 60-day, 6% method (a) for 60 days, (b) for a period of time that is a multiple or factor of 60, (c) when the time can be broken down into multiples of 60, and (d) when the interest rate is a factor or multiple of 6% and the time is 60 days,
(6) compute simple interest by use of tables for (a) a 360-day year and (b) a 365-day year,
(7) compute the maturity value of a loan when the amount of the loan, time, and rate are known,
(8) compute the principal (amount loaned) when the maturity value, time, and rate are known,
(9) compute the interest rate on a loan when the maturity value, time, and principal are known,
(10) compute the time on a loan when the rate, principal, and maturity value are known,

(11) compute compound interest without the use of tables,
(12) read compound interest tables,
(13) compute maturity value and compound interest by use of tables,
(14) compute and compare nominal and effective interest rates.

UNIT 1. SIMPLE INTEREST

Simple interest is the amount paid on a sum of money (borrowed or loaned) which remains unchanged for a specified period of time. The amount borrowed or loaned is called the *principal*; the *interest rate* or charge is quoted as an annual rate unless otherwise stated; the *time* may be expressed in days, months, or years.

1. Mr. Bowen borrowed $500 for 26 days at 6%.

   Principal = _____, interest rate = _____, time = _____.

   _

   Principal = $500, interest rate = 6%, time = 26 days

Ordinary and Accurate Simple Interest

Although there are four methods of calculating simple interest when time is expressed in days, only three are in common usage. They are identified as follows and are referred to in this manner throughout the book.

(a) *Ordinary simple interest* is based on a 360-day year and a 30-day month. This method is used most often on installment loans for purchases such as real estate or on other loans which are repaid periodically.

(b) *Banker's* or *commercial interest* is based on a 360-day year and exact number of days. The use of this method results in a greater return to the creditor (lending company, agency, or individual) and therefore is favored. When no statement is made in a loan agreement, this method generally applies.

(c) *Accurate interest* is based on a 365-day year and exact number of days. This method is always used by the Federal Government. Also, depending on the policy applied to certain kinds of loan, some banks and other lending agencies use this method.
(Accurate interest is sometimes referred to as "exact interest." Only the term "accurate interest" is used in this book.)

(d) The fourth method is based on a 365-day year and a 30-day month. This method is never used except by agreement among all parties concerned.

346 UNIT 1

2. Ordinary simple interest is based on a _____ day year and a _____ day month.

   Banker's or commercial interest is based on a _____ day year and _____ number of days.

   Accurate interest is based on a _____ day year and _____ number of days.

   360-day year and a 30-day month.
   360-day year and exact number of days.
   365-day year and exact number of days.

   ## Calculating Time

3. Since the interest charge cannot be calculated unless the time is known, it is necessary to determine the number of days for which a loan is made. Whether a 30-day month or the exact number of days is used depends on the method used.

   What type of simple interest problem would use either of the two methods on the facing page? _____

   Ordinary simple interest

4. Find the approximate time in days for the following:

   (a) March 2 to July 15 of the same year. _____

   (b) June 12, 1970 to September 11, 1970. _____

   (c) February 3, 1971 to June 10, 1971. _____

   (d) January 1, 1971 to January 31, 1972. _____

   See page 348 for the answers.

METHODS OF DETERMINING APPROXIMATE NUMBER OF DAYS

Example	Method I	Method II
Find the time from June 6 to December 15	June 6 to December 6 (6 months) = 180 days December 6 to December 15 = +9 days Time = 189 days	Month Day 12 15 December 15 −6 −6 June 6 6 9 180 days + 9 days = 189 days
Find the time from April 20 to September 4	April 20 to September 20 (5 months) = 150 days September 4 to September 20 = −16 days Time = 134 days	Month Day 8 34[a] September 4 9̶ 4̶ September 4 −4 −20 April 20 4 14 120 days + 14 days = 134 days

Find the time from March 3, 1968 to February 16, 1969	March 3, 1968 to February 3, 1969 (11 months) = 330 days
	February 3, 1969 to February 16, 1969 = +13 days
	Time = 343 days
		Year Month Day
		     8 14
		1969 2[b] 16 February 16
		−1968 −3 −3 March 3
		      11 13
		330 days + 13 days = 343 days.

[a] Since 20 cannot be subtracted from 4, borrow a month (30 days) and proceed as shown.
[b] Since 3 cannot be subtracted from 2, a year or 12 months was borrowed from 1969.

(a)
month	day
7	15 July
3	2 March
4	13

(4 × 30) + 13 days = 133 days

(b)
month	day
8	41
9	11 September
6	12 June
2	29

(2 × 30) + 29 = 89 days

(c)
month	day
6	10 June
2	3 February
4	7

(4 × 30) + 7 = 127 days

(d)
year	month	day
1972	1	31
1971	1	1
1	0	30

1 year = 360 days
360 + 30 = 390 days or 13 months

These answers may, of course, also be obtained by Method 1, frame 3.

5. *Exact time basis.* In determining the *exact* time (number of days) during the life of a loan, it is necessary to count each day (excluding the first but including the last). If the month of February is included in the time period and it is a leap year, add an extra day.

Example: Find the number of days from May 6 to July 20.

Solution:

Month	Number of Days
May (6–31)	25
June	30
July	20
Time (days)	75

The number of days from July 3 to December 21, 1971 is ——————.

- -

Month	Number of Days
July (3–31)	28
August	31
September	30
October	31
November	30
December	21
Total	171

Calculating Exact Number of Days
Between Two Dates by Use of a Table

The method of counting days as illustrated in frame 5 is awkward and time consuming, especially for long periods. Consequently, as in other kinds of computational work, tables have been developed whenever possible to simplify the problem. The following table is one of several used to find the number of days between two dates.

THE NUMBER OF EACH DAY OF THE YEAR

Day of Month	Jan.	Feb.*	Mar.	Apr.	May	June	July	Aug.	Sept.	Oct.	Nov.	Dec	Day of Month
1	1	32	60	91	121	152	182	213	244	274	305	335	1
2	2	33	61	92	122	153	183	214	245	275	306	336	2
3	3	34	62	93	123	154	184	215	246	276	307	337	3
4	4	35	63	94	124	155	185	216	247	277	308	338	4
5	5	36	64	95	125	156	186	217	248	278	309	339	5
6	6	37	65	96	126	157	187	218	249	279	310	340	6
7	7	38	66	97	127	158	188	219	250	280	311	341	7
8	8	39	67	98	128	159	189	220	251	281	312	342	8
9	9	40	68	99	129	160	190	221	252	282	313	343	9
10	10	41	69	100	130	161	191	222	253	283	314	344	10
11	11	42	70	101	131	162	192	223	254	284	315	345	11
12	12	43	71	102	132	163	193	224	255	285	316	346	12
13	13	44	72	103	133	164	194	225	256	286	317	347	13
14	14	45	73	104	134	165	195	226	257	287	318	348	14
15	15	46	74	105	135	166	196	227	258	288	319	349	15
16	16	47	75	106	136	167	197	228	259	289	320	350	16
17	17	48	76	107	137	168	198	229	260	290	321	351	17
18	18	49	77	108	138	169	199	230	261	291	322	352	18
19	19	50	78	109	139	170	200	231	262	292	323	353	19
20	20	51	79	110	140	171	201	232	263	293	324	354	20
21	21	52	80	111	141	172	202	233	264	294	325	355	21
22	22	53	81	112	142	173	203	234	265	295	326	356	22
23	23	54	82	113	143	174	204	235	266	296	327	357	23
24	24	55	83	114	144	175	205	236	267	297	328	358	24
25	25	56	84	115	145	176	206	237	268	298	329	359	25
26	26	57	85	116	146	177	207	238	269	299	330	360	26
27	27	58	86	117	147	178	208	239	270	300	331	361	27
28	28	59	87	118	148	179	209	240	271	301	332	362	28
29	29		88	119	149	180	210	241	272	302	333	363	29
30	30		89	120	150	181	211	242	273	303	334	364	30
31	31		90		151		212	243		304		365	31

*Add 1 for leap years after February 28.

6. Let us use the table and calculate the exact time (number of days) between May 15 and September 29.

(a) In the column headed "September" find the number that is in line with "29," as shown in the "Day of Month" column. It is 272. This means that September 29 is the 272nd day of the year.
(b) In the same manner we determine that May 15 is the 135th day of the year.
(c) The number of days between these two dates is 272 − 135 = 137 days.

Find the exact number of days between March 2 and November 21.

_____

325 − 61 = 264 days.

By use of the table, how many days are there from October 10 to February 14 of the following year?

Solution: December 31 = 365 days
 Less October 10 = 283 days
         82 days from October 10 to December 31
 plus February 14 = 45 days
         127 days from October 10 to February 14

7. How many days are there from November 26 to February 20 of the next year?
_____

_____

Days from November 26 to December 31 = 365 − 330 = 35.
February 20 = 51st day in the year.
Then 35 + 51 = 86 days from November 26 to February 20.

8. Find the exact time between January 12 and March 4, 1972.
(The year 1972 is a leap year.)

(a) According to the table, March 4 is the 63rd day of the year. Since 1972 is a leap year, however, February will have an extra day. Therefore March 4 will fall on the 64th day of the year instead of the 63rd.
(b) January 12 = 12 days. The number of days between the dates given = 64 − 12 = 52.

Find the exact number of days between January 6 and May 13, 1972. _____

_____

May 13, 1972 = 134th day of the year.
Number of days = 134 − 6 = 128.

9. Find the *approximate* time and *exact* time for the following. Use any method.

		Approximate time	Exact time
(a)	September 17, 1969, to June 9, 1970	_____	_____
(b)	April 1, 1970, to April 12, 1971	_____	_____
(c)	May 5, 1971, to October 19, 1971	_____	_____
(d)	March 29, 1972, to July 27, 1972	_____	_____
(e)	November 21, 1971, to March 2, 1972	_____	_____

- -

	Approximate time	Exact time
(a)	262	265
(b)	371	376
(c)	164	167
(d)	118	120
(e)	101	102

Calculating Interest

Simple Interest Formula

$$\text{Interest} = \text{principal} \times \text{rate} \times \text{time}$$

OR

$$I = Prt,$$

where I = interest in dollars,
P = principal (amount loaned or borrowed),
r = interest expressed as a percent,
t = time (period during which the borrower used the principal).

The unit of time must correspond to the rate. Therefore, if the rate is understood to be on an annual basis, the time must be expressed in terms of a year. Rates are quoted as annual rates unless otherwise stated; for example:

$$5 \text{ months} = \frac{5}{12}, \qquad 62 \text{ days} = \frac{62}{360 \text{ or } 365}$$

when used in the interest formula.

10. When time is expressed in *years*.

 Example: Find the interest on $300.00 for $2\frac{1}{2}$ years at 5%.

 Solution: $I = Prt = \$300.00 \times .05 \times 2.5 = \$37.50$.

 What is the interest on $250.00 for 3 years at 6%?

 $I = Prt = \$\underline{\hspace{1cm}} \times \underline{\hspace{1cm}} \times \underline{\hspace{1cm}} = \$\underline{\hspace{1cm}}$.

 $I = \$250.00 \times .06 \times 3 = \$45.00$.

11. When time is expressed in *months*, it must be converted to years.

 Example: Find the interest on $500.00 at 4% for 3 months.

 Solution: $I = \$500.00 \times .04 \times \dfrac{3}{12} = \$5.00$.

 Find the interest on $425.00 at 5% for 4 months.

 $I = \underline{\hspace{1cm}} \times \underline{\hspace{1cm}} \times \underline{\hspace{1cm}} = \underline{\hspace{1cm}}$.

 $I = \$425.00 \times .05 \times \dfrac{4}{12} = \$7.08$.

12. When time is expressed in *days*, it must be converted to years.

 Example: Find the interest on $3000 at 3% for 90 days.

 Solution: (a) If a 360-day year is used (ordinary or commercial interest),

 $$I = \$3000.00 \times .03 \times \dfrac{90}{360} = \$22.50.$$

 (b) If a 365-day year is used (accurate interest), then

 $$I = \$3000.00 \times .03 \times \dfrac{90}{365} = \$22.19.$$

Find (a) the ordinary interest and (b) the accurate interest on $1200.00 at 7% for 40 days.

(a) $I = $ _____ .

(b) $I = $ _____ .

- -

(a) $I = \$1200.00 \times .07 \times \dfrac{40}{360} = \$9.33$

(b) $I = \$1200.00 \times .07 \times \dfrac{40}{365} = \$9.21$

Simple Interest Formula and Cancellation Method

The formula $I = Prt$ may also be written

$$I = \frac{P \times r \times \text{days}}{360 \text{ or } 365}$$

and the cancellation method used.

Example: Find the interest on $350.00 at 4.5% for 72 days on a 360-day basis.

Solution: The numerator and denominator are divided by common factors when possible to simplify the calculations.

(a) $I = \dfrac{35\cancel{0} \times .045 \times 72}{36\cancel{0}}$ (divide 350 and 360 by 10).

(b) $I = \dfrac{35\cancel{0} \times .045 \times \overset{2}{\cancel{72}}}{\cancel{36}\cancel{0}} = \$3.15$ ($72 \div 36 = 2$).

13. Calculate the interest by this method on $600.00 at $3\tfrac{1}{2}\%$ for 52 days on a 360-day year.

    $I =$

- -

$I = \dfrac{\overset{5}{\cancel{\$600}} \times .035 \times 52}{\underset{3}{\cancel{360}}} = \$3.03$.

Find the (a) *ordinary*, (b) *banker's*, and (c) *accurate* interest on $1200 at 6% for a loan dated May 16 and due August 16 of the same year.

(a) Ordinary interest: $P = \$1200$, $r = .06$, approximate days = 90.

$$I = \frac{\overset{300}{\cancel{\$1200}} \times .06 \times \overset{\cancel{90}}{}}{\underset{\cancel{4}}{\cancel{360}}} = \$18.00.$$

(b) Banker's or commercial interest: $P = \$1200$, $r = .06$, exact days = 92.

$$I = \frac{\overset{20}{\cancel{\$1200}} \times \overset{.01}{\cancel{.06}} \times 92}{\underset{\cancel{60}}{\cancel{360}}} = \$18.40.$$

(c) Accurate interest: $P = \$1200$, $r = .06$, days (exact time) = 92.

$$I = \frac{\overset{240}{\cancel{\$1200}} \times .06 \times 92}{\underset{73}{\cancel{365}}} = \$18.15.$$

14. Compute the (a) ordinary, (b) banker's, and (c) accurate interest on $950 at 5% for a loan dated August 16 and due November 14.

   $P = \$$ _____, $r = $ _____, approximate days = _____, exact days = _____.

   (a) $I =$

   (b) $I =$

   (c) $I =$

   $P = \$950.00$, $r = .05$, approximate days = 88, exact days = 90.

   (a) $I = \dfrac{\$950 \times .05 \times 88}{360} = \$11.61$

   (b) $I = \dfrac{\$950 \times .05 \times 90}{360} = \$11.88$

   (c) $I = \dfrac{\$950 \times .05 \times 90}{365} = \$11.71$

   Notice that banker's interest brings the greatest return because there are more days than for ordinary interest and 360 (the divisor) is less than 365.

EXERCISE 36

Answers appear at the end of this exercise. If your answers do not agree with those shown, check your calculations before referring to the solutions that follow.

I. Find the simple interest on the following:
1. $2000 at $3\frac{1}{2}$% for 3 years _____
2. $4800 at 4% for $4\frac{1}{2}$ years _____
3. $455 for 3 months at $4\frac{1}{2}$% _____
4. $500 for 5 months at 5% _____
5. $250 at $6\frac{1}{2}$% for 2 years and 3 months ($2\frac{1}{4}$ years) _____

II. Find the *ordinary* simple interest (360-day year, 30-day month) on the following:
1. $642 for 60 days at 4% _____
2. $2000 for 62 days at 7.2% _____
3. $360 at $5\frac{1}{2}$% for 84 days _____
4. $750 from June 10 to August 17 at 6% _____
5. $800 at 7% from November 14 to February 12 _____

III. Find the *banker's* or *commercial* interest (360-day year, exact days) for the following:
1. $750 from June 10 to August 17 at 6% _____
2. $1200 at 3% from May 12 to June 18 _____
3. $800 at 7% from November 14 to February 12 _____
4. $1640 at 7% from July 19 to September 12 _____
5. $900 at 5% from March 16 to May 21 _____

IV. Find the *accurate* interest (365-day year, exact number of days) on the following:
1. $3000 at 6% for 90 days _____
2. $3500 at 9% from January 2 to June 5 _____
3. $7000 at 5% for 72 days _____
4. $600 at 6% from March 7 to September 15 _____
5. $1200 at $5\frac{1}{2}$% from May 12 to October 3 _____

Answers

I.		II.		III.		IV.	
1.	$210.00	1.	$ 4.28	1.	$ 8.50	1.	$ 44.38
2.	864.00	2.	24.80	2.	3.70	2.	132.90
3.	5.12	3.	4.62	3.	14.00	3.	69.04
4.	10.42	4.	8.38	4.	14.35	4.	18.94
5.	36.56	5.	13.69	5.	8.25	5.	26.04

Solutions

I.
1. $\$2000 \times .035 \times 3 = \$210.00$
2. $\$4800 \times .04 \times 4.5 = \$864.00$
3. $\$455 \times .045 \times \frac{3}{12} = \$5.12$
4. $\$500 \times .05 \times \frac{5}{12} = \$10.42$
5. $\$250 \times .065 \times 2.25 = \$36.56$

II.
1. $\$642 \times .04 \times \frac{60}{360} = \$4.28$
2. $\$2000 \times .072 \times \frac{62}{360} = \$24.80$
3. $\$360 \times .055 \times \frac{84}{360} = \$4.62$
4. $\$750 \times .06 \times \frac{67}{360} = \$8.38$
5. $\$800 \times .07 \times \frac{88}{360} = \$13.69$

III.
1. $\$750 \times .06 \times \frac{68}{360} = \$8.50$
2. $\$1200 \times .03 \times \frac{37}{360} = \$3.70$
3. $\$800 \times .07 \times \frac{90}{360} = \$14.00$
4. $\$1640 \times .07 \times \frac{45}{360} = \$14.35$
5. $\$900 \times .05 \times \frac{66}{360} = \$8.25$

IV.
1. $\$3000 \times .06 \times \frac{90}{365} = \$44.38$
2. $\$3500 \times .09 \times \frac{154}{365} = \$132.90$
3. $\$7000 \times .05 \times \frac{72}{365} = \$69.04$
4. $\$600 \times .06 \times \frac{192}{365} = \$18.94$
5. $\$1200 \times .055 \times \frac{144}{365} = \$26.04$

The 60-Day, 6% Method of Calculating Ordinary or Banker's Interest

When a loan is made for 60 days at 6%, the interest is always 1% of the principal. This is due to the fact that $.06 \times \frac{60}{360} = .01$.

Example: Find the ordinary interest on $575 at 6% for 60 days.

Solution: $I = \$575.00 \times (.06 \times 60/360) = \$575.00 \times .01 = \$5.75$.

Therefore the interest at 6% for 60 days on

$$\$ 326.50 = \$ 3.27, \quad \$ 39.50 = \$0.40,$$
$$4050.00 = 40.50, \quad 127.75 = 1.28.$$

15. The interest at 6% for 60 days on

$\$57.67 = \$$_____, $\$210.05 = \$$_____, $\$921.00 = \$$_____.

- -

$0.58, $2.10, $9.21

The 6%, 60-day rule can be applied to multiples or factors of 60; for example, the interest on $500.00 at 6% for

60 days = $ 5.00 (1% of $500)
120 days = 10.00 (2 × interest for 60 days)
180 days = 15.00 (3 × interest for 60 days)
90 days =   7.50 (1½ × interest for 60 days)
40 days =   3.33 (⅔ × interest for 60 days)
20 days =   1.67 (⅓ × interest for 60 days)
10 days =   .83 (⅙ × interest for 60 days)

16. The interest on $625.00 at 6% for

   60 days = _____ (____% of $625).

   30 days = _____ (____ × interest for 60 days).

   10 days = _____ (____ × interest for 60 days).

   120 days = _____ (____ × interest for 60 days).

- -

60 days = $ 6.25 (1% of $625).
30 days =   3.13 (½ × interest for 60 days).
10 days =   1.04 (⅙ × interest for 60 days).
120 days = 12.50 (2 × interest for 60 days).

This method also applies when a loan at 6% is made and the time is easily broken down into multiples or factors of 60.

The interest on $1250 at 6% for 92 days can be found as follows:
$$92 \text{ days} = 60 + 30 + 2.$$
Interest for 60 days = $12.50
Interest for 30 days =   6.25 (½ of $12.50)
Interest for 2 days =   0.42 (1/30 of $12.50)*
Interest for 92 days = $19.17

The interest for 47 days on $600 can be found as follows:
$$47 \text{ days} = 30 + 20 - 3.$$
Interest for 60 days = $6.00
Interest for 30 days = $3.00 (½ of $6.00)
Interest for 20 days = +2.00 (⅓ of $6.00)
Interest for 3 days = −0.30 (1/10 of 30 days' interest)
Interest for 47 days = $4.70

---

*The interest for 20 days = ⅓ of $12.50 or $4.19; the interest for 2 days = 1/10 of this amount or $0.42.

17. Compute the interest on $900 at 6% for 83 days; 83 days = 60 + 20 + 3.

   Interest for 60 days = $_____.

   Interest for 20 days = _____.

   Interest for 3 days = _____ ($\frac{1}{10}$ of 30 days' interest).

             total = $_____.

Interest for 60 days = $ 9.00
Interest for 20 days = $ 3.00   ($\frac{1}{3}$ of $9.00)
Interest for 3 days = $ 0.45   ($\frac{1}{10}$ of interest for 30 days; $\frac{1}{10}$ of $4.50)
        Total $12.45

18. Find the interest when the interest rate is a multiple or factor of 6% and the time is 60 days.

   Example: Find the interest on $800.00 for 60 days at:
      6% = $ 8.00
      3% =   4.00 ($\frac{1}{2}$ of 6%).
      2% =   2.67 ($\frac{1}{3}$ of 6%).
      9% = 12.00 ($1\frac{1}{2}$ × interest at 6%).
     12% = 16.00 (2 × interest at 6%).

   Find the interest on $750 for 60 days at

   6% = _____,   3% = _____,   1% = _____,

   12% = _____,   2% = _____.

6% = $ 7.50.   3% = $3.75 ($\frac{1}{2}$ of 6%).   1% = $1.25 ($\frac{1}{6}$ of 6%).
12% = $15.00 (2 × 6%).   2% = $2.50 ($\frac{1}{3}$ of 6%).

    The shortcuts illustrated in frames 16 to 18 are useful for simple problems. They need to be practiced, however, if results are to be dependable. Otherwise the time and effort to determine the best number combinations for them are not justified and it would be easier to use the interest formula $I = Prt$.

19. Try these. Find the *ordinary* simple interest for each of the following loans by the 60-day, 6% method.

   (a) $450 at 6% for 90 days $_____
   (b) $475 at 6% for 26 days   _____
   (c) $5500 at 2% for 60 days   _____
   (d) $500 at 3% for 120 days   _____
   (e) $198 at 9% for 60 days   _____

   (a) $ 6.75 ($1\frac{1}{2} \times$ interest for 60 days, $1\frac{1}{2} \times 4.50$)
   (b)   2.06 ($\frac{1}{3}$ of $4.75 + $\frac{1}{10}$ of $4.75)
   (c)   18.33 ($\frac{1}{3}$ of $55.00)
   (d)   5.00 (1% of $500)
   (e)   2.97 ($1\frac{1}{2} \times$ $1.98)

Simple Interest Tables

The use of tables greatly simplifies the computational work required to determine interest charges. Several commercial tables are available for this purpose. Those shown here are representative. They list the interest charges per $100 (to 4 decimals) for any number of days, at rates of 3% to 8%, based on a 360-day year and a 365-day year. Time not listed may be obtained by combining time periods shown that add to the time desired or, when subtracted one from the other, result in the time desired. This applies to rates as well.

Use the 360-day year table (page 392).

Example: Find the interest on $560.00 for 23 days at 4%.

Solution: In column headed "Time," find 23 days. In line with 23 days find the number in column headed 4%, i.e., 0.2556.

  Interest on $100.00 at 4% for 23 days = $0.2556 (from table).
  Interest on $560.00 at 4% for 23 days = (560 ÷ 100) × $0.2556
                              OR   5.60 × $0.2556 = $1.43136
                                                   = $1.43.

20. Find the interest on $964.00 for 16 days at $6\frac{1}{2}$% by use of the table.

   Interest = _____.

Interest on $100.00 at $6\frac{1}{2}\%$ = $0.2889 (from table).
Interest on $964.00 at $6\frac{1}{2}\%$ = 9.64 × 0.2889 = $2.78.

21. Find the interest on $6000.00 at $7\frac{1}{2}\%$ for 75 days (360-day year).

    Solution: Since 75 days is not listed in the tables, any combination of time that results in 75 days may be used; i.e., 2 months + 15 days.

    Interest on $100.00 at $7\frac{1}{2}\%$ for 2 months = $1.2500
    for 15 days = 0.3125
    75 days = $1.5625
    Interest on $6000.00 at $7\frac{1}{2}\%$ for 75 days = 60 × $1.5625
    = $93.75.

Find the interest on $4200 at 6% for 56 days.
56 days = 1 month (30 days) + 26 days.

Interest on $100 at 6% for 1 month = $_____ (from table),
for 26 days = _____ (from table),
for 56 days = $_____.

Interest on $4200 at 6% for 56 days = _____.

Interest on $100 at 6% for 1 month = $0.5000
Interest on $100 at 6% for 26 days = 0.4333
Interest on $100 at 6% for 56 days = $0.9333
Interest on $4200 at 6% for 56 days = 42 × $0.9333 = $39.20.

22. Find the interest on $400 at 2% for 12 days (360-day year).

    Solution: Since 2% is not included in the table, any combination of rates that results in 2% may be used; e.g., 6 − 4 or 8 − 6.

    Interest on $100 at 6% for 12 days = $0.2000
    at 4% for 12 days = −0.1333
    at 2% for 12 days = $0.0667
    Interest on $400.00 at 2% for 12 days = 4 × $0.0667 = $0.27.

Find the interest on $3800 at 9% for 25 days. (Combinations that equal 9% in the table are 4% + 5% or 6% + 3%.)

Interest on $100 at 4% for 25 days = $_____,

at 5% for 25 days = _____,

at 9% for 25 days = $_____.

Interest on $3800 at 9% for 25 days = _____ × _____ = $_____.

- -

Interest on $100 at 4% for 25 days = $0.2778
at 5% for 25 days =   0.3472
at 9% for 25 days = $0.6250
Interest on $3800 at 9% for 25 days = 38.00 × $0.6250 = $23.75.

23. Use the 365-day year table (page 393).

    Example: Find the interest on $1300.00 at 6% for 19 days.

    Solution: In column headed "Time" find 19 days. In line with 19 days find the number in column headed 6%, i.e., 0.3123.

    Interest on $100.00 at 6% for 19 days = $0.3123.
    Interest on $1300.00 at 6% for 19 days = 13 × $0.3123 = $4.06.

    What is the interest on $5500 at $5\frac{1}{2}$% for 15 days?

    $I = $ _____.

- -

$I = 55 \times \$0.2260 = \$12.43.$

24. Find the *accurate* interest on $2575.00 at $5\frac{1}{2}$% for 116 days. (116 days is not listed in the table. Any combination of time that equals 116, such as 90 + 26 or 120 − 4, may be used.)

    Interest on $100 at $5\frac{1}{2}$% for 90 days = $_____,

    for 26 days = _____,

    for 116 days = $_____.

    Interest on $2575 at $5\frac{1}{2}$% for 116 days = _____.

- -

Interest on $100 at $5\frac{1}{2}$% for 90 days = $1.3562
for 26 days = 0.3918
for 116 days = $1.7480

Interest on $2575 at $5\frac{1}{2}$% for 116 days = 25.75 × $1.7480 = $45.01.

25. Find the accurate interest on $300 at 10% for 18 days. (Use any combination of rates, such as 5 + 5, 7 + 3, or 6 + 4, that will result in a rate of 10%.)

$I =$ _____ × _____ = $_____ .

- -

$I = 3.00 \times \$0.4932 = \$1.48.$

EXERCISE 37

Use of Tables

Answers appear at the end of this exercise. If your answers do not agree with those shown, check your calculations before referring to the solutions that follow.

I. Find the amount of simple interest on each of the following loans by using (a) the 360-day table (page 392) for problems 1 to 3, inclusive, and (b) the 365-day table (page 393) for problems 4 to 6, inclusive. (c) Verify problems 3 and 6 by the interest formula.

No.	Principal	Rate (%)	Time (days)	Interest
1	$ 460	3	18	$_____
2	100	$8\frac{1}{2}$	21	_____
3	300	4	36	_____
4	850	$3\frac{1}{2}$	65	_____
5	2050	5	31	_____
6	1000	9	40	_____

II. Find the interest on the following loans by using the appropriate table.

No.	Principal	Rate (%)	Time Period	Interest	Interest ($)
1	$1300	3	Aug. 10, 1966–Dec. 15, 1966	Commercial	$_____
2	2400	4	Feb. 4, 1970–Mar. 15, 1970	Accurate	_____
3	725	$6\frac{1}{2}$	Apr. 20, 1971–Oct. 8, 1971	Ordinary	_____
4	550	8	May 19, 1972–Jan. 20, 1973	Commercial	_____
5	3000	7	Dec. 20, 1971–Mar. 5, 1972	Accurate	_____
6	3725	$5\frac{1}{2}$	Oct. 10, 1972–May 21, 1973	Accurate or Banker's (see frame 21)	_____

III. Word problems:

1. Bank A offers all personal unsecured loans on a 365-day year and Bank B uses a 360-day year. If Mr. Smith wishes to borrow $5000 for 90 days at 8%, which bank offers the best proposition? Why? By how much?

   _____
   _____
   _____

2. Using the banker's 60-day method, find the interest on (a) $1500 at 6% for 30 days, (b) $250 at 3% for 120 days, and (c) $3600 at 6% for 10 days.

   (a) _____
   (b) _____
   (c) _____

3. On May 5 Mr. Howe borrowed $650 at 7% for 90 days. When the note was due, however, Mr. Howe could pay only $350 on the principal, plus the interest. The bank accepted this payment, canceled the original note and made out a new 90-day loan at 7% for $300. (a) When was the last loan due? (b) What was the total interest charge from May 5 until the second loan was paid?

(a) _____

(b) _____

4. A finance company charges 6% on home loans. If a family borrows $12,000, what is the interest for the first month?

_____

5. Find the ordinary and accurate interest on $2400 for 45 days at $4\frac{1}{2}$%.

Ordinary interest _____

Accurate interest _____

6. Find the ordinary interest, the banker's interest, and the accurate interest on $950 at 5% from October 2 to February 11 of the next year?

_____

Answers

I.		II.		III.	
1.	$0.69	1.	$ 13.76	1.	Bank A, $1.37 less interest
2.	0.50	2.	10.26	2.	(a) $7.50, (b) $2.50, (c) $6.00
3.	1.20	3.	21.99	3.	(a) November 1, (b) $16.63
4.	5.30	4.	30.07	4.	$60.00
5.	8.71	5.	43.73	5.	Ordinary interest $13.50
					Accurate interest $13.32
6.	9.86	6.	125.17	6.	Ordinary interest $17.02
					Banker's interest $17.42
					Accurate interest $17.18

Solutions

I. 1. $4.60 \times .1500 = \$0.69.$ Verification of 3 and 6 by use of the formula.
    2. $1.00 \times .4959 = \$0.50.$
    3. $3.00 \times .4000 = \$1.20.$ 3. $300 \times .04 \times \dfrac{36}{360} = \$1.20.$
    4. $8.50 \times .6233 = \$5.30.$
    5. $20.50 \times .4247 = \$8.71.$
    6. $10.00 \times .9863 = \$9.86.$ 6. $1000 \times .09 \times \dfrac{48}{365} = \$9.86.$

II. Solutions are given by use of the formula and table.

1. $\$1300 \times .03 \times \dfrac{127}{360}$ OR $13.00 \times \$1.0583 = \$13.76.$

2. $\$2400 \times .04 \times \dfrac{39}{365}$ OR $24.00 \times \$0.4274 = \$10.26.$

3. $\$725 \times .065 \times \dfrac{168}{360}$ OR $7.25 \times \$3.0333 = \$21.99.$

4. $\$550 \times .08 \times \dfrac{246}{360}$ OR $5.50 \times \$5.4667 = \$30.07.$

    (use 8 months $(4 + 4) + 6$ days or any combination that equals 8 months).

5. $\$3000 \times .07 \times \dfrac{76}{365}$ OR $30.00 \times \$1.4576 = \$43.73.$

6. $\$3725 \times .055 \times \dfrac{224}{365}$ OR $37.25 \times \$3.3754 = \$125.73.$

III. 1. Bank A, interest $= \$5000 \times .08 \times \dfrac{90}{365} = \$98.63.$

    Bank B, interest $= \$5000 \times .08 \times \dfrac{90}{360} = \$100.00.$

    Bank A offer is best by $1.37.

2. (a) Interest on $1500 at 6% for 60 days = $15.00; therefore the interest on $1500 at 6% for 30 days $= \tfrac{1}{2}$ of $15.00 = $7.50.
    (b) Interest on $250 at 3% for 120 days is the same as interest at 6% for 60 days or $2.50.
    (c) Interest on $3600 at 6% for 10 days $= \tfrac{1}{6}$ of the amount earned for 60 days or $\tfrac{1}{6} \times \$36.00 = \$6.00.$

3. (a) The last note was due 180 days from May 5, i.e., November 1.
    (b) Interest on the first note $= \$650 \times .07 \times \dfrac{90}{360} = \$11.38.$

    First payment $= \$350.00 + \$11.38 = \$361.38.$

    Interest on second note $= \$300 \times .07 \times \dfrac{90}{360} = \$5.25.$

    Total interest $= \$11.38 + \$5.25 = \$16.63.$

4. Since the annual interest rate is 6%, the rate for a month is $\frac{1}{12}$th of 6%, or $\frac{1}{2}$%. Then the interest for one month on $12,000 = $12,000 × .005 = $60.00 OR I = $12,000 × .06 × $\frac{1}{12}$ = $60.00.

5. Ordinary interest = $2400 × .045 × $\frac{45}{360}$ = $13.50.

   Accurate interest = $2400 × .045 × $\frac{45}{365}$ = $13.32.

   Using the tables, ordinary interest = 24.00 × $0.5625 = $13.50,
   accurate interest = 24.00 × $0.5548 = $13.32.

6. Approximate time from October 2 to February 11 = 129 days.
   Exact time from October 2 to February 11   = 132 days.

   By use of tables: Ordinary interest = 9.50 × $1.7917 = $17.02.
   Banker's interest = 9.50 × $1.8333 = $17.42.
   Accurate interest = 9.50 × $1.8083 = $17.18.

   By formula: Ordinary interest = $950 × .05 × $\frac{129}{360}$ = $17.02.

   Banker's interest = $950 × .05 × $\frac{132}{360}$ = $17.42.

   Accurate interest = $950 × .05 × $\frac{132}{365}$ = $17.18.

Finding Maturity Value, Principal, Rate, and Time

MATURITY VALUE

When a loan matures it is due and payable in full. The amount to be repaid is called the maturity value and equals the principal plus the interest earned. As a formula, it is expressed as

$$\text{Maturity value} = \text{principal} + \text{interest}$$

OR

$$S = P + I$$

where S = maturity value or future sum,
P = principal (amount borrowed or loaned),
I = interest earned.

Example: Mr. Adams borrowed $500.00 at 6% for 6 months. What sum was due at the maturity date?

Solution: $I = Prt$ = $500.00 × .06 × $\frac{6}{12}$ = $15.00.
$S = P + I$ = $500.00 + $15.00 = $515.00 (maturity value).

26. A. Mann borrowed $700.00 at $5\frac{1}{2}\%$ for 9 months. What was the maturity value?

$I =$ _____.

$S =$ _____.

- -

$I = \$700.00 \times .055 \times \frac{9}{12} = \$28.88.$
$S = \$700.00 + \$28.88 = \$728.88.$

27. The Peoples Bank loaned the Hipple Co. $6000 at $6\frac{1}{2}\%$ for 90 days. If this loan was repaid when due, how much did the bank receive (commercial interest)?

Solution: $I = Prt = \$6000.00 \times .065 \times 90/360 = \$97.50.$
$S = P + I = \$6000.00 + \$97.50 = \$6097.50$ (maturity value).

Mr. Evers borrowed $500 from the local bank for 120 days at 8%. What sum did he repay at maturity date?

$I =$ _____.

$S =$ _____.

- -

$I = \$500 \times .08 \times \frac{120}{360} = \$13.33$ OR $I = 5.00 \times \$2.6667 = \$13.33$ (from tables).
$S = \$500 + \$13.33 = \$513.33.$

28. The Thrifty Savings & Loan Company lent $650 to Mr. James at 6% on May 15. If it was due on August 13, what was the maturity value (banker's or commercial interest)?

Number of days = _____.

$I =$ _____.

$S =$ _____.

- -

Number of days from May 15 to August 13 = 90.
$I = \$650 \times .06 \times \frac{90}{360} = \$9.75$ OR $6.50 \times \$1.50 = \$9.75$ (from tables).
$S = \$650.00 + \$9.75 = \$659.75.$

PRINCIPAL

To find the principal of a loan it is necessary to know the interest rate, amount of interest, and time period. When these factors are known, the principal may be found by substituting these values in the interest formula. If $I = Prt$, then $P = I \div rt$.

Example: When time is expressed in *years*:
find the principal necessary to earn $15 at 5% in 2 years.

Solution: $P = I \div rt = \$15 \div (.05 \times 2) = \$15 \div .10 = \$150$ (principal).

Proof: $I = Prt = \$150 \times .05 \times 2 = \$15.00$.

29. What sum of money will M. Hopkins need to earn $1500 in 5 years at 6%?

    $P = $ _____ .

    Proof: _____ .

    $P = \$1500 \div (.06 \times 5) = \$1500 \div .30 = \$5000$
    Proof: $I = \$5000 \times .06 \times 5 = \$1500$

30. When time is expressed in *months*, find the principal necessary to earn $60 at $4\frac{1}{2}\%$ in 4 months.

    Solution: $P = I \div rt = \$60 \div (.045 \times \frac{1}{3}) = \$60 \div .015 = \$4000$ (principal).

    Proof: $I = \$4000 \times .045 \times \frac{4}{12} = \$60.00$.

    If H. Ames earned $90 on an investment in 9 months, how much would he have to invest if the rate were 8%?

    $P = $ _____ .

    Proof: _____ .

    $P = \$90 \div (.08 \times \frac{9}{12}) = \$90 \div .06 = \$1500$.
    Proof: $I = \$1500 \times .08 \times \frac{9}{12} = \$90.00$.

Find the principal when time is expressed in *days*.
Find the principal necessary to yield $25 at 6% in 20 days (ordinary interest).

Solution: $P = I \div rt = \$25 \div (.06 \times \frac{20}{360}) = \$25 \div \frac{1}{300} = \$7500$ (principal).

Proof: $I = \$7500 \times .06 \times \frac{20}{360} = \$25.00$.

31. Find the principal necessary to earn $14.00 at 7% in 180 days?

    $P = $ _____ .

    Proof: _____ .

$P = \$14 \div (.07 \times \frac{180}{360}) = \$14 \div .035 = \$400$.
Proof: $I = \$400 \times .07 \times \frac{180}{360} = \$400 \times .035 = \$14.00$
  OR $I = 4.00 \times \$3.50 = \$14.00$ (from table).

RATE

As in finding the principal, use the basic interest formula and substitute known factors to find the rate. $I = Prt$; therefore $r = I \div Pt$.

Example: What rate of interest will earn $76.80 on $640.00 in 3 years?

Solution: $r = I \div Pt = \$76.80 \div (640.00 \times 3) = .04$ or 4% (interest rate).

Proof: $I = \$640 \times .04 \times 3 = \$76.80$.

32. At what interest rate will $3500 earn $875 in 5 years?

    $r = I \div Pt = $ _____ .

    Proof: $I = Prt = $ _____ .

$r = \$875 \div (\$3500 \times 5) = \$875 \div \$17,500 = .05 = 5\%$.
Proof: $I = Prt = \$3500 \times .05 \times 5 = \$875$.

33. At what rate must $720.00 be loaned to yield $29.70 in 9 months?

    Solution: $r = I \div Pt = \$29.70 \div (720 \times \frac{9}{12}) = .055 = 5\frac{1}{2}\%$ (interest rate).

    Proof: $I = \$720 \times .055 \times \frac{9}{12} = \$29.70$.

A. Brown wants to earn $325 in 6 months. If he has $6500 to invest, what interest rate is needed?

$r =$ _____.

Proof: $I = Prt =$ _____.

- -

$r = \$325 \div (\$6500 \times \frac{6}{12}) = \$325 \div \$3250 = .10 = 10\%$.
Proof: $I = Prt = \$6500 \times .10 \times \frac{1}{2} = \$325$.

34. What rate of interest will earn $6.40 on $1200.00 in 32 days (use 360-day year):

   Solution: $r = I \div Pt = \$6.40 \div (1200.00 \times \frac{32}{360} = .06 = 6\%$ (interest rate).
   Proof: $I = \$1200 \times .06 \times \frac{32}{360} = \$6.40$.

What rate of interest will earn $13.00 on $900.00 in 80 days (360-day year)?

$r =$ _____.

Proof: _____.

- -

$r = \$13 \div (\$900 \times \frac{80}{360}) = \$13 \div \$200 = .065 = 6.5\%$.
Proof: $I = \$900 \times .065 \times \frac{80}{360} = \$13.00$.

TIME

In the same manner in which the principal and interest rate were determined time is found by substituting the known factors in the basic formula. Time may be expressed in months, days, or years.

$$I = Prt; \text{ therefore } t = I \div Pr.$$

Since interest rates are quoted by the year unless otherwise stated, the time is in terms of years. If the result is less than 1, it may be converted to days or months, as illustrated in the following examples.

Example: How long will it take $3500.00 to earn $437.50 at 5%?

Solution: $t = I \div Pr = \$437.50 \div (3500.00 \times .05) = 2\frac{1}{2}$ years.

Proof: $I = \$3500 \times .05 \times 2.5 = \$437.50$.

UNIT 1

35. E. Redding has $4500 invested at 7%. How long will he have to wait to earn $630?

$t = I \div Pr$ = _____.

Proof: $I = Prt$ = _____.

- -

$t = \$630 \div (\$4500 \times .07) = \$630 \div \$315 = 2$ years.
Proof: $\$4500 \times .07 \times 2 = \$630$.

36. Find the time required for $425.00 to earn $25.50 at 8%.

Solution: $t = I \div Pr = \$25.50 \div (425.00 \times .08) = .75$ years.
Converted to months, .75 years = .75 × 12 = 9 months.
Converted to days (360-day year), .75 years = .75 × 360
= 270 days.

Proof: $I = \$425 \times .08 \times \frac{270}{360} = \$25.50$ OR
$I = \$425 \times .08 \times .75 = \$25.50$.

How long will it take for $650 to earn $21.67 at 5%?

$t =$ _____

Proof: _____

- -

$t = I \div Pr = \$21.67 \div (\$650 \times .05) = \$21.67 \div \$32.50 = .6667$ years or $\frac{2}{3}$ years.
.6667 × 360 = 240.012 or 240 days OR $\frac{2}{3}$ × 360 = 240 days.

Proof: $I = Prt = \$650 \times .05 \times \frac{240}{360} = \$21.67$.

EXERCISE 38

Answers appear at the end of this exercise. If your answers do not agree with those shown, check your calculations before referring to the solutions that follow.

I. Find the principal and maturity value for the following loans at simple ordinary interest:

No.	Interest	Rate (%)	Time	Principal	Maturity Value
1	$35.00	$3\frac{1}{2}$	8 months	_____	_____
2	26.25	6	15 months	_____	_____
3	8.05	7	18 days	_____	_____
4	14.50	5	120 days	_____	_____

II. Find the ordinary interest rate on the following loans:

No.	Principal	Interest	Time	Interest Rate
1	$1800.00	$ 35.10	117 days	_____
2	700.00	7.00	72 days	_____
3	3000.00	30.00	6 months	_____
4	1500.00	367.50	$3\frac{1}{2}$ years	_____

374 UNIT 1

III. Find the time required to earn the interest charges shown. Convert all fractions of a year to days, using a 360-day year.

No.	Principal	Interest	Rate (%)	Time (days)
1	$1240.00	$18.60	6	_____
2	6000.00	37.50	5	_____
3	3600.00	70.20	6	_____
4	800.00	35.00	$3\frac{1}{2}$	_____

IV. Solve the following.

1. From March 3 to June 1 $8120.00 earned $91.35. What was the commercial interest rate?

2. Find the maturity value on a loan of $675 at 4%, dated July 15 and due September 25? (Use banker's interest.)

3. Find the commercial interest on the following amounts by the 60-day, 6% method: (a) $160 at 3% for 60 days, (b) $750 at 12% for 30 days, and (c) $90 at 6% for 90 days.

(a) _____

(b) _____

(c) _____

4. Find the accurate interest on $375 at 5% from May 10 to July 15.

5. Mr. Haines bought a TV set from the Hi Fi Company for $650 cash or $670 if paid at the end of 3 months. If he borrowed $650 for 3 months at 5% (commercial interest) and paid the cash price, how much would he save?

Answers

	Principal	Maturity Value		Interest Rate
I. 1.	$1500.00	$1535.00	II. 1.	6%
2.	350.00	376.25	2.	5%
3.	2300.00	2308.05	3.	2%
4.	870.00	884.50	4.	7%

III. 1. 90 days
    2. 45 days
    3. 117 days
    4. 450 days or 1 year, 90 days

IV. 1. $4\frac{1}{2}\%$
    2. $680.40
    3. (a) $0.80
       (b) $7.50
       (c) $1.35
    4. $3.39
    5. $11.87

Solutions

I. $P = I \div rt$.

1. $P = \$35.00 \div (.035 \times \frac{8}{12}) = \$1500.00$.
$S = \$1500.00 + \$35.00 = \$1535.00$.

2. $P = \$26.25 \div (.06 \times \frac{15}{12}) = \$350.00$.
$S = \$350.00 + \$26.25 = \$376.25$.

3. $P = \$8.05 \div (.07 \times \frac{18}{360}) = \$2300.00$.
$S = \$2300.00 + \$8.05 = \$2308.05$.

4. $P = \$14.50 \div (.05 \times \frac{120}{360}) = \$870.00$.
$S = \$870.00 + \$14.50 = \$884.50$.

II. $\quad r = I \div Pt$.

1. $r = \$35.10 \div (\$1800 \times \frac{117}{360}) = .06 = 6\%$.
2. $r = \$7.00 \div (\$700 \times \frac{72}{360}) = .05 = 5\%$.
3. $r = \$30.00 \div (\$3000 \times \frac{6}{12}) = .02 = 2\%$.
4. $r = \$367.50 \div (\$1500 \times 3.5) = .07 = 7\%$.

III. $\quad t = I \div Pr$.

1. $t = \$18.60 \div (\$1240 \times .06) = .25$ years; $\quad .25 \times 360 = 90$ days.
2. $t = \$37.50 \div (\$6000 \times .05) = .125$ years; $\quad \frac{1}{8} \times 360 = 45$ days.
3. $t = \$70.20 \div (\$3600 \times .06) = \frac{117}{360}$ years; $\quad \frac{117}{360} \times 360 = 117$ days.
4. $t = \$35.00 \div (\$800 \times .035) = 1\frac{1}{4}$ years; $\quad 1.25 \times 360 = 450$ days or 1 year, 90 days.

IV.
1. Time = 90 days, $r = \$91.35 \div (\$1820 \times \frac{90}{360}) = .045 = 4.5\%$.
2. Time = 72 days, $I = \$675 \times .04 \times \frac{72}{360} = \$5.40$.
   $S = \$675.00 + \$5.40 = \$680.40$.
3. (a) Interest on \$160 at 6% for 60 days = \$1.60.
   Interest on \$160 at 3% for 60 days = $\frac{1}{2} \times \$1.00 = \$0.80$.
   (b) Interest on \$750 at 6% for 30 days = $\frac{1}{2}$ of 6% = $\frac{1}{2} \times \$750 = \$3.75$.
   Interest on \$750 at 12% for 30 days = $2 \times \$3.75 = \$7.50$.
   (c) Interest on \$90 at 6% for 90 days = $1\frac{1}{2} \times 6\% = 1\frac{1}{2} \times \$0.90 = \$1.35$.
4. Time (May 10–July 15) = 60 days.
   $I = \$375 \times .05 \times \frac{66}{365} = \$3.39$
   OR
   $I = 3.75 \times \$0.9041 = \$3.39$ (using tables).
5. $I = \$650 \times .05 \times \frac{3}{12} = \$8.13$.
   \$650.00 + \$8.13 = \$658.13 if he borrowed the money. This is better than \$670 by \$11.87.

UNIT 2. COMPOUND INTEREST

Simple interest is computed on a fixed amount or principal for a specified period of time and rate. Compound interest is computed on a principal that changes at stated intervals when interest is added to it. This interval may be any time period during the year: annual, semiannual, quarter, month, or day.* When simple interest is added

---

*The use of computers has brought many changes in banking procedures. The services of many clerks were required to calculate and post interest compounded quarterly; the computer can now convert money daily in a fraction of the time. This is the usual practice of banks as well as of savings and loan associations in some areas of the United States. When this system is used, individual accounts are credited at the end of each quarter with the interest earned.

to the principal, it is said to be *converted*—it becomes part of the principal. The number of *conversion periods* is the number of times the interest is converted during the year.

The difference between the original principal and the amount it has become at the end of any period of time is called *compound interest*.

1. When simple interest is added to the principal, it is said to be _____.
   When simple interest is added to the principal twice a year, the number of conversion periods is ____.

   ----

   converted, 2

2. When interest is compounded semiannually, it means that there are 2 conversion periods. If interest is compounded quarterly, there are ____ conversion periods.
   If interest is converted every month, it is compounded ____ times in a year. The number of conversion periods and the number of times interest is converted to principal is (the same/not the same)? _____

   4
   12
   Same

Computing Compound Interest

Let us assume that $100 is to be converted annually at 6%. What will the compound interest equal at the end of 3 years?

$100.00   original principal
   6.00   interest, first year ($100.00 × .06)
$106.00   principal at end of first year
   6.36   interest, second year ($106,00 × .06)
$112.36   principal at end of second year
   6.74   interest, third year ($112.36 × .06)
$119.10   principal at end of third year

Compound interest = $119.10 − $100.00 = $19.10

3. Compute the compound interest on $200 for 2 years at 5%.

$200.00   original principal

_____   interest, first year

$_____   principal at end of first year

_____   interest, second year

$_____   principal at end of second year

Compound interest = $_____ − $_____ = $_____ .

- -

$200.00   original principal
  10.00   interest, first year ($200 × .05)
─────
$210.00   principal at end of first year
  10.50   interest, second year (210 × .05)
─────
$220.50   principal at end of second year

Compound interest = $220.50 − $200.00 = $20.50.

4. If a person deposited $100 in a savings account, how much would he have at the end of a year if money is worth* 6% and is compounded (a) semiannually or (b) quarterly? What will the compound interest be in each case?

   Solution: (a) If the annual interest is 6%, the interest for half a year is 3%. In this case there are 2 conversions per year.

   $100.00   original principal
     3.00   interest, 6 months ($100.00 × .03)
   ─────
   $103.00   principal, end of 6 months
     3.09   interest, second 6-month period ($103.00 × .03)
   ─────
   $106.09   principal, end of year

   Compound interest = $106.09 − $100.00 = $6.09.

─────────────────────────

*"Money is worth" is a common expression. It is another way of saying that the rate of interest is (in this case) 6%.

(b) If money is converted quarterly, there are 4 conversion periods. Then the interest rate per conversion period will equal $1\frac{1}{2}\%$ ($6\% \div 4$).

$100.00 original principal
  1.50 interest, first quarter ($100.00 × .015)
$101.50 principal, end of first quarter
  1.52 interest, second quarter ($101.50 × .015)
$103.02 principal, end of second quarter
  1.55 interest, third quarter ($103.02 × .015)
$104.57 principal, end of third quarter
  1.57 interest, fourth quarter ($104.57 × .015)
$106.14 principal, end of fourth quarter of the year

Compound interest = $106.14 − $100.00 = $6.14

5. In frame 4 there were _____ conversion periods for example (a) and _____ conversion periods for example (b).
The compound interest is (more/less) as the number of conversion periods increases. _____
In example (a) the annual interest rate is 6%; therefore the rate for 6 months = $\frac{1}{2}$ of 6% = 3%. If the annual interest rate = 8%, the interest rate for 6 months = _____%; for 3 months it = _____%.

- -

2, 4
more
4%, 2%

Conversion periods: When computing compound interest, it is important to be able to change the annual rate to the conversion period rate quickly, both when solving a problem as illustrated or when using the Compound Interest Table; for example,

Annual Interest Rate	Conversion Periods per Year	Interest Rate per Conversion Period
8% converted annually	1	8%
8% converted semiannually	2	4%
8% converted quarterly	4	2%
5% converted semiannually	2	$2\frac{1}{2}\%$
5% converted monthly	12	$\frac{5}{12}\%$ or $.41\frac{2}{3}\%$

What is the interest rate per conversion period for the following:

Annual Interest Rate	Conversion Periods per Year	Interest Rate per Conversion Period
10	2	____%
10	4	____%
9	4	____%
6	1	____%
7	2	____%

5%
$2\frac{1}{2}$%
$2\frac{1}{4}$
6%
$3\frac{1}{2}$%

6. If money is converted semiannually, there are 2 conversion periods in a year, 4 in 2 years (2 × 2), 10 in 5 years (5 × 2), etc. How many conversion periods are there in

   8 years if money is converted annually ____,

   10 years if money is converted quarterly ____,

   15 years if money is converted semiannually ____?

8, 40, 30

Compound Interest Tables

As can be observed in frame 3, it becomes a tedious chore to compute the compound interest for sums in excess of 4 or 5 conversion periods.

Use of a Compound Interest Table reduces the arithmetical processes to a minimum. The column headed "n" represents the number of conversion periods; the interest rates are the rates per conversion period. The table shown on pages 394–397 includes rates from $\frac{1}{2}$% to $8\frac{1}{2}$% for 50 conversion periods.

Practice in reading the table is helpful in solving any problem when they are used.

Assume that money was loaned at 5%, compounded semiannually for 6 years. How much would $1.00 be worth at the end of that time?

(1) In 6 years there are 2 × 6 or 12 conversion periods if money is compounded semiannually; the interest rate per conversion period = 5% ÷ 2 = 2½%.
(2) Find the column headed by 2½%. Read down the column to the line opposite 12 in the n column.
(3) The number = 1.34488882. This means that $1.00 has increased to $1.34+ in 6 years at 5% compounded semiannually.
(4) The interest earned on $1.00 = ($1.34+) − $1.00 = $0.34+

7. (a) How much is $1.00 worth (correct to 5 decimals) at the end of 4 years at 6% compounded quarterly _____? Compounded monthly _____?
   (b) How much is $1.00 worth at the end of 15 years at 7% compounded annually _____? Semiannually _____?
   (c) What is the interest earned on $1.00 to the nearest cent for each case in questions (a) and (b)?

   (a) _____, _____; (b) _____, _____.

- -

(a) $n = 16$, rate per conversion period = 6% ÷ 4 = 1½%, factor = 1.26899.
    $n = 48$, rate per conversion period = 6% ÷ 12 = ½%, factor = 1.27049.
(b) $n = 15$, rate per conversion period = 7%, factor = 2.75903.
    $n = 30$, rate per conversion period = 7% ÷ 2 = 3½%, factor = 2.80679.
(c) Interest for (a) = $0.27 and $0.27, respectively (nearest cent).
    Interest for (b) = $1.76 and $1.81, respectively (nearest cent).

8. How much will $500 amount to in 5 years at 6% compounded quarterly? Find the interest earned.

   Solution: Conversion periods (n) = 20   (4 × 5 years).
   Conversion interest rate = 1½%   (6% ÷ 4).

   Find the column headed by 1½%. Read down the column to the line opposite 20 in the n column. The amount shown = 1.346855. This means that $1.00 will increase to $1.346855 in 5 years when compounded quarterly at 6%; the interest earned is $0.35 to the nearest cent. Therefore to find the sum to which $500 will increase, multiply $1.346855 by 500:

   500 × $1.346855 = $673.427500 = $673.43.

   The interest earned = $673.43 − $500.00 = $173.43.

How much will $400 equal in 6 years at 7% compounded semiannually? How much is the interest earned?

Conversion periods = _____.

Conversion period interest rate = _____.

Table factor (5 decimals) = _____.

S(sum) = $400 × _____ = $_____.

Interest earned = $_____ − $_____ = $_____.

- -

Conversion periods = 6 × 2 = 12.
Conversion interest rate = 7% ÷ 2 = $3\frac{1}{2}$%.
Table factor = 1.51107 (5 decimals corrected).
S = $400 × 1.51107 = $604.43.
Interest earned = $604.43 − $400.00 = $204.43.

9. What is the difference between simple interest on $1000 at 5% for 3 years and compounded interest on $1000 at 5% compounded semiannually for 3 years?

   Solution: Simple interest = $1000 × .05 × 3 = $150.00.
   Compound interest: $n = 6$, interest per period = $2\frac{1}{2}$%.
   Table factor (5 decimals) = $1.15969.
   Interest = $0.15969 per $1.00 during this time.
   Therefore compound interest = $1000 × $0.15969 = $159.69.
   Difference = $159.69 − $150.00 = $9.69.

What is the difference between simple interest on $1000 at 8% for 2 years and compound interest on the same amount at 8% compounded quarterly for 2 years?

Simple interest = _____

Compound interest = _____
   (use 5 decimal factor)

Difference = $_____ − $_____ = $_____.

- -

Simple interest = $1000 × .08 × 2 = $160.00.
$n = 8$, conversion period rate = 2%, table factor (5 decimals) = 1.17166.
Compound interest = $1000 × 0.17166 = $171.66.
Difference = $171.66 − $160.00 = $11.66.

10. How long approximately will it take money to double itself at 6% compounded semiannually? Conversion period interest rate = 3%.

Under column headed 3% in the tables, look for a sum that is almost or equal to $2.00. We find that $1.00 = $2.03 + at 24 periods. Since money is converted semiannually, this is 12 years approximately.

In how many years approximately will it take money to double itself at

4% compounded annually? _____

6% compounded quarterly? _____

8% compounded semiannually? _____

----

18 years
Between 11 and 12 years [(46 or 47 periods) ÷ 4]
9 years (18 periods ÷ 2)

Nominal and Effective Interest Rates

The *effective* rate is the annual rate that will produce the same interest in a year as the *nominal* rate converted a certain number of times; for example, 6% converted semiannually produces $6.09 per $100. Therefore *6% is the nominal rate and 6.09% is the effective rate*. This is the same as saying that a rate of 6% converted semiannually yields the same interest as a rate of 6.09% on an annual basis.

To make comparisons between different nominal rates, they must be reduced to a common base. Such comparisons can be made when all rates are expressed as effective rates.

What simple interest rate will earn the same interest in a year as 5% converted semiannually? Refer to the table and read the value given for 2 conversion periods at 2½%. This value = 1.050625. It means that a simple interest rate of 5.0625% will earn the same amount in a year as 5% converted twice a year. In this case the effective rate = 5.0625%; the nominal rate = 5%.

11. What are the effective interest rates for the following (record answers correct to 2 decimals as %):

    4% converted quarterly   __4.06%__

    6% converted semiannually _____

    10% converted quarterly   _____

    8% converted quarterly   _____

    6.09%
    10.38%
    8.24%

12. Which is the best investment program; 8% compounded quarterly or 9% compounded semiannually?

Nominal Rate	Table Factor (5 decimals)	Effective Rate (2 decimals)
(a) 8% compounded quarterly	_____	_____ %
(b) 9% compounded semiannually	_____	_____ %

    (a) Table factor = 1.08243, effective rate = 8.24%.
    (b) Table factor = 1.09203, effective rate = 9.20%.
    The best program is (b) since it earns 9.20 cents per dollar, compared with 8.24 cents in (a).

EXERCISE 39

Answers appear at the end of this exercise. If your answers do not agree with those shown, check your calculations before referring to the solutions that follow.

1. How many years, approximately, will it take money to double itself at 4% compound semiannually?

   _____

2. If 200 dollars were deposited in a bank at 5% compounded semiannually, how much will be on deposit at the end of 5 years? How much interest was earned?

   On deposit _____

   Interest   _____

3. If the rate of interest is 6%, how many conversion periods are there in 5 years if money is converted semiannually? Quarterly? Monthly? Yearly? What is the interest rate per period of time for each of these conversion periods?

   _____

   _____

   _____

   _____

4. How much more will $100 earn at 6% converted quarterly, compared with semiannually for a year?

   _____

5. How much does $100 earn at 5% converted annually for 10 years?

   _____

386   UNIT 2

6. How many years must $2000 be invested at 4% compounded annually to earn $1746 (nearest whole dollars)?

_____ years

7. A building and loan association pays interest on deposits at the rate of 3% compounded semiannually. How much, at this rate, would a deposit of $1200 equal at the end of 6 years?

_____

8. A man borrows $500 on September 10, 1970. If he pays interest at 6% converted monthly, how much must he pay on April 10, 1972 (use a 30-day month)?

_____

9. What sum will be needed to repay a loan of $1600 at an interest rate of 5% converted semiannually at the end of 2 years? (Carry rate to 6 decimals.)

_____

10. What is the effective interest rate equivalent to 7% converted semiannually, to 8% converted quarterly, and to 9% converted semiannually (nearest hundredth of 1%)?

_____

_____

_____

11. How much interest will $5000 earn in 15 months at 6% compounded quarterly? (Use 6 decimals in table factor.)

_____

12. An investment of $2000 earned 4% converted quarterly for 3 years, then 5% converted semiannually for the next 2 years. Find the total of the investment fund at the end of the 5 years and the interest earned. (Use 6 decimals in table factor.)

_____ in fund

_____ interest

Answers

1. $17\frac{1}{2}$ years
2. On deposit $256.02
   Interest $ 56.02
3. 3 %, 10
   $1\frac{1}{2}$%, 20
   $\frac{1}{2}$%, 60
   6 %, 5
4. $0.05
5. $62.89
6. 16 years
7. $1434.74
8. $549.70
9. $1766.10
10. 7.12%
    8.24%
    9.20%
11. $386.42
12. In fund $2487.61
    Interest $ 487.61

Solutions

1. Refer to the compound interest tables for 2%. Notice that $1.00 is worth $2.00 (nearest dollar) at the end of 35 periods if compounded semiannually at 4%. Then 35 periods represent $17\frac{1}{2}$ years.
2. Conversion period rate = $2\frac{1}{2}$%, conversion periods = 10.
   Factor from compound interest table for 10 periods at $2\frac{1}{2}$% = 1.28008.
   Amount on deposit = $200 × 1.28008 = $256.02.
   Interest = $256.02 − $200.00 = $56.02.

3.

	Conversion Periods	Interest Rate per Conversion Period
Semiannually = 5 × 2	10	6% ÷ 2 = 3%
Quarterly = 5 × 4	20	6% ÷ 4 = $1\frac{1}{2}$% or 1.5%
Monthly = 5 × 12	60	6% ÷ 12 = $\frac{1}{2}$% or 0.5%
Yearly = 5	5	6%

4. If money is converted quarterly, the number of conversion periods = 4 for one year and the interest rate per period is $\frac{1}{4}$ of 6% or $1\frac{1}{2}$%. According to the tables, $100 will earn $6.14. If money is converted semiannually, the number of conversion periods = 2 for one year and the interest rate per period is $\frac{1}{2}$ of 6% or 3%. According to the tables, $100 will earn $6.09 Difference = $0.05 (answer).

5. Periods = 10, rate = 5%, S = $1.62889 for $1.00.
Then for $100, the interest = $162.89 − $100.00 = $62.89.

6. $1746 ÷ 2 = $873 for $1000 or $87.30 for $100 at 4%. According to the tables, the time required = 16 years. (Use compound interest tables, 4% column, and look for nearest number to 1.873 for $1.00. It is 1.8729 +.)

7. Conversion periods = 12, rate per conversion period = $1\frac{1}{2}$%.
S = $1200 × 1.19562 = $1434.74.

8. Time = 19 months. Since money is converted monthly, the total number of conversion periods = 19. The interest rate per period is $\frac{1}{12}$ of 6% or $\frac{1}{2}$%. The factor in the table for $\frac{1}{2}$% for 19 periods = 1.09940; therefore the total amount to be paid on April 10 = $500 × 1.09940 = $549.70.

9. Conversion period rate = $2\frac{1}{2}$%, n = 4, rate in table for 4 periods at $2\frac{1}{2}$% = 1.103813. Then S = $1600 × 1.103813 = $1766.10.

10. Refer to table.
For 7% find factor for $3\frac{1}{2}$% for 2 periods. Effective rate = 7.12%.
For 8% find factor for 2% for 4 periods. Effective rate = 8.24%.
For 9% find factor for $4\frac{1}{2}$% for 2 periods. Effective rate = 9.20%.

11. S = $5000 × 1.077284 = $5386.42.
Interest = $5386.42 − $5000.00 = $386.42 OR $5000 × .077284 = $386.42.

12. 4% converted quarterly = 1% per period; 3 years = 12 periods.
5% converted semiannually = $2\frac{1}{2}$% per period; 2 years = 4 periods.
S = $2000 × 1.126825 = $2253.65 at the end of the first 3 years.
Amount in fund at the end of 5 years; S = $2253.65 × 1.103813 = $2487.61.
Interest earned = $2487.61 − $2000.00 = $487.61.

EXERCISE 40

Chapter Summary

Answers appear at the end of this exercise. If your answers do not agree with those shown, check your calculations before referring to the solutions that follow.

1. Find the ordinary, banker's, and accurate interest on a loan for $3000 at 6%, dated June 12 and due December 20 of the same year. (Use the formula and verify by use of the tables.)

    Ordinary _____

    Banker's _____

    Accurate _____

2. A man borrows $95.00. He repays the loan (principal plus interest) 6 months later with a payment of $100.00. What interest rate did he pay (nearest tenth of 1%)?

    _____

3. Mr. Kempton borrowed $300 for 3 months at $5\frac{1}{2}$%. How much was the payment when the loan was due?

    _____

4. Find the principal necessary to earn $11.25 in 3 months at 3%. Prove your answer, using the formula $I = Prt$.

    _____

5. If a person deposited $250 at 4% compounded quarterly, how much would he have at the end of 10 years? (Use rate rounded to 4 decimals.)

6. What is the effective rate of interest equivalent to 10% converted quarterly? (Record answer to nearest hundredth of 1 percent.)

7. How much interest will $3000 earn at 7% converted annually in 5 years and semiannually for 5 years? (Use rate rounded to 6 decimals.)

8. How much does $100 earn at 6% compounded quarterly for 10 years? (Read table to 5 decimals.)

Answers

1. Ordinary $94.00
   Banker's $95.50
   Accurate $94.19
2. 10.5%
3. $304.13
4. $1500.00
5. $372.23
6. 10.38%
7. $1207.66
   $1231.80
8. $81.40

Solutions

1. (a) Number of approximate days (30 day month) from June 12 to December 20 = 188.

   $$\frac{\$3000 \times .06 \times 188}{360} = \$94.00.$$

   Use of tables: 6 months (180 days) = 3.0000
   8 days = .1333
   188 days = 3.1333

   Interest = $30.00 × 3.1333 = $93.999 = $94.00.

   (b) Number of exact days from June 12 to December 20 = 191.

   $$\text{Interest} = \frac{\$3000 \times .06 \times 191}{360} = \$95.50.$$

   Use of tables: 6 months (180 days) = 3.0000
   11 days = .1833
   191 days = 3.1833

   Interest = $30.00 × 3.1833 = $95.499 = $95.50.

   (c) $$\text{Interest} = \frac{\$3000 \times .06 \times 191}{365} = \$94.19.$$

   Use of tables: 100 days = 1.6438
   90 days = 1.4795
   1 day = .0164
   191 days = 3.1397

   Any other combination that adds to 191 may be used. The total and result will be the same.

   Interest = $30.00 × 3.1397 = $94.1910 = $94.19.

2. $I = Prt$. $I = \$100 - \$95 = \$5$, $P = \$95$, $t = 6$ months or $\frac{1}{2}$ year.
   $r = I \div Pt = \$5 \div (\$95 \times \frac{1}{2}) = \$5 \div 47.5 = .1052 = 10.5\%$ (nearest tenth of 1%).

3. $I = \dfrac{\$300 \times .055 \times 3}{12}$ or $300 × .055 × .25 = \$4.13$.
   Amount paid = $300.00 + $4.13 = $304.13.

4. $I = Prt$, $P = I \div rt$. $I = \$11.25$, $t = 3$ months or $\frac{1}{4}$ year, $r = .03$.
   Then $P = \$11.25 \div (.03 \times .25) = \$11.25 \div .0075 = \$1500.00$.
   Proof: $I = \$1500 \times .03 \times .25 = \$11.25$.

5. $250 × 1.4889 = $372.23.

6. 10% converted quarterly. Conversion period rate = $2\frac{1}{2}\%$, conversion periods = 4 per year. Effective rate (reading from the tables) = 10.38%.

7. Compounded annually for 5 years, $3000 × 0.402552 = $1207.66.
   Compounded semiannually for 5 years, $3000 × 0.410599 = $1231.80.

8. Conversion periods = 40, Conversion period rate = $1\frac{1}{2}\%$.
   Tables show 1.81402. Interest earned = $81.40.

SIMPLE INTEREST TABLE   Interest on $100, Based on a 360-Day Year

Time (Days)	3%	3½%	4%	4½%	5%	5½%	6%	6½%	7%	7½%	8%
1	.0083	.0097	.0111	.0125	.0139	.0153	.0167	.0181	.0194	.0208	.0222
2	.0167	.0194	.0222	.0250	.0278	.0306	.0333	.0361	.0389	.0417	.0444
3	.0250	.0292	.0333	.0375	.0417	.0458	.0500	.0542	.0583	.0625	.0667
4	.0333	.0389	.0444	.0500	.0556	.0611	.0667	.0722	.0778	.0833	.0889
5	.0417	.0486	.0556	.0625	.0694	.0764	.0833	.0903	.0972	.1042	.1111
6	.0500	.0583	.0667	.0750	.0833	.0917	.1000	.1083	.1167	.1250	.1333
7	.0583	.0681	.0778	.0875	.0972	.1069	.1167	.1264	.1361	.1458	.1556
8	.0667	.0778	.0889	.1000	.1111	.1222	.1333	.1444	.1556	.1667	.1778
9	.0750	.0875	.1000	.1125	.1250	.1375	.1500	.1625	.1750	.1875	.2000
10	.0833	.0972	.1111	.1250	.1389	.1528	.1667	.1806	.1944	.2083	.2222
11	.0917	.1069	.1222	.1375	.1528	.1681	.1833	.1986	.2139	.2197	.2444
12	.1000	.1167	.1333	.1500	.1667	.1833	.2000	.2167	.2333	.2500	.2667
13	.1083	.1264	.1444	.1625	.1806	.1986	.2167	.2347	.2528	.2708	.2889
14	.1167	.1361	.1556	.1750	.1944	.2139	.2333	.2528	.2722	.2917	.3111
15	.1250	.1458	.1667	.1875	.2083	.2292	.2500	.2708	.2917	.3125	.3333
16	.1333	.1556	.1778	.2000	.2222	.2444	.2667	.2889	.3111	.3333	.3556
17	.1417	.1653	.1889	.2125	.2361	.2597	.2833	.3069	.3306	.3542	.3778
18	.1500	.1750	.2000	.2250	.2500	.2750	.3000	.3250	.3500	.3750	.4000
19	.1583	.1847	.2111	.2375	.2639	.2903	.3167	.3431	.3694	.3958	.4222
20	.1667	.1944	.2222	.2500	.2778	.3056	.3333	.3611	.3889	.4167	.4444
21	.1750	.2042	.2333	.2625	.2917	.3208	.3500	.3792	.4083	.4375	.4667
22	.1833	.2139	.2444	.2750	.3056	.3361	.3667	.3972	.4278	.4533	.4889
23	.1917	.2236	.2556	.2875	.3194	.3514	.3833	.4153	.4472	.4792	.5111
24	.2000	.2333	.2667	.3000	.3333	.3667	.4000	.4333	.4667	.5000	.5333
25	.2083	.2431	.2778	.3125	.3472	.3819	.4167	.4514	.4861	.5208	.5556
26	.2167	.2528	.2889	.3250	.3611	.3972	.4333	.4694	.5056	.5417	.5778
27	.2250	.2625	.3000	.3375	.3750	.4125	.4500	.4875	.5250	.5625	.6000
28	.2333	.2722	.3111	.3500	.3889	.4278	.4667	.5056	.5444	.5833	.6222
29	.2417	.2819	.3222	.3625	.4028	.4431	.4833	.5236	.5639	.6042	.6444
(Months)											
1	.2500	.2917	.3333	.3750	.4167	.4583	.5000	.5417	.5833	.6250	.6667
2	.5000	.5833	.6667	.7500	.8333	.9167	1.0000	1.0833	1.1667	1.2500	1.3333
3	.7500	.8750	1.0000	1.1250	1.2500	1.3750	1.5000	1.6250	1.7500	1.8750	2.0000
4	1.0000	1.1667	1.3333	1.5000	1.6667	1.8333	2.0000	2.1667	2.3333	2.5000	2.6667
5	1.2500	1.4583	1.6667	1.8750	2.0833	2.2917	2.5000	2.7083	2.9167	3.1250	3.3333
6	1.5000	1.7500	2.0000	2.2500	2.5000	2.7500	3.0000	3.2500	3.5000	3.7500	4.0000

*Each month equals 30 days.

SIMPLE INTEREST TABLE   Interest on $100, Based on a 365-Day Year

Time (Days)	3%	3½%	4%	4½%	5%	5½%	6%	6½%	7%	7½%	8%
1	.0082	.0096	.0110	.0123	.0137	.0151	.0164	.0178	.0192	.0205	.0219
2	.0164	.0192	.0219	.0247	.0274	.0301	.0329	.0356	.0384	.0411	.0438
3	.0247	.0288	.0329	.0370	.0411	.0452	.0493	.0534	.0575	.0616	.0658
4	.0329	.0384	.0438	.0493	.0548	.0603	.0658	.0712	.0767	.0822	.0877
5	.0411	.0480	.0548	.0616	.0685	.0753	.0822	.0890	.0959	.1027	.1096
6	.0493	.0575	.0658	.0740	.0822	.0904	.0986	.1068	.1151	.1233	.1315
7	.0575	.0671	.0767	.0863	.0959	.1055	.1151	.1247	.1342	.1438	.1534
8	.0658	.0767	.0877	.0986	.1096	.1205	.1315	.1425	.1534	.1654	.1753
9	.0740	.0863	.0986	.1110	.1233	.1356	.1479	.1603	.1726	.1849	.1973
10	.0822	.0959	.1096	.1233	.1370	.1507	.1644	.1781	.1918	.2055	.2192
11	.0904	.1055	.1205	.1356	.1507	.1658	.1808	.1959	.2110	.2260	.2411
12	.0986	.1151	.1315	.1479	.1644	.1808	.1973	.2137	.2301	.2466	.2630
13	.1068	.1247	.1425	.1603	.1781	.1959	.2137	.2315	.2493	.2671	.2849
14	.1151	.1342	.1534	.1726	.1918	.2110	.2301	.2493	.2685	.2877	.3068
15	.1233	.1438	.1644	.1849	.2055	.2260	.2466	.2671	.2877	.3082	.3288
16	.1315	.1534	.1753	.1973	.2192	.2411	.2630	.2849	.3068	.3288	.3507
17	.1397	.1630	.1863	.2096	.2329	.2562	.2795	.3027	.3260	.3493	.3726
18	.1479	.1726	.1973	.2219	.2466	.2712	.2959	.3205	.3452	.3699	.3945
19	.1562	.1822	.2082	.2342	.2603	.2863	.3123	.3384	.3644	.3904	.4164
20	.1644	.1918	.2192	.2466	.2740	.3014	.3288	.3562	.3836	.4110	.4384
21	.1726	.2014	.2301	.2589	.2817	.3164	.3452	.3740	.4027	.4315	.4603
22	.1808	.2110	.2411	.2712	.3014	.3315	.3616	.3918	.4219	.4521	.4822
23	.1890	.2205	.2521	.2836	.3151	.3466	.3781	.4096	.4411	.4726	.5041
24	.1973	.2301	.2630	.2959	.3288	.3616	.3945	.4274	.4603	.4932	.5260
25	.2055	.2397	.2740	.3082	.3425	.3767	.4110	.4452	.4795	.5137	.5479
26	.2137	.2493	.2849	.3205	.3562	.3918	.4274	.4630	.4986	.5342	.5699
27	.2219	.2589	.2959	.3329	.3699	.4068	.4438	.4808	.5178	.5548	.5918
28	.2301	.2685	.3068	.3452	.3836	.4219	.4603	.4986	.5370	.5753	.6137
29	.2384	.2781	.3178	.3575	.3973	.4370	.4767	.5164	.5562	.5959	.6356
30	.2466	.2877	.3288	.3699	.4110	.4521	.4932	.5342	.5753	.6164	.6575
31	.2548	.2973	.3397	.3822	.4247	.4671	.5096	.5521	.5945	.6370	.6795
40	.3288	.3836	.4384	.4932	.5479	.6027	.6575	.7123	.7671	.8219	.8767
50	.4110	.4795	.5479	.6164	.6849	.7534	.8219	.8904	.9589	1.0274	1.0959
60	.4932	.5753	.6575	.7397	.8219	.9041	.9863	1.0685	1.1507	1.2329	1.3151
70	.5753	.6712	.7671	.8630	.9589	1.0548	1.1507	1.2466	1.3425	1.4384	1.5343
80	.6575	.7671	.8767	.9863	1.0959	1.2055	1.3151	1.4247	1.5343	1.6438	1.7534
90	.7397	.8630	.9863	1.1096	1.2329	1.3562	1.4795	1.6027	1.7260	1.8493	1.9726
100	.8219	.9589	1.0959	1.2329	1.3699	1.5069	1.6438	1.7808	1.9178	2.0548	2.1918

COMPOUND INTEREST TABLE. Amount of $1 at Compound Interest:
$S = (1 + i)^n$

n	½%	1%	1½%	2%	n
1	1.0050 0000	1.0100 0000	1.0150 0000	1.0200 0000	1
2	1.0100 2500	1.0201 0000	1.0302 2500	1.0404 0000	2
3	1.0150 7513	1.0303 0100	1.0456 7838	1.0612 0800	3
4	1.0201 5050	1.0406 0401	1.0613 6355	1.0824 3216	4
5	1.0252 5125	1.0510 1005	1.0772 8400	1.1040 8080	5
6	1.0303 7751	1.0615 2015	1.0934 4326	1.1261 6242	6
7	1.0355 2940	1.0721 3535	1.1098 4491	1.1486 8567	7
8	1.0407 0704	1.0828 5671	1.1264 9259	1.1716 5938	8
9	1.0459 1058	1.0936 8527	1.1433 8998	1.1950 9257	9
10	1.0511 4013	1.1046 2213	1.1605 4083	1.2189 9442	10
11	1.0563 9583	1.1156 6835	1.1779 4894	1.2433 7431	11
12	1.0616 7781	1.1268 2503	1.1956 1817	1.2682 4179	12
13	1.0669 8620	1.1380 9328	1.2135 5244	1.2936 0663	13
14	1.0723 2113	1.1494 7421	1.2317 5573	1.3194 7876	14
15	1.0776 8274	1.1609 6896	1.2502 3207	1.3458 6834	15
16	1.0830 7115	1.1725 7864	1.2689 8555	1.3727 8571	16
17	1.0884 8651	1.1843 0443	1.2880 2033	1.4002 4142	17
18	1.0939 2894	1.1961 4748	1.3073 4064	1.4282 4625	18
19	1.0993 9858	1.2081 0895	1.3269 5075	1.4568 1117	19
20	1.1048 9558	1.2201 9004	1.3468 5501	1.4859 4740	20
21	1.1104 2006	1.2323 9194	1.3670 5783	1.5156 6634	21
22	1.1159 7216	1.2447 1586	1.3875 6370	1.5459 7967	22
23	1.1215 5202	1.2571 6302	1.4083 7715	1.5768 9926	23
24	1.1271 5978	1.2697 3465	1.4295 0281	1.6084 3725	24
25	1.1327 9558	1.2824 3200	1.4509 4535	1.6406 0599	25
26	1.1384 5955	1.2952 5631	1.4727 0953	1.6734 1811	26
27	1.1441 5185	1.3082 0888	1.4948 0018	1.7068 8648	27
28	1.1498 7261	1.3212 9097	1.5172 2218	1.7410 2421	28
29	1.1556 2197	1.3345 0388	1.5399 8051	1.7758 4469	29
30	1.1614 0008	1.3478 4892	1.5630 8022	1.8113 6158	30
31	1.1672 0708	1.3613 2740	1.5865 2642	1.8475 8882	31
32	1.1730 4312	1.3749 4068	1.6103 2432	1.8845 4059	32
33	1.1789 0833	1.3886 9009	1.6344 7918	1.9222 3140	33
34	1.1848 0288	1.4025 7699	1.6589 9637	1.9606 7603	34
35	1.1907 2689	1.4166 0276	1.6838 8132	1.9998 8955	35
36	1.1966 8052	1.4307 6878	1.7091 3954	2.0398 8734	36
37	1.2026 6393	1.4450 7647	1.7347 7663	2.0806 8509	37
38	1.2086 7725	1.4595 2724	1.7607 9828	2.1222 9879	38
39	1.2147 2063	1.4741 2251	1.7872 1025	2.1647 4477	39
40	1.2207 9424	1.4888 6373	1.8140 1841	2.2080 3966	40
41	1.2268 9821	1.5037 5237	1.8412 2868	2.2522 0046	41
42	1.2330 3270	1.5187 8989	1.8688 4712	2.2972 4447	42
43	1.2391 9786	1.5339 7779	1.8968 7982	2.3431 8936	43
44	1.2453 9385	1.5493 1757	1.9253 3302	2.3900 5314	44
45	1.2516 2082	1.5648 1075	1.9542 1301	2.4378 5421	45
46	1.2578 7892	1.5804 5885	1.9835 2621	2.4866 1129	46
47	1.2641 6832	1.5962 6344	2.0132 7910	2.5363 4351	47
48	1.2704 8916	1.6122 2608	2.0434 7829	2.5870 7039	48
49	1.2768 4161	1.6283 4834	2.0741 3046	2.6388 1179	49
50	1.2832 2581	1.6446 3182	2.1052 4242	2.6915 8803	50

COMPOUND INTEREST TABLE Amount of $1 at Compound Interest:
$S = (1 + i)^n$ — (continued)

n	2½%	3%	3½%	4%	n
1	1.0250 0000	1.0300 0000	1.0350 0000	1.0400 0000	1
2	1.0506 2500	1.0609 0000	1.0712 2500	1.0816 0000	2
3	1.0768 9063	1.0927 2700	1.1087 1788	1.1248 6400	3
4	1.1038 1289	1.1255 0881	1.1475 2300	1.1698 5856	4
5	1.1314 0821	1.1592 7407	1.1876 8631	1.2166 5290	5
6	1.1596 9342	1.1940 5230	1.2292 5533	1.2653 1902	6
7	1.1886 8575	1.2298 7387	1.2722 7926	1.3159 3178	7
8	1.2184 0290	1.2667 7008	1.3168 0904	1.3685 6905	8
9	1.2488 6297	1.3047 7318	1.3628 9735	1.4233 1181	9
10	1.2800 8454	1.3439 1638	1.4105 9876	1.4802 4428	10
11	1.3120 8666	1.3842 3387	1.4599 6972	1.5394 5406	11
12	1.3448 8882	1.4257 6089	1.5110 6866	1.6010 3222	12
13	1.3785 1104	1.4685 3371	1.5639 5606	1.6650 7351	13
14	1.4129 7382	1.5125 8972	1.6186 9452	1.7316 7645	14
15	1.4482 9817	1.5579 6742	1.6753 4883	1.8009 4351	15
16	1.4845 0562	1.6047 0644	1.7339 8604	1.8729 8125	16
17	1.5216 1826	1.6528 4763	1.7946 7555	1.9479 0050	17
18	1.5596 5872	1.7024 3306	1.8574 8920	2.0258 1652	18
19	1.5986 5019	1.7535 0605	1.9225 0132	2.1068 4918	19
20	1.6386 1644	1.8061 1123	1.9897 8886	2.1911 2314	20
21	1.6795 8185	1.8602 9457	2.0594 3147	2.2787 6807	21
22	1.7215 7140	1.9161 0341	2.1315 1158	2.3699 1879	22
23	1.7646 1068	1.9735 8651	2.2061 1448	2.4647 1554	23
24	1.8087 2595	2.0327 9411	2.2833 2849	2.5633 0416	24
25	1.8539 4410	2.0937 7793	2.3632 4498	2.6658 3633	25
26	1.9002 9270	2.1565 9127	2.4459 5856	2.7724 6978	26
27	1.9478 0002	2.2212 8901	2.5315 6711	2.8833 6858	27
28	1.9964 9502	2.2879 2768	2.6201 7196	2.9987 0332	28
29	2.0464 0739	2.3565 6551	2.7118 7798	3.1186 5145	29
30	2.0975 6758	2.4272 6247	2.8067 9370	3.2433 9751	30
31	2.1500 0677	2.5000 8035	2.9050 3148	3.3731 3341	31
32	2.2037 5694	2.5750 8276	3.0067 0759	3.5080 5875	32
33	2.2588 5086	2.6523 3524	3.1119 4235	3.6483 8110	33
34	2.3153 2213	2.7319 0530	3.2208 6033	3.7943 1634	34
35	2.3732 0519	2.8138 6245	3.3335 9045	3.9460 8899	35
36	2.4325 3532	2.8982 7833	3.4502 6611	4.1039 3255	36
37	2.4933 4870	2.9852 2668	3.5710 2543	4.2680 8986	37
38	2.5556 8242	3.0747 8348	3.6960 1132	4.4388 1345	38
39	2.6195 7448	3.1670 2698	3.8253 7171	4.6163 6599	39
40	2.6850 6384	3.2620 3779	3.9592 5972	4.8010 2063	40
41	2.7521 9043	3.3598 9893	4.0978 3381	4.9930 6145	41
42	2.8209 9520	3.4606 9589	4.2412 5799	5.1927 8391	42
43	2.8915 2008	3.5645 1677	4.3897 0202	5.4004 9527	43
44	2.9638 0808	3.6714 5227	4.5433 4160	5.6165 1508	44
45	3.0379 0328	3.7815 9584	4.7023 5855	5.8411 7568	45
46	3.1138 5086	3.8950 4372	4.8669 4110	6.0748 2271	46
47	3.1916 9713	4.0118 9503	5.0372 8404	6.3178 1562	47
48	3.2714 8956	4.1322 5188	5.2135 8898	6.5705 2824	48
49	3.3532 7680	4.2562 1944	5.3960 6459	6.8333 4937	49
50	3.4371 0872	4.3839 0602	5.5849 2686	7.1066 8335	50

continued

COMPOUND INTEREST TABLE Amount of $1 at Compound Interest:
$S = (1 + i)^n$ — (continued)

n	4½%	5%	5½%	6%	n
1	1.0450 0000	1.0500 0000	1.0550 0000	1.0600 0000	1
2	1.0920 2500	1.1025 0000	1.1130 2500	1.1236 0000	2
3	1.1411 6613	1.1576 2500	1.1742 4138	1.1910 1600	3
4	1.1925 1860	1.2155 0625	1.2388 2465	1.2624 7696	4
5	1.2461 8194	1.2762 8156	1.3069 6001	1.3382 2558	5
6	1.3022 6012	1.3400 9564	1.3788 4281	1.4185 1911	6
7	1.3608 6183	1.4071 0042	1.4546 7916	1.5036 3026	7
8	1.4221 0061	1.4774 5544	1.5346 8651	1.5938 4807	8
9	1.4860 9514	1.5513 2822	1.6190 9427	1.6894 7896	9
10	1.5529 6942	1.6288 9463	1.7081 4446	1.7908 4770	10
11	1.6228 5305	1.7103 3936	1.8020 9240	1.8982 9856	11
12	1.6958 8143	1.7958 5633	1.9012 0749	2.0121 9647	12
13	1.7721 9610	1.8856 4914	2.0057 7390	2.1329 2826	13
14	1.8519 4492	1.9799 3160	2.1160 9146	2.2609 0396	14
15	1.9352 8244	2.0789 2818	2.2324 7649	2.3965 5819	15
16	2.0223 7015	2.1828 7459	2.3552 6270	2.5403 5168	16
17	2.1133 7681	2.2920 1832	2.4848 0215	2.6927 7279	17
18	2.2084 7877	2.4066 1923	2.6214 6627	2.8543 3915	18
19	2.3078 6031	2.5269 5020	2.7656 4691	3.0255 9950	19
20	2.4117 1402	2.6532 9771	2.9177 5749	3.2071 3547	20
21	2.5202 4116	2.7859 6259	3.0782 3415	3.3995 6360	21
22	2.6336 5201	2.9252 6072	3.2475 3703	3.6035 3742	22
23	2.7521 6635	3.0715 2376	3.4261 5157	3.8197 4966	23
24	2.8760 1383	3.2250 9994	3.6145 8990	4.0489 3464	24
25	3.0054 3446	3.3863 5494	3.8133 9235	4.2918 7072	25
26	3.1406 7901	3.5556 7269	4.0231 2893	4.5493 8296	26
27	3.2820 0956	3.7334 5632	4.2444 0102	4.8223 4594	27
28	3.4296 9999	3.9201 2914	4.4778 4307	5.1116 8670	28
29	3.5840 3649	4.1161 3560	4.7241 2444	5.4183 8790	29
30	3.7453 1813	4.3219 4238	4.9339 5129	5.7434 9117	30
31	3.9138 5745	4.5380 3949	5.2580 6861	6.0881 0064	31
32	4.0899 8104	4.7649 4147	5.5472 6238	6.4533 8668	32
33	4.2740 3018	5.0031 8854	5.8523 6181	6.8405 8988	33
34	4.4663 6154	5.2533 4797	6.1742 4171	7.2510 2528	34
35	4.6673 4781	5.5160 1537	6.5138 2501	7.6860 8679	35
36	4.8773 7846	5.7918 1614	6.8720 8538	8.1472 5200	36
37	5.0968 6049	6.0814 0694	7.2500 5008	8.6360 8712	37
38	5.3262 1921	6.3854 7729	7.6488 0283	9.1542 5235	38
39	5.5658 9908	6.7047 5115	8.0694 8699	9.7035 0749	39
40	5.8163 6454	7.0399 8871	8.5133 0877	10.2857 1794	40
41	6.0781 0094	7.3919 8815	8.9815 4076	10.9028 6101	41
42	6.3516 1548	7.7615 8756	9.4755 2550	11.5570 3267	42
43	6.6374 3818	8.1496 6693	9.9966 7940	12.2504 5463	43
44	6.9361 2290	8.5571 5028	10.5464 9677	12.9854 8191	44
45	7.2482 4843	8.9850 0779	11.1265 5409	13.7646 1083	45
46	7.5744 1961	9.4342 5818	11.7385 1456	14.5904 8748	46
47	7.9152 6849	9.9059 7109	12.3841 3287	15.4659 1673	47
48	8.2714 5557	10.4012 6965	13.0652 6017	16.3938 7173	48
49	8.6436 7107	10.9213 3313	13.7838 4948	17.3775 0403	49
50	9.0326 3627	11.4673 9979	14.5419 6120	18.4201 5427	50

COMPOUND INTEREST TABLE
$S = (1 + i)^n$ — (continued)

Amount of $1 at Compound Interest:

n	6½%	7%	7½%	8%	n
1	1.0650 0000	1.0700 0000	1.0750 0000	1.0800 0000	1
2	1.1342 2500	1.1449 0000	1.1556 2500	1.1664 0000	2
3	1.2079 4963	1.2250 4300	1.2422 9688	1.2597 1200	3
4	1.2864 6635	1.3107 9601	1.3354 6914	1.3604 8896	4
5	1.3700 8666	1.4025 5173	1.4356 2933	1.4693 2808	5
6	1.4591 4230	1.5007 3035	1.5433 0153	1.5868 7432	6
7	1.5539 8655	1.6057 8148	1.6590 4914	1.7138 2427	7
8	1.6549 9567	1.7181 8618	1.7834 7783	1.8509 3021	8
9	1.7625 7039	1.8384 5921	1.9172 3866	1.9990 0463	9
10	1.8771 3747	1.9671 5136	2.0610 3156	2.1589 2500	10
11	1.9991 5140	2.1048 5195	2.2156 0893	2.3316 3900	11
12	2.1290 9624	2.2521 9159	2.3817 7960	2.5181 7012	12
13	2.2674 8750	2.4098 4500	2.5604 1307	2.7196 2373	13
14	2.4148 7418	2.5785 3415	2.7524 4405	2.9371 9362	14
15	2.5718 4101	2.7590 3154	2.9588 7735	3.1721 6911	15
16	2.7390 1067	2.9521 6375	3.1807 9315	3.4259 4264	16
17	2.9170 4637	3.1588 1521	3.4193 5264	3.7000 1805	17
18	3.1066 5438	3.3799 3228	3.6758 0409	3.9960 1950	18
19	3.3085 8691	3.6165 2754	3.9514 8940	4.3157 0106	19
20	3.5236 4506	3.8696 8446	4.2478 5110	4.6609 5714	20
21	3.7526 8199	4.1405 6237	4.5664 3993	5.0338 3372	21
22	3.9966 0632	4.4304 0174	4.9089 2293	5.4365 4041	22
23	4.2563 8573	4.7405 2986	5.2770 9215	5.8714 6365	23
24	4.5330 5081	5.0723 6695	5.6728 7406	6.3411 8074	24
25	4.8276 9911	5.4274 3264	6.0983 3961	6.8484 7520	25
26	5.1414 9955	5.8073 5292	6.5557 1508	7.3963 5321	26
27	5.4756 9702	6.2138 6763	7.0473 9371	7.9880 6147	27
28	5.8316 1733	6.6488 3836	7.5759 4824	8.6271 0639	28
29	6.2106 7245	7.1142 5705	8.1441 4436	9.3172 7490	29
30	6.6143 6616	7.6122 5504	8.7549 5519	10.0626 5689	30
31	7.0442 9996	8.1451 1290	9.4115 7683	10.8676 6944	31
32	7.5021 7946	8.7152 7080	10.1174 4509	11.7370 8300	32
33	7.9898 2113	9.3253 3975	10.8762 5347	12.6760 4964	33
34	8.5091 5950	9.9781 1354	11.6919 7248	13.6901 3361	34
35	9.0622 5487	10.6765 8148	12.5688 7042	14.7853 4429	35
36	9.6513 0143	11.4239 4219	13.5115 3570	15.9681 7184	36
37	10.2786 3603	12.2236 1814	14.5249 0088	17.2456 2558	37
38	10.9467 4737	13.0792 7141	15.6142 6844	18.6252 7563	38
39	11.6582 8595	13.9948 2041	16.7853 3858	20.1152 9768	39
40	12.4160 7453	14.9744 5784	18.0442 3897	21.7245 2150	40
41	13.2231 1938	16.0226 6989	19.3975 5689	23.4624 8322	41
42	14.0826 2214	17.1442 5678	20.8523 7366	25.3394 8187	42
43	14.9979 9258	18.3443 5475	22.4163 0168	27.3666 4042	43
44	15.9728 6209	19.6284 5959	24.0975 2431	29.5559 7166	44
45	17.0110 9813	21.0024 5176	25.9048 3863	31.9204 4939	45
46	18.1168 1951	22.4726 2338	27.8477 0153	34.4740 8534	46
47	19.2944 1278	24.0457 0702	29.9362 7915	37.2320 1217	47
48	20.5485 4961	25.7289 0651	32.1815 0008	40.2105 7314	48
49	21.8842 0533	27.5299 2997	34.5951 1259	43.4274 1899	49
50	23.3066 7868	29.4570 2506	37.1897 4603	46.9016 1251	50

CHAPTER TEN
Notes and Drafts

This chapter deals with the purpose and use of notes and drafts and how bank discounting procedures are applied. When you have completed this chapter, you will be able to

(1) recognize a promissory note, draft, and negotiable instrument and apply such terms as proceeds, bank discount, payee, maker of a note, face of note, maturity value, and term of discount,
(2) compute the proceeds of a note discounted at the bank and originating with the borrower,
(3) compute the proceeds of a note discounted at the bank and held by the payee,
(4) compute the interest rate that is equivalent to a given discount rate,
(5) compute the discount rate that is equivalent to a given interest rate,
(6) distinguish between a sight and time draft,
(7) distinguish between the terms "after date" and "after sight" on a time draft,
(8) determine the maturity date on a time draft when terms state (a) after date, (b) after sight,
(9) compute the proceeds on (a) a noninterest-bearing draft and (b) an interest-bearing draft.

UNIT 1. PROMISSORY NOTES

A promissory note is written evidence of a debt by the borrower. It is also a common form of a negotiable instrument, which means that it may be transferred from one person or company to another or sold to a bank.

A negotiable instrument (a) must be signed by the maker, (b) must have an exact due date, (c) must be an unconditional promise to pay a definite sum of money, and (d) must be payable to order or to bearer.

Notes are usually written on a standard form but may be written on a plain piece of paper if all of the above legal requirements for a negotiable instrument are met. The majority of promissory notes are usually for short periods of time such as 30, 60, or 90 days. They may be interest-bearing or noninterest-bearing. When the note bears no interest, it is so indicated.

1. A negotiable instrument is one that can be transferred from one person to another in return for equivalent value.

    A common form of negotiable instrument is the _____.

    -

    Promissory note

    The promissory note shown here is typical.

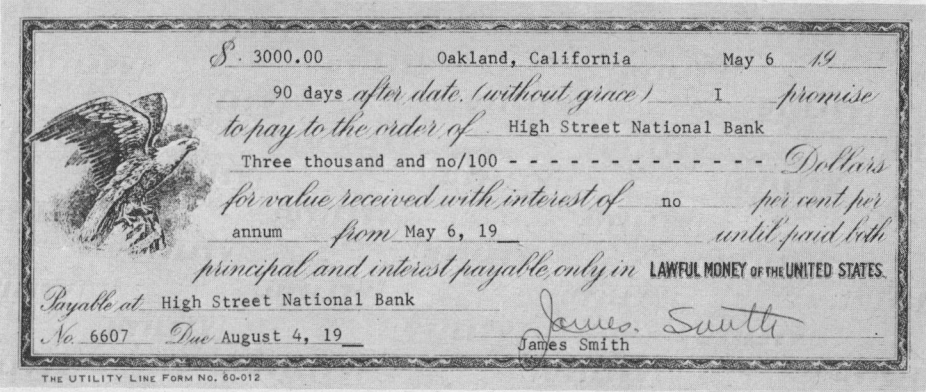

Face of note = $3000 (amount borrowed)
Term of note = 90 days
Due date or maturity date = August 4 (90 days after May 6, the day the note was dated.)
The maker   James Smith (the borrower)
The payee   High Street National Bank (the lender)

2. Identify the parts of the following note:

> $ 2500.00   White Rock, Oregon   June 1   19___
> 60 days *after date (without grace)* I *promise*
> *to pay to the order of* James National Bank
> Two thousand five hundred and no/100 -------- *Dollars*
> *for value received with interest of* no *per cent per*
> annum *from* June 1, 19___ *until paid both*
> *principal and interest payable only in* LAWFUL MONEY of the UNITED STATES.
> *Payable at* James National Bank
> No. 7009   *Due* July 31   Allen Bowen
>   Allen Bowen

Face of note _____   Maker _____

Term of note _____   Payee _____

Due date _____

$2500.00,   Allen Bowen
60 days,   James National Bank
July 31

Notes "sold" to a bank are of two types—those that originate with the borrower and those that the borrower holds from a third party in payment of a debt.

Notes Discounted at the Bank that Originate with the Borrower

Mr. James needs $500 to pay for the expansion of his shop, which is to include a new department. He expects new business to bring in enough additional income to meet this expense six months hence. Since his credit is good, the local bank agrees to lend him this amount on his personal note *after* deducting a charge for the service. This charge is called *bank discount* and is calculated in the same way that interest is determined. However, unlike interest, the *discount is calculated on the maturity value* rather than the principal. It is collected when the loan is made—not at maturity date. Since a note of this kind does not bear interest, the principal and maturity value are the same.

3. The principal and maturity value of Mr. James's note is $_____.

The charge made by the bank is called _____.

This charge is calculated on the _____ of the note.

It is collected (when the loan is made/at maturity) _____.

$500
bank discount
maturity value
when the loan is made

It is common practice for the loan department of a bank to use a discount rate, not an interest rate, for papers of the kind illustrated (see above). Bank discount is sometimes called "interest in advance," since it is collected when the loan is made and not at maturity.

Mr. Adams borrowed $500 for 60 days on his personal note. The bank charged him a discount rate of 6% for this service and gave him the balance.

Discount = .06 × $500 × $\frac{60}{360}$ = $5.00 (charge made by the bank)

The amount Mr. Adams received = $500.00 − $5.00 = $495.00. $495.00 is called the *proceeds* of the note.

When a note is handled in this manner, it is said to be *discounted*.

4. Mr. Smith borrowed $3000 for 90 days. If his note was discounted at 5%, what were the proceeds? (Face of note and the maturity value are the same, since this note bears no interest.)

Bank discount = _____ × _____ × _____ = $_____.

Proceeds = $_____ − $_____ = $_____.

Bank discount = .05 × $3000 × $\frac{90}{360}$ = $37.50.

Proceeds = $3000.00 − $37.50 = $2962.50.

5. Mr. Olmstead borrowed $4500 for 30 days from the local bank. The bank charged a 6% discount rate. How much did Mr. Olmstead actually receive (the proceeds)?

Bank discount = $4500 × .06 × $\frac{30}{360}$ = $22.50.
Proceeds = $4500.00 − $22.50 = $4477.50.

6. Assume that the discount rate is 8%; find the proceeds for the following note.

[Promissory note: $600.00, Highland, Illinois, August 3, 19__. 3 months after date (without grace) I promise to pay to the order of First National Bank. Six hundred and no/100 Dollars for value received with interest of no per cent per annum from August 3, 19__ until paid both principal and interest payable only in LAWFUL MONEY OF THE UNITED STATES. Payable at First National Bank. No. 1009 Due November 3, 19__. Arthur Hastings]

In this case the time is expressed in terms of months. Bank discount, like bank or commercial interest, is calculated on the *exact* number of days.

August 3 to November 3 = _____ days.

Bank discount = _____.

Proceeds = _____.

August 3 to November 3 = 92 days.
Bank discount = $600 × .08 × $\frac{92}{360}$ = $12.27.
Proceeds = $600.00 − $12.27 = $587.73.

7. A note dated June 6 for 6 months is due _____. How many days are there in this period? _____. What are the proceeds if the maturity value is $2000 and the discount rate is 5½%?

   Bank discount = _____.

   Proceeds = _____.

   -

   Note matures December 6. There are 183 days in this period.
   Bank discount = .055 × $2000 × $\frac{183}{360}$ = $55.92.
   Proceeds = $2000.00 − $55.92 = $1944.08.

8. Complete the following statements:

   (a) Bank discount is sometimes called _____.
   (b) Bank discount is computed on the (maturity value/principal) _____.

   (c) Bank discount is computed on (approximate/exact) days _____.
   (d) Proceeds = $_____ less $_____.

   -

   interest in advance
   maturity value
   exact
   maturity value less discount

Notes Discounted at the Bank Held by the Payee

Under some circumstances a company or individual accepts a personal note in payment of an obligation. It may be held by the payee until maturity when it is paid by the maker or it may be discounted at the bank (converted to cash) at some earlier date. If it is discounted, the bank holds the note until maturity and collects from the maker. If the maker fails to meet this obligation, the payee is held responsible.

Example: Mr. James, a farmer, needed some equipment that cost $1500. He could not pay for it, however, until 6 months later when his crop was sold. Accordingly, he went to the A & Z Farm Equipment Supply Company and made the necessary purchase in exchange for his personal note for 6 months at 6% interest. Two months later the A & Z Farm Equipment Supply Company "sold" the note to its bank. The bank collected the amount due on the note from Mr. James at maturity. If Mr. James (the maker) had been unable to pay the note when due, then the A & Z Farm Equipment Supply Co. (the payee) would have been liable for the debt.

The following example further illustrates this type of transaction.

[Promissory note: $600.00, Chicago, Illinois, June 12, 19__. 2 months after date (without grace) I promise to pay to the order of John Brown Six hundred and no/100 Dollars for value received with interest of 6 per cent per annum from June 12, 19__ until paid both principal and interest payable only in LAWFUL MONEY of the UNITED STATES. Payable at Third National Bank. No. 72 Due August 12, 19__. Signed Robert Smith.]

This note was given to John Brown (payee) by Robert Smith (maker) in lieu of a money payment for services or merchandise. Mr. Brown accepted this note with the understanding that he would collect the $600 plus interest at 6% from Mr. Smith at the end of 2 months. Before the note was due, however, he needed cash for unexpected expenses. Therefore he could not wait until the maturity date to collect this debt.

If his credit rating and standing with his bank were good, he could have the note discounted. Suppose he took it to his bank on July 15, where it was discounted at $5\frac{1}{2}\%$. The bank held the note until maturity and collected from Mr. Smith. The question is: "What were the proceeds of the note" (amount paid to Mr. Brown by the bank)?

When a note is discounted, the time is figured in exact days from the date it is "sold" (discounted) up to and including the date of maturity. This period of time is called the *term of discount*.

Face of note $600.00

Interest $\underline{6.00}$* [(6% of $600.00 for 2 months) or (.60 × $600 × $\frac{2}{12}$)]

Maturity value $606.00

Date of maturity August 12 (2 months from June 12)
Term of discount 28 days (July 15 to August 12; discounted July 15)
Rate of discount $5\frac{1}{2}$%
Discount $2.59 ($606.00 × .055 × $\frac{28}{360}$)
Proceeds $603.41 ($606.00 − $2.59)

9. Furnish the information requested below this illustration. This note was discounted on January 2 at $5\frac{1}{2}$%.

$500.00   Manchester, Wisconsin November 11 19___
3 months after date (without grace) I promise
to pay to the order of Mann Bros.
Five hundred and no/100 - - - - - - - - - - - - - - - Dollars
for value received with interest of   6   per cent per
annum   from November 11, 19___   until paid both
principal and interest payable only in LAWFUL MONEY OF THE UNITED STATES.
Payable at First National Bank
No. 306   Due February 11, 19___   John E. Hope
                                    John E. Hope
THE UTILITY LINE FORM NO. 60-012

Maker of note	_____	Date of discount	_____
Payee	_____	Term of discount	_____
Assignee (bank)	_____	Rate of discount	_____
Maturity date	_____	Bank discount	_____
Maturity value	_____	Proceeds	_____

*If days are used, calculate on the basis of a 360-day year unless stated otherwise.

Maker of note	John E. Hope	Date of discount	January 2
Payee	Mann Bros.	Term of discount	40 days
Assignee	First National Bank	Rate of discount	$5\frac{1}{2}\%$
Maturity date	February 11	Bank discount	$= \$507.50 \times .055 \times \frac{40}{360} = \$3.10.$
Maturity value	$\$500 + (6\%$ of $\$500$ for 3 months) $= \$507.50$	Proceeds	$= \$507.50 - \$3.10$ $= \$504.40.$

Interest Rate Equivalent to Discount Rate

If Mr. Smith has his personal note for $3000 discounted at the bank at 5% for 90 days, he receives $2962.50 (proceeds). He paid 5% on $3000 but had the use of only $2962.50. Therefore he actually paid an interest rate greater than 5% on the money he received. The sum of $2962.50 represents the principal in calculating the interest rate.

$$r = I \div Pt$$

$$I = \$3000.00 - \$2962.50 = \$37.50, \qquad P = \$2962.50, \qquad t = \tfrac{90}{360}.$$

The interest rate $(r) = \$37.50 \div (\$2962.50 \times \tfrac{90}{360}) = .0506 = 5.06\%$.

This means that the 5.06% interest rate is equivalent to a 5% discount rate. Mr. Smith actually paid 5.06% for the use of the money he received when his note was discounted at 5%.

Formulas have been derived for use in calculating the interest rate for any given discount rate and for calculating the discount rate for any given interest rate.

To find the interest rate that corresponds to a discount rate

$$r = \frac{d}{1 - dt}$$

where r = interest rate,
d = discount rate,
t = time.

Using the example above,

$$r = \frac{.05}{1 - [(.05)(\tfrac{90}{360})]} = \frac{.05}{1 - .0125} = \frac{.05}{.9875} = .0506 = 5.06\%.$$

10. Calculate the interest rate that corresponds to a discount rate of (a) 4% for 6 months, (b) 6% for 30 days. (Round answer to nearest hundredth of 1%.)

   (a) $r =$
   (b) $r =$

(a) $r = \dfrac{.04}{1 - [(.04)(\frac{6}{12})]} = \dfrac{.04}{1 - .02} = \dfrac{.04}{.98} = .0408 = 4.08\%.$

(b) $r = \dfrac{.06}{1 - [(.06)(\frac{30}{360})]} = \dfrac{.06}{1 - .005} = \dfrac{.06}{.995} = .0602 = 6.02\%.$

Observe that the corresponding interest rate is always greater than the discount rate.

11. Find the discount rate that corresponds to an interest rate. The discount rate is derived from the following formula:

$$d = \dfrac{r}{1 + rt}$$

where d = discount rate,
r = interest rate,
t = time.

Example: What is the discount rate that is equivalent to an interest rate of 8% for 120 days?

Solution: $d = \dfrac{.08}{1 + [(.08)(\frac{120}{360})]} = \dfrac{.08}{1 + .0267} = \dfrac{.08}{1.0267} = .0779 = 7.79\%.$

Find the discount rate that is equivalent to an interest rate of $6\frac{1}{2}\%$ for 1 year. (Record answer to nearest hundredth of 1%)

$d =$

$d = \dfrac{.065}{1 + (.065)(1)} = \dfrac{.065}{1.065} = .06103 = 6.10\%$

EXERCISE 41

Answers appear at the end of this exercise. If your answers do not agree with those shown, check your calculations before referring to the solutions that follow.

1. Find the proceeds on each of the following noninterest-bearing notes.

	Face of Note	Time to Run	Date of Note	Discount Date	Rate of Discount	Proceeds
(a)	$ 250.00	60 days	July 17	August 2	$4\frac{1}{2}\%$	_____
(b)	1450.00	3 months	October 11	November 23	8 %	_____
(c)	653.00	90 days	March 26	May 15	$5\frac{1}{2}\%$	_____
(d)	800.50	5 months	January 5	March 4	6 %	_____

2. Mr. Cox held a 60-day note for $4200 with interest at 5%. This note was discounted at his bank 25 days before maturity at 6%. What were the proceeds?

3. A noninterest-bearing note for $2400 was discounted 30 days before it was due. If the proceeds were $2389, what was the discount rate?

4. A 6-months note for $1500, bearing interest at 6% and dated May 17, was discounted at 8% on September 22. What were the proceeds?

5. Mr. Sams, a building contractor, needed $45,000 for 120 days for a construction project. The bank accepted his note for this amount at a discount rate of $4\frac{1}{2}\%$. How much did Mr. Sams receive from the bank? What is the equivalent interest rate (to 2 decimals in terms of percent)?

6. Mr. Hays gave Rincon Manufacturing Co. a 90-day note for $1250 on October 10. If it was discounted at the bank on November 15 at $6\frac{1}{2}\%$, what were the proceeds?

7. If a bank charges $6\frac{1}{2}\%$ for discounting notes, how much can a borrower receive now if he must repay a loan of $1300 in 3 months?

8. What interest rates are equivalent to the discount rates of 6% and 8% on a sum of money due in 1 year? (Record answers to the nearest tenth of 1%.)

9. Mr. Ames needs $1860 which he plans to repay a year later. How much must he borrow if the bank discounts his note at 7%?

10. What interest rate is Mr. Ames (problem 9) actually paying? (Record answer correct to nearest hundredth of 1%.)

Answers

1. (a) $ 348.07
   (b) $1434.21
   (c) $ 649.01
   (d) $ 788.09
2. $4217.35
3. $5\frac{1}{2}\%$
4. $1525.77
5. $44,325
   4.57%
6. $1237.81
7. $1278.87
8. 6.4%, 8.7%
9. $2000.00
10. 7.53%

Solutions

1. (a) Face of note = $350.00. Maturity date = September 15.
   Term of discount (August 2 to September 15) = 44 days.

   $$\text{Discount} = \frac{\$350 \times .045 \times 44}{360} = \$1.925 = \$1.93.$$

   Proceeds = $350.00 − $1.93 = $348.07.

   (b) Face of note = $1450. Maturity date = January 11.
   Term of discount = 49 days.

   $$\text{Discount} = \frac{\$1450 \times .08 \times 49}{360} = \$15.79.$$

   Proceeds = $1450.00 − $15.79 = $1434.21.

   (c) Face of note = $653.00, Maturity date = June 24.
   Term of discount (May 15 to June 24) = 40 days.

   $$\text{Discount} = \frac{\$653 \times .055 \times 40}{360} = \$3.99$$

   Proceeds = $653.00 − $3.99 = $649.01.

(d) Face of note = $800.50. Maturity date = June 5.
Term of discount (March 4 to June 5) = 93 days.

$$\text{Discount} = \frac{\$800.50 \times .06 \times 93}{360} = \$12.41.$$

Proceeds = $800.50 − $12.41 = $788.09.

2. Interest = $4200 × .05 × $\frac{60}{360}$ = $35.00.
Maturity value = $4235.00.
Discount = $4235 × .06 × $\frac{25}{360}$ = $17.65.
Proceeds = $4235.00 − $17.65 = $4217.35.

3. Discount = $2400 − $2389.09 = $11.00.
$r = I \div Pt$ = $11.00 ÷ ($2400 × $\frac{30}{360}$) = .055 or $5\frac{1}{2}\%$.

4. Interest = $1500 × .06 × $\frac{1}{2}$ = $45.00.
Maturity value = $1545.00, Maturity date = November 17.
Term of discount (September 22 to November 17) = 56 days.
Discount = $1545.00 × .08 × $\frac{56}{360}$ = $19.23.
Proceeds = $1545.00 − $19.23 = $1525.77.

5. Discount = $45,000 × .045 × $\frac{120}{360}$ = $675.
Proceeds = $45,000 − $675 = $44,325.
Interest rate = $675 ÷ ($44,325 × $\frac{120}{360}$) = .04568 or 4.57%.

6. Maturity date = January 8.
Term of discount (November 15 to January 8) = 54 days.
Discount = $1250 × .065 × $\frac{54}{360}$ = $12.19.
Proceeds = $1250.00 − $12.19 = $1237.81.

7. Discount = $1300 × .065 × $\frac{3}{12}$ = $21.13.
Proceeds = $1300.00 − $21.13 = $1278.87.

8. Interest rate = $\frac{d}{1-dt} = \frac{.06}{1-.06} = \frac{.06}{.94}$ = .064 = 6.4%.

Interest rate = $\frac{d}{1-dt} = \frac{.08}{1-.08} = \frac{.08}{.92}$ = .087 = 8.7%.

9. If Mr. Ames' note is discounted at 7% and the proceeds are $1860, the proceeds must equal 93% of the amount to be borrowed. Amount to be borrowed = $1860 ÷ .93 = $2000.

10. $r = \frac{.07}{1-[(.07)(1)]} = \frac{.07}{.93}$ = .07526 = 7.53%.

UNIT 2. DRAFTS

The draft, like the promissory note, is another negotiable instrument often used in commerce. Drafts are drawn for a specific purpose and, with the exception of the bank draft,* involve the buying and selling of goods. They are sometimes called "trade acceptances" or "bills of exchange." These drafts are drawn for the amount of a specific purchase by the seller (the *maker* or *drawer*) on the buyer (the *drawee*) and generally specify the place of payment (such as a specific bank).

1. A draft (except a bank draft) involves the _____ of goods.

    Such drafts are sometimes called _____ or _____.

    The drawer or maker of a draft is the _____.

    The drawee of a draft is the _____.

    ----

    buying and selling
    trade acceptance or bill of exchange
    seller
    buyer

The following illustration is one form of a trade acceptance. The acceptance date † may be written across the front of the draft or in a space provided as illustrated.

---

*A bank draft is an order by one bank on another bank to pay a third party a specified sum of money.
†The determination of the due or maturity date is discussed in the following frames. The *face* of draft is $500.26.

TRADE ACCEPTANCE

No. 187 — Oakland, California — April 24, 19__

To: Bayview Hardware Company — Crescent City, California

On 30 days after date Pay to the order of Ourselves

Five hundred and 26/100 — — — — — — — — — — Dollars ($500.26)

The transaction which gives rise to this instrument is the Purchase of Goods by the Acceptor from the Drawer. The Drawer may accept this Bill payable at any Bank, Banker or Trust Company in the United States which he may designate.

Accepted at Crescent City on April 28, 19__
Payable at North City National Bank
Location Crescent City, California
J. E. Lawson for Bayview Hardware Co.

Brandon Brothers
By M. S. Brandon

The *drawer* or *maker* (seller) is Brandon Brothers.
The *drawee* (buyer) is Bayview Hardware Company.
The *payee* is the seller (Brandon Brothers).
The *acceptor* of the draft is the buyer (Bayview Hardware Company).

2. Identify the parts of the following draft (trade acceptance):

TRADE ACCEPTANCE

No. 98 — San Francisco, California — July 16, 19__

To: Aker Products — Carson City, Nevada

On one month after date Pay to the order of Ourselves

Three hundred seventy-eight and no/100 — — — — — — — Dollars ($378.00)

The transaction which gives rise to this instrument is the Purchase of Goods by the Acceptor from the Drawer. The Drawer may accept this Bill payable at any Bank, Banker or Trust Company in the United States which he may designate.

Accepted at Carson City on July 20, 19__
Payable at Carson City Home Bank
Location Carson City, Nevada
A. B. Aker

Homecrafts Inc.
By A. J. Hampton

Face of draft _____
Maker _____
Payee _____
Acceptor _____
Drawee _____

$378.00
Homecrafts Inc.
Homecraft Inc.
Aker Products
Aker Products

Since sight drafts are payable when presented, we concern ourselves only with time drafts. The due date or maturity date on a time draft is computed in accordance with the terms as stated on the draft.

(a) "Two months after date" means that the draft is due and payable 2 months after the date of the draft.

Examples: (1) A draft dated October 12 is due and payable 30 days *after date*. The maturity date is November 11.

(2) A draft dated October 12 is due and payable 2 months *after date*. The maturity date is December 12.

(b) "2 months after sight" means that the draft is due and payable 2 months *after it is accepted*.

Examples: (1) A draft dated October 12 is due and payable 30 days *after sight*. If it is accepted on October 15, the maturity date is 30 days after October 15, which is November 14.

(2) A draft dated February 3 is due and payable 3 months *after sight*. It is accepted on February 10. The maturity date is 3 months after February 10, which is May 10.

3. When would the following time drafts be payable?

(a) A draft dated May 2, due and payable 60 days after date.

_____

(b) A draft dated July 10, due and payable 2 months after date.

_____

(c) A draft dated May 2, due and payable 60 days after sight if accepted June 1.

_____

(d) A draft dated January 17, due and payable 2 months after sight, if it is accepted January 31.

_____

_ _

(a) July 1 (60 days after May 2)
(b) September 10 (2 months after July 10)
(c) July 31 (60 days after June 1)
(d) March 31 (2 months after January 31)

Interest-bearing and Noninterest-bearing Drafts

Drafts may or may not bear interest. Also, they may be discounted ("sold to a bank") in the same manner as promissory notes. However, the bank may also charge a fee, which is a small percent of the face of the draft. The face of the draft, less the discount and collection fee, is called the *proceeds*.

Finding the Proceeds of a Noninterest-Bearing Draft

4. J. A. Iverson, coffee merchant, sold 210,000 pounds of coffee to The Best Grade Coffee Co. for $27,300. A draft was sent to and accepted by the buyer which granted them 30 days after date in which to pay for the shipment. The First National Bank, acting as the collection agent for J. A. Iverson, charged $\frac{1}{4}\%$ for its services. What were the proceeds if the draft was paid when due?

   Collection fee = $\frac{1}{4}\%$ of $27,300   = $_____.

   Proceeds = $27,300.00 − _____ = $_____.
                            collection fee

   -

   Collection fee = .0025 × $27,300 = $68.25 (A convenient method of calculating a fraction of 1% is to take 1% and divide by the fraction. In this case, 1% of $27,300 = $273; $\frac{1}{4}$ × $273 = $68.25.)
   Proceeds = $27,300.00 − $68.25 = $27,231.75.

5. Drafts, like promissory notes, may be discounted at the bank. The bank holds the draft to maturity at which time it collects from the buyer. Let us assume that S. A. Hipple, Cotton Merchants, Galveston, Texas, sold 700 bales of cotton amounting to $58,960.50 to the Parker Cotton Mills, Charlotte, N. C. A draft was sent to the Parker Cotton Mills which granted them 30 days after sight in which to pay for this shipment. The draft was dated September 28 and was accepted on October 10. If the draft was discounted on October 16 at 7% and the bank charged a $\frac{1}{4}\%$ collection fee, the proceeds would be computed as follows:

TRADE ACCEPTANCE

No. 189-AA Galveston, Texas September 28, 19___
(CITY OF DRAWER) (DATE)

To: Parker Cotton Mills Charlotte, North Carolina
(NAME OF DRAWEE) (ADDRESS OF DRAWEE)

On 30 days after sight Pay to the order of S. A. Hipple
(DATE OF MATURITY) (NAME OF PAYEE)

Fifty-eight thousand nine hundred sixty and 50/100 Dollars ($58,960.50)

The transaction which gives rise to this instrument is the Purchase of Goods by the Acceptor from the Drawer. The Drawee may accept this Bill payable at any Bank, Banker or Trust Company in the United States which he may designate.

Accepted at Charoltte, N.C. on Oct. 10, 19___
(CITY) (DATE)

Payable at First National Bank S. A. Hipple
(NAME OF BANK) DRAWER

Location Charlotte, N.C.

C. B. Howe for Parker Cotton By J. R. Gaines
(SIGNATURE OF ACCEPTOR) Mills J. A. Gaines

THE UTILITY LINE FORM NO. 149

Maturity date (30 days after October 10)   = November 9.
Term of discount (October 16 to November 9) = 24 days.
Discount (7% of $58,960.50 for 24 days)   = $275.15.
Collection fee ($\frac{1}{4}$% of $58,960.50)   = $147.40.
Proceeds = $58,960.50 − ($275.15 + $147.40) = $58,537.95.

(a) Who accepted the draft?   _____

(b) Who received the proceeds?   _____

(c) How much did the bank collect at maturity?   _____

(d) Who pays for the collection fee and the discount?   _____

(a) Parker Cotton Mills
(b) S. A. Hipple
(c) $58,960.50
(d) S. A. Hipple

6. A draft for $625, dated April 12, was drawn by Allen on Smith. It was due 4 months after date. On July 1 it was discounted at the bank at 6% and the proceeds deposited to Allen's account. What was the amount of the deposit?

   Maturity date = _____.

   Term of discount (_____ to _____) = _____ days.
                   date of discount   maturity date

   Discount = $625 × _____ × _____ = $_____.
                    rate   time

   Proceeds = $_____ − $_____ = $_____.

   \-

   Maturity date = August 12.
   Term of discount (July 1 to August 12) = 42 days.
   Discount = $625 × .06 × $\frac{42}{360}$ = $4.38.
   Proceeds = $625.00 − $4.38 = $620.62.

7. A draft, due and payable 60 days after sight, was drawn on Harper Bros. by Victrome Co. for $350.00. It was drawn on October 4 and accepted October 15. On November 12 it was discounted at the bank at 5%. The collection fee was $\frac{1}{5}$%. Find the proceeds.

   Maturity date (_____ days from _____) = _____.

   Term of discount (_____ to _____) = _____ days.

   Discount = $_____ × _____ × _____ = $_____.

   Collection fee = ($\frac{1}{5}$% of $_____) = $_____.

   Proceeds = $_____ − $_____ = $_____.

   \-

   Maturity date (60 days from October 15) = December 14.
   Term of discount (November 12 to December 14) = 32 days.
   Discount = $350 × .05 × $\frac{32}{360}$ = $1.56.
   Collection fee ($\frac{1}{5}$% of $350) = $0.70.
   Proceeds = $350.00 − ($1.56 + $0.70) = $347.74.

Finding the Proceeds of an Interest-Bearing Draft

8. J. Robertson and Co. sold furniture to Haverson Stores in the amount of $13,560. A draft dated July 10 was submitted in payment with terms of "90 days after date," bearing interest at 6%. If the draft was discounted on August 30 at $6\frac{1}{2}$% and the bank charged a collection fee of $\frac{1}{10}$%, the proceeds would be computed as follows:

Face of note	= $13,560.00
Interest (6% of $13,560.00 for 90 days)	= 203.40
Maturity value	= $13,763.40
Maturity date (90 days after July 10)	= October 8
Term of discount (August 30 to October 8)	= 39 days
Discount ($6\frac{1}{2}$% of $13,763.40 for 39 days)	= $96.92
Collection fee ($\frac{1}{10}$% of $13,763.40)	= $13.76
Proceeds = $13,763.40 − ($96.92 + $13.76)	= $13,652.72

(a) The discount is computed on the (face of note/maturity value) _____.

(b) Term of discount is the (exact/approximate) number of days. _____.

(c) Proceeds = _____ less discount and bank charge.
                face of note/maturity value

(a) maturity value
(b) exact
(c) maturity value

9. Find the proceeds of a draft drawn on July 11 in the amount of $544.20 bearing interest at 4% due 3 months after date. It was discounted on August 2 at 5%. The bank charged a $\frac{1}{8}$% collection fee.

    Face value of draft = _____.

    Interest = _____.

    Maturity value = _____.

    Maturity date = _____.

    Term of discount = _____.

    Discount = _____.

    Collection fee = _____.

    Proceeds = _____.

Face value of draft = $544.20.
Interest = $544.20 × .04 × $\frac{3}{12}$ = $5.44.
Maturity value = $544.20 + $5.44 = $549.64.
Maturity date = October 11.
Term of discount (August 2 to October 11) = 70 days.
Discount = $549.64 × .05 × $\frac{70}{360}$ = $5.34.
Collection fee = $\frac{1}{8}$% of $549.64 = $0.69.
Proceeds = $549.64 − ($5.34 + $0.69) = $543.61.

EXERCISE 42

Answers appear at the end of this exercise. If your answers do not agree with those shown, check your calculations before referring to the solutions that follow.

1. On April 10 Johnson Bros. accepted a 60-day sight draft, amounting to $562.50, drawn on them by Perkins & Co. Perkins & Co. had the draft discounted at the bank at 6% on April 15. What were the proceeds?

2. A draft in the amount of $425.00 due 90 days after sight was accepted on October 10 and discounted on November 1 at 5%. If the bank charged a $\frac{1}{3}$% collection fee, what were the proceeds?

3. James Owen accepted a draft, dated December 10, drawn by Parker Bros. for $815.50 at 6% payable 4 months after date. Parker Bros. had the draft discounted at the bank on January 10 at $6\frac{1}{2}$%. A charge of $\frac{1}{8}$% for collecting it when due was also made. What were the proceeds?

4. A draft for $800 due in 3 months and bearing interest at $4\frac{1}{2}$%, was discounted 60 days before it was due. If the discount rate was 5%, what were the proceeds?

5. Find the proceeds for the following drafts.

	Face Value	Date	When Due	Acceptance Date	Discount Date	Discount Rate	Proceeds
(a)	$1500.00	4–15	4 months after date	April 25*	May 10	4%	$_____
(b)	$ 750.40	12–18	60 days after date	January 4*	January 22	5%	_____
(c)	$3275.00	6–20	60 days after sight	July 1	July 15	$5\frac{1}{2}$%	_____

(a) _____
(b) _____
(c) _____

*Unless the terms state "days or months *after sight*," the due date is always calculated from the date of the draft for these problems, regardless of the date of acceptance. See page 414.

Answers

1. $557.34
2. $419.57
3. $817.25
4. $802.26
5. (a) $1483.83
   (b) $ 747.79
   (c) $3251.98

Solutions

1. Maturity value = $562.50.
   Maturity date (60 days after April 10) = June 9.
   Term of discount (April 15 to June 9) = 55 days.

   Discount = $562.50 × .06 × $\frac{55}{360}$ = $5.16
   Proceeds = $562.50 − $5.16 = $557.34

2. Maturity value = $425.00.
   Maturity date (90 days after October 10) = January 8.
   Term of discount (November 1 to January 8) = 68 days.

   Discount = $425 × .05 × $\frac{68}{360}$ = $4.01.
   Collection fee ($\frac{1}{3}$% of $425) = $1.42.
   Proceeds = $425.00 − ($4.01 + $1.42) = $419.57.

3. Face of draft = $815.50 bearing 6% interest.
   Maturity date (4 months after December 10) = April 10.
   Term of discount (January 10–April 10) = 90 days.

   Interest = $815.50 × .06 × $\frac{4}{12}$ = $16.31.
   Maturity value = $815.50 + $16.31 = $831.81.

   Discount = $831.81 × .065 × $\frac{90}{360}$ = $13.52.
   Collection fee ($\frac{1}{8}$% of $831.81) = $1.04.

   Proceeds = $831.81 − ($13.52 + $1.04) = $817.25.

4. Face of draft = $800 bearing interest at $4\frac{1}{2}$%.
   Term of discount = 60 days.

   Interest = $800 × .045 × $\frac{1}{4}$ = $9.00.
   Maturity value = $800.00 + $9.00 = $809.00.

   Discount = $809 × .05 × $\frac{60}{360}$ = $6.74.
   Proceeds = $809.00 − $6.74 = $802.26.

5. (a) Maturity date (4 months after April 15) = August 15.
       Term of discount (May 10 to August 15) = 97 days.

       Discount = $1500 × .04 × $\frac{97}{360}$ = $16.17.
       Proceeds = $1500.00 − $16.17 = $1483.83.

   (b) Maturity date (60 days after December 18) = February 16.
       Term of discount (January 22 to February 16) = 25 days.

       Discount = $750.40 × .05 × $\frac{25}{360}$ = $2.61.
       Proceeds = $750.40 − $2.61 = $747.79.

   (c) Maturity date (60 days after July 1) = August 30.
       Term of discount (July 15 to August 30) = 46 days.

       Discount = $3275 × .055 × $\frac{46}{360}$ = $23.02.
       Proceeds = $3275.00 − $23.02 = $3251.98.

EXERCISE 43

Chapter Summary

Answers appear at the end of this exercise. If your answers do not agree with those shown, check your calculations before referring to the solutions that follow.

1. James Bros. accepted a note as payment on a debt from Hiffin & Son amounting to $850, bearing interest at 6% for 3 months. A month later James Bros. took the note to the bank, where it was discounted at 6%. How much did they receive?

2. Mr. Howden wishes to borrow $5225 for one year. What size loan should he obtain if the bank charges a discount rate of 5%? Prove.

3. Jones obtained a loan of $4500 for a year and received $4275 as the proceeds. At what rate was the loan discounted? What simple interest rate was charged? (Record interest rate correct to nearest 10th of 1%.)

4. What are the proceeds on a draft for $1750, dated June 20, due 3 months after date, accepted July 7, and discounted August 10 at $5\frac{1}{2}$% with a collection fee of $\frac{1}{5}$%?

424 CHAPTER SUMMARY

5. Find the proceeds on a draft amounting to $457.40, due 60 days after sight, accepted November 18, and discounted November 24 at $6\frac{1}{2}\%$.

Answers

1. $854.12
2. $5500.00
3. 5%, 5.3%
4. $1735.54
5. $452.94

Solutions

1. Interest on note = $850 × .06 × $\frac{3}{12}$ = $12.75.
   Maturity value of note = $850 + $12.75 = $862.75.
   Term of discount = 2 months.
   Discount = $862.75 × .06 × $\frac{2}{12}$ = $8.63.
   Proceeds = $862.75 − $8.63 = $854.12.

2. $5225 = 95% of the loan.
   Then 100% = $5225 ÷ .95 = $5500.
   Proof: $5500 × .05 = $275; $5500 − $275 = $5225.

3. Amount of discount = $4500 − $4275 = $225.
   Discount rate = $225 ÷ $4500 = .05 or 5%.
   Interest rate = $225 ÷ $4275 = .0526 or 5.3%.

4. Due date (3 months after June 20) = September 20.
   Term of discount (August 10 to September 20) = 41 days.
   Discount = $1750 × .055 × $\frac{41}{360}$ = $10.96.
   Collection fee = $\frac{1}{5}\%$ of $1750 = $3.50.
   Proceeds = $175.00 − ($10.96 + $3.50) = $1735.54.

5. Maturity date (60 days from November 18) = January 17.
   Term of discount (November 24 to January 17) = 54 days.
   Discount = $457.40 × .065 × $\frac{54}{360}$ = $4.46.
   Proceeds = $457.40 − $4.46 = $452.92.

CHAPTER ELEVEN
Installment Purchases and Periodic Loan Payment Plans

OBJECTIVES

Buying or borrowing on the installment plan has become a way of life. Credit on the installment plan makes it possible to enjoy more of the desired things of life while paying for them. Also, the increased use of credit cards has encouraged buying to a great extent.

The use of credit is a necessary part of our economy but for the consumer it can be ruinous if not used wisely. A prospective borrower should shop for credit if he is going to use it to the best advantage. Interest rates and all other charges against a loan or a purchase should be compared. The consumer should be aware of cost differences, not just the amount of the monthly payment.

When you have completed this chapter, you will be able to

(1) recognize and apply terms, such as credit, amortized, flat sum charges, and installment, used in installment buying and periodic loan payment plans,
(2) compute the cost of buying on the installment plan when (a) the periodic payments are stated, (b) a flat sum is added to the unpaid balance, and (c) an interest charge is made on the unpaid balance,
(3) compare cash and installment prices,
(4) compute the true interest rate (effective rate) on installment purchases by use of the

   (a) constant ratio formula $r = \dfrac{2mI}{P(n+1)}$,

   (b) average balance method $r = I \div \dfrac{(P_1 + P_2)t}{2}$,

(5) compute installment payments and the true interest rate when a flat rate of interest is charged on the unpaid balance,
(6) compute installment payments if interest is calculated on the unpaid balance and the same amount is applied to the principal with each payment, plus the interest on the balance,

(7) compute installment payments on an amortized loan by the average principal balance method,
(8) compute the principal balance due on an amortized loan after each payment has been made.

UNIT 1. INSTALLMENT PURCHASES

When any article or service is bought on the installment plan, a carrying or credit charge is added to the purchase price and equal payments are made periodically until the obligation is paid in full. One kind of carrying charge is a *flat sum* which is a specified dollar amount added to the cost at the time of purchase. The other is an interest charge on the unpaid balance for each payment period. The contract invariably provides for a penalty if payments are late and gives the seller title to the goods sold until paid for in full.

Credit Charge (dollar amount or flat sum)

1. Credit charges *equal* price paid on a "time" plan *less* cash price. Mr. Haines could buy a TV set for $220 cash, but, if he bought it over a period of 8 months, it would cost him $238.

   The credit charge = $_____ − $_____ = $_____.

   _

   $238 − $220 = $18

The installment payment schedule shown here is representative of those in use today.

This chart lists (a) carrying charge and monthly payment for 12 months and (b) carrying charge and monthly payment for 18 months for purchases of $300 or more.

Example: Mr. Brown made a purchase amounting to $326.50. He paid $75 down and the balance over 12 months. What were the carrying charge and monthly payment (installment payment)?

Solution: Unpaid balance = $326.50 − $75.00 = $251.50.
According to the schedule, $251.50 is between $250.01 and $260.00
Therefore the carrying charge = $26.00,
    the monthly payment = $24.00.

SCHEDULE A—EASY PAYMENT CHART

Unpaid Balance	Carrying Charge	Up to 12 Monthly Payments*	Unpaid Balance	Carrying Charge	Up to 12 Monthly Payments*	Up to 18 Months	
						Carrying Charge	Monthly Payment*
Up to $20.00	$ 2.00	$ 5.00	$250.01–260	$26.00	$24.00		
$ 20.01–30	3.00	5.00	260.01–270	27.00	25.00		
30.01–40	4.00	5.00	270.01–280	28.00	26.00		
40.01–50	5.00	5.00	280.01–290	29.00	27.00		
50.01–60	6.00	6.00	290.01–300	30.00	28.00		
60.01–70	7.00	7.00	300.01–310	31.00	29.00	$46.50	$20.00
70.01–80	8.00	8.00	310.01–320	32.00	30.00	48.00	21.00
80.01–90	9.00	9.00	320.01–330	33.00	31.00	49.50	22.00
90.01–100	10.00	10.00	330.01–340	34.00	32.00	51.00	22.00
100.01–110	11.00	11.00	340.01–350	35.00	33.00	52.50	23.00
110.01–120	12.00	11.00	350.01–360	36.00	34.00	54.00	23.00
120.01–130	13.00	12.00	360.01–370	37.00	35.00	55.50	24.00
130.01–140	14.00	13.00	370.01–380	38.00	36.00	57.00	25.00
140.01–150	15.00	14.00	380.01–390	39.00	37.00	58.50	25.00
150.01–160	16.00	15.00	390.01–400	40.00	38.00	60.00	26.00
160.01–170	17.00	16.00	400.01–410	41.00	39.00	61.50	27.00
170.01–180	18.00	17.00	410.01–420	42.00	40.00	63.00	28.00
180.01–190	19.00	18.00	420.01–430	43.00	41.00	64.50	29.00
190.01–200	20.00	19.00	430.01–440	44.00	42.00	66.00	29.00
200.01–210	21.00	20.00	440.01–450	45.00	43.00	67.50	30.00
210.01–220	22.00	21.00	450.01–460	46.00	44.00	69.00	30.00
220.01–230	23.00	22.00	460.01–470	47.00	45.00	70.50	31.00
230.01–240	24.00	22.00	470.01–480	48.00	46.00	72.00	31.00
240.01–250	25.00	23.00	480.01–490	49.00	47.00	73.50	32.00
			490.01–500	50.00	48.00	75.00	32.00

Check if balance is over $300 and 18 months desired ☐

*All monthly payments are for the amount shown; last payment is for the odd amount remaining due.

2. According to the chart, what would the charge be for credit on the following purchases:

		Down payment	Unpaid balance	Carrying charge	
(a)	$219.00	$25.00	$_____	$_____	
(b)	128.18	12.00	_____	_____	
(c)	475.50	50.00	_____	_____	for 12 months
				_____	for 18 months

(a) $194.00, $20.00
(b) 116.18, 12.00
(c) 425.50, 43.00, $64.50

When a schedule is not used and the advertisement states the down payment, if any, and the monthly payment for a given number of months, it is then necessary to determine what the charges for credit are in order to compare the installment price with the cash price.

Example: A tractor is advertised at $675 cash or $25 down and the balance in payments of $30 each for 24 months. What is the carrying charge or installment charge?

Solution:

Down payment	$ 25
Monthly payments ($30 × 24)	720
Installment price	$745 = (downpayment + monthly payments)
Cash price	675
Installment charge	$ 70 = (installment price − cash price)

3. An outboard motor was advertised for sale as follows: "Used, 35 horsepower outboard motor, good condition, $275 cash or $50 down and 6 payments of $42.50 each. Phone ____." If purchased on time, what is the installment charge?

Down payment	$_____
Monthly payments	_____
Installment price	$_____
Cash price	_____
Installment charge	_____

Down payment	$ 50
Monthly payments	255
Installment price	$305
Cash price	275
Installment charge	$ 30

4. Find the installment charge for an article listed as follows:
"Cash price $98.65, downpayment $14.50, 6 installments of $16.00 each."

$$\frac{}{\text{(installment price)}} = \frac{}{\text{(downpayment)}} + \frac{}{\text{(total monthly payments)}}.$$

$$\frac{}{\text{(installment charge)}} = \frac{}{\text{(installment price)}} - \frac{}{\text{(cash price)}}.$$

- -

$110.50 = $14.50 + $96.00.
$11.85 = $110.50 − $98.65.

Credit charges may be (a) a *flat sum* (as illustrated in frames 2 to 4) which is added to the unpaid balance after a down payment has been made at the time of purchase or (b) an *interest charge* on the unpaid balance per payment period.

The following is an example of (b) in which the interest charge is expressed as a percent of the unpaid monthly balance.

A coat may be purchased for $80 cash or over a period of 6 months with a charge of $1\frac{1}{2}\%$ on the unpaid balance per month. If a downpayment of $20 is made, what are the (a) monthly payment schedule, (b) total cost on the installment plan, and (c) difference between the cash and installment price?

Solution: Balance due = cash price − downpayment = $80 − $20 = $60.
Monthly payment on the balance = $60 ÷ 6 = $10.

(a)

Month	Balance	Installment Payment	Service (Charge ($1\frac{1}{2}\%$))	Total Payment
1	$60.00	$10.00	$0.90*	$10.90
2	50.00	10.00	0.75†	10.75
3	40.00	10.00	0.60	10.60
4	30.00	10.00	0.45	10.45
5	20.00	10.00	0.30	10.30
6	10.00	10.00	0.15	10.15
Total	xxx	$60.00	$3.15	$63.15

*$1\frac{1}{2}\%$ of $60.
†$1\frac{1}{2}\%$ of $50 etc. for remaining months

(b) Total cost on the installment plan = $63.15 + $20.00 = $83.15.
(c) Installment charge = installment price − cash price
= $83.15 − $80.00 = $3.15.

5. Mr. Barnes bought merchandise amounting to $118.25 from the Home Department Store on the installment plan with no down payment. A charge is made of 1% on the unpaid monthly balances. Given the following installment payments, prepare a schedule as illustrated on page 429.

Month	Balance	Installment Payment	Service Charge (1%)	Total Payment
1	$118.25	$20.00	$1.18	$21.18
2	_____	20.00	_____	_____
3	_____	20.00	_____	_____
4	_____	20.00	_____	_____
5	_____	20.00	_____	_____
6	_____	18.25	_____	_____
Total	xxxxx	$_____	$_____	$_____

Total credit charge = $_____.

Month	Balance	Installment Payment	Service Charge (1%)	Total Payment
1	$118.25	$ 20.00	$1.18	$ 21.18
2	98.25	20.00	.98	20.98
3	78.25	20.00	.78	20.78
4	58.25	20.00	.58	20.58
5	38.25	20.00	.38	20.38
6	18.25	18.25	.18	18.43
Total	xxxx	$118.25	$4.08	$122.33

Total credit charge = $4.08.

6. Mrs. Page bought a piano, priced at $1250 plus $4\frac{1}{2}\%$ tax on the following terms: 10% of cash price down and 18 months in which to pay the balance. A service charge of 12% was added. What was the monthly installment? What was the total cost of the piano?

Solution:

Cash price	$1250.00
Sales tax ($4\frac{1}{2}\%$)	56.25
Total price	$1306.25
Downpayment	125.00
Balance (paid on time)	$1181.25
Plus 12% service charge	141.75
Balance due on installment	$1323.00

Amount of each installment = $1323.00 ÷ 18 = $73.50.*
Total cost of piano = cash price + sales tax + credit charges
= $1250.00 + $56.25 + $141.75 = $1448.00.

Baines Co. offered swivel chairs for $45.00 cash plus 4.4% sales tax or $10.00 down with the balance, plus a carrying charge of $2.25, to be paid in 3 monthly installments (a 3-month account). What would be the total cost of one chair bought on the time plan? What would the amount of each payment be?

Cash price $_____   Total cost = $_____.

Sales tax (4.4%)   _____

Total cash price   _____   Monthly payments =

down payment   _____ $_____, $_____, $_____

Balance due $_____   (make adjustment in last payment).

Carrying charges   _____

Amount to be paid
in 3 installments $_____

- -

Cash price	$45.00	Total cost = $45.00 + $1.98 + 2.25 = $49.23.
Sales tax (4.4%)	1.98	Monthly payments = $13.08, $13.08, $13.07.
Total cash price	$46.98	
Down payment	10.00	
Balance due	$36.98	
Carrying charges	2.25	
Amount to be paid on installments	$39.23	

---

*If there had been a fraction of $1.00 remaining, it would have been added to the last payment.

EXERCISE 44

Answers appear at the end of this exercise. If your answers do not agree with those shown, check your calculations before referring to the solutions that follow.

1. A TV set can be bought for $320 cash or $32 down and 12 payments of $25 each. How much is the carrying charge?

2. Miss Orr can buy a coat for $110 cash or, on a 90-day account that would include a service charge of $7.00. If the time plan is used, what would be the amount of the installments if paid in 3 equal amounts?

3. A radio may be bought for $76.50 cash or $10.00 down and $12.00 per month for 6 months. How much is the carrying charge?

4. Mr. Johns bought a table for $170.00. He made a downpayment of $20.00 and agreed to pay the balance in installments of $30.00 a month plus a 1% carrying charge on the unpaid balance. How much did he pay in total carrying charges?

5. An article costing $38.00 plus a 3% excise tax and a 4% sales tax may be purchased for $10.00 down and 3 payments of $11.60. (a) What was the total cash price? (b) What was the total price on the installment plan?

(a) _____
(b) _____

Answers

1. $12.00
2. $39.00
3. $ 5.50
4. $ 4.50
5. (a) $40.71
   (b) $44.80

Solutions

1. Price on the installment plan = $32 + (12 \times $25) = $332.
   Cash price = $320. Difference = $332 - $320 = $12 (carrying charge).
2. $117.00 \times \frac{1}{3} = 39.00$ each installment.
3. Price on time basis = $10.00 + ($12 \times 6) = $82.00.
   Carrying charge = $82.00 - $76.50 = $5.50.

4.

Month	Balance	Payment on Balance	Interest charge
1	$150.00	$ 30.00	$1.50
2	120.00	30.00	1.20
3	90.00	30.00	.90
4	60.00	30.00	.60
5	30.00	30.00	.30
Total	xxxx	$150.00	$4.50

5. Cash price = $38.00 + $1.14 = $39.14
   Sales tax (4% of $39.14)   =   1.57
   Total cash price   = $40.71
   Installment price = (3 × $11.60) + $10.00 = $44.80.

Effective or True Interest Rates

Credit costs on installment purchases vary and are deceiving. They are usually stated as a percent but often are expressed in some other manner such as "so many dollars a month," "low daily cost," and "easy monthly payments to meet your budget." The customer needs to compare credit charges with the cost of a loan to finance a purchase. So, although carrying charges* are not interest, we reduce them to a common base called the true interest rate or *effective rate of interest*.

---

*Strictly speaking, carrying charges are not interest.

7. When the installment contract calls for $1\frac{1}{2}\%$ a month on the unpaid balance, the *true annual interest* is equal to 18%. Since the interest for one month is $1\frac{1}{2}\%$, for a year it must equal $12 \times 1\frac{1}{2}\%$ or 18% (effective interest rate). Accordingly, the *effective* or *true annual interest rate* for 1% per month is 12%, for $\frac{3}{4}\%$ per month is 9%, and so on. Then the true annual interest rate (effective interest rate) for

$\frac{1}{2}\%$ per month is _____%,

$\frac{3}{8}\%$ per month is _____%,

2% per month is _____%,

6% $(12 \times \frac{1}{2}\%)$
$4\frac{1}{2}\%$ $(12 \times \frac{3}{8}\%)$
24% $(12 \times 2\%)$

8. When credit charges are expressed as a flat fee, which is added to the purchase price and then repaid in a number of equal installments, the problem of determining the *effective* or *true annual interest rate* can become involved, especially for accounts for less or more than a year. There are several methods. The *constant ratio formula* employed by the Federal Reserve System and recommended by Consumers Union as well as a system called the *average balance method* are used in this book.

Constant Ratio Formula

$$r = \frac{2mI}{P(n+1)},$$

where r = effective interest rate,
m = number of installments per year
(12 if monthly, 52 if weekly),
I = finance or credit charges (dollar amount),
P = net amount of credit on an installment loan after deduction of downpayment or actual cash received,
n = number of payments required.

Example: A heater may be bought for $39.90 cash or on an easy time plan that requires a down payment of $5.00 and $3.10 per month for a year. If the time payment plan is used, what is the annual interest rate?

Solution: $m = 12$, since the payments are made each month.
$n = 12$, since there are 12 payments in a year on a monthly basis.

Cash price   = $39.90
Down payment = 5.00
Balance due   = $34.90

Cost on installment plan = ($3.10 × 12) + $5.00 = $42.20.
Credit charges   = $42.20 − $39.90 = $2.30.

Substituting in the formula,
$$r = \frac{(2)(12)(\$2.30)}{(\$34.90)(12 + 1)} = .122 = 12.2\%.$$

8. A piece of machinery may be bought for $670 cash or $70 down and 12 monthly payments of $52. What is the interest rate on the time plan? (Record answer to the nearest 10th of 1%.)

$m =$ _____.   Balance due (P in formula) = $_____ − $_____ = $_____.
$I = \$$_____.   Installment payments = $_____ × 12 = $_____.
$P = \$$_____.   Installment charge   = $_____.
$n = \$$_____.
Then $r =$ _____ = _____%.

- -

$m = 12$ Balance due (P in formula) = $670 − $70 = $600.
$I = \$ 24$ Installment payments = $52 × 12 = $624.
$P = \$600$ Installment charges = $24.
$n = 12$
$$r = \frac{(2)(12)(\$24)}{(\$600)(12 + 1)} = .0738 = 7.4\%.$$

9. A radio may be bought for $76.50 cash or $10.00 down and $12.00 a month for 6 months. (a) How large is the carrying charge? (b) What is interest rate? (Record answer correct to the nearest 10th of 1%.)

   (a) Total cost on the installment plan = (____ × $_____) + $_____

       = $_____.

       Carrying charge = $_____ − $_____ = $_____.

   (b) $r = \dfrac{2mI}{P(n+1)}$.

       $m =$ _____ (always 12, regardless of the time as long as payments are made monthly).

       $I =$ $_____.

       $n =$ _____ (number of payments).

       $P =$ $_____ (balance due after down payment).

       Then $r =$ _____.

(a) Total cost on the installment plan = (6 × $12.00) + $10.00 = $82.00.
    Carrying charges = $82.00 − $76.50 = $5.50.

(b) $m = 12$.
    $I = \$5.50$.
    $n = 6$.
    $P = \$66.50$ ($76.50 − 10.00).
    $r = \dfrac{(2)(12)(\$5.50)}{(\$66.50)(6+1)} = 28.4\%$.

Average Balance Method

When this method is used, interest is found on the average of the principal balance at the beginning of the time plan and the principal balance due on the last payment.

$$r = I \div \dfrac{(P_1 + P_2)t}{2},$$

where r = interest rate,
         I = installment or credit charge,
         P_1 = beginning principal balance,
         P_2 = ending principal balance,
         $\dfrac{P_1 + P_2}{2}$ = average principal balance,
         t = time in years (term of the contract).

Notice that this formula is actually the basic interest formula $I = Prt$. Solving for r, $r = I \div Pt$, in which case P = the average principal balance.

Solution of the problem in frame 9 is by this method:

P_1 = cash price − down payment = $66.50.
P_2 = $66.50 ÷ 6* = $11.08.
$\dfrac{P_1 + P_2}{2}$ = ($66.50 + $11.08) ÷ 2 = $38.79.
I = (see solution, frame 9a) = $ 5.50.
t = 6 months = $\tfrac{1}{2}$ year.

Substituting in the formula,
$r = \$5.50 \div (\$38.79 \times \tfrac{1}{2}) = \$5.50 \div \$19.395 = 28.4\%$.

10. Solve the problem in frame 8 by the average balance method. Your answer will be the same, that is 7.4%, if calculated correctly.

Installment charge (I) = $_____.

Beginning principal balance (P_1) = $_____.

Ending principal balance (P_2) = $_____.

Average principal balance = $_____.

t (time) = _____ (years).

r = _____ (correct to nearest 10th of 1%).

I = $24.
P_1 = $600.
P_2 = $50.
Average principal balance = ($600 + $50) ÷ 2 = $325.
t = 1 year.
r = $24.00 ÷ $325.00 = .0738 = 7.4%.

---

*Divide the beginning principal balance (P_1) by the number of payments that are to be made. In this case, the number of payments equals 6.

11. A jeweler advertised a watch that could be purchased for $95 cash or $15 down and the balance in 36 weekly installments of $2.50. What is the interest rate on the installment plan to nearest 10th of 1% by (a) the constant ratio formula, (b) the average balance formula ($m = 52$, since payments are made weekly).

(a) Constant ratio formula

$m = $ _____.

$I = \$$_____. $r = $ _____ = _____%.

$P = \$$_____.

$n = $ _____.

(b) $I = \$$_____.

$P_1 = \$$_____. $r = $ _____ = _____%.

$P_2 = \$$_____.

$(P_1 + P_2) \div 2 = \$$_____.

$t = $ _____.

- -

(a) $m = 52$.
$I = \$10.00$. $r = \dfrac{(2)(52)(\$10)}{(\$80)(36 + 1)} = .351 = 35.1\%$.
$P = \$80.00$.
$n = 36$.

(b) $I = \$10.00$.
$P_1 = \$80.00$. $r = \$10.00 \div [(\$41.11)(\tfrac{36}{52})] = .351 = 35.1\%$.
$P_2 = \$80.00 \div 36 = \$2.22$.
$(P_1 + P_2) \div 2 = \$41.11$.
$t = \tfrac{36}{52}$ since time must be expressed in terms of a year.

EXERCISE 45

Answers appear at the end of this exercise. If your answers do not agree with those shown, check your calculations before referring to the solutions that follow.

Use either formula in calculating the interest rate. Record all interest rates correct to the nearest tenth of 1%.

1. What is the annual interest rate on an installment contract for the following monthly charges on the unpaid balance: 1%, $1\frac{1}{4}\%$, 2%, $\frac{1}{2}\%$, $\frac{3}{4}\%$, and $1\frac{1}{2}\%$?

2. An article that cost $280 was bought on the following terms: $20 down payment, the balance in 18 monthly installments, and a carrying charge of $30. What was the annual interest rate? (In this problem $m = 12$ if the constant ratio formula is used.)

3. The cash price of a desk is $65.00 or, if bought on the installment plan, 10% down and the balance in 6 monthly payments of $10.50. If the time plan is used, what is the annual interest rate?

4. Mrs. Rappen bought some carpet priced at $450 cash from the J. C. Furniture Company. Terms were $70 down and the balance in 12 monthly payments of $35 each. If Mrs. Rappen bought the carpet on time, what was the total cost? What was the annual interest rate?

5. A rifle may be purchased for $10.00 down and $3.50 a month for 9 months. What are the total cost and the annual interest rate on this basis if the cash price is $37.50 ($m = 12$)?

6. A stove sells for $330.00 cash or $40.00 down and $10.50 a month for 36 months. Find the annual interest rate ($m = 12$). Solve by both the constant ratio formula and the average principal balance method.

Answers

1. 12%, 15%, 24%, 6%, 9%, and 18%   2. 14.6%
3. 26.4%   4. $490.00, 19.4%
5. $41.50, 34.9%   6. 19.7%

Solutions

1. Multiply each rate by 12 to obtain the answer.
2. Unpaid balance (P in constant ratio formula) = $280 − $20 = $260. Charges for credit = $30, $m = 12$, $n + 1 = 19$.
$$r = \frac{(2)(12)(\$30)}{(\$260)(19)} = 14.6\%.$$
3. Unpaid balance = $65.00 − $6.50 = $58.50.
Installment price = (6 × $10.50) + $6.50 = $69.50.
Installment charge = $69.50 − $65.00 = $4.50.
$m = 12$, $n + 1 = 7$.
$$r = \frac{(2)(12)(\$4.50)}{(\$58.50)(7)} = 26.4\%.$$
4. Unpaid balance = $450 − $70 = $380.
Installment price = (12 × $35) + $70 = $490.
Installment charge = $490 − $450 = $40.
$m = 12$, $n + 1 = 13$.
$$r = \frac{(2)(12)(\$40)}{(\$380)(13)} = .194 = 19.4\%.$$

5. Beginning balance = $37.50 - $10.00 = $27.50.
   Installment price = (9 × $3.50) + $10.00 = $41.50.
   Installment charge = $41.50 - $37.50 = $4.00.
   $$r = \frac{(2)(12)(\$4.00)}{(\$27.50)(10)} = 34.9\%.$$
6. *Constant ratio formula*
   Installment price = ($10.50 × 36) + $40.00 = $418.00.
   Installment charge = $418.00 - cash price of $330.00 = $88.00.
   Unpaid balance = $330 - $40 = $290.
   $m = 12$, $I = \$88$, $n + 1 = 37$.
   $$r = \frac{(2)(12)(\$88)}{(\$290)(37)} = 19.7\%.$$
   Average principal balance method
   $I = \$88.00$.
   $P_1 = \$330 - \$40 = \$290$.
   $P_2 = \$290 \div 36 = \$8.06$.
   (t) time = 36 months = 3 years.
   Average principal balance = $(P_1 + P_2) \div 2 = \$298.06 \div 2 = \$149.03$.
   $$r = I \div \frac{(P_1 + P_2)t}{2} = \$88.00 \div (\$149.03)(3) = 19.7\%.$$

UNIT 2. PERIODIC LOAN PAYMENT PLANS

In the preceding section we considered some aspects of installment credit as it applies to the purchase of goods and services. We now consider installment credit as it applies to the borrowing of money.

There are numerous lending agencies that make personal loans. Rates depend on the size of the loan, length of time, security, purpose, and credit rating of the borrower. Many banks charge a minimum fee for any loan, regardless of size and time involved. Many lending agencies charge a fee (percent of the loan) to pay for the cost of handling the application in addition to the interest on the unpaid balance.

Except for loans on real estate purchases, installment loans are usually short term—3 years or less. Some, however, are made up to 5 years for home repairs.

The most favorable loan is one in which the only cost is the interest on the unpaid balance. Many loans, in addition to the interest, include charges in the payments such as insurance to protect the lender against loss and other costs pertinent to the transaction.

Finding Installment Payments and the True Interest Rate When a Flat Rate of Interest Is Charged

On loans in which the interest charge is added and then divided into 12 equal payments the actual interest rate is about double that quoted; for example, if $4\frac{1}{2}\%$ is added, the true interest rate is 9%; if 8% is added, the true rate is 14.8%; if 6% is added, the true rate is 11.1%. Such charges are sometimes called flat rates.

Example: Mrs. Holmes obtained a loan of $300 under the 6% plan (6% of the total loan for each year) to be repaid in 24 equal monthly installments. Find the carrying charge, the monthly installment, and the interest rate charged.

Solution: Carrying charge (6% of $300 for 2 years) = $36.
Principal + carrying charge = $336.
Monthly installment ($336 ÷ 24) = $14.
$m = 12, n = 24$.

Substituting in the constant ratio formula,

$$r = \frac{(2)(12)(36)}{(\$300)(24 + 1)} = .115 = 11.5\% \text{ interest rate.}$$

1. Mr. Collins obtained a loan from a local finance company for $400 plus a flat rate of $7\frac{1}{2}\%$ for 3 years. (a) What was the amount of the installment payments? (b) What interest rate did he pay? (Record rate correct to nearest tenth of 1%.)

    Carrying charge = $_____$.

    Principal + carrying charge = $_____$.

    (a) Installment = $_____$.

    (b) $m = _____, n = _____$.

    $r = _____$.

- -

Carrying charge = $400 × .075 × 3 = $90.00.
(a) Installment = (principal + carrying charge) ÷ 36 = $13.61.
(b) $m = 12, n = 36$.
$$r = \frac{(2)(12)(\$90)}{(\$400)(37)} = .146 = 14.6\%.$$

2. Assume that the following charges (flat rates) are made on $500 for a year and that the loan in each case is to be repaid in 12 equal monthly installments: (a) 3%, (b) 5%. What is the monthly payment and the true annual interest rate that the borrower is paying in each case? (Record interest rate correct to the nearest tenth of 1%.)

(a) Carrying charges = $_____.

Monthly payments = $_____.

$r =$ _____.

(b) Carrying charges = $_____.

Monthly payments = $_____.

$r =$ _____.

- -

(a) Carrying charges (3% of $500)   = $ 15.00.
Principal + carrying charges   = $515.00.
Monthly payments ($515 ÷ 12) = $ 42.92.

$$r = \frac{(2)(12)(\$15)}{(\$500)(13)} = 5.5\%.$$

(b) Carrying charges (5% of $500)   = $ 25.00.
Principal + carrying charges   = $525.00.
Monthly payments ($525 ÷ 12) = $ 43.75.

$$r = \frac{(2)(12)(\$25)}{(\$500)(13)} = 9.2\%.$$

Finding Installment Payments when Interest Is Calculated on the Unpaid Balance

A loan may be liquidated by payments in which the same amount is applied to the principal in each period, plus the interest on the unpaid balance, or the loan may be *amortized*, in which case all payments are equal (including principal and interest).

When the same amount is applied to the principal with each payment, plus the interest on the balance (an example is given on page 444).

Example: Mr. Dodge obtained a loan of $180 from his credit union which he was to repay in monthly installments of $30 plus 1% on the unpaid balance until liquidated. The following is a schedule of his payments:

Payment Number	Principal Balance	Payment On Principal	Interest (1%)	Total Payment
1	$180.00	$30.00	$1.80	$31.80
2	150.00	30.00	1.50	31.50
3	120.00	30.00	1.20	31.20
4	90.00	30.00	.90	30.90
5	60.00	30.00	.60	30.60
6	30.00	30.00	.30	30.30
Total	xxxx	$180.00	$6.30	$186.30

At the end of 6 months the loan has been paid in full plus interest in the amount of $6.30.

3. Mr. Johns borrowed $200 from a friend and agreed to repay the loan in $50 installments each month, plus $\frac{3}{4}$% interest on the unpaid balance. Complete the following schedule.

Payment Number	Principal Balance	Payment On Principal	Interest ($\frac{3}{4}$%)	Total Payment
1	$200.00	$50.00	$1.50	$51.50
2	_____	_____	_____	_____
3	_____	_____	_____	_____
4	_____	_____	_____	_____
Total	xxxx	$_____	$_____	$_____

- -

Payment Number	Principal Balance	Payment On Principal	Interest ($\frac{3}{4}$%)	Total Payment
1	$200.00	$50.00	$1.50	$51.50
2	150.00	50.00	1.13	51.13
3	100.00	50.00	.75	50.75
4	50.00	50.00	.38	50.38
Total	xxxxxx	$200.00	$3.76	$203.76

4. Amortized loans are usually for large amounts and spread over a period of years.

   Mr. and Mrs. Rucker bought a home for $45,000, with $10,000 down and the balance at 6% for 20 years.

   (a) If they paid for this purchase in equal installments, the loan is _____.

   (b) How much is the unpaid balance at time of purchase? _____

   (c) Is the loan illustrated in the preceding frame an amortized loan? _____
   Why? _____
   _____

   (d) If a loan is not amortized, successive payments (increase/decrease) _____? Why? _____

- -

(a) amortized
(b) $35,000
(c) No, because the payments are not equal.
(d) Decrease because the interest decreases as the unpaid balance decreases.

5. When a loan is amortized.

   Mr. and Mrs. Warren purchased a home for $30,000. They made a down payment of 20% and borrowed the balance at 6% for 20 years on an amortized basis. How much is their monthly payment?

Price of home	$30,000	
Down payment	6,000	(20% of $30,000)
Balance	$24,000	(sum borrowed)

   The total interest on this loan may be calculated by the average principal balance method.

   $I = Prt$. In this case P = average principal balance = $\dfrac{P_1 + P_2}{2}$.

   P_1 = beginning principal balance = $24,000
   P_2 = ending principal balance = $ 100   (24,000 ÷ 240, number of months in 20 years).
   $P = \dfrac{P_1 + P_2}{2}$ = average principal balance = $12,050   [($24,000 + $100) ÷ 2].

Then, since $I = Prt$,

I = interest on average principal balance
over the 20-year period = $14,460 ($12,050 × .06 × 20).
Total amount to be repaid = $P + I$ = $38,460 ($24,000 + $14,460).
Monthly payment = total amount to be
repaid ÷ number of monthly payments = $160.25 ($38,460 ÷ 240).

This method results in an answer that is a little less than the true amount except for very short periods of time.

5. A couple bought 12 acres of orchard land at $2500 an acre from the owner. They made a down payment of 10%. The owner agreed to carry the balance at $6\frac{1}{2}\%$ to be paid in equal monthly installments for 10 years. Find the amount of the monthly payment.

Principal balance due = $_____ − $_____ = $_____.

Beginning principal balance = $_____.

Ending principal balance = $_____.

Average principal balance = $_____.

Interest on the average principal balance = _____.

Total amount to be repaid = _____.

Monthly payment = _____.

Principal balance due = $30,000 − $3,000 = $27,000.
Biginning principal balance = $27,000.
Ending principal balance = $27,000 ÷ 120 = $225.
Average principal balance = ($27,000 + $225) ÷ 2 = $13,612.50.
Interest on average principal balance = $13,612.50 × .065 × 10 = $8,848.13.
Total amount to be repaid = $27,000 + $8,848.13 = $35,848.13.
Monthly payment = $35,848.13 ÷ 120 = $298.73.

6. We found that Mr. and Mrs. Warren (page 445) made payments of $160.25 each month. The interest rate was 6%. The amount of the loan was $24,000. How much of the first and second month payments were applied to principal and how much to interest?

With each succeeding month, the amount applied to the principal increases, whereas the interest decreases since the balance of the loan becomes increasingly smaller.

Payment	Balance	Payment	Amount Applied to Interest ($\frac{1}{2}$%)	Principal
First month	$24,000.00	$160.25	$120.00	$40.25
Second month	23,959.75	160.25	119.80	40.45

First month interest = $24,000 × .005 = $120.00,
        principal = $160.25 − $120.00 = $40.25.
Second month interest = $23,959.75 × .005 = $119.80,
        principal = $160.25 − $119.80 = $40.45.

How much is the interest and what amount is applied to the principal for the third and fourth payments on this loan?

Third month interest = _____,
    principal = _____.

Fourth month interest = _____,
    principal = _____.

Third month interest = $23,919.30* × .005 = $119.60,
    principal = $160.25 − $119.60 = $ 40.65.

Fourth month interest = $23,878.65† × .005 = $119.39,
    principal = $160.25 − $119.39 = $ 40.86.

---

*$23,959.75 − $40.45 = $23,919.30
†$23,919.30 − $40.65 = $23,878.65

7. The Lindsays purchased a home for $28,500. They paid 10% down and financed the balance at 8% over a period of 15 years on the installment plan. Find the monthly payment and the amount applied to principal for the first month if the loan was amortized.

Monthly payment $_____.

First month's payment, amount applied to interest = $_____,
amount applied to principal = $_____.

Amount borrowed = $28,500 − (10% of price) = $25,650.
In 15 years there are 180 payment periods. Therefore the ending principal balance = $25,650 ÷ 180 = $142.50.
Average principal balance = ($25,650 + $142.50) ÷ 2 = $12,896.25.
Interest for life of loan = $12,896.25 × .08 × 15 = $15,475.00.
Total amount to be paid = $15,475.00 + $25,650.00 = $41,125.00.
Installments = $41,125.50 ÷ 180 = $228.48.
Interest for the first month = ($25,650 × .08) ÷ 12 = $171.00.
Amount applied to principal, first month = $228.48 − $171.00 = $57.48.

EXERCISE 46

Answers appear at the end of this exercise. If your answers do not agree with those shown, check your calculations before referring to the solutions that follow.

1. Mr. Marshall purchased a hand cultivator for $190 from a garden equipment company on time. He was charged a flat fee of 8% for 6 months. This obligation was to be paid off in 6 equal monthly installments. Find (a) the carrying charge, (b) the monthly installment, and (c) the true interest rate to the nearest 10th of 1%.

    (a) _____

    (b) _____

    (c) _____

2. Mr. John belongs to a credit union. He borrows $150 and pays back $25 a month plus 1% carrying charge on the unpaid balance. How much does he pay in total carrying charges and what is the true rate of interest? Prepare a payment schedule.

    _____

3. Mary Redding bought a home for $28,500. She made a down payment of 20%. The remainder was amortized at 7% for 10 years. (a) How much of the first month's payment was applied to principal? How much to interest? (c) What was the installment payment?

    (a) Applied to interest _____

    (b) Applied to principal _____

    (c) Installment payment _____

4. If the loan (problem 3) had not been amortized, how much would the first month's payment equal (principal plus interest)?

    _____

Answers

1. (a) $7.60   (2) $5.25, 12%
   (b) $32.93
   (c) 13.7%
3. (a) Applied to principal $124.05   (4) $323.00
   (b) Applied to interest $133.00
   (c) Installment payment $257.05

Solutions

1. (a) $190 \times .08 \times .50 = \$7.60$.
   (b) $(\$190.00 + \$7.60) \div 6 = \$32.93$.
   (c) $r = \dfrac{2mI}{P(n+1)} = \dfrac{2(12)(\$7.60)}{(\$190)(6+1)} = .1371 = 13.7\%$.

   or

   $r = I \div \dfrac{(P_1 + P_2)t}{2} = \$7.60 \div \dfrac{(\$190.00 + \$31.67)}{2} \times \dfrac{1}{2} = 13.7\%$.

2.

Payment Number	Principal Balance	Payment On Principal	Payment Interest (1%)	Total Payment
1	$150.00	$25.00	$1.50	$26.50
2	125.00	25.00	1.25	26.25
3	100.00	25.00	1.00	26.00
4	75.00	25.00	.75	25.75
5	50.00	25.00	.50	25.50
6	25.00	25.00	.25	25.25
Total	—	$150.00	$5.25	$155.25

    Interest rate = $12 \times 1\% = 12\%$ (see page 434, frame 7).

    Proof: $r = \dfrac{2(12)(\$5.25)}{(\$150)(6+1)} = .12 = 12\%$ (not required).

3. Amount of loan = $28,500 - (20\% \text{ of } \$28,500) = \$22,800$.
   Number of payments = $10 \times 12 = 120$.
   Average monthly payment on principal (ending principal balance) = $\$22,800 \div 120 = \$190.00$.
   Average principal balance = $(\$22,800 + \$190) \div 2 = \$11,495$.
   Interest = $\$11,495 \times .07 \times 10 = \$8046.50$.
   Total amount to be repaid = $\$22,800.00 + \$8,046.50 = \$30,846.50$.
   Monthly payment = $\$30,846.50 \div 120 = \$257.05$.
   Interest for the first month = $(\$22,800 \times .07) \div 12 = \$133.00$.
   Amount applied to principal for first month = $\$257.05 - \$133.00 = \$124.05$.

4. 20% of $28,500 = $5700.
   Balance due = $28,500 − $5700 = $22,800 (amount of loan).
   Interest on $22,800 for one month (first month) = ($22,800 × .07) ÷ 12.
   = $133.00.
   Payment on principal = $22,800 ÷ 120 = $190
   Total payment for the first month = $190 + $133 = $323.00.
   Notice (problem 3) that this is considerably more than when the loan is amortized on an equal payment plan, i.e., $323.00 compared with $257.05.

EXERCISE 47

Chapter Summary

Answers appear at the end of this exercise. If your answers do not agree with those shown, check your calculations before referring to the solutions that follow.

1. Mr. and Mrs. Rogers obtained a loan for home improvements in the amount of $2000 which was to be repaid in 3 years. The annual interest rate was 10%. On an amortized basis, what were the monthly installment payments?

    _____

2. Mr. Hupp borrowed $200 from the local finance company at $2\frac{1}{2}\%$ per month on the unpaid balance. If he repaid the loan in 4 monthly payments of $50, plus interest, what were (a) the amount of each payment and what (b) the total interest cost?

    (a) _____
    (b) _____

3. Mr. C. Matteson holds a small mortgage for $2600 at 7%. If this obligation is paid in 15 years, (a) how much are the monthly payments on an amortized basis and (b) how much did Mr. Matteson receive in interest during the life of the loan?

    (a) _____
    (b) _____

4. A bank offers unsecured personal loans at a flat rate of 8%. If a man borrowed $350 for a year and repaid it in 12 equal installments (a) how much were the payments? (b) What was the true annual interest rate?

    (a) _____
    (b) _____

5. Mr. Guthrie borrowed $200, which he repaid in 12 monthly installments of $19.50. What was the annual interest rate?

6. Miss Cole wanted a fur coat worth $720. She could buy it from the store for 10% down and 12 monthly payments of $65. Would it be more economical for her to borrow $720 at 8% for the same period of time to be repaid in 12 installments? If so, how much would she save?

7. Assume that the following charges (flat rates) are made on $400 for a year and that the loan in each case is to be repaid in 12 equal monthly installments: 3% and 9%. What true annual interest rate is the borrower paying?

8. A store advertised cameras for $98, 10% down and the balance in weekly payments of $4 for 24 weeks. What was the interest rate ($m = 52$)?

Answers

1. $64.12
2. (a) $55.00, $53.75, $52.50, $51.25
   (b) $12.50
3. (a) $ 22.07
   (b) $1372.58
4. (a) $31.50
   (b) 14.8%
5. 31.4%
6. Yes. A saving of $74.40
7. 5.5%, 16.6%
8. 36.8%

Solutions

1. $2000 to be paid in 3 years, 10% interest charge, 36 payments.

   Beginning principal balance = $2000.00.
   Ending principal balance   = $2000 ÷ 36 = $55.55.
   Average principal balance   = ($2000 + $55.55) ÷ 2 = $1027.78.
   Interest for life of loan   = $1027.78 × .10 × 3 = $308.33.
   Total amount to be paid   = $2000.00 + $308.33 = $2308.33.
   Monthly payments   = $2308.33 ÷ 36 = $64.12.

2.
	Balance	Payment	Interest	Total Payment
1	$200.00	$50.00	$5.00	$55.00
2	150.00	50.00	3.75	53.75
3	100.00	50.00	2.50	52.50
4	50.00	50.00	1.25	51.25

3. Number of payments = 15 × 12 = 180.
   Beginning principal balance = $2600.
   Ending principal balance = $2600 ÷ 180 = $14.44.
   Average principal balance = $2614.44 ÷ 2 = $1307.22.
   Interest = $1307.22 × .07 × 15 = $1372.58.
   Monthly payments = ($2600.00 + $1372.58) ÷ 180 = $22.07.

4. Interest = $350 × .08 = $28.00.
   Payments = ($350.00 + $28.00) ÷ 12 = $31.50.

   Interest rate = $\dfrac{(2)(12)(\$28)}{(\$350)(13)} = 14.8\%$.

5. $r = \dfrac{(2)(12)(\$34)}{(\$200)(13)} = 31.4\%$.

6. Cash price = $720.00, installment price = (12 × $65) + $72 = $852.
   Down payment = 10% of $720 = $72.
   Installment charge = $852 − $720 = $132.
   Interest on $720 at 8% for 12 months = $720 × .08 = $57.60.
   Saving if money is borrowed, i.e., $132.00 − $57.60 = $74.40.

7. 3% rate of interest on $400 for a year = $12.00.

   Therefore $r = \dfrac{(2)(12)(\$12)}{(\$400)(13)} = 5.5\%$ true annual interest rate.

   The remaining problems in this question are computed in the same manner with the constant ratio formula.

8. Total of weekly payments = $4.00 × 24 = $96.00.
   Down payment = $9.80.
   Installment cost = $96.00 + $9.80 = $105.80.
   Cash price = $98.00.
   Installment charge = installment cost − cash price = $105.80 − $98.00 = $7.80.

   $r = \dfrac{(2)(52)(\$7.80)}{(\$88.20)(25)} = 36.8\%$.

FINAL EXAMINATION

1. (a) The price per share of a certain security was $27.50. It increased to $40.00 within 3 years. What was the increase in the amount and percent during that time? (Record answer correct to nearest tenth of 1%.)

   _____

   (b) A store sold 15% of its monthly quota in 1 day. If the monthly quota was $32,500, what were the sales for the day?

   _____

2. (a) Mr. Thomas owns rental property worth $20,000.00. What are the (1) annual depreciation and (2) rate of depreciation if the straight-line method is used over a period of 30 years?

   (1) _____

   (2) _____

   (b) A calculating machine that cost $1215 is to be written off in 10 years. If the scrap value is estimated at $175, what is the book value at the end of 4 years by using (1) the declining-balance method of depreciation and (2) the sum-of-the-digits method of depreciation?

   (1) _____

   (2) _____

3. (a) The assessed valuation of property in a city equals $50,600,000. If $4,500,000 are to be raised in property taxes, what is the tax rate in dollars per $100? Per $1000? As a percent? (Carry division to 5 decimals.)

   _____

   _____

   _____

(b) Mr. Lindsay lived in a district in which the tax rate was $0.092 per dollar of assessed valuation. If the assessment rate was 22% and he paid $364.32 in taxes, what was the market value of Mr. Lindsay's home?

_____

4. (a) Mr. Hale earned $750 a month. If during one month he was on leave without pay for one week, how much did he earn?

_____

(b) Miss Wright earns $520 a month as a clerk on the basis of a 40-hour week. During one month she worked 5 hours overtime. If she is paid time and a half for overtime, (1) how much did she earn for the month? (2) What were her FICA taxes (use 5.85% rate)?

(1) _____

(2) _____

5. (a) Barker Bros. received an invoice for goods purchased from the Top Quality Manufacturing Company in the amount of $416.50, less 15% and $2\frac{1}{2}$% with terms of 2% 10-EOM. If the invoice was dated March 2 and paid April 10, what was the amount remitted in payment?

_____

(b) The Glamour Shop marked down all dresses 30% in a fall clearance sale. Mrs. Hale purchased one that was originally priced at $47.50. In addition, she paid a 6% sales tax. How much was her total payment?

_____

6. (a) The Havens Electric Shop is a dealer for the A-line coffee percolators. The cost is $12.65 each less 10% and 5%. Compute the selling price if a 70% markup is based (1) on the selling price and (2) on the cost price.

(b) What is the markdown rate on a rug that normally sells for $425 if the price has been reduced to $295? (Carry rate to 3 places corrected.)

7. (a) Find the annual premium on a policy for $12,000 at $3.42 per $1000.

(b) Mr. Hale bought insurance on his home for one year. The insurance company canceled the policy after 90 days. How much was the refund to Mr. Hale if his premium was $96.50?

8. (a) Miss Smith applied for a personal loan of $250 at her bank to be repaid in 6 months. If the bank discounted the loan at 5%, how much did she receive?

(b) Baines Bros. accepted a 4-month note for $320 at 6% for Hope & Co. in payment of a debt. The note was dated June 10. On August 22 Baines Bros. "sold" the note at a discount rate of $6\frac{1}{2}$%. What were the proceeds?

9. Mr. Smith purchased a car for $4250. He was allowed $500 for his old car as a down payment. The balance was paid in 25 equal monthly payments of $180. What was the interest rate (nearest 10th of 1%)? Use any method.

10. Mary bought a watch that sold for $75.00 cash which she paid for in five equal monthly payments including interest. If the interest rate was 18%, what was the installment payment?

Answers

1. (a) $12.50, 45.5%
   (b) $4875.00
2. (a) (1) $666.67
       (2) $3\frac{1}{3}$%
   (b) (1) $497.66
       (2) $572.09
3. (a) $8.893 per $100
       $88.93 per $1000
       8.893%
   (b) $18,000
4. (a) $576.92
   (b) (1) $542.50
       (2) $31.74
5. (a) $338.27
   (b) $35.25
6. (a) $36.07, $18.39
   (b) 30.6%
7. (a) $41.04
   (b) $72.71
8. (a) $243.75
   (b) $323.51
9. 18.5%
10. $15.68

Solutions

1. (a) Increase per share = $40.00 − $27.50 = $12.50.
    % increase = $12.50 ÷ $27.50 = 45.5%.
   (b) Sales for the day = $32,500 × .15 = $4,875.00.
2. (a) (1) Annual depreciation = $20,000 ÷ 30 = $666.67.
       (2) Rate of depreciation = $\frac{1}{30}$ = $0.033\frac{1}{3}$ = $3\frac{1}{3}\%$.
   (b) (1) Rate of depreciation by the declining balance method = 20%
       Book value: end of first year = $1215.00 − (20% of $1215.00)
       = $ 972.00.
       end of second year = $ 972.00 − (20% of $ 972.00)
       = $ 777.60.
       end of third year = $ 777.60 − (20% of $ 777.60)
       = $ 622.08.
       end of fourth year = $ 622.08 − (20% of $ 622.08)
       = $ 497.66.
       (2) $S = 55$. Depreciation for the first 4 years = $\frac{34}{55}$ ($1215 − $175)
       = $\frac{34}{55}$ ($1040) = $642.91.
       Book value, end of 4th year = $1215.00 − $642.91 = $572.09.
3. (a) Tax rate per dollar = $4,500,000 ÷ $50,600,000 = .08893.
       Tax rate per $100 = $8.893, per $1000 = $88.93, as a % = 8.893%.
   (b) Assessed valuation = taxes ÷ tax rate = $364.32 ÷ .092 = $3960.00.
       Market price = assessed valuation ÷ assessment rate
       = $3960.00 ÷ .22 = $18,000.
4. (a) $750.00 ÷ $4\frac{1}{3}$ = $173.08 weekly pay.
       $750.00 − $173.08 = $576.92, since he was not paid for one week.
   (b) (1) $520 ÷ $4\frac{1}{3}$ = $120 weekly rate.
       $120 ÷ 40 = $3.00 hourly rate.
       $3.00 × $1\frac{1}{2}$ = $4.50 overtime rate.
       $4.50 × 5 = $22.50 overtime earnings.
       $520.00 + $22.50 = $542.50 total earnings.
       (2) $542.50 × .0585 = $31.74
5. (a) $416.50 less 15% and $2\frac{1}{2}\%$ = $345.17   net amount
       less 2% =   6.90   cash discount
       $338.27   amount remitted
   (b) $47.50 less 30% = $33.25
       plus 6% =   2.00   sales tax.
       $35.25   total payment.
6. (a) $12.65 less 10% and 5% = $10.82 net cost.
       On selling price: $10.82 = 30% of selling price,
       $10.82 ÷ .30 = $36.07 selling price.
       On cost price: cost = 100%.
       Then $10.82 × 1.70 = $18.39 selling price.
   (b) $425 − $295 = $130 amount of markdown; $130 ÷ $425 = .306 or 30.6%.

7. (a) 12 × $3.42 = $41.04.
   (b) $96.50 × $\frac{90}{365}$ = $23.79 cost of insurance,
       $96.50 − $23.79 = $72.71 refund.
8. (a) $250 × .05 × $\frac{1}{2}$ = $6.25 discount
       $250.00 − $6.25 = $243.75 proceeds
   (b) Maturity value = $320 + ($320 × .06 × $\frac{4}{12}$) = $326.40.
       Maturity date, October 10 (4 months from June 10).
       Term of discount 49 days (August 22 to October 10).
       Discount = $326.40 × .065 × $\frac{49}{360}$ = $2.89.
       Proceeds = $326.40 − $2.89 = $323.51.
9. Balance due $4250 − $500 = $3750.
   Total of payments $180 × 25 = $4500.
   Installment charge $4500 − $3750 = $750.

   $r = \dfrac{2mI}{P(n+1)}$, where $m = 12$, $n = 25$, $P = \$3750$, $I = \$750$.

   then $r = \dfrac{(2)(12)(\$750)}{(\$3750)(26)} = 18.5\%$.

   OR

   $r = I \div \dfrac{(P_1 + P_2)}{2} t$, where $I = \$750$, $P_1 = \$3750$,

   $t = \frac{25}{12}$, $P_2 = \$3750 \div 25 = \$150$,

   $\dfrac{P_1 + P_2}{2} = \$1950$.

   Then $r = \$750 \div (\$1950)(\frac{25}{12}) = 18.5\%$.

10. Ending principal balance $75 × $\frac{1}{5}$ = $15.
    Average principal balance   ($75 + $15) × $\frac{1}{2}$ = $45.
    Interest on average principal balance $45 × .18 × $\frac{5}{12}$ = $3.38.
    Monthly installment   ($75.00 + $3.38) × $\frac{1}{5}$ = $15.68.

Index

Accurate interest, 345, 354
Accurate time, 348
Addition, 10
  checking, 14, 18
  crossfooting, 17
  decimals, 10
  fractions, 61-65
  integers, 10
  short methods of, 12
  subtotals, 13
Additional first-year depreciation, 229
Aliquot parts, 75-77
Amortization, 445
Approximate time, 347
Approximating numbers, see Estimating numbers
Assessed valuation, 280
Automobile insurance, 326
  cancellation, 328
  classifications, 327
  comprehensive, 327
  liability, 327
  physical damage, 327
  premiums, 328
  property damage liability, 327
Average principal balance, 436
  method of finding interest rate, 436

Bank discount, 400
Bank drafts, 412
Banker's interest, 354, 356
Bodily injury liability, 327
Book value, 203

Cancellation, fractions, 68, 69
  insurance, 322, 328
  method of figuring interest, 353
Carriers, insurance, multiple, 308
Carrying charge, 426
Cash discount, 145-155
  partial payments on invoices, 154
Cash payroll, 265
Chain discount, 129-133
Change memorandum, 267
Checking, methods of, addition, 14, 18
  division, 34

  multiplication, 25
  subtraction, 20
Claims, insurance, 307
Coinsurance, 313
Collision insurance, 327
Commercial interest (banker's), 354, 356
Commission, payroll, 260
Common denominator, 63
Common fractions, 56
Complement, of a number, 131, 137
Complex fractions, 56
Compound interest, 376
  tables, 394-397
Comprehensive automobile insurance, 327
Constant ratio formula, 434
Conversation periods, 377, 379
Credit charges, 426-431
Crossfooting, 17, 18

Day of the year, 349
Decimals or decimal fractions, 73
  addition, 10
  division, 31
  multiplication, 24
  subtraction, 20
Declining-balance method of, depreciation, 221
Denominator, common, 61
  least common, 63
Depreciation, 202
  additional first-year, 229
  declining-balance, 221
  straight-line, 205
  sum-of-the-years digits, 211
Discounts, bank, 400-405
  cash, 145-155
  chain, 129-133
  partial payments (cash), 154
  single equivalent, 141
  table, 163-164
  term, 404
  trade, 119-144
Discounting, drafts, 415, 418
  notes, 404
Division, 30
  checking, 34
  decimals, 31

fractions, 70-71
integers, 30
mixed numbers, 70
short methods of, 35, 36
Drafts, bank, 412
sight, 414
time, 414
Drawee, notes and drafts, 404, 412
Drawer or maker, notes and drafts, 404, 412

Effective interest rates, 383, 433
Endowment life insurance, 332
Estimating numbers, addition, 42
multiplication, 46
division, 47
subtraction, 44
Exact time, 349
Extra dating, 151

Face amount, note, 399
policy, 303
Federal income tax withholding, 250
percentage method, 251
tax withholding tables, 276
wage-bracket method, 251
FICA taxes, 248
Fire insurance, 302
cancellation, by insured, 322
by insurer, 323
coinsurance, 313
multiple carriers, 308
premiums, 304
short-rate table, 320
short-term policies, 319
Flat interest rate, 429
Fractions, 54
addition, 61-64
aliquot parts, 75-77
changing form, 58-60
common, 56
complex, 56
decimal, 73
division, 69-71
improper, 55
mixed, 55
multiplication, 67-69
proper, 55
reducing, 57
simple, 56
subtraction, 66

Gross profit, 167, 191-195

Improper fractions, 55
Income taxes, 250
Installment buying, 426
Installment charges, 426-431
Installment payments, 426-431, 442

Insurance, automobile, 326
fire, 302
life, 330
Interest, compound, 376
simple, 345
Interest-bearing notes and drafts, 403, 418
Interest formula (simple), 351
Interest rate, discount rate equivalent, 406
effective, 383
nominal, 383

Least common denominator, 63
Liability insurance, 327
Life insurance, 330
endowment, 332
limited-payment life, 332
premiums, 333
straight life, 331
term, 331
Limited-payment life insurance, 332
List price, 119, 120

Maker, notes and drafts, 399, 412
Markdown, dollar amounts, 185-188
rate, 185, 186
Markup, dollar amounts, 167-185
on cost, 170
on selling price, 170
Markup rate, 168
on cost, 169
on selling price, 169
Maturity date, draft, 414
note, 399
Maturity value, interest-bearing notes, 405
noninterest-bearing notes, 400
simple interest, 367
Mixed numbers, 55
Monthly installments, 426, 442
Multiple carriers (insurance), 308
Multiplication, 22
checking, 25
common fractions, 67-69
decimals, 24
integers, 22
short methods in, 25, 27, 29

Negotiable instruments, 398
Net decimal equivalent, tables, 163-164
Net price, 122
Net profit, 191-195
Nominal interest rate, 383
Noninterest-bearing notes and drafts, 400
Notes, interest-bearing, 403
noninterest-bearing, 400

Operating expenses, 191-195
Ordinary interest, 354
Overtime pay, 237

INDEX

Partial payments (cash discounts), 154
Payee, notes and drafts, 399, 412-413
Payroll, 236
  cash, 265
  commissions, 260
  deductions, 249
  piece-rate payroll system, 259
  time-payment or hourly rate system, 236
Percent, 103
Percentage, 89, 102
Periodic payment plans, 441
Policy, insurance, 303
Postdating, 150
Premium, insurance, 305, 333
Principal, 369
Proceeds, draft, 415
  note, 401, 404
Profit and loss, 191
Promissory notes, 398
Proper fractions, 55
Property damage liability insurance, 327
Property taxes, 281

Rate, carrying charge, 426
  discount, 400-406
  insurance, automobile, 328
    fire, 303, 305, 320
    life, 330, 333, 334
  interest, compound, 376
    effective, 383
    nominal, 383
    simple, 345
  markdown, 185
  markup, 167-185
  percent, 103
  short-rate table, 320
  tax, property, 282
    sales, 292
Reading numbers, 7
Reducing fractions, 57
Rounding numbers, 40

Sales taxes, 292
Salvage value, 204
Scrap value, 204
Selling price, 173, 174
Short method of, addition, 12
  division, 35, 36
  muliplication, 25, 27, 29
Short-term insurance, 319
  cancellation, 322
Sight draft, 414
Simple interest, accurate, 345, 354
  banker's or commercial, 354, 356
  formula, 351
  ordinary, 354
  rate, 370
  six percent, 60-day method, 356
  table, 360-day year, 392
  table, 365-day year, 393
Single discount equivalent, 141
Social Security Tax, 249
  tax table, 274
Straight-life insurance, 331
Straight-line method of depreciation, 205
Subtotals, 13
Subtraction, 21
  checking, 20
  decimals, 20
  fractions, 66
  mixed numbers, 66
  whole numbers, 21
Sum-of-the-years-digits method of depreciation, 211

Tables, aliquot parts, 76
  compound interest, 394-397
  decimal equivalents of common fractions, 76
  discounts (net decimal equivalents of chain discounts), 163-164
  federal income tax withholding, 276
  life insurance, 330
  the number of each day of the year, 349
  short-rate table, 320
  simple interest, 360-day year, 392, 393
  social security employee tax table, 274
Taxes, excise tax, 295
  federal income, 250
  property, 281
  sales, 292
  social security, 249
Tax rate, federal income withholding, 276
  property, 282
  sales, 292
  social security (FICA), 248
Term life insurance, 331
Term of discount, 404
Terms of sale, 145-153
Time, approximate, 347
  exact, 349
Time draft, 414
Trade discount, 119-145
  series (chain), 129-133
  single, 121-125
  tables, 133-135, 163-164

Value, book, 203
  salvage, scrap, 204

Wage-bracket method (income tax withholding), 251
Writing numbers, 8